I Shall
Come Again

Volume I
Time Prophecies of
the Second Coming

Hushidar Motlagh, Ed. D.

Foreword by the Hon. Dorothy W. Nelson
Judge, U. S. Court of Appeals

Global
Perspective
Mt. Pleasant, Michigan

I Shall Come Again

ISBN 0-937661-16-3 (cloth)
ISBN 0-937661-15-5 (paper)
Library of Congress Catalog Card No. 98-94039

Acknowledgments of permission to reprint previously copyrighted material appear on pages 495-498.

Cover design by Rowshan Maani

SECOND EDITION

Cover: The two stars symbolize the twin luminaries of our time, the Báb and Bahá'u'lláh, whose message spread like lightening from the East to the West.

To order copies of this book and other works by this author, in the United States call or fax:

1-800-949-1863

If you prefer, order online from any country:

www.globalperspective.org

For further information and possible change of our address, visit our website or send us an E-mail to:

info@globalperspective.org

Our present address:
**Global Perspective, 1106 Greenbanks Dr.
Mt. Pleasant, MI 48858, USA**

In Commemoration of the Hundredth
Anniversary of the Passing of
Bahá'u'lláh, this Book is Dedicated to:

The Glory of God

Whatever you do, do it all for *the glory of God* [emphasis added to all passages on this page].   I Corinthians 10:31 NIV

Did I not tell you that if you have faith you will see *the glory of God*?   John 11:40 NEB

Great is *the glory of the Lord*.   Psalms 138:5

Sing to the Lord a new song; sing to the Lord, all the earth. Sing to the Lord, praise his name; proclaim his salvation day after day. *Declare his glory* among the nations...
                                  Psalms 96:1-2 NIV

For the earth shall be filled with the knowledge of *the glory of the Lord*, as the waters cover the sea.   Habakkuk 2:14

And we rejoice in the hope of *the glory of God*.
                                  Romans 5:2 NIV

I have come in the shadows of *the clouds of glory*...
                                  Bahá'u'lláh

I believe that the Scriptures do reveal unto us, in plain language, that Jesus Christ will appear again on this earth ...in *the glory of God*.   William Miller
                      Views of the Prophecies and
                      Prophetic Chronology, 1842, p. 33

Works by This Author
About the Bahá'í Faith

Six-volume series on proofs and prophecies
I Shall Come Again
Lord of Lords
King of Kings
In the Clouds of Glory
The Spirit that Acknowledges Jesus Christ
By My Fruits You Shall Know Me

Introductory books on the Bahá'í Faith
One God, Many Faiths; One Garden, Many Flowers
Heaven's Most Glorious Gift
Destiny is a Choice
On Wings of Destiny
Choosing Your Destiny
Bahá'í Faith: Teachings for Inner Peace and Purpose
Bahá'í Faith: Teachings for Global Peace and Unity

Books for Christians
Seek and Ye Shall Find
The Glory of the Son
The Glory of the Father
Come Now, Let Us Reason Together
The News Every Christian Should Know

Compilations
The Glorious Journey to God
The Remembrance of God
Unto Him Shall We Return

Others
Teaching: The Crown of Immortal Glory
Proclaim the Most Great Name
Does Your Fishbowl Need Fresh Water?
A Messenger of Joy

Contents

Part I
Preparing for the Journey

Part II
Proofs: Time Prophecies

Part III
God's Covenant With Humanity

Appendices

Foreword

This work offers proofs of the most remarkable event in human history—the Advent of the Prince of Peace, the Desire of the Ages, the Redeemer of the World. It presents hundreds of scriptural prophecies and proofs fitting a pattern that clearly indicates that the Return expected by the followers of all the world's great religions has already occurred. The prophecies and promises have been fulfilled in the advent of Bahá'u'lláh (the Glory of God) and His Herald, the Báb (the Gate), who appeared in the mid-19th century and established the Bahá'í Faith—a universal religion dedicated to world unity.

The references offered in this work to prove the validity of Bahá'u'lláh's claim to be the great world Redeemer come mostly from the Bible. Prophecies from the Scriptures of other religions have also been presented, for they have all foretold His coming. Scientific explanations and mathematical calculations further substantiate this claim. The overwhelming weight of the evidence presented here cannot be ignored. It challenges the reader to investigate further Bahá'u'lláh's Revelation.

The author was born to a Jewish family that later became Bahá'í. His grandfather, after making an extensive study of proofs and prophecies, recognized Bahá'u'lláh as the expected Messiah of the Jews in the last days. Although influenced by his grandfather, the author pursued his own independent search into the Bahá'í Revelation. After years of study, he became convinced of the validity of Bahá'u'lláh's claim and teachings.

It seems ironic to him that his Jewish ancestors met many Christians who would say: "The Messiah has come!" And now he is saying to the descendants of those same Christians: "The Messiah has come *again*!"

This book points out that the prophets and seers of past ages longed to witness the dawning of this glorious time in history— the Day of the Lord. Bahá'ís believe that this blessed Day has indeed dawned, that Christ *has* returned, and that all the prophecies have been fulfilled!

At the opening of this glorious age (1844), a few followed the warnings of the Scriptures; they stayed awake and watchful and caught a glimpse of its glory. But the vast majority, as predicted by the prophets, were caught by surprise—asleep and dreaming of a loud trumpet blast that would awaken them, hoping for an unseen hand that would raise them to the heavens on high.

Seekers who study Bahá'u'lláh's world order—the Kingdom of God on earth prayed for by Christ—find it practical, indeed ideal. Who could rationally deny the need for global unity, for a universal language, and for world peace? But even though Bahá'u'lláh's teachings are in harmony with the needs of the age and scientific understanding, and even though the Bahá'í life inspires spiritual transformation, there need to be objective proofs of the validity of Bahá'u'lláh's prophetic Mission. That is the purpose of this book.

Bahá'u'lláh offers a message of hope and fulfillment, of love, peace, and harmony; a message that can transform our planet into a veritable paradise, that can bring the heart of humanity into fellowship with God.

How glorious a world in which justice, love, and peace prevail; a world whose inhabitants worship one God, acknowledge one Faith, speak in one language, and abide by one Law. How wondrous a world in which prejudice is uprooted, fanaticism forsaken, illiteracy eradicated, poverty eliminated, work exalted, and idleness despised. How blessed a world in which religion and science stand together as perfect partners in fostering human progress; a world in which the station of woman is acknowledged as man's equal. How enchanting a world from whose heart worldliness is effaced, crime cast out, enmity expelled, and war banished. How splendid a world in which the love of God dominates and moves the hearts of all its inhabitants—a love from which will spring every noble act, every pure and worthy deed.

Such is the world whose advent all the prophets have foretold; such is the day for whose dawning the Bahá'ís have offered countless lives; such is the peace for whose triumph the Báb suffered and gave His youthful life; and such is the kingdom for whose coming Bahá'u'lláh endured forty years of affliction, exile, and imprisonment. What a blessed gift to live in this glorious time!

Dorothy W. Nelson

He Who Overcomes

Revelation 3:12

Behold, I come quickly...*He who overcomes*...I will make him a pillar in the temple of my God...And I will also write on him my new name.

Revelation 3:11-12 NKJ

Recently, a series of interviews entitled, *Prophecy Today, Christian Leaders Look at the Signs of the Time*, was conducted with several distinguished Christians. Leaders of various denominations, both Catholic and Protestant, were asked to link the events of our time to biblical prophecy.

Among the leaders interviewed was Dr. James Kennedy, one of the most distinguished Christian scholars and founder of the Westminster Academy. He is known to many Christians through his writings as well as his weekly television and radio broadcasts that reach millions in 3,300 communities in the United States and 21 other countries. When asked "What do you believe are some of the major mistakes we tend to make in our study of prophecy?", he said:

The great Princeton theologian of the last century, Dr. Charles Hodge, said something which I have always thought is worth remembering. ***He said that though the Old Testament is filled with some 333 prophecies concerning the first coming of Christ; in spite of that, nobody got it right.*** And as you know, they crucified Christ because of a misunderstanding about what the Messiah was really coming to do. And we should because of that be somewhat humbled and modest in our attempts to interpret prophecies concerning the second coming of Christ. ***It is quite possible that all of us [Christian leaders] are wrong*** as well. [Emphasis added.][1]

To see the present clearly, we must look at the past; to understand our lives, we must understand the lives of those who have lived before us:

> People are fond of saying that "the past is dead," but it is actually the future that is dead—and we make it come alive only by applying what we have learned from the living past to the present.   Sydney Harris

> Without retrospect, no real prospect is possible.
>   Richard Niebuhr

Much wisdom comes from history:

> Days should speak, and multitudes of years should teach wisdom...   Job 32:7

A Christian publication declares:

> The Bible does tell us, of course, that we should use the past as the right kind of spiritual rearview mirror. We should learn from our own or others' errors.

> The Hebrew or Old Testament Scriptures, said Paul, provide us this opportunity. "For whatever things were written before were written for our learning"... (Romans 15:4). Paul said the spiritual errors ancient Israel made "were written for our admonition" (I Cor. 10:11).[2]

Has history repeated itself in our time? Is it possible that the masses of people have once again missed their Redeemer "because of a misunderstanding about what He was really coming to do?" Are Christian leaders of our time willing to acknowledge Dr. Kennedy's *message of humility* in interpreting biblical prophecy?

> *...he shall save the humble person.* [Emphasis added throughout this section.]   Job 22:29

> Show me your ways, O Lord, teach me your paths; guide me in your truth and teach me, for you are God my Savior, and my hope is in you all day long...*He guides the humble* in what is right and teaches them his way.
> Psalms 25:4-5, 9 NIV

> Deliver me, O Lord, I beseech thee...The Lord preserves the simple-hearted; *I was brought low and he saved me*.
> Psalms 116:4, 6 NEB

> Seek the Lord, all you humble of the land, you who do what he commands. Seek righteousness, *seek humility; perhaps you will be sheltered on the day of the Lord's anger*.   Zephaniah 2:3 NIV

> ...the Lord has anointed me *to preach good news to the poor* [the meek, ARV].   Isaiah 61:1 NIV
> See also Luke 4:18

Christian scholar Dr. Barry Chant in his book *The Return* illustrates the need for humility by this example:

> Imagine four theologians sitting in a library one day, when a pigeon flutters down and lands on the window sill. "Aha," says one, "a symbol of peace."

> "No," suggests another. "In Scripture, the dove is always a symbol of the Holy Spirit."

> "Not always." interjects the third scholar. "It reminds me of the freedom we have in Christ."

> "I cannot agree with any of you," argues the fourth. "That bird obviously reminds us of the return of Christ."

Now, so far, there is no problem. Each man has a perfect right to his view and each may have good reason for it. But let us imagine that this is what happens next—

The fourth man goes on to say, "Listen, you may not agree, but I'm telling you that you are all wrong. There is only one possible significance in the landing of that bird. It is the message of the parousia [the coming and presence of Christ]!"

Another then says, "Wait a minute! I have had such an experience of liberation in Christ that there can be no other meaning for me than spiritual freedom. That bird has nothing whatsoever to do with some eschatalogical event!"

And then the second speaker chips in. "You men obviously know nothing whatever of the Scriptures. The dove is the...sign of the Spirit. To say anything else is to border on heresy! I insist that you consider my viewpoint and that you seriously question your own views."

And then the one who spoke first says, "Listen to me, all of you. From time immemorial, the dove has been a sign of peace. I have history and tradition on my side. And I'm prepared to fight anyone to prove it!"[3]

Dr. Chant then concludes:

Voltaire, an atheistic philosopher once said, "I disapprove of what you say, but I will defend to the death your right to say it." We need a similar attitude in the area of eschatology.[4]

Bahá'u'lláh begins *The Book of Certitude*—which examines the proofs of His Mission—with the topic of *detachment*:

No man shall attain the shores of the ocean of true understanding except he be detached from all that is in heaven and on earth. Sanctify your souls, O ye peoples of the world, that haply ye may attain that station which God hath destined for you...[5]

And he concludes another of His books (*The Hidden Words*) with the topic of **detachment**:

> I bear witness, O friends! that the favor is complete, the argument fulfilled, the proof manifest and the evidence established. *Let it now be seen what your endeavors in the path of detachment will reveal.*[6]

What is "detachment"? It is best defined by communication specialists Ronald Adler and Neil Towne. They state that in all human relationships and regarding all subjects the most essential ingredient for effective communication is:

> ...the ability and disposition to be open-minded—*to set aside for the moment his or her own beliefs, attitudes, and values and consider those of the other person.* This is especially difficult when the other person's position is radically different from your own. The temptation is to think (and sometimes say), "That's crazy!" "How can you believe that?"...attitudes like these often aren't helpful even if your position is correct. *Being open-minded is often difficult because people confuse understanding another's position with accepting it.*[7]

Countless attachments surround us and entangle us. There is attachment to:

- Names and labels
- Traditions
- The opinion of authority figures (pastors, parents, celebrities)
- Security, popularity, or power
- Personal inclinations or prejudices
- The voice of the majority
- The voice of ego
- Ignorance
- Illusions and unverified assumptions
- Despair, apathy, and cynicism
- The glitter and glamor of the world

Even one of these attachments can entangle our freedom and strangle our vision of truth. Bahá'u'lláh refers to many attachments, but the one He emphasizes in *The Book of Certitude* is dependence on the opinion of others:

> ...man can never hope to attain unto the knowledge of the All-Glorious, can never quaff from the stream of divine knowledge and wisdom, can never enter the abode of immortality, nor partake of the cup of divine nearness and favor, unless and until he ceases to regard the words and deeds of mortal men as a standard for the true understanding and recognition of God and His Prophets.[8]

Noted psychologist, Dr. Wayne Dyer, discusses the necessity of detachment:

> Certainly it is fine to have strong opinions about anything that you choose, but the moment you become attached to these ideas and thereby define yourself by them, you shut out the possibility of hearing another point of view. This attachment to ideas and to making others wrong is the history of the being called Human Being, and it accounts for untold wars and misery since the beginning of recorded history.
>
> Seldom do people stop and truly hear what the other person has to say. Seldom if ever do we change our mind based upon solid ideas presented by others.[9]
>
> We can respect and even appreciate the past and the ways of our ancestors. We can love them for having chosen to go their own way. *But to be attached to having to live and think the way others before you did, because you showed up looking like them in forms, is to deny yourself enlightenment.*[10]

Detachment is freedom, attachment is slavery; freedom from what others expect us to be, slavery to their judgment of who *we* should be and our own judgment of how *they* should be. Detachment is an absolute necessity because of this pervasive principle:

Every way of a man is right in his own eyes.

Proverbs 21:2

Attachment is perhaps the greatest weakness in human nature, and *overcoming* it—attaining *de*tachment—is man's greatest victory, his supreme purpose, glory and honor. Both the difficulty and the glory of "overcoming" are of such magnitude that the Book of Revelation refers to them eight times. Here are two of these references:

> I am coming soon...Him who *overcomes*...I will write on him the name of my God...I will also write on him my new name. He who has an ear, let him hear what the Spirit says to the churches.   Revelation 3:11-13 NIV

> To him who *overcomes*, I will give the right to sit with me on my throne...   Revelation 3:21 NIV
>
> See also Rev. 2:7, 11, 17, 26; 3:5; 21:7

The Cause of God hath come as a token of His grace. Happy are they who act; happy are they who understand; happy the man that hath clung unto the truth, detached from all that is in the heavens and all that is on earth.[11]

Bahá'u'lláh

The only acceptable attachment is to God:

> ...they that tread the path of faith...must cleanse themselves of all that is earthly [detachment]...They should put their trust in God, and, holding fast unto Him [attachment], follow in His way.[12]   Bahá'u'lláh

The Scriptures ask us to *"test everything"* (I Thess. 5:21 NIV), to *"test the spirits to see whether they are from God"* (I John 4:1 NIV), to *"prove all things"* and to *"hold fast that which is good"* (I Thess. 5:21). The necessity of testing is confirmed in all sacred Scriptures:

> Take heed to carefully consider the words of every soul, then hold fast to the proofs which attest the truth.[13]

The Báb

What follows is an attempt to comply with those directives and guidance; to put the new Messenger to the test; to see whether He who claims to be the Spirit of truth, the return of Christ, the expected Savior and Redeemer of the world, is indeed from God. It is an attempt that has taken the author over thirty years—and thousands of hours of research and writing. It tells a story so remarkable that it happens only once in thousands of years.

It is about a Messenger, Bahá'u'lláh, the Glory of God:

- Who sacrificed His freedom and comfort to liberate the human race from the fetters of war, prejudice, and injustice.

- Who endured every conceivable loss, pain, and suffering for nearly 40 years, yet never wavered in His claim.

- Who, without help, withstood and overcame three of the most powerful and despotic kings of the earth.

- Who did not attend school, yet wrote words of exquisite grace and wisdom with astonishing speed.

- Who lived in prison and exile most of His life, yet composed Writings equal to a hundred volumes, unveiling the knowledge, wisdom, and inspiration that humanity needs to live in peace for the next thousand years and more.

- A Messenger who has already influenced millions with His teachings, hailed by great thinkers from many lands as the ultimate remedy for the afflictions of the world.

- A Teacher whose teachings, within the span of a century, have given rise to a global community based on the highest ethical standards—a community that extends to the farthest reaches of the earth—with members in over 200 countries and dependencies.

- A Redeemer about whose advent the Bible speaks more than a thousand times, predicting the events of His life and His Revelation; *events that, according to the facts presented in this volume and the next, could happen by* *chance only once in 10^{80} times—a figure that equals the estimated number of elementary particles (protons, neutrons, and electrons) in the observable universe.* (See Volume II, *Lord of Lords*.)

If Bahá'u'lláh's claim is false, we need to know, and no harm will come from knowing. If it is true, we also need to know. For knowing God's latest Manifestation of Truth— the Prince of Peace—is a privilege and a bounty with which nothing can ever compare. Only through Him can the purpose of human life be known—a purpose that is the wellspring of the deepest and most enduring joy.

Paul said we need three things—faith, hope, and love. We must have faith that the Comforter (John 15:26) would not leave us comfortless in an hour of dire need, we must have love for truth, and hope that we can find it.

I will not leave you comfortless: I will come to you.
Christ (John 14:18)

This work consists of six volumes that cover the objective proofs of Bahá'u'lláh's Revelation. By *objective* is meant the evidences or proofs that are equally accessible to everyone, that can be examined and verified by *all* seekers of truth. At the other extreme, and totally different from these, are *subjective* evidences, which result from personal spiritual transformations or encounters. Such evidences are *not* equally accessible to all seekers of truth, and as a rule, cannot be repeated, tested, and verified. They must be accepted mainly on faith. These have not received the status of primary proofs in this book, yet because of the credence given to them by many seekers, they have not been ignored.

The Contents of This Volume

This volume examines primarily the time prophecies of the Bible that point to the second coming of Christ. Sixteen biblical prophecies that specify 1844 as the year of the

coming of the Redeemer of the world are examined. Nine
time prophecies that further confirm 1844 are also provided
from the Scriptures of other religions. The section on proofs
begins with an account of one of the most tragic and dramatic events in the religious history of the world: the revival
of the hope of the imminent return of Christ in the mid-19th
century and the bitter disappointment experienced by those
who failed to find the object of their search.

After an examination of the time prophecies—which is the
main theme of this volume—several chapters present a
number of facts and questions of concern to seekers:

- Why has the Bahá'í Faith *not* been acknowledged by all
  or most of humanity?

- Why have most of the religious leaders not seriously
  investigated Bahá'u'lláh's Message?

- What is God's eternal covenant with humanity?

Preliminary Material

No book can meet the needs of *all* seekers of truth. Volume
I, therefore, begins with some preliminary material, which
lays a groundwork for the study of scriptural proofs, and
provides some factual background for those with little or no
exposure to the Bahá'í Faith. It addresses seven central
questions:

- What did Jesus mean when He repeatedly gave this
  warning: "Watch!"? (Chapter 1)

- What did Jesus mean when He said "I shall come like a
  thief"? (Chapter 2)

- What attitudes and attributes, according to the Scriptures,
  characterize the true seeker? (Chapter 3)

- What is the message of the Bahá'í Faith and who are its
  Central Figures? (Chapter 4)

• Does God speak in the same way humans do? What features characterize the unique language of the divine? (Chapter 5)

• Can the interpreters of the Word of God tell with certainty which prophecies are literal, which prophecies are symbolic? (Chapter 6)

• Is it possible to single out from the Scriptures as well as historical records the main difference between what people have expected from God's Messengers and Redeemers and what they are given? Does the same difference exist today? (Chapter 7)

These seven chapters constitute an independent unit. They are placed at the beginning of the book for this purpose only: ***to prove that it is possible to arrive late for the banquet of the Kingdom, and to miss the Bridegroom.*** Readers not in need of this message may wish to proceed directly to Part II, which carries the main theme of Volume I: the fulfillment of time prophecies pointing to the advent of the Redeemer of the World.

The Subsequent Volumes

Volumes II and III—*Lord of Lords*, and *King of Kings*—deal with many other biblical predictions pertaining to the return of Christ: His new name, the chief events of His life, and the prevailing conditions of the appointed time. (See the table of contents of those Volumes at the end of this book.)

Volume IV—*The Spirit That Acknowledges Jesus Christ*—presents the identical prophecies of the Bible and the Qur'án concerning the return of Christ. It attempts to eradicate the prevailing misconceptions about Islam in the West and to demonstrate the Qur'án's confirmation of the Bible and glorification of Christ and His mother, as well as Noah, Abraham, Moses, and the Hebrew prophets. It establishes that the spiritual teachings of the Bible and the Qur'án are not just similar; they are identical.

Volume V—*In the Clouds of Glory*—demonstrates the sharp contrast between divine and human language. It explores the meaning of the symbolic prophecies that point to the return of Christ. It shows how the symbols interrelate and interact, demonstrates the harmony of seemingly contradictory words, and resolves some of the most enduring mysteries of the Scriptures.

Volume VI—*By My Fruits Ye Shall Know Me*—examines many other scriptural standards by which a Messenger from God can be known.

In this work, the words **Messenger, Redeemer, Manifestation (of God), Savior,** and **divine Teacher** are used interchange-ably. Some writers apply the word **Christ** to **the divine Spirit** manifested in Jesus, and the word **Jesus** to the Redeemer's **personal identity.** Such a distinction is not always followed in this book. The author has emphasized some scriptural passages by putting them in **bold** print.

Some authorities doubt the authenticity of the words of Jesus. That position is not upheld here. First, Bahá'u'lláh confirms the Gospel as "genuine" and "heavenly."[14] Second, the Word of God is unique and distinctive. It stands out clearly above the word of His creatures. The passages attributed to Jesus testify to this distinction.

To enhance clarity, two modern translations of the Old and New Testaments are used: *The New English Bible* (NEB), and *New International Version* (NIV). The wording in different editions of *The New International Version* varies slightly. For passages from *The King James Version* (KJV), identifying abbreviations are not used. To clarify or emphasize special meanings, in a few instances, *The Amplified Bible* (AB), *The New American Bible* (NAB), and *The New King James Version* (NKJ) have also been used.

Appreciations and Acknowledgments

Sources of Guidance and Inspiration

Bahá'u'lláh's *Book of Certitude*, more than any other, has been my guide and inspiration. I have also drawn from *Gleanings from the Writings of Bahá'u'lláh*, *Selections from the Writings of the Báb*, and 'Abdu'l-Bahá's works, especially *Some Answered Questions*. It is impossible to estimate my debts to these sources. To fully acknowledge my indebtedness would require referring to the names of Bahá'u'lláh, the Báb, and 'Abdu'l-Bahá on almost every page.

This acknowledgment does not imply that all the views presented here stem from the Bahá'í sacred Writings, or that they constitute an "official" Bahá'í interpretation of those Scriptures.

I make no claim that this work is free from errors. I have made many corrections and expect to be corrected by others for decades to come. What matters is not if I have erred in judging specific facts or interpretations, but if I have erred in judging the concluding message of this book. That judgment is for everyone to make for himself *only after he has examined all the facts presented here*. The concluding message of this book should not and cannot be invalidated by my shortcomings. For we all err "and come short of the glory of God" (Romans 3:23).

Contributors of Thought and Talent

I am indebted most for the contributions made by: Jim Allen, Kenneth Augustine, Dr. Fredrick Bonds, Waldo Boyd, Dr. Carlos Castillo, Dr. R. Jackson Armstrong-Ingram, Michael S. Centner, John Dale, Jr., Dr. William Diehl, Alan Gamble, Irma Gray, John Huddleston, Dr. Enrico Indiogine, Dr. Thomas Kalantar, Kern Kuipers, Joe Killeen, Bruce Limber, Virginia Martig, Dr. Dorothea Martin, Dr. William Maxwell, Dr. Dorothy Nelson, Gail Radley, Richard Reid, Robert Riggs, Dr. Thomas Rowe, Dr. Robert Stockman, Michael W. Thomas, and Jane Zehnder-Merrell.

I also wish to express my appreciation to other contributors of thought or talent: Mahmud, Ahmad, Parviz, May, and Navid Motlagh.

Part I

Preparing for the Journey

Finding and Following the
Searchlights of Truth

But when the Son of Man comes, will he find faith on earth?　　　　　*Luke 18:8 NEB*

As things were in Noah's days, so will they be when the Son of Man comes.　　　　　*Matthew 24:37 NEB*

...I shall come upon you like a thief...　*Revelation 3:3 NEB*

It will be good for those servants whose master finds them watching when he comes.　　　*Luke 12:37 NIV*

That is the day when I come like a thief! Happy the man who stays awake...　　　*Revelation 16:15 NEB*

Be on the alert...　　　　　　　*Luke 21:36 NEB*

...do not let him find you sleeping.　　*Mark 13:36 NIV*

Take ye heed, watch and pray...　　　*Mark 13:33*

Watch ye therefore, and pray always...　　*Luke 21:36*

...whatsoever ye shall ask in prayer, believing, ye shall receive.　　　　　　　*Matthew 21:22*

...Unto them that look for him [Christ] shall he appear the second time...　　　　*Hebrews 9:28*

1

Be Always on the Watch
Luke 21:36 NIV

"Watch!"
What Does That Mean?

The Olivet Discourse (Matt., Chapters 24 and 25)✝ contains the most comprehensive and emphatic pronouncement Jesus made during His ministry to prepare Christians for His return. This chapter introduces the parts of this discourse that encourage Christians to investigate the good news of "the coming of the Kingdom of God on earth." *It shows that in the light of Christ's clear and definitive instructions, Bahá'u'lláh's claim deserves the most serious investigation by all Christians,* especially those who wish to follow the counsels of their Lord and Savior. Succeeding chapters and volumes will examine other themes of Jesus' discourse, among them the fulfillment of some of His most specific predictions in Bahá'u'lláh's Revelation.

✝ It also appears in Mark, Chapter 13, and Luke, Chapter 21. But each of the latter contains only about a third of the verses found in Matthew.

The Olivet Discourse was uttered in response to the disciples' concern and curiosity about the future:

> When he was sitting on the Mount of Olives the disciples came to speak to him privately. 'Tell us,' they said, 'when will this happen? And what will be the signal for your coming and the end of the age?'   Matthew 24:3 NEB

Perhaps the most critical word Jesus used in His discourse to awaken the Christians to the reality of His return is this: "Watch!"

> Be on guard! Be alert!...keep watch...do not let him find you sleeping. What I say to you, I say to everyone: ***"Watch!"***   Christ (Mark 13:33-37 NIV)

> ***Be always on the watch***...that you may be able to stand before the Son of Man.   Luke 21:36 NIV

What did He mean by that word? Did He mean: look always heavenward, and gaze into space? Certainly not! To comprehend Jesus' prophecies, it is absolutely essential to decode this critical word.

As Dr. Ray Stedman,[1] a Christian scholar, observes, in His discourse Jesus uses three different parables to explain His intentions in saying "Watch!" All of them contain the answer to this question: the Master is away for a long time. How should we find and recognize Him when He returns? All of them explain the meaning of the key word, "Watch!"

The first of the three parables points to the role of those in positions of leadership. Religious leaders have a sublime station, as high and bright as the stars of heaven (Daniel 12:3). They also have duties commensurate with their position of honor. Perhaps the most awesome task Jesus has entrusted to them is that of preparing Christians for His return. As a reward for complying with His counsel, He has promised to "put them in charge of ***all*** His possessions:"

> Who then is the faithful and wise servant [leader], whom
> the master has put in charge of the servants in his house-
> hold [the church]✛ to give them their food at the proper
> time? It will be good for that servant whose master finds
> him doing so when he returns. I tell you the truth, he will
> put him in charge of all his possessions.
>
> Christ (Matthew 24:45-47 NIV)

To be placed in charge of **all** the Master's possessions is the
highest and most honored reward anyone can receive. But the
reward must be earned:

> That servant who knows his master's will and does not
> get ready or does not do what his master wants will be
> beaten with many blows...From everyone who has been
> given much, much will be demanded; and from the one
> who has been entrusted with much, much more will be
> asked.
>
> Christ (Luke 12:47-48 NIV)

Both the rewards and the punishments assigned to those in
positions of power are extraordinary. Leaders are responsible
not only for themselves but, to some extent, for the spiritual
destiny of those they lead.

Daniel, too, predicts a bright destiny for those leaders who
walk by the light of wisdom and understanding:

> The wise leaders shall shine like the bright vault of
> heaven, and those who have guided the people in the true
> path shall be like the stars for ever and ever...keep the
> words secret and seal the book till the time of the end...
> only the wise leaders shall understand.
>
> Daniel 12:3, 4, 10 NEB

Many religious leaders speak in glowing terms about the
return of Christ. They plant the hope of His return in the
hearts of millions. This is commendable. But to conform to

✛ ...every teacher of the law [of the Lord] who has been instructed about
the kingdom of heaven is like the owner of a house... Matthew 13:52 NIV

the Master's counsels, they need to take one more step: transform this positive force—hope—into action and search. Some
religious leaders hesitate in this endeavor. Others instill
avoidance. The climate of fear and avoidance that is thus
created affects not only the lay people but the leaders as well.
It generates an attitude of apathy, the feeling that truth need
not be sought; it is something that one is either born into or
forced to recognize by the power of the supernatural.

The second parable, in which Jesus teaches the reality of His
return, is that of the banquet of the Kingdom, or the wise
and foolish maidens—perhaps the most touching of all His
parables (Matt. 25:1-13). He utters this parable to teach *not*
fear of being deceived, but fear of *being deprived of His
Glory* at His second coming.

To keep the seekers' attention on the topic—the closing of
the age and His return—Jesus prefaces the parable with this
passage: "When that day comes the kingdom of Heaven will
be like this" (Matt. 25:1 NEB). That is, when the promised
day dawns, the Kingdom of God on earth will begin as this
parable portrays. As *Unger's Bible Dictionary* states:

> ...the "kingdom of heaven" in its earthly manifested form
> was postponed until Christ's Second Advent...According to
> the clear teaching of the Bible it will be realized only in
> connection with the Second Advent. The testimony of
> Scripture agrees completely with this fact...the kingdom of
> heaven is no other than the rule of God on the earth...[2]

Jesus then relates the story of ten maidens who waited a long
time to meet the Bridegroom [Christ]. In preparing for the
Bridegroom and His wedding banquet they took their lamps
and went out to meet Him. Five of them carried oil, the rest
did not. The five maidens who carried oil He praised as being
wise, the rest as unwise. Both the wise and unwise maidens
waited a long time for the Bridegroom whom they wished to
meet. The only difference between them was the extra oil
the wise ones carried. Why carry oil? Accompanying the

Bridegroom and entering His banquet were deemed by the wise maidens as the greatest glory and honor. They made every effort to be prepared. They *took every precaution* to be sure they could keep their lamps burning *as long as possible*. They knew that without lighted lamps they could neither see the Bridegroom nor enter His banquet.

The unwise maidens felt that *their only duty was waiting and wishing*. To them what mattered was the lamp of the church; carrying oil did not seem essential. *They did not believe they could miss the Bridegroom or be kept out of His banquet*.

The Bridegroom finally arrived in the dark and secrecy of midnight. The wise maidens with lighted lamps received the unparalleled honor of accompanying the Bridegroom to the banquet. The others—who had been complacent, who had *not feared missing the Bridegroom*, who had not taken extra precautions—arrived too late. They met closed doors, and their pleas to enter the banquet went unheeded.

What the parable teaches is this: waiting and wishing are not sufficient. Almost all Christians are waiting for Christ to return and wish to meet Him. But only those who have taken advantage of *every* opportunity to enlighten themselves, only those who carry the oil of wisdom, not just the lamp of the church can accompany Him to His banquet. *It is indeed possible to miss the Bridegroom*.

In all the verses quoted, the attribute of *wisdom* stands out. All the verses indicate that:

- Only the *wise* leaders shall understand (Daniel 12:10 NEB).

- Only the *wise* leaders shall shine (Daniel 12:3 NEB).

- Only the *wise* maidens can enter the banquet of the Kingdom (Matt. 25:1-13).

- Only the faithful and *wise* servants [leaders] are put in charge of the Master's possessions (Matt. 24:45-47).

This verse also links deliverance to wisdom:

...whoso walketh *wisely*, he shall be delivered.

Proverbs 28:26

Still another passage from Isaiah points to a link not only
between wisdom and understanding of prophecies but also the
scarcity of wisdom among the "wise men" of our time:

> All prophetic vision has become for you like a sealed
> book...*the wisdom of their wise men shall vanish* and the
> discernment of the discerning shall be lost.

Isaiah 29:11-14 NEB

It is evident that wisdom is required when a vital choice is at
stake, especially one that demands discernment. In this case
the choice is investigating the good news of the coming of
the Master, or ignoring the news. A sincere desire to learn
the facts—investigation—is the first step toward attaining
wisdom:

"The true beginning of wisdom is the desire to learn"
(Wisdom of Solomon 6:17 NEB). "A wise man will hear, and
will increase learning" (Prov. 1:5). "The ear of the wise
seeketh knowledge" (Prov. 18:15). "The wise shall inherit
glory" (Prov. 3:35).

The parable of the banquet of the Kingdom teaches one more
lesson. It indicates that each individual must carry out his
own independent investigation of truth. When the unwise
maidens found that their lamps were going out and they had
no oil, they asked their companions to give them some, but
none was given to them. The companions could not comply
with the request. The investigation and recognition of truth
must always come from one's *own soul*. As each person sees
the physical realm only with his own eyes, even so should
he see the spiritual. God has granted the gift of recognizing
His divine glory to every soul.

An example may further illustrate why the wise maidens
could *not* share their oil with their companions. Suppose you
see a spiritually gifted friend, full of love, knowledge, and

wisdom, on his deathbed. You say, "Dear friend, before you go please give me some of your spiritual wealth." What would you expect him to say? Would he not say, "I have gained that wealth at great cost and through many years. You too must work for yours." Earthly wealth can be bequeathed, but spiritual wealth cannot.

The responsibility and ability of each individual to find the truth is emphasized in all the scriptures:

> ...I have perfected in every one of you My creation, so that the excellence of My handiwork may be fully revealed unto men. It follows, therefore, that every man hath been, and will continue to be, able of himself to appreciate the Beauty of God, the Glorified. Had he not been endowed with such a capacity, how could he be called to account for his failure?[3]   Bahá'u'lláh

> Behold, I have set before thee an open door, and no man can shut it.   Christ (Revelation 3:8)

> This day I call heaven and earth as witnesses...that I have set before you life and death...Now choose life...the Lord is your life...   Deuteronomy 30:19-20 NIV

The parable of the wedding banquet raises this question: why did the Bridegroom, or any one of His invited guests, *not* open the door to the unwise maidens? Answer: should strangers go to a wedding to which they are not invited? The Bridegroom had made it clear that Christians who would not honor His wishes did not belong to His household. Those who faced closed doors, had ignored the Master's repeated warnings and counsels. They had made no attempt to join His household when the going was tough. Why should they be allowed to join the banquet?

It is impossible to conceive of a literary device more fitting than this simple but touching parable to teach the vital lessons it communicates. It is the quintessence of perfection.

The last of the three parables, that of *the talents* (Matt. 25:14-30), likens Jesus to a Master who leaves for a long journey. Before leaving, the Master calls His servants and entrusts them with His possessions. To each of them He gives according to his capacity or talents. Two of the servants, who had received the most, *double* their possessions by investing them. The third one, who had received the least, *buries* his.

"A long time afterwards their master returns to settle accounts with them." The two servants who had invested their posses- sions heard these glowing words from their Master: "You have proved trustworthy in a small way; I will now put you in charge of something big. Come and share your master's delight." What of the fearful servant who did *not* invest his possessions? He presented excuses that showed lack of trust in his Master. He said, "I was afraid and went out and hid my talent in the ground." His Master called him "wicked and lazy." Wicked because he pretended to trust Him in words but not in deeds, lazy because he would not take time to use his God-given talents for the very purpose for which they were given him. Then the Master punished the fearful servant by taking his meager possessions away from him and shutting him out of His heavenly Kingdom.

It is clear "investing" means using one's talents in the light of divine guidance to find and follow the Truth—in this case the Master Himself. The severe punishment imposed on the fearful servant points to the severity of his infraction: denying the very Master who granted him the cherished possessions.

The fearful servant had Jesus Christ in his heart, His Name at least, but did not obey His command or trust His counsels. At last, he lost even the very Name he had zealously guarded. The adventurous, enterprising servants *also* had Jesus Christ in their hearts. But since they trusted in His Command *"Watch!"*—which means nothing short of *"Investigate!"*— they *doubled* their possessions. They kept the Christ of the Gospel, and to that added the Christ of the new Revelation.

Whoever has will be given more; whoever does not have, even what he has will be taken from him.

Christ (Mark 4:25 NIV)

Jesus used still another parable to show God's displeasure with those who are not adventurous, who cling to what they already have for fear of losing it (Luke 19:11-27).

We can find one more message that the parable of the talents shares with that of the banquet of the Kingdom. The five maidens accompanied the Bridegroom to the banquet only because of a little "oil" or inner light and wisdom they carried along, only because of a little extra precaution they took. The two enterprising servants, who invested their capital, *also* entered the heavenly Kingdom for the same reason: "You have proved trustworthy *in a small way*," they were told. Both parables teach us that sometimes a little extra effort leads to phenomenal gains, in this case everlasting fellowship with the Master in His Kingdom. Sometimes, champions become Olympians by staying an inch or a fraction of a second ahead of other runners. An unknown woman made herself immortal by pouring a small, but precious, bottle of fragrant oil over Jesus' head (Matt. 26:6-13).

Many Christians do not investigate the Bahá'í Faith out of fear of losing what they already have. Some of them even hesitate to read a book such as this. *This is exactly how that one-talent servant thought*. He too was afraid that by investing his capital—investigating—he might lose his cherished possessions.

Of course, he felt he had "good reasons" for burying his wealth, *but the Master accepted none of them*. His Master had given him all the instructions, the signs, and clues: "behold, I have foretold you all things" (Mark 13:23). He knew that he must be watching for "the thief:" "I shall come upon you like a thief" (Rev. 3:3 NEB). *Watching is required only when someone or something can be missed*. He knew the command of the Scriptures: "Test everything" (I Thess.

5:21 NIV), "test the Spirits to see whether they are from God" (I John 4:1 NIV). He knew that once again the Master would appear to those who looked for him: "unto them that look for him shall he appear the second time" (Heb. 9:28).

He knew the blessed task his Lord had entrusted to him: "Happy that servant who is found at his task when his master comes!" (Matt. 24:46 NEB). What task? The task of looking for the Master: "Happy are those servants whom the master finds on the alert when he comes" (Luke 12:37 NEB). On the alert for what? For news of the coming of the Master; about the claim of the One who speaks, lives, and acts like the Master. "Keep your lamps burning" (Luke 12:35 NIV). What lamp? The lamp of search. He knew from the loving counsels of his Lord and Savior that with a little invest-ment of his time and talents he could sit with Him on His throne (Rev. 3:21) and receive the immortal crown of glory:

> And when the Chief Shepherd appears, you will receive the crown of glory that will never fade away.
>
> I Peter 5:4 NIV

Why then did this servant hesitate to search, to be daring? Why did he relinquish his responsibility? Why did he "bury" his "talents"? It is clear our Creator dearly loves and rewards courage, the spirit of adventure and openness. Avoidance and fear of the search for truth have no place in His Presence. In the Book of Revelation, too, Jesus warns that He will keep "the fearful" out of His Kingdom. *The first* obstacle to the kingdom of heaven, He specifies, is fear felt by His followers; *the second* is unbelief; *the third* is abominable deeds:

> He that overcometh [the obstacles] shall inherit all things; and I will be his God, and he shall be my son. But *the fearful*, and *the unbelieving,* and *the abominable*...shall have their part in the lake which burneth with fire [of separation from God]...   Christ (Revelation 21:7-8)

What kind of fear deserves such a severe punishment? None except this: the fear of searching for truth, the fear of losing the security that goes with inertia, with preserving the status quo, the fear of stepping into the Kingdom:

> Fear not, little flock; for it is your Father's good pleasure to give you the kingdom. Christ (Luke 12:32)

The consequence of this fear is often a lukewarm and apathetic attitude.

> I know your deeds, that you are neither cold nor hot. I wish you were either one or the other!
> Christ (Revelation 3:15 NIV)

> I know that you have little strength, yet you have kept my word and have not denied my name.
> Christ (Revelation 3:8 NIV)

The parable of the talents and the above quoted prophecy from Revelation both specify the same severe punishment for fearful believers. One describes the punishment as going to a place where there is sorrow and anger ("weeping and grinding of teeth"); the other as sinking in a burning desire for God and a consuming sense of remorse and grief for rejecting Heaven's brightest gift, for saying "no" to the call of the Lord, for refusing to examine even briefly His mighty words to get a glimpse of His great power and glory. The intention of the Master in using strong metaphors, such as "grinding of teeth," "scorching fire," or "burning lake" is not to frighten His beloved servants for whom He gave His life. His intention is to motivate them, to set them free from the fetters of fear and complacency. For He knows they will be afflicted with both. He knows that even the sound of the words "Christ has come again!" casts fear in their hearts.

After uttering the three parables, Jesus goes on to conclude His discourse (Matt. 25:31-46) with a brief profile of His own destiny when He comes again. He refers to **both** the glory that will accompany Him and the sufferings that He and His humble servants must endure again.

He states that when His new followers will be in pain and suffering, some people will offer them a helping hand, while others will ignore them. On those who offer help, He bestows the same sublime gift He grants to *the wise maidens and the wise servants*: "His Father's blessings" and "the kingdom that had been made ready for them since the world began." To them He says, "when I was hungry, you gave me food; when thirsty, you gave me drink; when I was a stranger you took me into your home, when naked you clothed me; when I was ill you came to my help, when in prison you visited me" (Matt. 25:35-36 NEB). When those servants ask the King, "When did we see you ill or in prison, and come to visit you?" (Matt. 25:39 NEB), He responds, "I tell you this: anything you did for one of my brothers here, however humble, you did for me" (Matt. 25:40 NEB).

On those who felt indifferent to the King's anguish and adversities, or refused to lend a helping hand to His humble and suffering servants, He inflicts a severe punishment: He deprives them of His glorious Kingdom (Matt. 25:41). To them He says:

> "The curse is upon you...for when I was hungry you gave me nothing to eat, when thirsty nothing to drink; when I was a stranger you gave me no home, when naked you did not clothe me; when I was ill and in prison you did not come to my help." And they too will reply, "Lord, when was it that we saw you hungry or thirsty or a stranger or naked or ill or in prison, and did nothing for you?" And he will answer, "I tell you this: anything you did not do for one of these, however humble, you did not do for me."
>   Christ (Matthew 25:41-46 NEB)

Why would people cause pain and suffering to their Redeemer? Why would they reject Him? Why would they mistreat His servants?

> There will be terrible times in the last days. People will be lovers of themselves, lovers of money...lovers of pleasure

rather than lovers of God—having a form of godliness but denying its power...They are the kind who...are...always learning but never able to acknowledge the truth. Just as Jannes and Jambres opposed Moses, so also these men oppose the truth... II Timothy 3:1-8 NIV

To reveal the state of the world at the time of His second coming, Jesus said:

As things were in Noah's days, so will they be when the Son of Man comes. Christ (Matthew 24:37 NEB)

The New American Bible version of the same verse reads:

The coming [parousia] of the Son of Man will repeat what happened in Noah's time. Matthew 24:37

The Greek word used here is *parousia*, which according to scholars means both *coming* and *presence*. As one source indicates: "*parousia* does not mean the moment of coming but covers the entire duration of the visit."[4] *Harper's Bible Dictionary* defines *parousia* as "arrival, coming, or being present."[5]

Isaiah too makes the same prediction:

These days recall for me the days of Noah... Isaiah 54:9 NEB

Noah was present among the people, yet they were unaware of *His* presence. To them He was as invisible as "a thief." They kept doing what they would usually do—"they ate and drank and married" (Luke 17:27 NEB); "they knew nothing until the flood came" (Matt. 24:39 NEB). Their minds were dulled by complacency, and their souls occupied with worldly cares. Those same obstacles are predicted to be pervasive at the time of the second advent:

Keep a watch on yourselves; do not let your minds be dulled by dissipation and drunkenness and worldly cares ...Be on the alert... Christ (Luke 21:34-36 NEB)

There is a close link between this prophecy and the one pointing to the destiny of Noah. The link is this:

- Certain veils will conceal the identity of Christ.
- These veils will be *spiritual*.

It is clear, "being on the alert" or "on the watch" can be attained by removing the veils, by cultivating a sincere desire to know the truth, and by paying attention to news of the Master's arrival.

Some Christians believe that as long as they belong to a certain church or espouse a particular set of beliefs, they will be the chosen ones. When Christ returns, He will take them to heaven (the rapture). They assume that only the Redeemer does the choosing, based on people's previous beliefs. There is little anyone can do except wait and hope that he or she will be one of the chosen ones. In one of His parables Jesus says:

> Be like men who wait for their master's return from a wedding-party, ready to let him in the moment he arrives and knocks. Happy are those servants whom the master finds on the alert when he comes. Christ (Luke 12:36-37 NEB)

What does Jesus mean by "knocks"? It is clear He means *the Redeemer will call you, invite you to His presence, or ask you to investigate His identity*. When someone knocks, the man or woman of the house has the freedom to either open the door or to leave it closed. What does Jesus mean by "let him in"? It is equally clear, He means *let him into your heart, be receptive, be open-minded*. Again the freedom of choice is evident. When a person knows the Voice, he opens the door without fear. If he cannot recognize it, he must investigate the caller. Not responding to him is the same as rejecting him. As these verses imply, people's freedom to choose or reject their Redeemer will not be taken away from them. This is how it has been and always will be. This subject is so critical, it is discussed in greater depth later.

(See God's eternal covenant with humanity: *I Have Set My Rainbow in the Clouds*, Chapter 21.) In the Book of Revelation, which is mainly about the return of the Redeemer of our time, Jesus confirms the human freedom to accept Him or reject Him:

> Here I stand knocking at the door; if anyone hears my voice and opens the door, I will come in and sit down to supper with him and he with me. To him who is victorious [in opening his heart] I will grant a place on my throne, as I myself was victorious and sat down with my Father on his throne. Hear, you who have ears to hear, what the Spirit says to the churches!   Christ (Revelation 3:20-22 NEB)

The Master simply *invites* the people to His banquet. He does not force them to attend. If they close their hearts to Him, He too will close His banquet to them:

> Blessed the insatiate soul who casteth away his selfish desires for love of Me and taketh his place at the banquet table which I have sent down from the heaven of divine bounty...[6]   Bahá'u'lláh

> I tell you that not one of those who were invited [but did not come] shall taste my banquet.   Christ (Luke 14:24 NEB)

The imagery Jesus uses to encourage investigation is always tinged with a most urgent and emphatic tone:

> Be ready for action, with belts fastened and lamps alight... ready to let him in the moment he arrives and knocks... Even if it is the middle of the night or before dawn...
> Christ (Luke 12:35-38 NEB)

This is the kind of readiness often required of soldiers or in emergencies. Why so much emphasis on speed?

The event is so vital and the consequence so far reaching that there must not be even a moment's hesitation between hearing the news of the coming of the Master and the initiation of the search and discovery mission.

On that day no one who is on the roof of his house, with
his goods inside, should go down to get them. Likewise,
no one in the field should go back for anything.

Christ (Luke 17:31 NIV)

To summarize, "watch" is a state of mind opposite to "sleep."
Sleeping implies negligence, unawareness, an inability to see
or hear; the absence of a desire to think, to know, and to
investigate. To be asleep is to be wrapped in one's fantasies
and illusions; to rest in the dark of one's wishes, dreams, and
desires. To be alert and watchful is to learn, to see, to inquire,
to test, to stay in touch with a larger dimension of life than
one's own preoccupations. The glory of the dawn always goes
unnoticed by the sleeper, but never by the careful watchman.

In the spring of 1833, eleven years before the advent of the
Báb, Miss Margaret MacDonald of Scotland disclosed the
message of a vision she claimed she had received about the
manner of Christ's return. Her vision offers further insight
into the meaning of the critical word "*Watch!*" and the purpose
of Jesus' prophetic parables. She recorded and printed an
account of her vision under the title "Recollections of the
first morning of the outpouring of the Spirit:"

It was first the awful state of the land that was pressed
upon me. I saw the blindness and infatuation of the people
to be very great...Now there is distress of nations, with
perplexity, the seas and the waves roaring, men's hearts
failing them for fear—now look out for the sign of the
Son of man. Here I was made to stop and cry out, O it
is not known what the sign of the Son of man is; the
people of God think they are waiting, but they know not
what it is. I felt this needed to be revealed, and that there
was great darkness and error about it...*I saw the error to
be, that men think that it will be something seen by the
natural eye; but 'tis spiritual discernment that is needed,
the eye of God in his people*. Many passages were
revealed, in a light in which I had not before seen them.

I repeated, 'Now is the kingdom of Heaven like unto ten virgins, who went forth to meet the Bridegroom, five wise and five foolish; they that were foolish took their lamps, but took no oil with them; but they that were wise took oil in their vessels with their lamps.' 'But be ye not unwise, but understanding what the will of the Lord is; and be not drunk with wine...but be filled with the Spirit.' This was the oil the wise virgins took in their vessels—this is the light to be kept burning—the light of God—that we may discern that which cometh not with observation to the natural eye. *Only those who have the light of God within them will see the sign of his appearance...I often said, Oh the glorious inbreaking of God which is now about to burst on this earth...It was a glorious light above the brightness of the sun, that shone round about me. I felt that those who were filled with the Spirit could see spiritual things, and feel walking in the midst of them, while those who had not the Spirit could see nothing—* so that two shall be in one bed, the one taken and the other left, because the one has the light of God within while the other cannot see the Kingdom of Heaven.[7] [Emphasis added.]

Some authorities maintain that Miss MacDonald's vision gave rise to the idea of "the rapture," to the expectation that Jesus will make two appearances, first secretly, and then later openly. More about this in Appendix III.

As stated, in the Book of Revelation Jesus offers many gifts to those who overcome the obstacles that prevent them from knowing their Lord. This is one of them:

To him who overcomes and does my will to the end...I will also give him the morning star.   Revelation 2:26,28 NIV

In 1852, a noted Christian author, John Darby wrote:

And who is it that sees the morning star? He who watches while it is night. All see the sun in its brightness; but those only who are not of the night, yet knowing that morally it is night and are looking for the morning star— those, and those only, see the morning star and get it as their portion.[8]

The meaning of the command "Watch!" and "Be on the alert!" become clearer when we study in the next chapter Jesus' purpose in saying, "I shall come upon you like a thief!"

2

I Shall Come Upon You Like a Thief

Revelation 3:3 NEB

Part I

I beseech God, exalted be His glory, that He may graciously awaken the peoples of the earth...[1]

Bahá'u'lláh

That is the day when I come like a thief! Happy the man who stays awake... Christ (Revelation 16:15 NEB)

Christian scholar Dr. Ray Stedman, in his book *Waiting for the Second Coming*, writes:

The first characteristic of the Day of the Lord, said Paul to the Thessalonians, is that it will come stealthily. It will come "like a thief in the night" (v. 2). I recall hearing of an incident where an entire family was sleeping upstairs one night when someone entered their home and stole several items of value; the thief came and left without their knowing it. That is the way a professional thief operates. He enters silently and unobtrusively and does his work. That, said Paul, is the way the Lord will come.[2]

He then concludes:

> What should be the result in our lives?...The apostle [Paul] stirs us from our apathy and from fantasies and dreams such as the world dreams..."Be alert," warns the apostle (v. 6). "Do not lose sight of reality. This is the hour when God is about to move on earth again. Snap out of your lethargy and tune in to His voice."[3]

The Master's Strategy

Why does the Master urge His servants to stay awake, to keep constant watch? The Master has a clear and definitive plan; to pursue it, He has devised a perfect strategy, an ingenious plot. His chief goal is to disclose His glory to His faithful and humble servants, while concealing it from others. To accomplish this goal, He offers certain simple but coded instructions that He knows only His faithful and humble servants can decipher; He gives certain emphatic warnings that He knows only *they* will heed.

No ordinary plotter can do this. Only a divine strategist can devise such instructions. Only *He* can conceal a blazing glory before whose radiance the sun, with all its splendor, pales into darkness. Only *He* can hide His identity from the great masses of perfectly sighted but inattentive and veiled viewers —those who look but see only their own desires, who think but within the domain of tradition, who listen but hear only the whisperings of their own selves, who dig deep into the earth, discover and detect long-forgotten facts from fading archaeological records but fail to discern the luminous face of their Lord. Only *He* has the wisdom to devise a strategy that can be deciphered by a few of His simple and humble servants, but remain a supreme mystery to others—among them some of His most well read, best educated, and noted followers. He is the Perfect Plotter, the Supreme Strategist of the universe, the All-Knowing, the All-Wise.

He knows that only His most humble servants will undertake the effort of searching for His concealed glory. He predicts that others will be busy with their daily affairs (Matt. 24:37-39)—working, vacationing, studying, saving, worrying and wondering why, in spite of all material means and comforts, life is so full of stress and distress. He knows that people will have more things to do than they have time for; that there will be too many attractions to allow them to be attracted to their Lord. To awaken them, He gives them this astonishingly clear and definitive clue, which He knows most people will not heed; if they did, His prophecy would not come true:

> The coming of the Son of Man will repeat what happened in Noah's time. Christ (Matthew 24:37 NAB)

To pursue His plan the Master must choose the most advantageous time—when people live in the darkest depths of unawareness. The Master had used this same strategy before. It had worked then; it must work again. While the great masses of people and their leaders had their sights set on a mighty Messiah crowned with jewels, a Prince adorned with swords, a King with myriads of angels at His command, He came in the guise of a poor and humble man with no home to protect Him from the heat of the blazing sun, with no bed to give Him rest through the long hours of the night. Only a handful discerned His divine glory. People do not change that much. If the strategy worked then, it must work again.

Those who were eloquent orators and gifted debaters, who could hold spellbound an audience with their brilliant interpretation of prophecies; those who were the unquestioned teachers of the Law, the masters of Hebrew and Greek; those who could quote verse after verse from memory with their exact location in the Scriptures—yes, scholars, leaders, and orators of great distinction who could do all these and more, could not discern the blazing glory of their Messiah, the One who was the light of the world. Why did their education *not* lead them to their Lord? "The letter they knew, but of the spirit they knew nothing."

The Jews looked at their suffering Master, but saw only mercy, misery, and meekness. Of misery and meekness, they had plenty. They lived like slaves in their own country. And mercy could not save them from the hands of an astute enemy. Only power could restore their pride.

They asked their Master to come down from the cross and prove His powers. They wondered why a Savior could not save Himself. While they were busy mocking the Son of God sent from heaven (John 6:38); while they were laughing and jeering at the One whom Bahá'u'lláh calls *the Lord of the visible and invisible*; while they were rejoicing that they had done away with an impostor, a handful of people, mostly unschooled, very ordinary people—peasants and fishermen— were bitterly mourning the painful and agonizing departure of their Lord, their only hope and desire. Yes, people do not change that much. The strategy worked then, it must work again.

Even if this drama repeats itself a thousand times, people will continue to do what others have done before them. They will repeat the exact words of their forefathers. They will say, "No, this time is different. This time our Master will be a *real* king. This time He will have a *real* throne. This time He will soar through the clouds of glory like a blazing shaft of light with the roar of thunder. He will *not* be crowned again with thorn and thistle. He will *not* fall again into the hands of His enemies. The stars of heaven will crown Him. He will *not* be held by the harsh hands of His foes, but by the soft embrace of a rainbow. He will *not* need again the help of the poor and lowly. At His command He will have the arrayed armies and angels of heaven." Most people do not learn from the experience of others, especially from what others experienced long ago.

The Master knows that when He comes, the darkness of despair and confusion will be so vast and deep that, without His help, even His most humble servants will fail to find Him. To guide their steps by the light of knowledge, He offers them hundreds of clues and warnings. He tells them that *that day* will come under the veil of clouds and darkness, and so will *the Master*.

Perhaps no one is as much concerned with preserving secrecy as a thief. Everything he does revolves around that goal. The strategy of a thief offers a perfect demonstration of the Master's strategy. These two warnings—about the secret coming of the Master, *and* the secret coming of His day—should not simply be read and glossed over, but pondered upon day and night. They should adorn a wall in every home:

> ...I shall come upon you like a thief...
>
> Christ (Revelation 3:3 NEB)

> Lo, I am going to come like a thief! Blessed—happy, to be envied—is he who stays awake (alert)...
>
> Christ (Revelation 16:15 AB)

> ...*the day* of the Lord will come like a thief in the night [emphasis added].   I Thessalonians 5:2 NIV

That day arrives secretly and passes secretly, even as a thief does. The sleepers are taken by surprise, unaware of what has happened. If they knew the exact time, secrecy could not be maintained. The event must occur when people least expect it:

> But understand this: If the owner of the house had known at what hour the thief was coming, he would not have let his house be broken into. You also must be ready, because the Son of Man will come at an hour when you do not expect him.   Christ (Luke 12:39-40 NIV)

The owner of the house or the ***householder*** here symbolizes a person in possession of the desired resources: knowledge, wealth, power, prestige. As we already noted, Jesus applies the term specifically to religious leaders (Matt. 24:45-47) or to the teachers of the word of God who are given instructions about "the kingdom of heaven," namely the coming of God's kingdom to the earthly realm:

> ...every teacher of the law [of the Lord] who has been instructed about the kingdom of heaven is like the owner of a house who brings out of his storeroom new treasures as well as old.   Christ (Matthew 13:52 NIV)

Those in positions of power tend to see themselves as "the householders" and the new Redeemer as "a thief" who comes to steal their spiritual and earthly heritage. Instinctively, they distrust Him and try to prevent Him from pursuing His plans. For instance, those who had the most to lose, conspired against Jesus. They thought that by crucifying Him they could stop His influence. They were the enemies of His plan. Yet without knowing it, they became the instruments of His plan.

Their counterparts tried to destroy Bahá'u'lláh by sending Him to the most deadly prison in the most desolate city in the Holy Land. Without knowing it, they too became the instruments of His plan. Instead of changing that which was pre-ordained, they brought about its fulfillment. The same kind of people imprisoned and executed the Báb for the same reasons, and faced the same consequence:

> Ye cannot alter the things which the Almighty hath prescribed unto Me. Naught shall touch Me besides that which God, My Lord, hath pre-ordained for Me. In Him have I placed my whole trust...[4]   The Báb

How can the thief preserve and pursue His pre-ordained plan? How can He keep His enemies in the dark? He can do this by clothing the bare facts of His coming with symbols. The secret must always be kept in such a way as to allow no one the opportunity to misuse or undermine any part of the divine plan. If the householder could decipher some of the thief's well-guarded secrets, then perhaps he could prevent the thief from "breaking into his home," into what he considers rightfully his own, the domain of his rule and power. If the householder could decode more than he is allowed, then perhaps he could prevent or alter the execution of the thief's plans.

The Day of Return is inscrutable unto all men until after the divine Revelation hath been fulfilled.[5]   Bahá'u'lláh

When King Herod learned from the wise men of the East that the king of the Jews was born, he feared the loss of his power, and plotted in vain to destroy the child before He could attain His divine destiny (Matt. 2:1-18). An angel in a dream inspired Joseph to take Jesus and Mary to Egypt, where they could live in safety. If this help had not come, Jesus could not have fulfilled His Mission. Because the secrets were kept, Herod was unable to alter the pre-ordained plan. Not only that, he himself served as an instrument in carrying out the plan. Without knowing it, he brought about the fulfillment of the prophecies (Matt. 2:15).

The kings and rulers in the 19th century also tried in vain to devise ingenious plots against the Báb and Bahá'u'lláh (see Volumes II and III):

Why do the nations rage and the peoples plot in vain? The kings of the earth take their stand and the rulers gather together against the Lord...   Psalms 2:1-2 NIV

The term *householder* also symbolizes any individual who does not wish to open his heart to the Master, and to let "his house be broken into." He is the person who does not feel threatened by the good news of the Kingdom, but would like to retain what he already has. Since he does not feel threatened, he does not try to hinder the thief. His main goal is simply to protect *himself*.

The Master, of course, honors his wishes and in no way does He try to enter his heart without his consent, without being invited. How can He do this? This, too, He can do by *"not* removing the veil," by living as other humans do, by being humble "like a servant" (Luke 22:27), and by *not* engaging in dramatic displays of His divine power, His supreme splendor. That is His best strategy.

No other analogy than "the householder who fears his house will be broken into" could better describe the way people feel when they are asked to renew their spiritual possessions, such as by adopting a new name. They know the Master's promise and pre-ordained plan: "the old order of things has passed away...I am making everything new!" (Rev. 21:4-5 NIV). Yet they feel threatened by the new order of things; they perceive it as a loss of their eternal heritage. They know the Master has asked them to stay awake, yet they remain absorbed in their dreams. Why?

> We may enjoy the dreaming part so much that we do not even want to consider that there is much more available if we awaken. Thus we choose to remain asleep, unaware of the grandness that is there for us in awakening. When we stay with the familiar we take no risks.   Dr. Wayne Dyer

Among the many who sleep with their hearts and homes firmly locked, among the multitudes who cherish the comfort of sleeping and the joy of dreaming, a few adventurous householders do just the opposite. They keep constant vigilance through the whole night with their hopes aglow and their hearts and homes open. They trim their lamps, and wear their beautiful white robes with fastened belts, ready for the call to the banquet. They keep their eyes on the door and set their hopes on heaven. They pray through the whole night, and wait for their heavenly Bridegroom to arrive at any moment and take them. They want to be *His* possession. That is their highest hope, their most cherished desire and honor.

Fear finds no room in their souls. They know no intruder can rob them, no earthly thief, no imposter can break in and steal the precious pearl of their faith. Their trust in their Lord is limitless, their confidence in His undying care and protection beyond measure.

When the heavenly thief knocks, they hear His call and know His voice. They jump with joy—as a bride who hears the voice of her adored One—and welcome Him to their arms, to their hearts and homes with the utmost ecstasy. As a reward for their faith, vigilance, and courage, the heavenly thief takes them all for Himself. He needs many jewels for the crown of His Kingdom. He seeks them and gathers them from the farthest reaches of the earth, from the houses and the fields, the meadows and mountains. And He does all this in full secrecy from the slumberers. How could they hear Him? How could they know? It is midnight. They are sound asleep and dreaming.

The heavenly thief knows that to remain invisible, He must take only the hearts and souls of His servants. *If He took their bodies, He would awaken some of the slumberers*. That would violate His most urgent concern: secrecy.

> Two men will be in the field; one will be taken and the other left. Two women will be grinding with a hand mill; one will be taken and the other left. Therefore keep watch...   Christ (Matthew 24:40-42 NIV)

Those taken are the first fruits of the vineyard of the Lord, ripe and ready for the kingdom.

> Then as I looked there appeared a white cloud, and on the cloud sat one like a son of man. He had on his head a crown of gold and in his hand a sharp sickle. Another angel came out of the temple and called in a loud voice to him who sat on the cloud: 'Stretch out your sickle and reap; for harvest-time has come, and earth's crop is over-ripe.' So he who sat on the cloud put his sickle to the earth and its harvest was reaped.   Revelation 14:14-16 NEB

What then does the Master's secret plan require from the sincere seekers of truth, from those who wish to welcome their Master, from those who do not mind "their house being broken into"? It requires perfect readiness, absolute receptivity and sensitivity. That is how Jesus concludes the analogy: "you also must be ready" (Luke 12:40 NIV). The seekers must be as prepared to play their role as the Master does His.

Of course the Master does not need to keep everything a secret. To the seekers of His Kingdom He has offered all the clues they need to find Him: "behold I have foretold you all things" (Mark 13:23). But they are the kind of clues that would neither help the householder to prevent the thief from carrying out His plan, nor force him into submission. The householder has the right to enjoy his own spiritual freedom, but not to violate the Master's. He has the right to keep *his* heart closed to the Master, but not to keep *Him* beyond the reach of *other* hearts.

It is an essential part of the Master's plan and an eternal requirement of His Covenant, to become known *only to those who sincerely seek Him by being faithful to His instructions, only to those who use all their talents, only to those who strive with their whole heart for the un-paralleled reward of finding their Lord*.

> ...thou shalt find him, if thou seek him with all thy heart and with all thy soul.   Deuteronomy 4:29

To be known is one of the Master's most cherished desires, but only to those servants *who leave their selves behind*.

> If anyone wishes to be a follower of mine, he must leave self behind...Whoever cares for his own safety is lost...
> Christ (Luke 9:23-24 NEB)

> If anyone would come after me, he must deny himself and take up his cross and follow me.
> Christ (Matthew 16:24 NIV)

No one who sets his hand to the plough and then keeps looking back is fit for the kingdom of God.

> Christ (Luke 9:62 NEB)

The heavenly Host does not wish to have any ungrateful or unprepared guests at His banquet:

> The kingdom of Heaven is like this. There was a king who prepared a feast for his son's wedding...When the king came in to see the company at table, he observed one man who was not dressed for a wedding. "My friend," said the king, "how do you come to be here without your wedding clothes?" He had nothing to say. The king then said to his attendants, "Bind him hand and foot; turn him out into the dark, the place of wailing and grinding of teeth." For though many are invited, few are chosen.
>
> Christ (Matthew 22:1-2, 11-14 NEB)

The Master wants to be followed *only* by those who set aside whatever pleases *them*—whether it is the quiet and comfort of tradition or "the ease of a passing day"—to pursue that which pleases *their Lord*. His plan is to test those who call on His name, to measure their purity in the crucible of trials. He intends to separate the Annases and Caiaphases from the Peters and Mary Magdalenes. He wishes to disclose people's inward motives:

> ...wait until the Lord comes. For he will bring to light what darkness hides, and *disclose men's inward motives* [emphasis added throughout]...   I Corinthians 4:5 NEB

It was for the same reason—to test His followers—that the Master hid Himself behind "the clouds of glory" on his first appearance:

> Many in Israel will stand or fall because of him [Jesus], and thus *the secret thoughts of many will be laid bare*.
>
> Luke 2:35 NEB

If the Master revealed His *full* glory, how could people feel
free to disclose their true selves, their inner motives? If the
Master "removed the veil," who could dare deny Him? How
could anyone *not* see or recognize Him?

> Were I to remove the veil, all would recognize Me as their
> Best Beloved, and no one would deny Me.[6]   The Báb

Why does Jesus use the word "if" in the following prophecy
addressed to the people of our time?

> *Wake up*! Strengthen what remains and is about to die, for
> *I have not found your deeds complete in the sight of my
> God*. Remember, therefore, what you have received and
> heard; obey it, and repent. But *if* you do not wake up, I
> will come like a thief...He who has an ear, let him hear
> what the Spirit says to the churches.
>
> > Christ (Revelation 3:2, 3, 6 NIV)

Does Jesus mean the way He comes depends on how people
will act? Does He mean that if Christians fail to watch for
Him, He will come like a thief, otherwise not like a thief?
The answer to this question can be found in the first two
words of the prophecy. Jesus begins by urging Christians to
"*Wake up*!" Evidently He knew they would be asleep at His
coming and must be awakened. He knew they would be
dreaming their own earthly dreams and would be unable to
see and recognize their Master's heavenly visions of truth and
glory. "If a little eyelid can conceal the world, what then can
the vast expanse of human thoughts and theories, advanced
and stored for centuries, conceal?"[7]

The answer to the meaning of "if" can also be found in
other prophecies where Jesus declares unconditionally that He
will indeed come like a thief (Rev. 16:15). Then what does
the word "if" imply? It implies this: the thief remains invisible only to those who stay asleep; He remains hidden only
to those who fail to watch for Him, who ignore the good news
of His coming. He need not hide Himself from others. Why
would He wish to conceal Himself from those who have been

faithful to His counsels, who have remained awake and alert to the news, *who have been looking for Him*?

> ...unto them that look for him shall he appear the second time... Hebrews 9:28

That a shroud enfolds all people, that a veil conceals the heavenly thief is confirmed also in this prophecy:

> ...the covering that covereth all peoples, and the veil that is spread over all nations. Isaiah 25:7 ARV

> Behold how great is the Cause, and yet how the people are wrapt in veils.[8] The Báb

> ...the peoples of the world are wrapt in palpable veils.[9] Bahá'u'lláh

> The accumulations of vain fancy have obscured men's ears and stopped them from hearing the Voice of God, and the veils of human learning and false imaginings have prevented their eyes from beholding the splendor of the light of His countenance.[10] Bahá'u'lláh

God's Wisdom ordains that only the "eye" that is humble, unafraid, and pure from preconceived, even though popular, notions should see the Lord.

> ...without holiness no one will see the Lord. Hebrews 12:14 NIV

Thus visibility or invisibility is a result of *people's* responses. *They* choose to see or not to see the heavenly thief. If they search for their Master with open hearts and minds, they will behold His heavenly glory, otherwise they will see nothing but the clouds of their own desires and fantasies.

> Awake, sleeper...and Christ will shine upon you. Ephesians 5:14 NEB

The Master remains forever both manifest and hidden.

...He is the Beginning and the End, the Manifest and the Hidden...[11]   The Báb

One more point: just before saying that He will come like a thief, Jesus declared:

Remember, therefore, what you have received and heard; obey it, and repent.   Christ (Revelation 3:3 NIV)

What does He ask the servant to obey? The context of the passage clearly shows He asks the servant to obey the commandment to stay awake and to investigate the good news of His Return. In the next verse He predicts that at His coming only *a few* will keep their "clothes" pure. Only *a few* will walk with Him dressed in white (Rev. 3:4).

The Most Manifest And the Most Hidden

To gain a glimmer of God's Wisdom, to understand how the Creator relates to humans, it is absolutely essential to recognize the immutable and universal "law of visibility and invisibility." The best evidence of God's unlimited and mysterious powers is this: ***He always remains both the most visible and the most invisible to human beings***. He is everywhere and in everything:

The glory and greatness of Almighty God are marvelously discerned in all His works and divinely read in the book of heaven.   Galileo Galilei

Everyone who is seriously involved in the pursuit of science becomes convinced that a Spirit is manifest in the Law of the Universe—a Spirit vastly superior to that of man, and one in the face of which we, with our modest powers, must feel humble.   Albert Einstein

Nature is too thin a screen; the glory of the omnipresent God bursts through everywhere.   Ralph Waldo Emerson

Every atom declares God's supreme grandeur; every star manifests His awesome splendor; every flower unfolds His wisdom and wonders. He shines with dazzling brightness, yet many cannot detect even the faintest glimmer of His glory. Among those incapable of finding any evidence of God are some of the most astute scientists who detect invisible atoms and distant galaxies billions of light years away, yet fail to detect God. Nothing could be more puzzling.

How profound our sense of wonder if we learned that millions of people with perfect eyes were unable to see, or that countless others with flawless hearing could not hear. That is how puzzling it is to know that many of the people with the sharpest minds—minds that penetrate the most abstruse mysteries of nature—cannot discern God. Yet this is so commonplace that we are used to accepting it with little, if any, surprise.

The ability to make and maintain the mysterious "law of visibility and invisibility" is perhaps the most marvelous evidence of the Creator's supreme power and wisdom. If this law were ever lifted, the whole purpose and design of creation would instantly crumble. This universal law holds true not only in the way God reveals Himself to humans, *but also in the way His Messengers or Mediators reveal themselves*. That some humans *give* their lives for those Messengers, whereas others *take* the lives of those Messengers is a clear evidence of this supreme mystery, of how well this immutable law is upheld.

> ...they [God's Messengers] all abide on the throne of divine Revelation, and are established upon the seat of divine Concealment.[12]   Bahá'u'lláh

> ...[they are] the throne of the revelation and concealment of God among His creatures...[13]   The Báb

> They are the mirrors that truly and faithfully reflect the light of God. Whatever is applicable to them is in reality

applicable to God, Himself, Who is both the Visible and
the Invisible.[14]   Bahá'u'lláh

Our Creator keeps a perfect balance between how much of
His glory He should reveal to inspire faith without disturb-
ing our freedom, and how much of His glory He should
conceal from those unreceptive to His call and unworthy of
attaining His presence. Thus the supreme gift of knowing
Him is not imposed and the bounty of loving Him does not
lose its luster.

> Truly you are a God who hides himself...   Isaiah 45:15 NIV

> He chose to hide His own Self behind a thousand veils,
> lest profane and mortal eyes discover His glory.[15]
>   Bahá'u'lláh

> He wraps himself in light as with a garment...He makes
> the clouds his chariot and rides on the wings of the wind.
>   Psalms 104:2-3 NIV

To the king who exiled Him, the Báb wrote:

> Were the veil to be removed from thine eye thou wouldst
> crawl unto Me on thy breast, even through the snow, from
> fear of the chastisement of God...[16]

Without *humility*, and constant *striving* and searching, the
"morning light" hides forever behind the "veils of glory:"

> Let us *humble* ourselves, let us *strive* to know the Lord,
> whose justice dawns like morning light, and its dawning
> is as sure as the sunrise.   Hosea 6:3 NEB

> ...if you search with all your heart, I [God] will let you
> find me...   Jeremiah 29:14 NEB

If people saw the Master's heavenly Kingdom, if they beheld
the glories of "immortal sovereignty" in His "Father's many
mansions" (John 14:2), how could they *not* feel forced to
carry the cross after Him, to become His perfect followers?

Did thou behold immortal sovereignty, thou wouldst strive to pass from this fleeting world. But to conceal the one from thee and to reveal the other is a mystery which none but the pure in heart can comprehend.[17]   Bahá'u'lláh

Should the greatness of this Day be revealed in its fullness, every man would forsake a myriad lives in his longing to partake, though it be for one moment, of its great glory— how much more this world and its corruptible treasures![18]
Bahá'u'lláh

The great mathematician, Blaise Pascal, discerned not only the mysteries of the visible but the invisible as well. Here he speaks about Christ but his thought expresses a universal principle that establishes the Creator's relationship with all humankind for all time:

It was...not right that Christ should appear in a manner manifestly divine and absolutely capable of convincing all men, but neither was it right that His coming should be so hidden that He could not be recognized by those who sincerely sought Him. He wished to make Himself perfectly recognizable to them. Thus wishing to appear openly to those who seek Him with all their heart and hidden from those who shun Him with all their heart, He has qualified our knowledge of Him by giving signs which can be seen by those who seek Him and not by those who do not.

The basic laws that govern the relationship between the Creator and the created never change.

Every part of this law must remain in force upon all mankind, and in all ages; as not depending either on time or place, or any other circumstances liable to change, but on the nature of God, and the nature of man, and their unchangeable relation to each other.   John Wesley

There is no pleasure or honor in entering hearts by force and fear. The Master's glory lies in this: to be invited and welcomed. If He wished, He could conquer the hearts of all humanity in an instant:

> Should it be Our wish, it is in Our power to compel, through the agency of but one letter of Our Revelation, the world and all that is therein to recognize, in less than the twinkling of an eye, the truth of Our Cause...[19]
>
> The Báb

> ...one drop out of the ocean of His bountiful grace is enough to confer upon all beings the glory of everlasting life. But inasmuch as the divine Purpose hath decreed that the true should be known from the false...He hath, therefore, in every season sent down upon mankind the showers of tests from His realm of glory.[20]   Bahá'u'lláh

"The arm of the Lord is not too short" to reach and lift all those who are fallen. It is the fallen who avoid His arm. His light dazzles the eyes. It is the eyes that avoid His light.

> Surely the arm of the Lord is not too short to save...your sins have hidden his face from you...   Isaiah 59:1-2 NIV

The sun with all its glory is veiled by a little eyelid. How much more can be veiled by the drifting mists of fancy and desire, by the glow and glitter of the world?[21]

> The light shines on in the dark, and the darkness has never mastered it.   John 1:5 NEB

Who Shall Sit Upon the Throne?

What is "the great Day of the Lord" like? It is a time when "many...shall be tried" (Daniel 12:10); when the work of each person "will be shown for what it is, because the Day will bring it to light. It will be revealed with fire, and the fire will test the quality of each man's work" (I Cor. 3:13 NIV).

> For there is nothing hidden that will not become public, nothing under cover that will not be made known and brought into the open.   Christ (Luke 8:17 NEB)

Those who recognize and follow the Redeemer are promised "thrones of their own" in the Kingdom of heaven:

> ...in the world that is to be...you my followers will have thrones of your own...　　　　Christ (Matthew 19:28 NEB)
> See also I Peter 5:4

Those who trust the Redeemer, who discern His power and glory in the garment of humility and weakness, who look beyond the barrier of flesh to see the divine in the human, can *also* behold the heavenly throne in all its splendor behind the veils of the world. Others see nothing but an empty promise. Who shall sit upon the throne and be crowned? Only those who stand the test:

> Blessed is the man who perseveres under trial, because when he has stood the test, he will receive the crown of life...　　　　James 1:12 NIV

In the earthly realm no one can escape tests and trials. Even the distinguished disciples were asked to pray for strength to face the loss of their Lord: "pray that you may be spared the test" (Matt. 26:41 NEB). Even the Redeemer Himself went through trials to set an example for others (Matt. 26:39-44).

> Even gold passes through the assayer's fire, and more precious than perishable gold is faith which has stood the test. These trials come so that your faith may prove itself worthy...when Jesus Christ is revealed.　　　I Peter 1:7 NEB

> ...from time immemorial even unto eternity the Almighty hath tried, and will continue to try, His servants, so that light may be distinguished from darkness...[22]　　　Bahá'u'lláh

The Redeemer presents an awesome challenge to those who call on His name: "Who can stand when he [the Redeemer] appears? For he will be like a refiner's fire" (Mal. 3:2 NIV). Only those who enter His fiery crucible with courage, faith, and patience can stand the test, can meet the demands of the Hour. Only *they* are granted the crown of immortal glory.

To attain the Master's presence and become worthy of His grace, those who seek His Kingdom must put *all* their spiritual talents to work. They must be ready to encounter and endure the hardest tests and trials. They must put tradition aside and become as nonjudgmental and pure as little children. For "whoever does not accept the kingdom of God like a child will never enter it" (Luke 18:17 NEB). They must constantly recall the Master's words: "Be careful, or your hearts will be weighed down with dissipation, drunkenness and the anxieties of life, and that day will close on you unexpectedly like a trap" (Luke 21:34 NIV).

> Only when the lamp of search, of earnest striving, of longing desire, of passionate devotion, of fervid love, of rapture, and ecstasy, is kindled within the seeker's heart, and the breeze of His loving-kindness is wafted upon his soul, will the darkness of error be dispelled, the mists of doubts and misgivings be dissipated, and the lights of knowledge and certitude envelop his being.[23]   Bahá'u'lláh

To live up to the awesome challenge the thief presents, the highest degree of alertness is required. The hearers must be ready to test *every* call, just as the detectives must be willing to follow *every* lead.

> On this journey [of the search for truth] the traveler abideth in every land and dwelleth in every region. In every face, he seeketh the beauty of the Friend; in every country he looketh for the Beloved. He joineth every company, and seeketh fellowship with every soul, that haply in some mind he may uncover the secret of the Friend, or in some face he may behold the beauty of the Loved One.[24]   Bahá'u'lláh

Power and Glory

One question remains. The Master gave all these clues and instructions to show that His return would not be dramatic. Why, then, did He say that He would come on clouds with great power and glory? This question has deeply puzzled Christian scholars. Some of them, such as Dr. Ray Stedman, have resolved the paradox this way: Christ will make two appearances, first "stealthily, without warning," and then later from heaven with power and glory.[25] Before reading further, perhaps you could resolve the puzzle on your own:

- The Master wants to carry out His plan with precision. He does not want the householder to have any opportunity to alter or undermine His original design.

- He wants to test His servants in every possible way, so that nothing hidden is left undisclosed. He wants to separate those who are willing to search for their Master from those who are content with the security of a well-established name.

- He does not wish to have any unprepared or ungrateful guests at His banquet.

- He does not wish to allow anyone the privilege of applying the prophecies to himself. If people were absolutely sure how the Master would come and on what "day and hour," some of them would imitate Him. They would advance an identical claim, at the same time, and in the same way.

What strategies should the Master adopt?

The Master is extremely kind and caring. He would not give an incomprehensible puzzle to His beloved servants: "my yoke is easy and my burden is light" (Matt. 11:30 NIV). He has left them many instructions. What they need is not a new course in theology, but a fresh mind uncluttered by preconceived notions. And if for any reason they fail to resolve the puzzle, He has promised to resolve it for them when He returns. Since everyone errs and "falls short of the glory of God" (Romans 3:23 NIV), it would be best if no one came to a final conclusion without first studying all the new clues and instructions the Master has promised to reveal upon His return:

...judge nothing before the appointed time; wait till the Lord comes. *He will bring to light what is hidden in darkness* [emphasis added]...   I Corinthians 4:5 NIV

In keeping with the preceding promise, Bahá'u'lláh, the Glory of God, decoded all the clues needed for resolving the divine puzzle.

Every hidden thing hath been brought to light, by the virtue of the Will of the Supreme Ordainer [emphasis added]...[26]   Bahá'u'lláh

Through Him hath appeared that which had been hidden from time immemorial and been veiled from the eyes of men.[27]   Bahá'u'lláh

We have decreed, O people, that the highest and last end of all learning be the recognition of Him Who is the Object of all knowledge; and yet, behold how ye have allowed your learning to shut you out, as by a veil, from Him Who is the Dayspring of this Light, through Whom every hidden thing hath been revealed.[28]   Bahá'u'lláh

Some of the mysteries Bahá'u'lláh has brought to light are presented later in this volume, many others in succeeding volumes.

People have always faced difficult puzzles. How best can they be deciphered? By mastering Hebrew and Greek? By reading the latest archeological research? By going to the most prestigious universities with the most scholarly publications on the Scriptures? This prophecy points specifically to the people of our time:

They are the kind who...are...always learning but never able to acknowledge the truth.   II Timothy 3:6-7 NIV

The people of Israel faced puzzles very similar to ours. Who solved their puzzles? Was it Annas and Caiaphas (the leading religious leaders and scholars of their time), or was it Peter (a fisherman) and Mary Magdalene (a peasant)? Who was more educated among Jesus' twelve apostles? Was it the man who betrayed Him or the man who could hardly keep track of the days of the week? Who recognized the glory of the Master? The unknown woman who cheered her Lord and immortalized her memory by pouring her precious perfume on Him, or the established teachers of the Law who jeered at Him?

> ...wherever the gospel is preached throughout the world, what she has done will also be told, in memory of her.
>
> Christ (Mark 14:9 NIV)

Who, then, can solve the divine puzzle? And who is crowned with salvation?

> For the Lord takes delight in his people; he crowns *the humble* with salvation [emphasis added].   Psalms 149:4 NIV

> Seek the Lord, all you humble of the land...Seek righteousness, *seek humility*; perhaps you will be sheltered on the day of the Lord's anger [our day].   Zephaniah 2:3 NIV

What More Could the Master Say?

Let us summarize some of the devices Jesus used to communicate the absolute necessity of finding and recognizing Him—in His second advent as in the first—through *investigation*:

A Command

- The command to "Watch!", to be always *awake* and *alert*—terms that say: "*Investigate!*"

Analogies

- The analogy of "the thief in the night" to convey secrecy, to declare this message: *investigate* the news of the coming of the Master just as a detective would follow every lead to find a thief (Matt. 24:43; Rev. 3:3).

- The analogy of "the sheep and the goats" to show a contrast between those in the Master's flock, namely the Christians, who will hear and welcome the chief Shepherd and those who will ignore His call (Matt. 25:32-34).

Historical Examples

- "The story of Noah and Lot" to show both the secret coming of the Master and the denial He must face again (Matt. 24:37-39).

Parables

- Three parables to explain further the meaning of the word "Watch!" (Matt. 24:42-51; 25:1-30).

- Two parables to portray the gradual growth or unfolding of the Redeemer's heavenly Kingdom on earth: the parable of "mustard seed," and that of "the leaven" (Matt. 13:31-33).

- Two parables to show both the secrecy of the Redeemer's return and the need for preparing and investigating the onset of His Kingdom: the parable of "the hidden treasure," and that of "a merchant looking for fine pearls" (Matt. 13:44-46).

- A second parable on the theme of a wedding banquet to teach that God will continue to honor the freedom He has granted to humanity, that people will indeed have a choice between receiving their Redeemer or rejecting Him (Luke 12:35-40).

- A third parable with the theme of a wedding banquet to point both to the suffering of the King's servants and the unresponsiveness of the people to His call (Matt. 22:1-14).

- The parable of "the doorkeeper" to emphasize the need for alertness to the news of the coming of the Master (Mark 13:32-37).

- The parable of the dragnet to point to the separation of the people at the end of the age (Matt. 13:47-50; see also Matt. 25:31-32).

- The parable of "the weeds and good seeds" to predict divisions and alterations the Master will find in His church at the time of His return. Such conditions will inevitably make it difficult for the servants to recognize their Master's voice, to understand His original instructions on finding and following Him (Matt. 13:24-30, 36-43).

Did Jesus not know what the state of the world and of His church would be at the time of His return? Why did He ask this question:

...when the Son of Man comes, will he find faith on earth?

Luke 18:8 NEB

We have a total of twelve parables all confirming one another, all leading to the same conclusion: *that the banquet of the kingdom will be open only to those who investigate the news of the coming of the Master with absolute sincerity, and that many Christians will fail to heed this warning.*

Descriptions

- A graphic description of the suffering that the Master and His humble followers must endure again (Matt. 25:35-46). Volume II presents an entire chapter on this topic.

- A list of the obstacles that will conceal the identity of the Master and the attributes that will lead the faithful servant to His presence (Luke 21:34-36).

The Consequences of Action and Inaction

- A graphic—but symbolic—description of the way God will reward those who *investigate* the good news of the Master's return and punish those who ignore this news.

To motivate Christians to awareness and action, nowhere
Jesus appeals as often and as strongly to reward and
punishment and to fear of God, as He does in His
prophecies of His second Advent (Matt. 24:48-51; 25:12,
30, 41, 46; 13:30, 40-43, 47-50; 22:13-14; II Thess. 1:9;
Rev. 14:7). The punishment He imposes is always the
most severe (separation from Him and His Kingdom); the
reward He promises is always the most splendid (the
crown of glory, and a place on His throne (I Peter 5:4;
Rev. 3:21). Why so much emphasis on reward and punishment? As we noted, the Scriptures teach that the key to
understanding the prophecies is *wisdom* (Daniel 12:10;
12:3; Matt. 25:1-4; 24:45-47). There is a clear connection
between *wisdom* and the *fear of God*:

> The fear of the Lord is the beginning of wisdom, and
> they who live by it grow in understanding.
>
> Psalms 111:10 NEB

> The essence of wisdom is the fear of God...[29]
>
> Bahá'u'lláh

It is evident that the Creator who is the Essence of Love
would not wish to be feared, but loved:

> "Thy paradise is My love..."[30] "The essence of wealth is
> love for Me; whoso loveth Me is the possessor of all
> things..."[31] "I belong to him that loveth Me..."[32]
>
> Bahá'u'lláh

What purpose then does "fear of God" serve? It serves to
move humans out of apathy, and out of attraction and attachment to the world. It is the voice that awakens the soul to
this call: "Since God is the goal, the hope, and desire of the
world, no one should be complacent in his duties toward
Him. No one should risk and suffer the loss of that which
humans were made for." This awakening by *fear* is healthy.
It protects the soul from the ravages of primitive and selfish
passions and desires. It draws the soul away from the glitter
of the world and leads it to the hope and peace of nearness

to God. Further, the fear of God releases the soul from the pressures and unreasonable expectations of society. Conformity comes from fearing people, courage from fearing God.

But this fear need not be intense or endure long. When the light of the knowledge of God casts its glory upon the soul, fear vanishes away as darkness is banished by the sun. The fear of the Lord turns into the love of the Lord.

> There is no fear in love...perfect love drives out fear...
>
>   I John 4:18 NIV

> A lover [of God] feareth nothing...[33]   Bahá'u'lláh

Fear overcome by *love* becomes a positive force. Isaiah predicted that the promised Redeemer "will delight in the fear of the Lord:"

> The Spirit of the Lord will rest on him—the Spirit of wisdom and of understanding, the Spirit of counsel and of power, the Spirit of knowledge and of the fear of the Lord—and he will delight in the fear of the Lord.
>
>   Isaiah 11:2-3 NIV

To summarize: the fear of God is the vanguard and the first glimmer of wisdom. It protects and leads humans to their divine destiny:

- It keeps the soul from falling until it grows and gains strength in the light of love.

- It awakens humans by reminding them of the consequences of apathy, inaction, and laxity toward their Creator. The purpose of this awakening is not to make people live in fear but rather to stir them to awareness and action.

- This fear leads humans to investigate, to acquire knowledge, and to understand God's way and wisdom. Without the light of understanding and knowledge, the soul is blind.

> The fear of the Lord is the beginning of knowledge...
>
>   Proverbs 1:7

- The light of knowledge eventually leads humans to perfect faith, trust, and love; for God is absolute beauty and perfection.

> He [the Lord] will be the sure foundation for your times, a rich store of salvation and wisdom and knowledge; the fear of the Lord is the key to this treasure.
>
> Isaiah 33:6 NIV

What is the common thread running through the parables of the Olivet Discourse and other instructions pointing to the second coming of Christ? That there is a clear contrast between people, between the wise and the unwise, the sheep and the goat, the daring and the fearful, the curious and the complacent, the good seed and the weed. And in all cases the reward or the punishment assigned to each of them is of the extreme: the highest reward, the harshest punishment. *It does not seem logical to divide people into only two groups except by this standard: whether they accept or reject the Master*. The heavenly reward and the harsh punishment assigned to each group is a further evidence of this.

This division, however, does not in any way imply that individuals *within* each of the two groups are equal or will be rewarded equally. Each of the two groups contains an infinite variety of people with infinite degrees of moral and spiritual maturity. Each individual is rewarded by the degree of his faith and deeds.

> I will judge between one sheep and another, and between rams and goats...I myself will judge between the fat sheep and the lean sheep.   Ezekiel 34:17, 20 NIV

The purpose of knowing the Master is spiritual transformation:

> What good is it, my brothers, if a man claims to have faith but has no deeds? Can such faith save him?...faith by itself, if it is not accompanied by action, is dead.
>
> James 2:14, 17 NIV

> The essence of faith is fewness of words and abundance
> of deeds...[34]   Bahá'u'lláh

Divine justice ordains that those who acknowledge the Master
by their words but deny Him by their deeds should not attain
the fruits of their faith. As for those who do not acknowledge
the Master, they will not be treated equally either, for their
motives and deeds are not the same. They too will reap the
fruits of their deeds. For God is not a God of justice alone;
His mercy and grace encompass the whole creation.

The Olivet Discourse contains all the directives of the Master
to His faithful servants. What more could the Master say to
reveal the reality of His return? What more could the Master do
to awaken His beloved servants, to move them *to investigate*?

> ...behold, I have foretold you all things.
>   Christ (Mark 13:23)

Thus Jesus admonished His faithful followers and concluded
His prophetic discourse as He looked down over Jerusalem
from the Mount of Olives with a few hopeful and humble disciples; a discourse for whose fulfillment countless Christians
have been waiting and praying for nearly two thousand years.

The Olivet Discourse carries an urgent tone. It is at once a
command from a King and a plea from a compassionate and
loving Guardian. It is Jesus' final directive. It is His will and
testament to all Christians:

> What I say to you, I say to everyone: Watch!
>   Christ (Mark 13:37 NIV)

Jesus finished His discourse with these words:

> You know that in two days' time it will be Passover, and
> the Son of Man is to be handed over for crucifixion.
>   Christ (Matthew 26:2 NEB)

The theme of the "thief in the night" is vast and vital. It is
explored further under Appendix III in this volume and again
in Volume V.

3

Be Strong, Fear Not
Isaiah 35:4

A ll through the Bible the faithful are asked to seek and
search, to investigate and inquire:

"Search the scriptures" (John 5:39); "Thou shalt meditate
therein day and night" (Joshua 1:8); "Those that seek me
early shall find me" (Prov. 8:17); "Seek ye the Lord while
he may be found" (Isa. 55:6); "You will find him, if
indeed you search with all your heart and soul" (Deut.
4:29 NEB); "unto them that look for him shall he appear
the second time" (Heb. 9:28).

What harm can come from looking, from inquiring? Avoidance,
apathy, and fear show a lack of faith:

Why are ye fearful, O ye of little faith?

Christ (Matthew 8:26)

This book is an attempt to seek and find a truth that is the ultimate goal and the crowning glory of human life on this planet—a goal that is the wellspring of the deepest and most enchanting joys, a glory that bestows a new life, abundant and everlasting:

> Then the King will say to those on his right, 'Come, you who are blessed by my Father; take your inheritance, the kingdom prepared for you since the creation of the world.'   Christ (Matthew 25:34 NIV)

It is a gift offered to those—

• Who thirst for truth:

> Whoever is thirsty, let him come; and whoever wishes, let him take the free gift of the water of life.
>   Christ (Revelation 22:17 NIV)
>   See also Isaiah 55:1

• Who strive to sustain their souls with knowledge:

> ...through knowledge shall the just be delivered.
>   Proverbs 11:9

• Who are guided by an open mind and gifted "with a noble and good heart:"

> But the seed on good soil stands for those with a noble and good heart, who hear the word, retain it, and by persevering produce a crop.   Christ (Luke 8:15 NIV)

• Who do not reject or judge a Redeemer by His name or place of origin:

> Judge not according to the appearance...
>   Christ (John 7:24)

• Who do not allow a known Name (Christ, Moses) to become an obstacle between them and the *new Name* (Bahá'u'lláh):

> He who is victorious [over obstacles]—I will make him a pillar in the temple of my God...will write the name

of my God upon him...and my own ***new name*** [emphasis added]. Revelation 3:12 NEB

• Who in their search for truth depend on ***proof*** and ***reason***:

Prove all things... I Thessalonians 5:21

Come now, and let us reason together, saith the Lord...
Isaiah 1:18

• Who are not influenced by popularity or concerned with the judgment of people:

...ye shall not be afraid of the face of man; for the judgment is God's... Deuteronomy 1:17

If I were still trying to please men, I would not be a servant of Christ. Galatians 1:10 NIV

• Who have high regard for prophetic utterances, and a deep desire to test their fulfillment:

...do not despise prophetic utterances, but bring them all to the test... I Thessalonians 5:20-21 NEB

• Who do not allow others to decide the truth for them, even if they are notable scholars or authorities:

...every man shall bear his own burden. Galatians 6:5

• Who in their search for truth are wakeful and watchful, taking advantage of every opportunity that may lead them to the object of their search:

Be always on the watch [investigate]...that you may be able to stand before the Son of Man.
Christ (Luke 21:36 NIV)

Blessed—happy, fortunate and to be envied—are those servants, whom the master finds awake and alert and watching when he comes. Christ (Luke 12:37 AB)

• And, finally, those who say: ***it is possible***! Perhaps during "the night," when people were "asleep," He came:

"That day is a day of...darkness and gloominess..." (Zeph. 1:15). And "every eye" that *was* awake during "the night" caught a glimpse of His great Glory. For a sleeper cannot see: "Awake, sleeper...and Christ will shine upon you" (Eph. 5:14 NEB). For some eyes may be open and still never see: "you may look and look, but you will never see" (Acts 28:26 NEB). And "the eye" that *can* "see" is always in the heart:

> Blessed are the pure in heart: for they shall see God.
>
> Christ (Matthew 5:8)

> ...without holiness no one will see the Lord.
>
> Hebrews 12:14 NIV

Requirements for Success

Just as with any task, chances of success improve with preparation. Without acquiring the essential skills and attitudes, the seeker of truth will find success unattainable. Among the various requirements, the following deserve special attention:

Freedom from Fear

In the first paragraph of the preface to a book published and distributed by one of the largest and most respected evangelical groups in the world (*Billy Graham Evangelistic Association*) appear these words:

> We are living in a disordered age. Most people, including Christians, are confused. They are bombarded by multitudes of voices and *no two of them are in agreement*, they are all saying different things. Which voice are we to believe or depend on? [Emphasis added].[1]

Virtually the same message was uttered by Bahá'u'lláh about a century earlier:

> *No two men can be found who may be said to be outwardly and inwardly united.* The evidences of discord and malice

are apparent everywhere, though all were made for harmony and union [emphasis added].[2]

The multitude of inharmonious voices that people hear destroys their trust. Lack of trust leads them to fear, and fear to avoidance and apathy.

Fear of falsehood is a justifiable concern. No one wants to be deceived, especially on questions of conscience and belief. We should, however, note that there is a clear difference between fear and phobia, between observing caution and magnifying caution to avoid making *any* search. The first (reasonable caution) leads to protection from falsehood; the second (intense fear or phobia) to separation from truth. Unfortunately, most people allow their fear of falsehood to overcome their love for truth.

Some Christians are so sensitized by fear of being deceived that if they read a hundred verses on the necessity of investigating the truth and one verse on fearing falsehood, they forget the hundred, but remember the one. The consequence is inaction, indifference, and apathy—a belief that the best defense is to avoid new ideas. They wonder why they should take chances and venture into the unknown when they already have something to depend on.

Since fear of falsehood directs the action and destiny of so many believers—even the most sincere—we should test it in as many ways as possible. We should put it to the test of the Scriptures, examine it by the standards of reason, and view it in the light of history:

• *The Test of Reason and Science*. In daily life we quickly learn that to judge something is to test it. Scientists follow the same course of action. To prove its effectiveness, a drug or a diet must be tested. Experimentation is the chief method of scientific search. Does not the same principle hold true with religion? Reason demands that judgment must come only *after* the "fruit" is examined.

...a tree is recognized by its fruit.   Matthew 12:33 NIV

Thus, by their fruit you will recognize them.
Matthew 7:20 NIV

• *The Lesson of History.* Why did people deny Jesus? Why did they deny Moses or Noah or Abraham, and all the other Messengers? Partly because of fear. They were so overcome by their fear of falsehood that they lost their sense of adventure and thirst for truth. They preferred apathy and inaction to concern and active involvement. They conformed to prevailing views and shifted responsibility from themselves. They allowed the prevailing views to stifle their spirit of adventure and their longing for truth. Were not the people of the time of Jesus also paralyzed by fear and avoidance?

Have no fear...for your Father has chosen to give you the Kingdom.   Christ (Luke 12:32 NEB)

• *The Testimony of the Scriptures.* The following verse from the Book of Revelation—a book that is primarily concerned with the events of the end-times—portrays clearly the consequences of being fearful to investigate:

He who *overcomes* will inherit all this, and I will be his God and he will be my son. But *the cowardly*...their place will be in the fiery lake of burning sulfur.
Revelation 21:7-8 NIV

The prophecy specifies "He who overcomes." Overcomes what? It is clear, overcomes "cowardliness or fear." What kind of fear? Fear of inquiry or investigation, fear of being deceived. Can the severe punishment—to burn in the fiery lake—be justified for any other fear? Can those rewards—to inherit all things—be justified for overcoming any fear other than the fear of the search for truth? Is there any fear whose dire consequences can be as drastic as ignoring the news of the coming of the Master? Has there been and will there ever be news greater than the news of the coming of the Lord?

What should be feared is falsehood, not knowledge. What should be feared is being deprived of the truth, *not the search for truth*. To inspire the spirit of strength and courage, Bahá'u'lláh quotes this biblical verse that is addressed to the people of our time:

> Say to them that are of a fearful heart, Be strong, fear not: behold, your God will come...and save you.
>
> Isaiah 35:4

The following verse also inspires strength and courage in those waiting for their Lord:

> Wait for the Lord; be strong, take courage, and wait for the Lord.   Psalms 27:14 NEB

The task of recognizing the divine Teachers is quite easy if we use the true standards, the ones that God Himself has specified. It is easy because when we examine human beings, we encounter an infinite range of degrees of perfection and imperfection. But when we test a Redeemer from God, we encounter only two degrees of choice. We contrast the divine against human, not human against human. A Redeemer is either divine or deceptive. This makes our search quite simple. We are not called upon to make fine discriminations between deceptively similar choices.

"My yoke is easy, and my burden is light" (Christ; Matt. 11:30). "He will never deal unjustly with any one, neither will He task a soul beyond its power"[3] (Bahá'u'lláh). "The evidence set forth by God can never be compared with evidences produced by any one of the peoples and kindreds of the earth"[4] (The Báb). "Truth can in no wise be confounded with aught else except itself...Nor can error be confused with Truth, if ye do but reflect upon the testimony of God"[5] (The Báb).

Following the Light of Reason

This requirement is stated eloquently by noted Christian scholar and leader, Dr. James Kennedy:

> When we do not stand ready with a reason for our hope and do not know why we believe what we believe, we give others the impression that Christianity is a religion based merely upon blind faith or emotional prejudice. Nothing could be farther from the truth! We often accuse those who reject Christianity without at least examining the evidence for it of being prejudiced. Then is it not also true that if a person accepts Christianity without examining the evidence, that too is nothing other than prejudice or credulity?[6]

Dr. Kennedy also encourages Christians to search for truth:

> The Bible tells us to examine all things and to hold fast to that which is good. Yet too frequently we are not willing to do that just because it takes a little intellectual effort on our part...[7]

Dr. Barry Chant and Winkie Pratney, Christian writers and scholars, state:

> [Jesus] intimates that His servants are not to be passive in their waiting [for His return]. They must show enterprise and investment, to use initiative with what has been given them (even perhaps to take calculated risk)...[8]

Postponing Judgment

To prejudge is to decide before examining all the evidence. Proofs of the validity of a divine Revelation are cumulative. None of them should be judged apart from the others, for each proof constitutes only *part* of the full profile. *The ultimate value of any given proof or precept must be judged only in the light of the entire spectrum of evidence presented*.

We should regard our role as that of a jury, seeking to find *all* the facts before coming to a verdict.

> Does our law...permit us to pass judgment on a man un-
> less we have first given him a hearing and learned the
> facts?   John 7:51 NEB

> So pass no premature judgment...   I Corinthians 4:5 NEB

Not everything can be fully explained at once. Questions of
concern are dealt with progressively in the course of these six
volumes. Therefore, if you find an idea objectionable, do not
come to a final conclusion; you may well find the issue
resolved later.

> Nothing will ever be attempted if all possible objections
> must be first overcome.   Samuel Johnson

While pursuing the truth, it is essential to set aside all
traditional expectations or orthodox interpretations. If the
prevailing expectations enjoy the status of an absolute
standard, then how can any other standard, however reasonable, be viewed with an open mind and tested impartially?
How can judgment be postponed?

Persisting

Success in any endeavor requires persistence. To stop before
completing an investigation will give only an incomplete or
distorted picture of the prophetic profile. Nothing short of
seeing *the whole profile* can be a reliable basis for judging.

Jesus used *the parable of the sower* to demonstrate the
qualities essential for finding the truth. Among the qualities
He emphasized was perseverance:

> But the seed on good soil stands for those with a noble and
> good heart, who hear the word, retain it, and by persever-
> ing produce a crop.   Christ (Luke 8:15 NIV)

Dr. Robert Schuler, the renowned author, clergyman, and the
best-known advocate of positive and possibility thinking,
considers constancy one of the four essential qualities for
success in any endeavor. The other three are: curiosity,
confidence, and courage.

What makes persistence or constancy so essential is the interrelation of the proofs. For each proof leads to another, like the critical parts of a delicately balanced bridge or a rising tower. We must walk over the bridge and rise to the height of the tower to gain a true vision of their glory and grandeur. "Let us run with patience the race that is set before us" (Heb. 12:1). "Only have faith, patience and courage—this is but the beginning...surely you will succeed, for God is with you!"[9] ('Abdu'l-Bahá). "If you...know how to give good gifts to your children, how much more will your Father in heaven give good gifts to those who ask him!" (Matt. 7:11 NIV). "Whatsoever ye shall ask in prayer, believing, ye shall receive" (Matt. 21:22). "Watch ye therefore, and pray always" (Luke 21:36).

Being Humble

In interpreting the Word of God we must be acutely aware of our weaknesses and fallibility. This rule applies to both the givers and receivers of knowledge. The freedom of the human spirit necessitates a diversity of thinking and understanding. We should welcome and even encourage this freedom, for it leads us to new dimensions of knowledge, wisdom, and truth. Yet the gains from diversity can come only if those who impart knowledge are gifted with humility and those who receive it are tempered with tolerance.

Let not the wise man glory in his wisdom... Jeremiah 9:23

Blessed are the meek: for they shall inherit the earth.
Christ (Matthew 5:5)

...the Lord has...sent me to bring glad tidings to the lowly ...To announce a year of favor from the Lord.
Isaiah 61:1-2 NAB

...he shall save the humble person.   Job 22:29

Show me your ways, O Lord, teach me your paths; guide me in your truth and teach me, for you are God my Savior, and my hope is in you all day long...He guides the humble in what is right and teaches them his way.

Psalms 25:4-5, 9 NIV

The giver of knowledge should say to the receiver, "It is an honor to offer you the gift of my labors. But please remember that only the box is mine—the gift comes from heaven. Look not at my flawed wrappings. Look at the perfect pearls of truth within that are not mine." To this acknowledgment, the receiver of knowledge should reply, "I, too, am surrounded by the wrappings of my own thoughts and fantasies that are also of my own creation. I will put all the wrappings—yours and mine—aside, so that only my spirit, as God gave it, touches the pearl."

The greatest friend of truth is Time, her greatest enemy is Prejudice, and her constant companion is Humility.

Charles C. Colton

The spark of truth comes, as the Master observes, from a clash of ideas. But the diverse ideas must be tempered with humility and tolerance, lest their clash lead to a sudden outburst, lest they create a battleground in which *people* take the place of *ideas*. This is how the great Gift of God has been cut into many competing sects. This is why many have used the sword to promote love, torture to preserve the truth, and the prison to please God.

People have interpreted the Scriptures from the time Moses revealed the Ten Commandments, and their interpretations have differed. This is fine, as long as they do not insist that their understanding of the words of God is the only truth. This especially holds true with prophecies, because as a rule they are concealed in codes. The Scriptures teach that *no one* has the right to declare his interpretation of prophecies infallible, for to *no one* is given full knowledge of their meaning:

...note this: no one can interpret any prophecy of Scripture by himself.

II Peter 1:20 NEB

Therefore judge nothing before the appointed time; wait
till the Lord comes. He will bring to light what is hidden
in darkness...   I Corinthians 4:5 NIV

Which of the following positions fulfills the above exhorta-
tions and warnings?

- I have no doubt about what Jesus meant, when He said "He
  would come from heaven." I have no doubt that at His
  coming, graves will open and the dead will rise...I have
  no doubt that all the prophecies are literal.

- I will begin my search with an open mind, without any
  preconceived notions. I will postpone my judgment concerning all my expectations until I have examined *all* the
  evidences presented by *the One who claims to be the Lord.*

If we truly accept the Word of God that "He saves the humble
person," not the proud, then, who has presented himself
humbly before the Lord, the person who holds the first position or the second?

The statement from Dr. James Kennedy, quoted in the
preface, reflects the true spirit of humility; it is a beacon of
enlightenment and awareness for every seeker of truth:

The great Princeton theologian of the last century, Dr.
Charles Hodge, said something which I have always
thought is worth remembering. *He said that though
the Old Testament is filled with some 333 prophecies
concerning the first coming of Christ; in spite of that,
nobody got it right.* And as you know, they crucified
Christ because of a misunderstanding about what the
Messiah was really coming to do. And we should because
of that be somewhat humbled and modest in our attempts
to interpret prophecies concerning the second coming of
Christ. *It is quite possible that all of us [Christian
leaders] are wrong as well.* [Emphasis added].[10]

Praying

Self-reliance shows strength; leaning on others implies weakness. Praying is turning to a higher source for help. Many hesitate or refuse to accept such a dependency. By so doing, they leave out the most reliable source of inspiration and guidance. Perhaps nowhere does praying play as decisive a role as it does in spiritual matters. Two conditions make dependence on God absolutely imperative:

- When the choice is very complex and requires profound wisdom.

- When the choice leads to long lasting or far-reaching consequences.

Can any decision compare in its consequence with accepting, ignoring, or denying a Messenger of God? Does a human being need more wisdom concerning *any* choice, *any* decision than in regard to recognizing a new Redeemer? When Jesus spoke about His return, did He not say, "pray"?

> Be always on the watch, and *pray* that you may be able to escape all that is about to happen, and that you may be able to stand before the Son of Man [emphasis added].
>
> Luke 21:34-36 NIV

Do not Jesus' words imply that for most people knowing Him the second time may be as difficult as it was the first time, that it may require more wisdom than a human being can gain on his own? Did He not also in the prayer concerning His return begin with, "Father...thy kingdom come" and end with "do not bring us to the test [temptation KJV]" (Luke 11:2-4 NEB)? Did He not also declare:

> ...the hour of temptation, which shall come upon all the world, to try them that dwell upon the earth.
>
> Revelation 3:10

A test always implies the possibility of pursuing an improper course of action. Even Jesus' enlightened disciples needed to pray to pass the tests or escape the temptations:

Pray that you will not fall into temptation.   Luke 22:40 NIV

The following verse is both a prophecy and a promise:

> And everyone who calls on the name of the Lord will be
> saved...   Joel 2:32 NIV

The Báb and Bahá'u'lláh have also encouraged dependence
on God and written hundreds of prayers for the spiritual
needs of humankind. Several prayers from both the Bahá'í
and Hebrew Scriptures are offered in the next section. The
prayers are for those who by hearing the good news of the
coming of the kingdom enter the "Valley of Decision" (Joel
3:14 NEB), and suddenly see on the horizon the dawning of
the most critical choice a human being may ever be called
upon to make.

The prayers are suited especially for us, the people of this
age, who live in the evening of time (Zech. 14:7), in the
twilight of uncertainty and confusion (Micah 7:4 NIV), when
"the ways to God have multiplied." "The light shines in the
darkness, but the darkness has not understood it" (John 1:5
NIV). "The Dawn hath broken, yet the people understand
not"[11] (Bahá'u'lláh).

> Prayer begins where human capacity ends.
>   Norman Vincent Peal

> God dwells far off from us, but prayer brings Him down
> to earth, and links His power with our efforts.
>   M. Gasparin

Prayers for Divine Guidance

> Show me your ways, O Lord, teach me your paths; guide
> me in your truth and teach me, for you are God my Savior,
> and my hope is in you all day long.   Psalms 25:4-5 NIV

> You are God my stronghold. Why have you rejected me?
> Why must I go about mourning...? Send forth your light
> and your truth, let them guide me; let them bring me to

your holy mountain, to the place where you dwell. Then will I go to the altar of God, to God, my joy and my delight. I will praise you with the harp, O God, my God. Why are you downcast, O my soul? Why so disturbed within me? Put your hope in God, for I will yet praise him, my Savior and my God. Psalms 43:2-5 NIV

May God be gracious to us and bless us and make his face shine upon us; may your ways be known on earth, your salvation among all nations...May the peoples praise you, O God; may all the peoples praise you. Then the land will yield its harvest, and God, our God, will bless us. Psalms 67:1-2, 5-6 NIV

Search me, O God, and know my heart; test me and know my anxious thoughts. See if there is any offensive way in me, and lead me in the way everlasting.
Psalms 139:23-24 NIV

O Thou Whose face is the object of my adoration, Whose beauty is my sanctuary, Whose habitation is my goal, Whose praise is my hope, Whose providence is my companion, Whose love is the cause of my being, Whose mention is my solace, Whose nearness is my desire, Whose presence is my dearest wish and highest aspiration, I entreat Thee not to withhold from me the things Thou didst ordain for the chosen ones among Thy servants. Supply me, then, with the good of this world and of the next.

Thou, truly, art the King of all men. There is no God but Thee, the Ever-Forgiving, the Most Generous.[12]
Bahá'u'lláh

O my God, my Lord and my Master! I have detached myself from my kindred and have sought through Thee to become independent of all that dwell on earth and ever ready to receive that which is praiseworthy in Thy sight. Bestow on me such good as will make me independent of aught else but Thee, and grant me an ampler share of

Thy boundless favors. Verily, Thou art the Lord of grace abounding.[13]   The Báb

Say: O my God! O Thou Who art the Maker of the heavens and of the earth, O Lord of the Kingdom! Thou well knowest the secrets of my heart, while Thy Being is inscrutable to all save Thyself. Thou seest whatsoever is of me, while no one else can do this save Thee. Vouchsafe unto me, through Thy grace, what will enable me to dispense with all except Thee, and destine for me that which will make me independent of everyone else besides Thee. Grant that I may reap the benefit of my life in this world and in the next. Open to my face the portals of Thy grace and graciously confer upon me Thy tender mercy and bestowals.[14]   The Báb

Perhaps the following course of action may prove helpful to many seekers of truth. After reading each chapter, you may wish to pause, pray, and meditate as long as needed to receive the inspiration you may need for the next step in your spiritual journey. God has assured us that if we pray sincerely and search with *all our hearts and souls*, the gift of guidance will be ours:

Which of you, if his son asks for bread, will give him a stone? Or if he asks for a fish, will give him a snake? If you, then...know how to give good gifts to your children, how much more will your Father in heaven give good gifts to those who ask him!   Christ (Matthew 7:9-11 NIV)

Call to me and I will answer you and tell you great and unsearchable things you do not know.   Jeremiah 33:3 NIV

...you will find him, if indeed you search with all your heart and soul.   Deuteronomy 4:29 NEB

Blessed are they who keep his statutes and seek him with all their heart.   Psalms 119:2 NIV

4

I Shall Come Again
John 14:3 NEB

Trust in God always; trust also in me. There are many dwelling-places in my Father's house...I am going there on purpose to prepare a place for you. And if I go and prepare a place for you, *I shall come again* and receive you to myself, so that where I am you may be also [emphasis added]...   Christ (John 14:1-3 NEB)

Return, O Lord, how long?...Let thy work appear unto thy servants, and thy glory unto their children. And let the beauty of the Lord our God be upon us...
Psalms 90:13, 16, 17

Come back, O Lord; set my soul free, deliver me for thy love's sake.   Psalms 6:4 NEB

The advent of the Lord, the Desire of all nations, the Prince of Peace, the return of the Son of man in the glory of His

Father, is the most recurring and emphatic promise of the Scriptures. "The desire of all nations shall come" (Hag. 2:7). "For the Son of man shall come in the glory of his Father" (Matt. 16:27). "Behold, I am coming soon! Blessed is he who keeps the words of the prophecy in this book" (Rev. 22:7 NIV). "I will not leave you as orphans; I will come to you" (John 14:18 NIV). "I go away, and come again unto you" (John 14:28).

> Then I saw another angel flying in midair, and he had the eternal gospel [good news] to proclaim to those who live on the earth—to every nation, tribe, language and people. He said in a loud voice, 'Fear God and give him glory, because the hour of his judgment has come.'
>
> Revelation 14:6-7 NIV

Dr. John White, in his book on Christ's return *Re-entry*, states:

> The teaching of the second coming of our Lord is dealt with some 1,845 times in the Bible, 318 of these being in the New Testament. The return of the Lord is the dominant theme of 17 Old Testament books and one epistle in the New. In fact, 7 out of every 10 chapters in the New Testament make a reference to the second coming.[1]

Dr. Billy Graham in his foreword to *Re-entry* states:

> The theme...of the second coming of Jesus Christ, is urgently needed in the preaching of the Church today... Probably no Gospel theme apart from 'Ye must be born again' is more relevant today, and I preach on some facet of this subject in virtually all of my crusades. Our world is filled with fear, hate, lust, greed, war and utter despair. Surely the second coming of Jesus Christ, His 're-entry,' is the only hope of replacing these depressing features with trust, love, universal peace and prosperity. For it the world, wittingly or inadvertently, waits.[2]

O Lord Show Thyself
Psalms 94:1 NEB

Come, Lord Jesus. Revelation 22:20 NIV

He, verily, is come with His Kingdom, and all the atoms cry aloud: "Lo! The Lord is come in His great majesty!"[3]

Bahá'u'lláh

Lo! He is come in the sheltering shadow of Testimony, invested with conclusive proof...Blessed is the man who turneth towards Him...[4] Bahá'u'lláh

Followers of the Gospel...behold the gates of heaven are flung open. He that had ascended unto it is now come. Give ear to His voice calling aloud over land and sea, announcing to all mankind the advent of this Revelation...[5]

Bahá'u'lláh

Behold how He hath come down from the heaven of His grace, girded with power and invested with sovereignty. Is there any doubt concerning His signs?[6] Bahá'u'lláh

By God! This is He Who hath at one time appeared in the name of the Spirit✣ [Christ]...[7] Bahá'u'lláh

The time foreordained unto the peoples and kindreds of the earth is now come. The promises of God, as recorded in the holy Scriptures, have all been fulfilled.[8] Bahá'u'lláh

Bahá'u'lláh proclaims in the clearest, most certain, and most emphatic terms His station as the supreme Savior and Redeemer of the World, the Promised One of all ages and religions, *the return of Christ* to Christians, and *the Glory of the Lord* to the followers of both the Torah and the Gospel. He claims a station referred to throughout the Scriptures as

---

✣ *The Spirit* and *the Spirit of God* are two common titles by which Bahá'u'lláh refers to Christ. "The spirit of the Lord is upon me [Jesus] because he has anointed me" (Luke 4:18 NEB). "He [Jesus] saw the Spirit of God descending like a dove to alight upon him" (Matt. 3:16 NEB).

the Return of the Son in the Glory of His Father, the Lord of the vineyard, the King of Glory, the Desire of all Nations, the Comforter, the Counselor, and the Prince of Peace.

Bahá'u'lláh proclaimed His Mission in Epistles (Tablets) addressed to humanity in general and to the religious and political leaders in particular. They are published by the Universal House of Justice under the title *The Proclamation of Bahá'u'lláh to the Kings and Leaders of the World.*[9]

The following quotations from those epistles and other sources demonstrate the authority and mission of Bahá'u'lláh:

He who is the Desired One is come in His transcendent majesty...Better is this for you than all ye possess.[10]

The Hour which We had concealed from the knowledge of the peoples of the earth...hath come to pass.[11]

He that was hidden from mortal eyes is come! His all-conquering sovereignty is manifest; His all-encompassing splendor is revealed. Beware lest thou hesitate or halt.[12]

This is the changeless Faith of God, eternal in the past, eternal in the future. Let him that seeketh, attain it; and as to him that hath refused to seek it—verily, God is Self-Sufficient, above any need of His creatures.[13]

Verily I say, this is the Day in which mankind can behold the Face, and hear the Voice, of the Promised One...It behoveth every man to blot out the trace of every idle word from the tablet of his heart, and to gaze, with an open and unbiased mind, on the signs of His Revelation, the proofs of His Mission, and the tokens of His glory.[14]

The most grievous veil hath shut out the peoples of the earth from His glory, and hindered them from hearkening to His call. God grant that the light of unity may envelop the whole earth.[15]

In His Epistle to Christians, Bahá'u'lláh asks them why they allow the name *Bahá'u'lláh* to stand as an obstacle in testing His claim. He reminds them that the people to whom Jesus was sent constantly prayed for their Redeemer's advent. They expressed the deepest desire to meet Him. Yet when He came, only a few among them, mostly from the disadvantaged of society—the poor and the powerless, the simple and the sinners—recognized His divine glory. Why did the deep love of the others who were expecting their adored Redeemer and Master *not* save them from denying Him? They read their Scriptures day and night. Why was their knowledge of no avail to them? Why did their repeated readings of the prophecies *not* guide them to truth?

> You study the scriptures diligently, supposing that in having them you have eternal life; yet, although their testimony points to me, you refuse to come to me for that life. Christ (John 5:39-40 NEB)

Bahá'u'lláh intimates that without asking these questions and resolving them, we cannot learn from the example of those who were once in our place, of those who thought that by ignoring or opposing Jesus they were doing the right thing, without ever realizing that they were depriving themselves of the greatest gift that Heaven may bestow upon humans. Without pondering these questions and resolving them, it is extremely difficult, even impossible, to overcome the many obstacles that our traditional beliefs place before us. We will be as confused and perplexed as our forebears who time and again rejected God's Messengers:

> You always resist the Holy Spirit! Was there ever a prophet your fathers did not persecute? They even killed those who predicted the coming of the Righteous One.
> Acts 7:51-52 NIV

> Great spirits have always encountered opposition from mediocre minds. Albert Einstein

In *The Book of Certitude*, Bahá'u'lláh presents a brief history
of the past Messengers and shows that they all encountered
people unprepared to accept or appreciate them. His purpose
in citing this history is to indicate that ***in recognizing a new
Redeemer, absolute humility and open-mindedness are
required.*** The past exerts a profound influence on our lives.
The overwhelming influence comes not from what we learn
from the past, but from what we don't.

> Those who cannot remember the past are condemned to
> repeat it.   George Santayna

> A page of history is worth a volume of logic.
>   Oliver Wendell Holmes

> What experience and history teach us is this—that people
> and governments have never learned anything from history,
> or acted on principles deduced from it.   Georg Hegel

How can history help us? By ***separating us from our immediate needs and concerns.*** How can we get a full picture
of a mountain? By standing at a distance. How can we see
the true meaning and significance of the events of our lives?
By patience, by allowing time to separate us from the events.
How often does it happen that at the time of making a vital
decision we see only ***part*** of the picture? Later we wonder
with amazement why we could not have seen more! How
many wars would have been prevented, how many lives
saved, if world leaders had read and heeded the lessons of
history? Bahá'u'lláh calls on Christians to take history as their
guide and inspiration, to pursue its light to the city of true
knowledge:

> Say,✛ O followers of the Son [Jesus]! Have ye shut out
> yourselves from Me by reason of My Name?...Day and
> night ye have been calling upon your Lord, the Omnipotent,
> but when He came from the heaven of eternity in His
> great glory, ye turned aside from Him...

✛ Here the word "Say" is equivalent to the biblical phrase: "Thus saith the Lord."

Consider those who rejected the Spirit [Jesus] when He came unto them with manifest dominion. How numerous the Pharisees who had secluded themselves in synagogues in His name, lamenting over their separation from Him, and yet when the portals of reunion were flung open... they disbelieved in God, the Exalted, the Mighty...No one from among them turned his face towards the Dayspring of divine bounty [Jesus] except such as were destitute of any power amongst men...Moreover, call thou to mind the one [the high priest] who sentenced Jesus to death. He was the most learned of his age in his own country, whilst he who was only a fisherman [Peter] believed in Him. Take good heed and be of them that observe the warning.[16]

"The one who sentenced Jesus" may refer either to Annas or Caiaphas, but more likely to Annas. Annas occupied the highest spiritual position for the Jews, Caiaphas the highest state position. They were both the most prestigious, influential, and learned Jewish religious leaders at the time of Jesus. According to *Nelson Bible Dictionary*:

Annas was...the most influential of the priests...[and] was officially succeeded by each of his five sons, one grandson, and his son-in-law Caiaphas, the high priest who presided at the trial of Jesus (Matt. 26:3, 57; John 18:13-14). During His trial, Jesus was first taken to Annas, who then sent Jesus to Caiaphas (John 18:13, 24). Both Annas and Caiaphas were among the principal examiners when Peter and John were arrested (Acts 4:6).[17]

According to *The Zondervan Bible Dictionary*:

Jesus offered the Kingdom to Israel, for they were its proper heirs...but the religious leaders, followed by most of the people, not only refused to enter its blessings but tried to prevent others from entering (Matt. 23:13). Nevertheless, many tax-collectors [who occupied a low position in people's eyes] and harlots did enter the Kingdom (Matt. 21:31).[18]

Is there a single one of our rulers who has believed in
him...?   John 7:48 NEB

How vast the number of the learned who have turned aside
from the way of God and how numerous the men devoid
of learning who have apprehended the truth and hastened
unto Him, saying, 'Praised be Thou, O Lord of all things,
visible and invisible.'[19]   Bahá'u'lláh

Seeing and knowing the truth—whether it is the recognition
of the Word of God or the very existence of God—does not
require scientific training, biblical scholarship, a master's
degree in debate and logic, a doctorate in philosophy or
theology. It requires *only a pure heart, only a sanctified
soul*:

Blessed are the pure in heart; for they shall see God.
                                            Christ (Matthew 5:8)

The understanding of His [God's] words...are in no wise
dependent upon human learning. They depend solely upon
purity of heart...and freedom of spirit...[20]   Bahá'u'lláh

Sanctify your souls, O ye peoples of the world, that haply
ye may attain that station which God hath destined for
you...[21]   Bahá'u'lláh

Sanctify your souls from whatsoever is not of God, and
taste ye the sweetness of rest within the pale of His vast
and mighty Revelation, and beneath the shadow of His
supreme and infallible authority.[22]   Bahá'u'lláh

Every human being—even the least educated from the most
primitive culture—is able to recognize the existence of God
and distinguish His Word from others. *The first* clue to the
Word of God *is its uniqueness*. Its *tone*, its *"voice,"* its *power*
and *authority* clearly set it apart from the words of others.

My own sheep listen to my voice; I know them and they
follow me.   Christ (John 10:27 NEB)

...he goes ahead and the sheep follow, because they know his voice. Christ (John 10:4 NEB)

...I have perfected in every one of you My creation, so that the excellence of My handiwork may be fully revealed unto men. It follows, therefore, that every man hath been, and will continue to be, able of himself to appreciate the Beauty of God, the Glorified. Had he not been endowed with such a capacity, how could he be called to account for his failure? If, in the Day when all the peoples of the earth will be gathered together, any man should, whilst standing in the presence of God, be asked: "Wherefore hast thou disbelieved in My Beauty and turned away from My Self," and if such a man should reply and say: "Inasmuch as all men have erred, and none hath been found willing to turn his face to the Truth, I, too, following their example, have grievously failed to recognize the Beauty of the Eternal," such a plea will, assuredly, be rejected. For the faith of no man can be conditioned by any one except himself.[23] Bahá'u'lláh

Bahá'u'lláh addresses Christians and declares to them *the return of that same Spirit that appeared in the name of Christ*:

...O concourse of Christians! We have, on a previous occasion, revealed Ourself unto you, and ye recognized Me not. This is yet another occasion vouchsafed unto you. This is the Day of God; turn ye unto Him...The Beloved One loveth not that ye be consumed with the fire of your desires...Ye make mention of Me, and know Me not. Ye call upon Me, and are heedless of My Revelation...O people of the Gospel! They who were not in the Kingdom have now entered it, whilst We behold you, in this day, tarrying at the gate. Rend the veils asunder by the power of your Lord, the Almighty, the All-Bounteous, and enter, then, in My name My Kingdom. Thus biddeth you He Who desireth for you everlasting life...We behold you, O children of the Kingdom, in darkness. This, verily, beseemeth you

not. Are ye, in the face of the Light, fearful because of
your deeds? Direct yourselves towards Him...Verily, He
(Jesus) said: 'Come ye after Me, and I will make you to
become fishers of men.' In this day, however, We say:
'Come ye after Me, that We may make you to become
quickeners of mankind.'[24]

Bahá'u'lláh Glorifies Christ

Bahá'u'lláh glorifies Christ in the most moving and majestic
terms:

> Know thou that when the Son of Man yielded up His
> breath to God, the whole creation wept with a great
> weeping. By sacrificing Himself, however, a fresh capacity
> was infused into all created things. Its evidences, as wit-
> nessed in all the peoples of the earth, are now manifest
> before thee. The deepest wisdom which the sages have
> uttered, the profoundest learning which any mind hath
> unfolded, the arts which the ablest hands have produced,
> the influence exerted by the most potent of rulers, are but
> manifestations of the quickening power released by His
> transcendent, His all-pervasive, and resplendent Spirit.

> We testify that when He came into the world, He shed the
> splendor of His glory upon all created things. Through
> Him the leper recovered from the leprosy of perversity
> and ignorance. Through Him, the unchaste and wayward
> were healed. Through His power, born of Almighty God,
> the eyes of the blind were opened, and the soul of the
> sinner sanctified.[25]

> Reflect how Jesus, the Spirit of God, was, notwithstand-
> ing His extreme meekness and perfect tender-heartedness,
> treated by His enemies. So fierce was the opposition
> which He, the Essence of Being and Lord of the visible
> and invisible, had to face, that He had nowhere to lay
> His head. He wandered continually from place to place,
> deprived of a permanent abode.[26]

The Báb and 'Abdu'l-Bahá too glorify the station of Christ and His teachings:

> O Spirit of God [Jesus]!...Verily God hath inspired Thee with divine verses and wisdom while still a child and hath graciously deigned to bestow His favor upon the peoples of the world through the influence of Thy Most Great Name...[27]   The Báb

> If you reflect upon the essential teachings of Jesus, you will realize that they are the light of the world...They are the very source of life and the cause of happiness to the human race.[28]   'Abdu'l-Bahá

Bahá'u'lláh eulogizes the station of Jesus as one "which hath been exalted above the imaginings of all that dwell on earth."[29] 'Abdu'l-Bahá describes that station as one of absolute perfection.[30] Here are some of the titles by which Bahá'u'lláh and 'Abdu'l-Bahá refer to Christ:

The Lord Christ
The Lord of all being
The Lord of the visible
 and invisible
The Spirit of God
The Divine Spirit
The Spirit
The Essence of Being

The Essence of detachment
The Essence of the Spirit
The Word of God
That Peerless Beauty
The Revealer of the
 unseen Beauty
The Daystar of the heaven
 of divine Revelation

Jesus did not destroy what was granted to the world before Him:

> Do not think that I have come to abolish the Law or the Prophets...but to fulfill them.   Matthew 5:17 NIV

Bahá'u'lláh too does not destroy what was given before. He rather restores, fulfills, and glorifies it. Jesus declared:

> And this is the will of him who sent me, that I shall lose none of all that he has given me, but raise them up at the last day.   John 6:39 NIV

The Origin of the Bahá'í Faith

This work is about proofs of the Bahá'í Faith, not its history and teachings. Those not acquainted with the basics of the new Revelation, will find it helpful to begin their search by studying first its history and teachings, and *then* the evidences of its validity. For proofs of a faith are most relevant when one already knows its basic principles. The Message is the goal, and proofs the means for reaching the goal.

For our purposes a brief reference or introduction to the central figures and the supreme institution of the Bahá'í Faith is in order:

- *The Bahá'í Faith* literally means *The Glorious Faith*—the Faith that manifests *the Glory of God*.

- *The Báb*. On May 23, 1844, a young man entitled the Báb (the Gate) declared the dawning of a new Day in the religious history of the world. The young man came from southern Persia. He announced that God would soon send a World Teacher and Savior to bring peace and order and to unify all humanity. Within the brief span of His ministry (1844-1850), the Báb attracted many followers, thousands of whom were massacred, mostly by the order of fanatical religious leaders of Islam. The Báb Himself was imprisoned and finally executed in 1850.

- *Bahá'u'lláh*. In 1863, a nobleman entitled Bahá'u'lláh (Glory of God) announced that He was the World Teacher and Redeemer promised by the Báb and expected by humanity since the dawn of history. Like His Herald, the Báb, Bahá'u'lláh encountered relentless opposition and oppression throughout His ministry. His imprisonment and exile lasted for 39 years. He often refers to His sufferings with a sense of submission and pride—submission because He welcomed that which was ordained for Him, pride because He suffered for the sake of others to bring hope and love to the heart of humanity and peace and justice to the world. Bahá'u'lláh's Writings equal a hundred volumes. They offer teachings and unveil "all the truth" (John 16:13) needed by humanity for at least a thousand years.

- ***'Abdu'l-Bahá***. Before His passing in 1892, Bahá'u'lláh appointed His eldest son, 'Abdu'l-Bahá (Servant of Glory), to serve as the Interpreter and Exemplar of His teachings and the Center of His Covenant. 'Abdu'l-Bahá is also known as the Mystery of God. His station is not that of the Báb or Bahá'u'lláh, but of a Perfect Exemplar or Model for all to emulate. 'Abdu'l-Bahá traveled through many countries to spread the teachings of the new Revelation.

- ***Shoghi Effendi***. Shoghi Effendi did not consider himself one of the central figures of the Bahá'í Faith, yet he occupied a position of preeminence in the development of the new faith. After the passing of 'Abdu'l-Bahá, he served as the appointed Guardian of the Faith. His chief accomplishment was the building of the Administrative Order of Bahá'u'lláh, which constitutes a pattern for the future World Order—an Order called by Jesus *the Kingdom of God*, and *the Kingdom of heaven*, meaning the coming of *the Kingdom of God* or *the Kingdom of heaven* on earth.

- ***The Universal House of Justice***. Shortly after Shoghi Effendi's passing, the responsibility for leadership in the Bahá'í Faith was delegated to a supreme elected institution designated by Bahá'u'lláh as *The Universal House of Justice*. Its members represent and receive the full support of the entire Bahá'í community living in over two hundred countries and territories around the globe.

The Goals of the Bahá'í Faith

When that time comes...I will gather all the nations together...   Joel 3:1-2 NEB

And I...am about to come and gather all nations and tongues, and they will come and see my glory...they will bring all your brothers, from all the nations...

Isaiah 66:18-20 NIV
See also Isaiah 10:13-14

Ye were created to show love one to another...Take pride not in love for yourselves but in love for your fellow-creatures. Glory not in love for your country, but in love for all mankind.[31]   Bahá'u'lláh

...the old order of things has passed away...I am making everything new!   Christ (Revelation 21:4-5 NIV)

Soon will the present-day order be rolled up, and a new one spread out in its stead.[32]   Bahá'u'lláh

The Bahá'í Faith seeks to attain these goals:

- To transform our divided planet into a global community crowned with harmony, peace, and justice

- To inspire the heart of humanity with a divine purpose, and an immortal hope, and

- To raise the ethical standards to levels never before achieved. (For a detailed study of these goals, see any introductory book on Bahá'í teachings. See also Volume VI of this work, *By My Fruits Ye Shall Know Me.*)

All these goals are pursued in fulfillment of this divine prayer and purpose:

Our Father in heaven, thy name be hallowed; thy kingdom come, thy will be done, on earth as in heaven.

Christ (Matthew 6:9-10 NEB)

Many prominent figures of our time have testified to the positive and dynamic influence of the Bahá'í Faith in leading the world toward these goals:

I sympathize with the Bahá'í Faith with all my heart because it has the Spirit of Christ in it...You hold...the key that will settle all of our difficulties...[33]

Dr. George Washington Carver

...the highest and purest form of religious teaching...I know of no other [faith] so profound.　　　Leo Tolstoy

The philosophy of Bahá'u'lláh deserves the best thought we can give it...　　　Helen Keller

In our times we can only survive, and our civilization can only flower, if we reorient the conventional wisdom and achieve the new insights...proclaimed by the Bahá'í Faith and...now also supported by the latest discoveries of the empirical sciences.　　　Dr. Ervin Laszlo
Editor of *The World Encyclopedia of Peace,* Renowned Authority on Systems Sciences and World Order

Bahá'u'lláh was...without question one of the supreme spiritual geniuses of history.　　　Dr. John Holmes
Minister

[The Bahá'í Faith] teaches the essential unity of mankind under one God...That is a force which cuts across politics, trade routes, racial groupings the world around.

It can be made a powerful force in the practical affairs of the world.　　　Hon. William O. Douglas
U.S. Supreme Court Justice

...the greatest movement working today for universal peace.　　　Dr. Auguste Forel
Renowned Swiss Scientist

5

Why Do You Not Understand My Language?

Christ (John 8:43 NEB)

He who is from the earth belongs to the earth and uses earthly speech.   John 3:31 NEB

Lack of communication is at the heart of many conflicts, failures, and tragedies. It affects all spheres of human life, including religion.

But why is there lack of communication? Many experts believe the root cause is a tendency *to act on unverified perceptions and assumptions*. The following story demonstrates the point. A man who was hard of hearing wanted to visit a patient in a hospital. He thought of several questions and presumed the likely answers from the patient. For instance, he thought to ask him, "How are you?" and assumed the patient would say, "I am feeling fine," etc. But this is actually what happened:

Visitor: How are you my friend?

Patient: I feel terrible!

Visitor: Thank God. How is your heart?

Patient: It misses some beats and it may stop at any moment.

Visitor: I am glad to hear that. Where are you going from the hospital?

Patient: To my grave!

Visitor: That is the most restful place to be. When you leave the hospital, who is going to take care of you?

Patient: The angel of hell!

Visitor: You are lucky to have someone like her. What will you be eating there?

Patient: Worms!

Visitor: That is my favorite food. Do you have any close friends who will come to talk with you?

Patient: Yes, his name is the Devil.

Visitor: You are lucky to have friends like that. What does your doctor say?

Patient: He says I will be dead in two weeks.

Visitor: Glad to hear it. Take care now.

The story may seem far-fetched, but it portrays vividly how conflicts and tragedies often take root and spread. It is believed that the atomic bomb was dropped on Hiroshima because the political leaders assumed the translation of a message conveyed by a Japanese news agency was accurate, when it was not:

Unfortunately the translators at the Domei News Agency could not know what Suzuki [the Premier] had in mind. As they hastily translated the prime minister's statement into English, they chose the wrong meaning. From the towers of Radio Tokyo the news crackled to the Allied world that the Suzuki cabinet had decided to "ignore" the Potsdam ultimatum.[1]

The cabinet was furious at the Premier's choice of words and the poor translation of his message by the news agency, but it was too late. "Tokyo radio had flashed it—to America! The punishment came swiftly."[2]

What is religion? It is communication between God and man. The problem is this: *people assume that God speaks in their language, which He does not. They also assume that God sees things as they do, which He does not.* No wonder people find it easier to be grateful to God in times of comfort and prosperity. When good fortune visits them, they say "God is right! I deserve this." But when trouble touches them they say "I can't understand why this is happening to me. Why would God allow this. I never did anything to deserve it!"

These unverified assumptions, that God speaks as we do and sees everything as we see, have caused immeasurable misery and suffering throughout the ages. *Such assumptions continue to prevail in our time.*

Why did people fail to understand Jesus whose marvelous words are models of grace and beauty? Would He—and does He—address the same words He addressed to the Jews (Why do you not understand my language?) to the Christians who are now interpreting His prophecies? Has the way people understand religion changed since the time of Jesus?

This chapter presents a comparative study of the "symbolic language" as used in both biblical and Bahá'í Scriptures. It offers passages from both Scriptures to decode the meaning of some of the most critical prophecies of the second advent. It demonstrates the validity of statements such as the following, which are made by an increasing number of Christian scholars:

> Too often, we try to interpret literally what should be taken symbolically.[3]   Dr. Barry Chant

The examples presented here share this common feature: they contain messages that imply miraculous and dramatic displays of powers over the laws of nature, over the ordinary course of events. The chapter shows:

- The remarkable similarity between the language of Christ and Bahá'u'lláh.

- The astonishing similarity between how the Jews interpreted the prophecies in the first century A. D. and how Christians interpret them today.

- The stark contrast between what people expect and the ways prophecies have been fulfilled.

It concludes that *the strongest obstacle in recognizing God's Messengers and Redeemers is and has always been an inability to discern the difference between how the Creator speaks and what His hearers would like to hear, how He acts and how people would like Him to act.*

> Man looks at the outward appearance, but the Lord looks at the heart.   I Samuel 16:7 NIV

> ...the letter killeth, but the spirit giveth life. II Corinthians 3:6

> For my thoughts are not your thoughts, neither are your ways my ways...   Isaiah 55:8

> ...how can My way accord with thine?[4]   Bahá'u'lláh

The Promise of a King and its Fulfillment

> [The Promise:]...the Lord God will give him [Jesus] the throne of his ancestor David, and *he will be king over Israel for ever*; his reign shall never end [emphasis added throughout the chapter].   Luke 1:31-33 NEB
> See also Luke 1:70-75

> Art thou a king then?...To this end was I [Christ] born...
> John 18:37

The preceding verses are an affirmation of the Old Testament prophecies and promises such as:

> ...I will raise up your offspring to succeed you, one of your own sons...I will establish his throne forever. I will be his father, and he will be my son...I will set him over my house and my kingdom forever; *his throne will be established forever.*   I Chronicles 17:11-14 NIV

> The Lord swore to David an oath which he will not break: 'A prince of your own line will I set upon *your throne.*'   Psalms 132:11 NEB

> But you, Bethlehem...out of you will come for me *one who will be ruler over Israel...*✛   Micah 5:2 NIV

> [The Fulfillment:] You cannot tell by observation when the kingdom of God comes...in fact the kingdom of God is among you.   Christ (Luke 17:20-21 NEB)

> My kingdom does not belong to this world.   Christ (John 18:36 NEB)

How did Jesus who was so poor as to say "Foxes have holes and birds of the air have nests, but the Son of Man has no place to lay his head" (Matt. 8:20 NIV), fulfill the Hebrew prophecies that the promised Redeemer "will be ruler over Israel"? How did Jesus receive "the throne of His ancestor David"? *Spiritually.* How could the Jews in the time of Jesus have acknowledged an interpretation contrary to their established beliefs? By making *wisdom* the guiding lamp of their lives, by being *humble* and *open-minded.* To them "carrying a little extra oil" of wisdom did not seem urgent. Yet that one small step would have led them to the presence of their Lord.

In spite of His seeming poverty and weakness, Jesus spoke like a conquering king:

> ...Jesus Christ, who is...the ruler of the kings of the earth.   Revelation 1:5 NIV

✛ Matthew 2:4-6 indicates that this prophecy was fulfilled by Jesus.

...I have conquered the world.   Christ (John 16:33 NEB)

We find Bahá'u'lláh speaking the same way:

> The Most Great Law is come, and the Ancient Beauty [Bahá'u'lláh] ruleth upon the throne of David.[5]

> Ye are but vassals, O kings of the earth! He Who is the King of Kings hath appeared, arrayed in His most wondrous glory...[6]

When Bahá'u'lláh announced the preceding words, He was a captive—an exile and a prisoner of the Ottoman Empire, under a most mighty and cruel king.

It is divine to judge *by the heart*:

> ...behold, a [King] greater than Solomon is here.
>   Christ (Matthew 12:42)

It is human to judge *by appearance*:

> Is not this the carpenter's son?   Matthew 13:55

The King who was greater than Solomon showed His greatness not by pomp and pride, but by humility: "he poured water into a basin, and began to wash his disciples' feet and to wipe them with the towel" (John 13:5 NEB). *This* is true glory and greatness. The One who was God's beloved Son and the Lord of the visible and invisible declared: "whoever wants to be first must be the willing slave of all—like the Son of Man" (Matt. 20:27 NEB).

While Bahá'u'lláh was being taken to prison, a woman "emerged from the midst of the crowd with a stone in her hand, eager to cast it at the face of Bahá'u'lláh." Bahá'u'lláh asked the guards to let her fulfill her heart's desire: "Deny her not what she regards as a meritorious act in the sight of God."[7] The Master puts the servant's need above His own. *This* is true power.

Both Christ and Bahá'u'lláh ascended the throne of a spiritual—not earthly—kingdom. But this was not what the people expected and are still expecting. Orthodox Jews after two thousand years of expectation and disappointment have not yet abandoned their hope for a King-Messiah.

The Promise of Freedom and its Fulfillment

> [The Promise:] So he promised: age after age he proclaimed by the lips of his holy prophets, that he would *deliver us* [the Jews] from our enemies...   Luke 1:70-71 NEB

> He [the Spirit of the Lord] has sent me...*to release the oppressed...*   Christ (Luke 4:18 NIV)

> [The Fulfillment:] Praise to the God of Israel! For he has turned to his people, saved them and *set them free*, and has raised up a deliverer [Jesus] of victorious power from the house of his servant David.   Luke 1:68-69 NEB
> See also Matt. 11:28-30

How did Jesus release the Jews who were the captives of the Roman oppression? *Spiritually.* Even the Deliverer Himself was oppressed by both the Romans and the Jews. Those who embraced His tidings of love, peace, and salvation were released from their foremost enemies: unbelief, pride, prejudice, selfishness, and hypocrisy. True liberty comes from following what God, the divine Deliverer, prescribes:

> Ye shall know the truth, and the truth shall make you free.
> Christ (John 8:32)

> ...where the Spirit of the Lord is, there is liberty.
> II Corinthians 3:17

> The liberty that profiteth you is to be found nowhere except in complete servitude unto God, the Eternal Truth. Whoso hath tasted of its sweetness will refuse to barter it for all the dominion of earth and heaven.[8]   Bahá'u'lláh

He is indeed a captive who hath not recognized the Supreme
Redeemer, but hath suffered his soul to be bound...in the
fetters of his desires.[9]   Bahá'u'lláh

...everyone who commits sin is a slave. Christ (John 8:34 NEB)

Descending from Heaven

Three common expectations among the Christians are that
Christ will (1) "Come from heaven," (2) "with power and
great glory," (3) "be seen by every eye." Comparing the
following passages from Christ and Bahá'u'lláh should cast
new light on the unique language of revelation, and the
intended meaning of Christ's promises.

We know Jesus was born physically on earth, yet He made
statements that seem to indicate otherwise:

> He who comes from heaven bears witness to what he has
> seen and heard, yet no one accepts his witness.
>   Christ (John 3:31-32 NEB)

> No one has ever gone into heaven except the one who came
> from heaven—the Son of Man.   Christ (John 3:13 NIV)

> I have come down from heaven...   Christ (John 6:38 NEB)

How did Christ come down from heaven? *Spiritually*.

Those who take literally "coming down from heaven" in
relation to the *second* advent can find their counterparts
among Jesus' contemporaries. For they also took literally the
above words in relation to Christ's *first* advent:

> Surely this is Jesus son of Joseph; we know his father and
> mother. *How can he now say*, *"I have come down from
> heaven"*?   John 6:42 NEB

Why did the people not understand Jesus' intention in saying
"I have come down from heaven"? *They tried to translate
the heavenly speech into the earthly*.

...he who is from the earth belongs to the earth and uses earthly speech.   John 3:31 NEB

In the following passage, Bahá'u'lláh again speaks in the language of revelation and declares that He has come from heaven "even as He had come down from it the first time:"

...God is my witness! The Promised One Himself [Bahá'u'lláh] hath come down from heaven, seated upon the crimson cloud with the hosts of revelation on His right, and the angels of inspiration on His left, and the Decree hath been fulfilled at the behest of God, the Omnipotent, the Almighty.[10]   Bahá'u'lláh

How did Bahá'u'lláh descend from heaven? *Spiritually*, even as that Spirit descended the first time:

He [Bahá'u'lláh], verily, hath again come down from heaven, *even as He came down from it the first time.*[11]

Power

Praise to the God of Israel! for he has...raised up a deliverer [Jesus] of victorious *power*...   Luke 1:68-69 NEB

All *power* is given unto me in heaven and in earth.
Christ (Matthew 28:18)
See also Mark 9:1

God is my witness! He, the Ancient of everlasting days is come, girded with majesty and *power*.[12]   Bahá'u'lláh

The All-Merciful is come invested with *power* and sovereignty.[13]   Bahá'u'lláh

The following words testify to Bahá'u'lláh's supreme power. Has anyone ever spoken with such authority?

I am the One Whom the tongue of Isaiah hath extolled, the One with Whose name both the Torah and the Evangel were adorned...The glory of Sinai hath hastened to circle round the Day-Spring of this Revelation, while from the heights of the Kingdom the voice of the Son of God is heard proclaiming: "Bestir yourselves, ye proud ones of the earth, and hasten ye towards Him." Carmel hath in this day hastened in longing adoration to attain His court, whilst from the heart of Zion there cometh the cry: "The promise of all ages is now fulfilled. That which had been announced in the holy writ of God, the Beloved, the Most High, is made manifest."...By the one true God, Elijah hath hastened unto My court and hath circumambulated in the day-time and in the night-season My throne of glory. Solomon in all his majesty circles in adoration around Me in this day, uttering this most exalted word: "I have turned my face towards Thy face, O Thou omnipotent Ruler of the world! I am wholly detached from all things pertaining unto me, and yearn for that which Thou dost possess." [14]

He, verily, is come with His Kingdom, and all the atoms cry aloud:...."Here am I, here am I, O Lord, My God!" whilst Sinai circleth round the House, and the Burning Bush calleth aloud: "The All-bounteous is come mounted upon the clouds!" [15]

What kind of power did Christ and Bahá'u'lláh have? *Spiritual*. This too was not what people valued and expected or are still expecting.

Glory

How did Christ view His crucifixion?

> The hour is come, that the Son of man should be *glorified*.
> > Christ (John 12:23)

> Father, the hour has come. *Glorify* thy Son...
> > Christ (John 17:1 neb)

How did Bahá'u'lláh perceive *His* sufferings?

I sorrow not for the burden of My imprisonment. Neither do I grieve over My abasement, or the tribulation I suffer at the hands of Mine enemies. By My life! They are My *glory*, a glory wherewith God hath adorned His own Self. Would that ye know it![16]   Bahá'u'lláh

And again:

I am not impatient in the troubles that touch me in my love for Thee...Nay, I have, by Thy power, chosen them for my own self, and I *glory* in them...[17]   Bahá'u'lláh

What kind of glory did Christ and Bahá'u'lláh have? *Spiritual.* This too was not what the people expected and valued and are still expecting.

Seeing

...he [Jesus] came to dwell among us, and *we saw* his glory...   John 1:14 NEB

But *we see* Jesus...crowned with glory and honor...
                                                   Hebrews 2:9

Who *saw* Jesus crowned with glory and honor? Only those— a few—who had *in*sight. At first "even his brothers had no faith in him" (John 7:5 NEB). It is the spirit and the heart that see the Glory of God. Seeing the truth requires *spiritual* sight:

Except a man be born again, he cannot *see* the kingdom of God.   Christ (John 3:3)

...without holiness no one will *see* the Lord.
                                                   Hebrews 12:14 NIV

...your sins have hidden his [the Lord's] face from you...
                                                   Isaiah 59:2 NIV

...whosoever sinneth hath not *seen* Him...   I John 3:6

Blessed are the *pure in heart*: for they shall *see* God.
                                                   Christ (Matthew 5:8)

...when a true seeker determineth to take the step of search in the path leading to the knowledge of the Ancient of Days, he must, before all else, cleanse and *purify his heart*...[18]
                                                                        Bahá'u'lláh

...had these people...*sanctified their eyes*...they surely would not have been deprived of *beholding* the beauty of God...[19]
                                                                        Bahá'u'lláh

I counsel you to buy from me...salve to put on your eyes, so you can *see*.   Christ (Revelation 3:18 NIV)

At His trial Jesus said:

...from now on, you will *see* the Son of Man seated at the right hand of God...   Christ (Matthew 26:64 NEB)

Who *saw* Jesus from then on sitting at the right hand of God? And how was He seen? With *insight* or *eyesight*? How did those who heard Jesus—both believers and unbelievers—interpret His words? Has anyone ever seen Him sitting at the right hand of God?

He that was hidden from mortal eyes is come! His all-conquering sovereignty is *manifest*; His all-encompassing splendor is *revealed*. Beware lest thou hesitate or halt.[20]
                                                                        Bahá'u'lláh

Behold Him [Bahá'u'lláh] *manifest and resplendent* as the sun in all its glory.[21]   Bahá'u'lláh

"Manifest and resplendent" to whom? Who saw Bahá'u'lláh's "all-encompassing" splendor? Only those who stayed awake with watchful eyes:

Behold, I come like a thief! Blessed is he who stays *awake*...   Christ (Revelation 16:15 NIV)

...do not let him find you sleeping...I say to everyone: '*Watch*!'   Christ (Mark 13:36-37 NIV)

Did Jesus mean watching with *physical* or *spiritual* eyes? Did He mean sleeping *eyes* or sleeping *spirits*? Did He mean sleeping in the dark of the night or in the dark of unawareness?

> Blessed the slumberer who is *awakened*...[22]   Bahá'u'lláh

> ...blessed are your eyes, for they *see*: and your ears, for they *hear*.   Christ (Matthew 13:16)

> Blessed the ear that hath *heard*...and the eye that hath *seen* and recognized the Lord...[23]   Bahá'u'lláh

Life, Death, and Resurrection

> I am the resurrection and I am life...no one who is alive and has faith *shall ever die*.   Christ (John 11:25-26 NEB)

> Whoso hath been re-born in this Day, *shall never die*...[24]
> Bahá'u'lláh

> ...if anyone keeps My word he *shall never see death*.
> Christ (John 8:51 NKJ)

Who are those who never die? The *spiritually* alive. They are resurrected through their faith and their love for God.

If there were no other example in the Bible, the next one in itself would be adequate to teach us God's unique way of communicating. In the last part of this most instructive passage Jesus promises to return "in His kingdom" during the lifetime of His contemporaries:

> For the Son of Man is going to come in his Father's glory with his angels, and then he will reward each person according to what he has done. I tell you the truth, *some who are standing here will not taste death before they see the Son of Man coming in his kingdom*.
> Christ (Matt. 16:27-28 NIV)

Was Jesus' promise fulfilled literally or spiritually? Did some of the people addressed by Him live to see "the coming of the

Son of Man in his kingdom"? Then what did He mean by
glory, *angels*, *reward*, *death*, *see*, and *kingdom*? Can these
words be viewed in any light other than spiritual? Was the
prophecy fulfilled in any other way?

The lack of literal fulfillment of the prophecy at the due time
(the life-span of those addressed by Jesus), has made Christian interpreters recognize Jesus' true intention in uttering the
prophecy. They believe it contains a spiritual rather than
literal message. For instance, a Christian scholar states that it
refers to "a spiritual coming of Christ, to an inner experience
of the soul in accordance with the inward nature of the kingdom."[25] Another Christian scholar declares that the people
who had insight could "behold with their inward eye those
wonderful words of God which Jesus calls His kingdom..."[26]

To understand God's word, we must think in His ways of
speaking. His language is unique:

> Blessed the man who, assured of My Word, *hath arisen
> from among the dead* to celebrate My praise.[27]
>
> Bahá'u'lláh

Suffering First, Glory Later

When the disciples asked: "Lord, are you at this time going
to restore the kingdom to Israel?" (Acts 1:6 NIV), Jesus did
not tell them what they wanted to hear. Instead of saying yes
or no, He simply pointed to the future, without giving a
definite date: "It is not for you to know the times" (Acts 1:7
NIV). On another occasion, the Jews asked Him a similar
question: "But we had been hoping that he [Jesus] was the
man to liberate Israel" (Luke 24:21 NEB). And this is the
answer *they* received: "How dull you are!...Was the Messiah
not bound to *suffer* thus *before entering upon his glory*?"
(Luke 24:25-26 NEB).

Just as Jesus said that the days of glory would come later,
so did Bahá'u'lláh:

The day is approaching when God will have exalted His Cause and magnified His testimony in the eyes of all who are in the heavens and...on the earth.[28]   Bahá'u'lláh

The day is approaching when We will have rolled up the world and all that is therein, and spread out a new order in its stead. He, verily, is powerful over all things.[29]

Bahá'u'lláh

The universe is pregnant with these manifold bounties, awaiting the hour when the effects of its unseen gifts will be made manifest in this world...[30]   Bahá'u'lláh

The reign of an earthly sovereign endures for his lifetime. The reign of a spiritual sovereign grows in His absence. *This* is true power and glory. A poor, homeless man from an obscure town is crucified with the utmost meekness, and with no one to defend Him. Nineteen centuries later, one of the most powerful monarchs of the earth says this about that homeless man:

I wish He would come during my lifetime so that I could take my crown and lay it at His feet.[31]   Queen Victoria

Ironically, Queen Victoria's wish came true: both the Báb and Bahá'u'lláh declared their Mission during her long reign (1837-1901). She received Bahá'u'lláh's message in an epistle addressed to her, but did not recognize Him.

A man suffers persecution and humiliation for forty years. He dies as a prisoner and exile in an obscure and desolate town. Decades after He has passed away, a monarch says this about Him and His teachings:

Indeed a great light came to me with the Message of Bahá'u'lláh...It is a wondrous Message...It is Christ's Message...Some of those of my caste wonder at and disapprove my courage to step forward pronouncing words not habitual for Crowned Heads to pronounce, but I advance by an inner urge I cannot resist. With bowed head

I recognize that I too am but an instrument in greater Hands
and rejoice in the knowledge.[32]   Queen Marie of Rumania
                                         (Granddaughter of Queen Victoria)

Edward Browne, the Cambridge scholar, who met Bahá'u'lláh,
said this about Him: "[Bahá'u'lláh is] the object of a devotion
and love which kings might envy and emperors sigh for in
vain!"[33] Humans desire crowns of jewels, Messengers crowns
of thorns. As Carlyle notes: "Every noble crown is, and on
Earth will forever be, a crown of thorns." This is how
Bahá'u'lláh viewed Jesus' poverty and abasement:

> Thousands of treasures circle round this poverty, and a
> myriad kingdoms of glory yearn for such abasement![34]

That a crucified homeless man could command the loyalty
of almost a third of the earth's population for countless
centuries is a wonder far more astonishing than anything an
earthly sovereign can ever achieve. What else but the presence
of suprahuman power can explain such an achievement? *This*
is true grandeur and glory.

Which is *true* glory? To conquer by *fire* or by *faith*, by
power or by *patience*? Who is the true sovereign, the one
who fears the triumph of his own evil powers over himself,
or the One who triumphs over the evil powers of the world?

> I have conquered an empire but have been unable to con-
> quer myself.   Peter the Great, Czar of Russia

Dr. James Kennedy, the renowned Christian orator who has
influenced millions by emphasizing the rational basis of
Christianity, makes this statement about the suprahuman
power of Jesus:

> Suppose that today in the cities of Europe or America
> missionaries were to appear telling us that just recently
> some obscure peasant had been put to death in Persia and
> was reputed to have risen from the dead and declared to
> be the eternal Creator of the cosmos. What chance do you
> think such missionaries would have in propagating such a

religion? *Can you not see that the probabilities against such a faith ever taking hold would be staggering?* But this is precisely what the Apostles did in the Roman Empire, and amazing as it is, they succeeded. They succeeded in overthrowing that pagan empire. *This feat simply demonstrates that there must have been inherent in this absurd and incredible declaration, some supernatural power. It was indeed the very power of the spirit of God*, who reached down and drew unto Himself those whom He would by irresistible power.[35]

Does the Bahá'í Faith meet the standard declared by Dr. Kennedy?

The Bahá'í Faith...has spread to over 362 countries, territories, and islands around the world. This worldwide Bahá'í community includes believers from nearly every race, background, nation, and culture. Indeed, the *1988 Britannica Book of the Year* states that over 14 major religious systems are each now found in over 80 countries. [Among them], Christianity, Islam, and the Bahá'í World Faith are the most global..."[36]

The same source presents these figures to show the spread of the Bahá'í Faith to various countries and territories in comparison with other faiths:

- Christianity   254
- Bahá'í Faith   205
- Islam   172
- Hinduism   88
- Buddhism   86

Both Christ and Bahá'u'lláh declared that they had no desire for the pomp and pageantry of this world, that earthly glory would follow, after they had ascended to the heavenly realms. *This too was not what the people expected and are still expecting.*

The Second Advent is Also Prophesied to Begin with Suffering

For the Son of Man in his day will be like the lightning...
But first he must suffer...Just as it was in the days of
Noah, so also will it be in the days of the Son of Man.
                              Christ (Luke 17:24-26 NIV)

For a detailed study of this prophecy, as well as many other
biblical passages that point to suffering, see Volume III, ***King
of Kings***, which offers several chapters on the subject. As we
noted in Chapter 1, Jesus also predicted pain and suffering
for ***the followers*** of the new Revelation.

Bahá'u'lláh often refers to His motives for enduring pain, to
His purpose in suffering:

> I have, all the days of My life, been at the mercy of Mine
> enemies, and have suffered each day, in the path of the
> love of God, a fresh tribulation.[37]   Bahá'u'lláh

> Verily, He [Bahá'u'lláh] hath consented to be sorely abased
> that ye may attain unto glory...He, in truth, liveth in the
> most desolate of abodes for your sakes...[38]   Bahá'u'lláh

> Behold Him [Bahá'u'lláh], an exile, a victim of tyranny,
> in this Most Great Prison ['Akká, in the Holy Land]. His
> enemies have assailed Him on every side, and will
> continue to do so till the end of His life. Whatever, there-
> fore, He saith unto you is wholly for the sake of God, that
> haply the peoples of the earth may cleanse their hearts
> from the stain of evil desire...and attain unto the knowl-
> edge of the one true God—the most exalted station to
> which any man can aspire. Their belief or disbelief in My
> Cause can neither profit nor harm Me. We summon them
> wholly for the sake of God.[39]   Bahá'u'lláh

> I yield Thee thanks, O my God, for that Thou has offered
> me up as a sacrifice in Thy path, and made me a target
> for the arrows of afflictions as a token of Thy love for

Thy servants...Whoso hath quaffed the living waters of
Thy favors can fear no trouble in Thy path, neither can
he be deterred by any tribulation from remembering Thee
or from celebrating Thy praise.[40]   Bahá'u'lláh

The Right to Interpret

Has God given us the right to interpret prophecies? Has He
also given us the right to consider our opinion *the right
one*?

Opinions differ very little on fundamentals of mathematics
and physics, but as we move to more subjective fields such
as psychology, sociology, education, philosophy, and religion,
we find a wide variation of views. Within religion we see
the greatest diversity of thought in the realm of prophecy,
for nothing is more mysterious. Of course, the mystery is
ingrained by choice, not by chance. Perhaps the only subject
comparable in complexity to prophecy is the interpretation
of dreams. (We should note that the greatest portion of
prophecies are also dreams and visions.)

As a Christian scholar notes "After reading some of the books
on the subject [of prophecy] it would be easy to suggest that
there are as many opinions as there are people." For instance,
some Christians believe rapture is real; others deny it
vehemently; and still others disagree about how or when it
can happen.

How then can one find a path to true knowledge? First, the
sheer complexity of prophetic language should make every
interpreter of the Word of God utterly humble. Once a very
learned man was found crying. His students asked him why.
He said "For fifty years I believed something to be true. I
just discovered I was wrong. I am afraid everything else I
know is of the same kind." Second, the interpreter of the
word of God should not look up to any "authority" or

school as his guide, even as he would not close his eyes and let someone lead him. And third, he should carefully observe God's own guidance, expressed in these verses:

> But first note this: no one can interpret any prophecy of Scripture by himself.   II Peter 1:20 NEB

The Amplified version of the same verse:

> [Yet] first [you must] understand this, that no prophecy of Scripture is [a matter] of any personal *or* private *or* special interpretation (loosening, solving) [brackets and parentheses belong to original source].

The main message of the verse is this: only God knows *for sure* the true meaning of a prophecy. God is universal and infinite; we are private and finite. People have a right to state their opinions, *as long as they do not insist that they are the only right ones.*

In spite of his superb wisdom, St. Paul acknowledged his own limitations in understanding the Word of God:

> For we know in part and we prophesy in part, but when perfection [Christ] comes, the imperfect disappears.
> I Corinthians 13:9-10 NIV

The need for being open-minded and non-dogmatic is also confirmed by some Christian scholars:

> *Whatever view we adopt, we should avoid dogmatism.* Many wise and godly people have studied the same passages in the Bible and come up with differing inter- pretations. It is obvious that they cannot all be right. Yet they may not all be wrong, either.[41]

The next verse offers still more enlightenment. It says if something is mysterious ("is hidden in darkness"), do not attempt to interpret it:

Therefore judge nothing before the appointed time; wait till the Lord comes. He will bring to light what is hidden in darkness and will expose the motives of men's hearts.

I Corinthians 4:5 NIV

Then what right do we have over prophecies? *The only right we have is this: to expect all of them without any exception to come true, all of them to come to pass.* A prophecy is uttered to be fulfilled. Otherwise, what purpose would it serve? *The right we do not have is this: to decide with certainty which prophecy is literal and which is symbolic; to insist that our interpretation is the right one.*

The power that protects us from stumbling or falling, the light that leads us to the true knowledge of God's Word is the recognition of our specific rights and responsibilities. Overstepping the boundaries that God has specified for us can lead us only to illusions and fantasies. For many faithful believers, the full recognition or acceptance of their *limited powers, rights, and boundaries* is extremely painful. Many reasons account for this:

- Those in positions of leadership and authority must project confidence and knowledge to the people they lead and inspire.

- The people they lead and inspire tend to reinforce that need. For they too need well-informed leaders on whom they can lean for spiritual guidance and security.

- Most people, especially those in positions of authority, feel uncomfortable with saying "I don't know." Acknowledging one's weaknesses is always painful.

- Coming up with new theories and insights is always exciting. We all like to be in the forefront of discovery.

All these complex needs, relationships, and weaknesses that affect all human beings, prompt many interpreters of the Word of God to cross their boundaries, to claim more than they are entitled to.

Those who trust their Lord, always submit to and are content with the limited rights He has given them. Those unwilling to acknowledge their weaknesses, recognize their boundaries, and stay within their rights are powerless to pursue the path of truth, the path that leads to the light of the Lord.

Separating the symbolic prophecies from the literal is not an easy task. On the basis of biblical prophecies, many Christians expect terrible wars between the forces of Christ and military forces of the earth. The main reason for war is people's refusal to accept God's plan of peace. It is a war the like of which the world has never seen. According to a source published and distributed by a Christian association,[42] the earthly side of the war is waged "by a fiendish army of 200,000,000." This great war is expected to lead to the death of many hundreds of millions of people, many times more than have been killed in all wars since the dawn of history.

Hal Lindsey, perhaps the most popular interpreter of prophecies in our time, states that as the result of such wars "blood will stand to the horses' bridles [over three feet] for a total of 200 miles northward and southward of Jerusalem (Rev. 14:20)." (Astonishingly, one of the two major branches of Islam entertains a similar expectation: that their promised Redeemer will engage in battles in which blood will reach the stirrups of His horse.)

Expecting Jesus and the host of His angels to wage war against earthly people is very common. The following brief example from *Understanding End Time Prophecy*, written by Norman Robertson, assistant Dean of Rhema Bible Training Center, offers more insight into literal interpretation. Examples of this kind are found abundantly in books on Bible prophecy:

> Jesus speaks the Word which releases a plague to smite the vast armies of the Antichrist and the 200 million strong Oriental army. They are immediately blinded; their eyes are consumed away in their sockets. They are immediately

dumb; their tongues are consumed away in their mouths. In fright, they reach out and grab one another for security. That only frightens them more, so they turn to fight among themselves. Their flesh begins to consume away from their bones. Their blood gushes to the earth, creating the pool of blood described in Revelation 14. It stretches over an area of about 185 miles in the valley of Megiddo and the Plains of Jezreel.[43]

Would the divine, loving, gentle Savior of the world allow or engage in such horrible wars? Who can *be sure* that such terrible and titanic wars are to be waged with bullets, bombs, and missiles on airfields and battle grounds, or if they are to be carried out with an exchange of ideas and thoughts in churches, temples, and on the airways of the world? Only the One who knows "what is hidden in darkness" (I Cor. 4:5 NIV).

Unsheathe the sword of your tongue from the scabbard of utterance, for therewith ye can conquer the citadels of men's hearts.[44]   Bahá'u'lláh

The Book of Revelation speaks of a sword that comes out of the mouth of the One called the Word of God (19:13, 15). Who can tell *for sure* if the sword is spiritual (the Word of God) or literal? Only the One who has the knowledge of all things.

The same book speaks of a city (a new Jerusalem) that descends from heaven. Who can tell *for sure* if this city is literal or spiritual (one based on God's plan but built by people)? Only the One gifted with divine guidance.

In Matthew 24:40-41, Jesus declares that at His coming some people will be taken away (the rapture). Who can tell *for sure* if it is the believers' hearts and souls that are lifted into the realm of faith, or their flesh and bone? *Only the Lord, the One who as evidence of His divine power fulfills each and every prophecy that God's Messengers and prophets have spoken; the One who fulfills them all—EITHER*

LITERALLY OR SYMBOLICALLY. *The choice of resolving the*
mysteries (what is literal, what is symbolic?) is all His. No
one has the right to present his private, personal interpretation as the truth. No one has the wisdom and the insight to
challenge His knowledge.

As we will see in the next chapter, even Jesus' enlightened
disciples sometimes had to struggle to reconcile their thoughts
and desires with their Master's. Despite their great wisdom,
they too could not always separate the symbolic from the literal.

Some Christian leaders and scholars are beginning to acknowledge that the pendulum of interpretation supported
by most churches has gone too far toward literalism. For
instance, Dr. Barry Chant, who has written extensively on
Christian issues including prophecy, declares:

> Too often, we try to interpret literally what should be
> taken symbolically.[45]...symbolic language is quite typical
> of prophecy. In the Old Testament, in fact, it is clearly
> stated that prophets speak in visions, dreams and riddles
> (Numbers 12:6). A 'riddle' was usually a saying that had
> some hidden or subtle meaning that was not obvious at
> first. In fact, sometimes its meaning would not be known
> at all until the matter was fulfilled.[46]

The most critical message of this chapter should be repeated
once again: *God has given us the right to expect the fulfill-*
ment of all prophecies, but He has given us neither the right
nor the wisdom to separate with certainty all the literal
prophecies from the symbolic. Even one major mistake can
cause us to become blind to the reality before us.

6

The Great and Terrible Day of the Lord

Malachi 4:5 NEB

Our age is one of extreme contrasts. Prophecies attribute two potentials or possibilities to our age: the most awful and terrible, and the greatest and most glorious. This brief verse from Malachi portrays the paradox of our time:

...the **great** and **terrible** [dreadful NIV] day of the Lord [emphasis added throughout the chapter]... Malachi 4:5 NEB

The two translations of the following verse cover the full range of the potentials of our time:

Alas! For that day is **great**, so that none is like it...
Jeremiah 30:7 NKJ

How *awful* that day will be! None will be like it.

Jeremiah 30:7 NIV

This chapter shows mainly the gloomy state of the present. An entire chapter in Volume IV will cover prophecies about the glory of the future, portraying a magnificent world, a world wherein love, justice, and peace dominate the hearts of humanity. A world radiant with the glory of God, for everything will be under God's rule.

...I saw the glory of the God of Israel...the land was radiant with his glory.   Ezekiel 43:2 NIV

This is the Day in which the earth shineth with the effulgent light of thy Lord...[1]   Bahá'u'lláh

...the earth was illuminated by his splendor.

Revelation 18:1 NIV

The Lord their God will save them on that day...They will sparkle...like jewels in a crown. How attractive and beautiful they will be!   Zechariah 9:16-17 NIV

Hallelujah! For our Lord God Almighty reigns. Let us rejoice and be glad and give him glory!   Revelation 19:7 NIV

The two portrayals of our time offer *extreme contrasts*, with the overwhelming weight on the side of glory rather than gloom. At this very instant we are experiencing the pangs of a new birth—one that has been the hope of humanity since the dawn of history and will be its crown of glory for countless ages to come. It is the birth of a kingdom divine, immortal, and everlasting; a kingdom patterned after the one in heaven. The pains must be proportionate to the gains.

But the "pains" are mostly "mental," as reachable and changeable as our thoughts and desires. They can be removed or lessened by a little change of attitude, by a desire to overcome the fear of exploring new frontiers of knowledge. The Book of Revelation promises the most exquisite gifts to those who *overcome their spiritual handicaps*; gifts as glorious as *receiving God's own name and sitting on His thron*e.

I am coming soon...Him who overcomes (Rev. 3:11-12 NIV):

• Will inherit all things (Rev. 21:7).

• I will be his God and he will be my son (Rev. 21:7).

• I will give the right *to sit with me on my throne* (Rev. 3:21).

• I will give the right to eat from the tree of life which is in the paradise of God (Rev. 2:7).

• I will make a pillar in the temple of my God (Rev. 3:12).

• I will...give him the morning star (Rev. 2:28).

• I...will acknowledge his name before my Father... (Rev. 3:5).

• I will never erase his name from the book of life... (Rev. 3:5).

• I will write on him the name of my God... (Rev. 3:12).

• I will write on him...the name of the city of my God (Rev. 3:12).

• I will also give him a white stone with a new name... (Rev. 2:17).

• *I will also write on him my new name*. He who has an [spiritual] ear, let him hear what the Spirit says to the churches (Rev. 3:12-13).

The Standards of Judgment

> The Lord does not look at the things man looks at. Man looks at the outward appearance, but the Lord looks at the heart.   I Samuel 16:7 NIV

To feel secure and at ease, human beings tend to accept and conform to the status quo. According to the Book of Zechariah, the Lord sends visitors throughout the earth to assess the spiritual state of the nations. The assessors declare: "We have gone throughout the earth and found the whole world at rest and in peace" (Zech. 1:11 NIV). The Lord then declares: "I am very angry with nations that feel secure [at ease, NEB]" (Zech. 1:15 NIV).

Who is the true judge of human beings? The Creator or the created? Our knowledge of our true potential for spiritual growth and greatness is always limited and our assessment of our attainments and failures subjective. To cope with difficult conditions, we often compromise or alter our standards to meet daily demands. Something that was unacceptable, unethical, or even unthinkable for one generation may become the norm for the next. "We don't see things as they are, but as we are."

Do God's standards also change? Only He knows the true and absolute standards of being human; only He knows our capacities for greatness and self-fulfillment; only He can assess the worth of the missed opportunities, the magnitude of His unclaimed blessings. Therefore, to know how well we are doing, we must always depend on *His* standards.

Consider these examples. At the time of this writing, over 30,000 people on our planet die *every day* from malnutrition and starvation. As Dr. Ervin Laszlo notes "one in every five human beings goes permanently hungry and lives in abject poverty." *If we did not have the resources to save them, we would not be accountable*. But we do. The accumulated wealth of the world in our time is beyond imagination. The rich ones of the earth could save all the hungry people of our planet with a stroke of a pen, with virtually no change in their wealth. They could also be saved with a fraction of one percent of the world's military budget. Our political leaders search for the biggest and latest bombers but ignore the rampant spread of blindness in little children, a terrible handicap that can be prevented with a few pennies worth of vitamin A.

To us the ignoring of such widespread death and disease in the context of enormous wealth is the norm. But what about God?

Likewise, when we find many people around us depressed, uninterested in knowledge, cynical, conforming, apathetic, or suffering in quiet desperation, then we accept those conditions as normal. Usually what is easy and what the majority follows shapes and reshapes our standards, and statistics often write the rules of living.

Making money often seems to be the prime motive and having money the prime purpose of living. How does God view wealth? A man of wealth came to Jesus and asked how he could gain eternal life. Jesus told him to keep the commandments (love thy neighbor, etc.). The man said he was keeping them already. (That is what *he* thought.) Jesus then tried his soul in the fiery crucible of testing: "If you want to be perfect, go, sell your possessions and give to the poor" (Matt. 19:21 NIV). Sadness overwhelmed the man's soul. He could not pass this test and walked away. He could give love but not gold. God saw his perfection in giving away his possessions. He saw his self-worth in keeping them.

O SON OF MAN!
Thou dost wish for gold and I desire thy freedom from it. Thou thinkest thyself rich in its possession, and I recognize thy wealth in thy sanctity therefrom. By My life! This is My knowledge, and that is thy fancy; how can My way accord with thine? [2]   Bahá'u'lláh

The Spiritual State of Our Time

Jesus predicted that at His return faithfulness to His covenant would be scarce:

"But when the Son of Man comes, will he find faith on earth?" (Luke 18:8 NEB). "At that time many will turn away from the faith" (Matt. 24:10 NIV). "The love of most will grow cold" (Matt. 24:12 NIV).

What love will grow cold? The love of God, religion, and truth.

> People will be lovers of themselves, lovers of money...not lovers of the good...having a form of godliness but denying its power.   II Timothy 3:2-5 NIV

Is religion today an accumulation of the ideas, illusions, and precepts of people or an expression of the principles of God? Is it based on true understanding or on rote learning?

> ...their religion is but a precept of men, *learnt by rote*...
> Isaiah 29:13 NEB
> See also Amos 8:12

In our time biblical scholarship has advanced beyond the dreams of past generations. The number of books published to help people understand the Bible is phenomenal. Many new translations of the Bible have appeared. Hundreds of colleges and universities offer degrees or courses in religion. Never before have there been so many Bible scholars with Ph.D.'s and D.D.'s. What kind of knowledge is being discovered and shared? Is it the kind that mostly "begins and ends in words," or the kind that leads to action? Is it the kind that promotes "rote learning" as Isaiah foretold (29:13), or the kind that fosters enlightenment?

> People [who live at the end of the age] *will be...always learning but never able to acknowledge the truth*...
> II Timothy 3:2-7 NIV

These prophecies should make anyone who reads them—no matter how learned—as humble as a little child. They imply:

• Following the popular views of prophecies may be unjustified.

• Openness of the mind and the heart to *new* ideas is absolutely essential.

Do the countless theories on prophecies enlighten or becloud the mind? Do they create insight or confusion? Why did Jesus declare that He would come on *the clouds*?

> They will see the Son of Man coming on the clouds...
>
> Matthew 24:30 NIV

What purpose do the clouds serve? They *veil* the heavenly lights. The Hebrew prophets also predicted the gloominess of our time:

> "That day will be a day of...darkness and gloom, *a day of clouds*..." (Zeph. 1:15 NIV). "Arise...your light has come, and the glory of the Lord rises upon you. See, *darkness covers the earth...and thick darkness is over the peoples*" (Isa. 60:1-2 NIV).

Jesus warned the seekers of His Kingdom and showed them how to lift the veils of gloom and darkness, so that the glory of the Lord could become visible:

> Keep a *watch* on yourselves; do not let your minds [hearts, NIV] be dulled by *dissipation* and *drunkenness* and worldly cares...Be on the alert, praying at all times...
>
> Luke 21:34-36 NEB

Jesus asked His faithful followers to observe two actions:

- Watch or investigate
- Pray continuously

He also urged them to overcome three obstacles:

- Dissipation, which the dictionary defines as "indulging in intemperate pursuit of pleasure"
- Preoccupation with worldly concerns, such as working, going to school, and raising a family
- Drunkenness

What does Jesus mean by "drunkenness"? Many in our age numb their souls with intoxicating drinks and drugs. But far more critical is spiritual intoxication—with one's own fantasies, which leads to separation from reality; and self-satisfaction, which leads to coldness, complacency, and apathy. The

Scriptures declare that the spiritual handicap of the people of our time is very serious; it is continual intoxication:

> "They are drunken, but not with wine; they stagger, but not with strong drink" (Isa. 29:9). "They grope in the darkness without light and are left to wander like a drunkard" (Job 12:25 NEB). "All the nations shall drink continually" (Ob. 1:16 NEB). "Wake up, you drunkards, and lament your fate...Alas! the day is near, the day of the Lord" (Joel 1:5,15 NEB). "The inhabitants of the earth were intoxicated" (Rev. 17:2 NIV). "They will walk like blind men" (Zeph. 1:17 NIV). (See also Rev. 18:3; Isa. 29:9-14; 49:26.)

To whom do these prophecies apply? Humility requires that each individual, no matter how learned, admit this in his heart: I too may have serious *spiritual handicaps of which I may be totally unaware*. I too may be living in the clouds. *I too may be afflicted with spiritual intoxication*. I too need to remain *sober*:

> Therefore let us not sleep, as do others; but let us watch and *be sober*.   I Thessalonians 5:6

Bahá'u'lláh repeatedly characterizes the spiritual state of mankind in passages such as these:

> *Drunken are the eyes* of those men that have openly refused to behold the face of God, the All-Glorious, the All Praised.[3]

> *Their eyes are drunken*; they are indeed a blind people.[4]

> We behold it [the world], in this day, at the mercy of rulers so *drunk with pride* that they cannot discern clearly their own best advantage, much less recognize a Revelation so bewildering and challenging as this.[5]

> Thou beholdest, O my God, how *bewildered in their drunkenness* are Thy servants who have turned back from Thy beauty and caviled at what hath been sent down from the right hand of the throne of Thy majesty.[6]

What is the consequence of "drinking"? The consequence is spiritual unconsciousness; it is an inability to recognize the signs of the times and the timely return of the Master:

> But suppose that servant...says to himself, 'My master is staying away a long time,' and he then begins...to eat and *drink with drunkards*. The master of that servant will... assign him a place with the hypocrites...
>
> Christ (Matthew 24:48-51 NIV)

Why is the servant placed with the hypocrites? Because he considers himself a faithful follower, yet he fails to abide by his Master's wishes, he refuses to investigate the news of His return. Hypocrisy always results from failure to put one's professed faith and belief into action.

This prophetic parable implies that many will continue to wait and wish for their Master's return, *after the set time has passed, and after the Master has returned* because they assume that their "master is delaying his coming" (NKJ). The parable of the ten maidens clearly supports this. The five maidens who took no oil, "slumbered and slept" (Matt. 25:5) because they thought the Bridegroom would be late. While they were dreaming about His late return, He came and left them absorbed in their dreams.

This prophecy clarifies the point:

> Suddenly, in an instant, the Lord Almighty will come...[it will be] as it is with a dream, with a vision in the night— as when a hungry man dreams that he is eating, but he awakens, and his hunger remains; as when a thirsty man dreams that he is drinking, but he awakens faint, with his thirst unquenched.   Isaiah 29:5-8 NIV

Many people prefer to be dreaming than to be awake, especially if they can choose their dreams. But as the prophecy declares, dreaming alone or feeling comfortable cannot satisfy the hunger of the spirit.

We may enjoy the dreaming part so much that we do not even want to consider that there is much more available if we awaken. Thus we choose to remain asleep, unaware of the grandness that is there for us in awakening. When we stay with the familiar we take no risks.[7] Wayne Dyer

Would the Bridegroom ever be late to His banquet? How can the One who calls Himself a faithful witness (Rev. 1:5) fail to fulfill His most urgent and glorious promise to His servants? No, the heavenly Host would never be late to His banquet. He appears late only to His "slumbering and sleeping" guests who are caught in their dreams.

He who is coming will come and will not delay.

Hebrews 10:37 NIV

The belief that the Master has delayed His return is not uncommon. Noted Christian author and leader, George Vandeman writes:

...Jesus could have returned to this earth any time after 1844...No time prophecy is holding Him back. Then why hasn't He returned?[8]

He then concludes that God is waiting to give people more time to repent. Here are two more examples from other writers:

If we put all the information together we must reach the inescapable conclusion that it [the time of the advent] will take longer than we thought, but when it comes it will happen sooner than we expect.[9]

God is holding back to give us that chance. It will not last forever.[10]

The idea of the late coming of the Master is not new. It has been held by the Jews for as long as 2000 years:

Rabbi Avrohom Feuer wrote, "The Talmud (Sanhedrin 97a) lists numerous signs which herald the imminent arrival of Messiah...all these signs have appeared, yet Messiah tarries."[11]

In the delay many have succumbed to drunkenness. Some are drunk with the wonders of modern technology, others with a specific ideology or theology, and still others with success, wealth, power, prestige, pride, self-conceit, or self-satisfaction. *Any* of these obstacles may preoccupy the mind and becloud the spirit. Any one of them can conceal the great glory of the Master, *can make Him totally invisible*.

Spiritual intoxication comes also from a stressful life. The people of our time live under constant stress and distress:

> "That day will be...a day of distress and anguish, a day of trouble and ruin" (Zeph. 1:15-16 NIV). "There will be a time of distress such as has not happened from the beginning of nations until then" (Dan. 12:1 NIV). "It will be a time of great distress" (Christ, Matt. 24:21 NEB). "There shall be great distress in the land" (Christ, Luke 21:23).

> The new wine dries up, the vines sicken, and all the revellers turn to sorrow...No one shall drink wine to the sound of song; the liquor will be bitter to the man who drinks it...mirth is banished from the land...*So shall it be in all the world, in every nation*...   Isaiah 24:7-13 NEB

The spiritual state of human beings will grow so grave as to affect the earth itself:

> The earth reels to and fro like a drunken man...
>
>   Isaiah 24:20 NEB

To compensate for pain and to cope with pressure, people have devised an assortment of escape routes. Some live from weekend to weekend, from vacation to vacation. Others go to bars, watch violent movies, rent scary videos, read romantic novels, or seek new sexual encounters; they join cults, form gangs, or practice voodoo and satanism; they resort to drugs, alcohol, or astrology; they run away from their families, abuse their children, or divorce their spouses; they escape from reality, and as a last resort attempt suicide.

Suicide as a means of escape is on the rise and occurs especially among young people. In the United States—one of the most prosperous countries in the world—*every day over a thousand young people try to take their own lives*. (The latest statistics place the figure at 500,000 a year.) At that rate there would be over 27,000 attempts around the planet *every day*.

Some people depend in vain on their wealth as a means of satisfying their spiritual hunger; others simply dream that if only they had more, happiness would be theirs:

> Their silver and gold will not be able to save them in the day of the Lord's wrath. They will not satisfy their hunger...
>
> Ezekiel 7:19 NIV

Many people complain about being too busy, yet are afraid of free time; they do not know how to cope with freedom. The stress of freedom makes some workers workaholics and sends many retirees to an early death.

According to a new Harris Poll, in a fifteen-year period the number of leisure hours per week declined 37 percent, from 26.2 to 16.6. The sharing of "quality time" among family members has reached its lowest point. Dr. Roberta Berns in her book *Child, Family, Community* writes: "According to Shaevitz working couples typically spend only 12 minutes a week talking to each other."[12] Another study indicates that married couples speak about 4 minutes a day with each other and 2 minutes a day with their children.

The unrelenting stress and distress of our time and the massive energies devoted to defuse them create in most people *a state of spiritual exhaustion*. A state of the mind such as this: "I am tense, tired, anxious, and in need of escape. I have no time for anything else." They try to go from one high to another before anxiety grips their soul. They take "nourishment" all the time, yet remain hungry. *They are constantly on the run yet feel entrapped*. This state of the mind often causes spiritual slumber. It manifests itself as apathy, coldness, and complacency, which are often concealed under a facade of self-satisfaction, covered with a shallow sense of well-being. The busy life, the constant search for a high, the demanding struggle for mere survival, *leave no room for self-awareness, reflection, curiosity, knowledge, and spiritual adventure.*

But where are to be found earnest seekers and inquiring minds?[13]   Bahá'u'lláh

If you ask someone on the street "Have you heard that Christ has come again?" His first thought may be, "This person is weird," and his first concern, "How can I escape from this unfortunate encounter without wasting a minute?" Not wanting any conflict or controversy, he may respond briefly and courteously and walk away. If the person who hears the message happens to be a "born-again" believer, he may actually be offended by the question itself, and feel sorry for the questioner. Before departing, he may simply say, "My brother I will pray for you." He runs away from this encounter without ever thinking *"My Master has asked me to watch for His coming and to be on the alert."* He departs or runs away from the news without recognizing his role in the unfolding of the divine drama, without suspecting that he is running away from the news of the coming of the One called "the Lion of the tribe of Juda" (Rev. 5:5), without realizing that his untimely departure has been graphically portrayed by the prophets:

It [the day of the Lord] will be as when a man runs from a lion, and a bear meets him, or turns into a house and leans his hand on the wall, and a snake bites him.
                                          Amos 5:19 NEB

They will *flee*...from dread of the Lord and the splendor of his majesty, when he rises to shake the earth [the stagnant hearts; see Volumes IV and V].   Isaiah 2:21 NIV

The thing that must come hath come suddenly; behold how they *flee* from it![14]   Bahá'u'lláh

Flee ye the One Who hath sacrificed His life that ye may be quickened?[15]   Bahá'u'lláh

The receiver of the message has been told to crown his heart
with courage, yet he fears:

> "Say to them that are of a fearful heart, be **strong, fear
> not**: behold, your God will come" (Isa. 35:4). "Be **strong**,
> take **courage**, and wait for the Lord" (Psa. 27:14 NEB).

The receiver of the message has been told *to take advantage
of every opportunity to seek His Lord*, to try to find Him
before "the silver cord is cut," yet he fails to pursue the news:

> Give ear and come to me; hear me, that your soul may
> live...Seek the Lord while he may be found...
>
> Isaiah 55:3, 6 NIV

Most of us are repelled by complacent people, those who
wear special blinders to conceal their surroundings, who just
mind their own business and do not get excited by any news
—whether it concerns pollution, poverty, or prejudice—who
starve for truth yet refuse to admit hunger, who live in dire
need of the spirit yet conceal their poverty with the mask of
self-satisfaction, who stand aloof from the world and respond
to a warm invitation as coldly as a snow-capped mountain.

In the next passage, Jesus shows His displeasure with them.
He appeals to His dearly beloved but unconcerned followers,
who stand unmoved by the news of His return. His message
portrays the divine discipline, uttered in the harshest yet
kindest words:

> I know your deeds, that you are neither cold nor hot. I
> wish you were either one or the other!...you are lukewarm
> ...You say, 'I am rich; I have acquired wealth and do not
> need a thing.' But you do not realize that you are...poor,
> blind and naked. I counsel you to *buy from me* gold refined
> in the fire, so you can become rich; and white clothes to
> wear, so you can cover your shameful nakedness; and
> *salve to put on your eyes, so you can see*.
>
> Those whom I love I rebuke and discipline. So be earnest,
> and repent. Here I am! I stand at the door and knock. If

anyone hears my voice and opens the door, I will come
in and eat with him, and he with me. To him who overcomes [the fear of opening the door], I will give the right
to sit with me on my throne...   Revelation 3:15-21 NIV

The invitation and the counsel found in the preceding passage
(to open one's heart to the news of the coming of the Master)
have been repeated once again in our time:

Say: We, in truth, have opened unto you the gates of the
Kingdom. Will ye bar the door of your houses in My
face?[16]   Bahá'u'lláh

If ye choose to follow Me, I will make you heirs of My
Kingdom...[17]   Bahá'u'lláh

Prophecies declare that among the masses of complacent and
stressed people, many remain alert and curious; they hunger
for truth, but they too are hampered. They do not know
where to turn. Who can help them?

The time is coming, says the Lord God, when...Men shall
stagger from north to south, they shall range from east to
west, seeking the word of the Lord, but they shall not find
it.   Amos 8:11-12 NEB

What "oppression" is more grievous than that a soul seeking the truth, and wishing to attain unto the knowledge of
God, should know not where to go for it and from whom
to seek it? For opinions have sorely differed, and the ways
unto the attainment of God have multiplied.[18]   Bahá'u'lláh

Dr. John White in *Re-entry* (published by Billy Graham
Evangelic Association, with a foreword by Dr. Graham)
devotes an entire chapter, "The Church and the Coming
Christ" to the decline of faith and the confusion of a divided
church in our time. As evidence, the author offers numerous
quotations from a wide range of Christian leaders and writers.
These are two brief examples from that chapter:

H. G. Wells, the historian [declared] "The world is now a
very tragic and anxious world...more people are asking
today (than ever before) and asking with a new intensity,
'What must I do to be saved?' The trouble with the Christian churches is that they give a confused, unconvincing
and unsatisfying answer."[19]...Visser't Hooft...the Secretary-
General of the World Council of Churches, characterizes
the Church today: "confusion reigns supreme—politically,
theologically, socially."[20]

Dr. White states that One of the most eloquent, if tragic
passages in the entire New Testament is where Jude forecasts
the state of the people in the last days.[21] Here is part of that
prophecy as quoted in *Re-entry*:

"They are like clouds driven up by the wind...They are
like stars which follow no orbit, and their proper place
is...the regions beyond the light" (Jude 12, 13, Phillips
Version).[22]

According to a widely distributed Christian magazine:

Today, Christianity is fragmented more than any other
major religion. Already 25,000 different churches, denominations, sects and cults divide Christianity, and *the World
Christian Encyclopedia* suggests that number is growing
by five every week [260 a year]!...If Jesus were to return
to earth today, where would *he* go to worship?...How can
this tangle of ideas represent him?[23]

In a Christian publication called *What Is the True Gospel?*
appears this statement:

Why should there be such perplexity—such *confusion*—
in every phase of life today? It should be the function of
religion to point the way. Yet here, too, we find only
confusion of tongues—hundreds of religious denominations and sects, in a babylon of disagreement.[24]

This prophecy too confirms the prevailing confusion in
our time:

...the day God visits you. ***Now is the time of their confusion.***
         Micah 7:4 NIV

The Great Tribulation

To examine further the mental and spiritual states of the people of our time, let us take a frequently quoted prophecy on this topic and view it in the light of both the Bahá'í teachings and the various schools of thought supported by Christian scholars. Let us take Jesus' prediction that at His return there will be ***great tribulation***:

> For then shall be great tribulation, such as was not since the beginning of the world to this time, no, nor ever shall be.
>   Matthew 24:21

Daniel predicts the same ominous occurrence:

> There will be a time of distress such as has not happened from the beginning of nations until then.   Daniel 12:1 NIV

If we look at specifics we find many variations of views, but in principle, as theologians have discovered, we have four schools of thought, each of them defended by hundreds of competent scholars. This is how, according to a Christian source, the four schools interpret "tribulation" and a list of the verses they use to support their views:

Praeterist: the tribulation was centered at the fall of Jerusalem in A.D. 70 (Luke 21:20-24).

Historicist: the tribulation represents the whole gospel age (John 16:33; 1 Tim. 3:12).

Futurist: the tribulation will be a short time of intensive trouble at the end of the age (Rev. 7:14; 13:5).

Idealist: there will always be tribulation and trouble for the people of God, although it will vary in intensity from time to time and from place to place (John 16:33; 2 Tim. 3:12; Rev. 1:9).[25]

In the Bahá'í view "tribulation"—also translated as "distress" (NIV), "misery" (ME), "trouble" (EB), and "affliction and oppression" (AB)—*is already in progress and climbing.* It points to the sufferings and pangs of hunger that the people of this age are enduring because of spiritual starvation. It means the stress and anguish of being deprived of divine guidance, of the joy and peace that come from knowing and loving God. Its distress calls can be heard everywhere. Its presence can be seen in the lives of people of all ages:

- In the widespread child abuse
- In the alienation of the youth
- In the crisis of the middle aged
- In the abuse and despair of the aged

Christian leaders often mourn the terrible distress and decline of the people of our time. Dr. Billy Graham in preface to his book *Till Armageddon* writes:

> The whole world is sighing and suffering on a scale perhaps not known in human history: the refugees, the starving, the "new slaves," the psychological woes, the emotional turmoils, the broken marriages, the rebellious children, the terrorism, the hostages, the wars, and a thousand other troubles which beset every country in the world. There are no people anywhere that are immune. The rich and famous suffer as well as the poor and obscure. As the late actor Peter Sellers said, "Behind the mask of all [of] us clowns is sadness and broken hearts." It seems that the human race may well be heading toward the climax of the tears, hurts, and wounds of the centuries—Armageddon![26]

Perhaps the best way to know the troubles and tribulations of our time is to look at some statistics about the state of the "mental" or psychological health of the world. As we shall see later in this chapter, the Hebrew prophets, Christ, and Bahá'u'lláh all predicted the diseased state of our world with flawless accuracy.

My purpose in presenting the distressing news is not to dwell on the negative but rather to inform and awaken. The first step to change is awareness. Few people realize *the scale* of the prevalence of pain and suffering in our time. *Perhaps awareness will stir action*. Furthermore, the information is given here in the light of God's judgment. What matters is not the facts but the meaning *behind* the facts, and the understanding that may come from the facts.

We can all tolerate so much bad news. When we pass the threshold of our tolerance, we tune out. That may be good for us but not for the world. We must be aware of the pain and suffering of *all* members of the human race. We must try to see everything as God would. Furthermore, hearing bad news is futile only *in the absence of hope. This book brings the news of the greatest hope for humanity since the dawn of history*. The bad news must be judged only with an eye on the good news.

> Like cold water to a weary soul is good news from a distant land.   Proverbs 25:25 NIV

> The test of first-rate intelligence is the ability to hold two opposed ideas in mind at the same time and still retain the ability to function. One should, for example, be able to see that things are hopeless and yet be determined to make them better.   F. Scott Fitzgerald

What is the state of mental and spiritual health of nations? A poll taken in June 1994 by *Newsweek* shows that three-fourths of Americans believe the United States is in moral and spiritual decline.

The following are some figures mostly from the United States, a country for which statistics are available. They probably represent the state of mental and spiritual health of *all* nations, except the least developed. They indicate that the troubles and tribulations of our age—especially in the last few decades—have been *on the rise*. (Unless indicated, the data is from U.S. population studies.)

- Psychiatric disorders are more prevalent today than ever before. Percentage of the population afflicted with these disorders at any given time: depression 17%; alcoholism 14%; social anxiety disorder 13%; simple phobia 11%; drug dependence 8%.

- According to National Center for Health Statistics, in a thirty-year period, the number of U.S. teenagers who attempted suicide increased three to five times. Their number has now climbed to about 500,000 a year.

- A *Who's Who* survey shows that one-third of outstanding students have considered suicide to solve their problems.

- A recent survey indicates that, "More than 50% of young adults between the ages of 16 and 24 say they have thought about killing themselves."

- In a four-year period, the number of adolescents admitted to private psychiatric hospitals increased about 350 percent.

- In a three-year period, alcohol use among high-school seniors increased 90 percent.

- In 1996, Columbia University reported that young women are using illegal drugs 15 times more often than their mothers did.

- In Canada suicide among all age groups doubled in 22 years. Among those 20 to 24 years, it increased threefold. Among those aged 15 to 19, it increased fourfold.

- In the United States, suicide is the second highest cause of death among college students.

- ABC television network recently reported that, for the first time in the United States, more people aged 15 to 19 are being killed by guns than by all other causes combined. The number of all those killed by guns in the United States stands at about 30,000 a year.

- Fifty percent of high-school graduates have tried some narcotic drugs. There has been 106 percent increase in substance abuse among teenagers since 1992.

- Teenage pregnancy has increased more than 600 percent in the last 40 years.

- Clinical depression in the United States costs 44 billion dollars a year.

- Eighty-two percent of young people have sexual relations before they marry.

- AIDS is spreading rapidly throughout the planet. It has infected 22 million people, and is now spreading at the rate of one victim every second. In Africa, every day 5,500 funerals are held for AIDS victims. One and a half million people died from AIDS in one year. The cost of treating those infected with HIV in the United States is about $20,000 per victim.

- Violence is accepted as a way of life. In a recent study, 8 percent of high school students stated that if someone insulted them, they had the right to kill him! Harris polls indicate that 9 percent of school children have fired a gun at someone, and 11 percent have been fired at. Three-fourths of them feared being killed by a gun.

- President Clinton recently stated that 40 years ago homicide was not even among the first ten causes of death for young people. Today it is the second highest cause of death for those between 15 and 25 years of age.

- Violence has also entered the workplace. Recently NBC reported that one-fourth of employees report being harassed or attacked, one-sixth of them with lethal weapons.

- Alcohol abuse kills 500 Americans *every day*. The cost of drinking (due to treatment and loss of productivity) stands at over $100 billion a year.

- Drunk driving is the number one killer of teenagers.

• A recent study shows that, in the United States, Canada, and many European countries, the rich have been getting richer and the poor poorer.

• UNICEF reports that every *hour* 940 children die from five infectious but preventable diseases.

• In recent years, the U.S. prison population has more than doubled. For certain crimes, criminals are set free almost as soon as they are arrested. Many prisons are already overpopulated.

• Violent crimes in the United States since 1960 have increased many times faster than the population. "Shortly after the gulf conflict ended, [President Bush] made this sobering observation at an anti-crime conference at the Justice Department: 'During the first three days of the ground offensive, more Americans were killed in some American cities than at the entire Kuwaiti front...One of our brave National Guardsmen may have actually been safer in the midst of the largest armored offensive in history than he would have been on the streets of his own hometown.'" Statistics from the FBI indicate that, in a given year, about one in every 16 Americans is the victim of a violent crime.

• In recent years, unruly behavior or "air rage" among airline passengers has tripled. The news media reported that a group of scientists representing various disciplines plan to meet once a year for three years to study "the rising tide of meanness and incivility" in the United States.

• Money spent on illegal drugs has reached an estimated 50 billion dollars per year, or about 136 million dollars a day. In the United States 12 million people use narcotic drugs.

• Every 20 seconds a car is stolen. Some of the thieves are young children. The police are so busy, they do not take car theft seriously.

• White-collar crime is at an all-time high. Government officials are preoccupied with so many problems and pressures, they don't have the will or the power to prevent white-collar crimes. They often go on unnoticed and unpunished. American taxpayers lost about $200 billion in the Savings and Loan scandal. Never before has a scandal of such magnitude been discovered.

- Income not reported to the IRS is estimated at $175 billion.

- The total cost of fraud in the repair business is beyond estimation. Experts maintain that 50 percent of repair bills are fraudulent.

- Perhaps the most painful fraud is in the health services, which, because of their huge cost—over one trillion a year—have been investigated more than any other. In the United States, the cost of fraud, overcharging, unnecessary surgery, unnecessary services and tests by the health profession is estimated at over $150 billion a year. This is about two and a half times the cost of the Gulf War, which was $61 billion.

  Who, then, can people trust? What goes on in corporations, repair businesses, medical services, and many other professions and institutions is not unique. It simply reflects the value system of a world that has lost its spiritual purpose. What would happen if these billions of dollars were used year after year for the prevention of disease, for daycare centers and education, for a better quality of life for all people?

- Some countries carry enormous debts. The United States borrows about $240 billion a year to pay the interest on its debt, which is now over $5,500 billion ($5.5 trillion). How much is five trillion? If converted into one dollar bills and placed in a straight line, the line would extend over five times the distance between the earth and the sun!

- In the last three decades the divorce rate has tripled. About 50 percent of children must cope with the separation of their parents. Court battles for custody and alimony take a terrible toll on parents and children alike. Today's newlyweds are likely to stay married for only 7.2 years.

• The traditional family is in grave danger. "More and more American men and women are choosing to just live together instead of marrying. The number of cohabiting couples increased by 740 percent between 1970 and 1989—with an 88 percent rise between 1987 and 1989 alone." One authority estimated that about 40 percent of first-born children are born out of wedlock. In a ten-year period, the birth rate among unwed mothers increased 75 percent.

• According to one report, on average, parents hold positive conversations with their children for about 12 minutes a week.

• In the United States, every year 350,000 children are abducted by their parents.

• In recent years rape has become the fastest growing crime. According to a television documentary, one out of every five women will eventually be raped. A recent study of 4,000 women indicates that one out of eight has been raped, and 25 percent of rapes occurred when the victim was 11 or younger. Another study indicates that "One out of every four American women is sexually abused before she reaches 18. Girls are twice as likely to be sexually abused as boys. Family members—fathers, stepfathers, uncles, grandfathers, and brothers—are the most frequent abusers of children under the age of 11."

• Other kinds of abuse have also continued to increase. In a ten-year period, the number of neglected and abused children has doubled. Every year about 2,000 children die from abuse and inflicted injuries. The number of both abused and neglected children is about 10 million.

• Every year, about 2.5 million elderly people are abused.

• In Canada, violence against women has doubled in the last few years.

• Even unborn babies have not escaped the pains and pressures of this age. Some of them are born addicted (100,000 a year in U.S.) and about 50 million are aborted every year around the globe. If we put these babies in a line (one foot for each baby), they would stretch for 9,470 miles, nearly two and a half times the radius of the earth!

How has the school environment changed in the last 50 years? The following estimates seem quite reasonable:

Teachers' Greatest Concerns in 1940	*Teachers' Greatest Concerns Today*
1. Talking out of turn	1. Drug abuse
2. Chewing gum	2. Alcohol abuse
3. Making noise	3. Pregnancy
4. Running in the halls	4. Suicide
5. Getting out of line	5. Rape
6. Wearing improper clothing	6. Robbery
7. Not putting waste paper in basket	

A disgruntled schoolteacher handed in her resignation with the following comment: "In our public schools today, the teachers are afraid of the principals, the principals are afraid of the superintendents, the superintendents are afraid of the board, the board members are afraid of the parents, the parents are afraid of the children, and the children are afraid of nobody."

Perhaps the groups touched most by the onrush of the troubles and tribulations of our time are our youth and children. Psychiatrist Mary Giffin, author of *A Cry for Help*, writes:

The median age of depressed patients has been dropping steadily. Today, more than half the patients in U.S. mental institutions are under twenty-one...one in five children may be suffering from symptoms of depression, outstripping that for the middle-aged and exceeded only by the rate of depression among the elderly.

Among depressed children, suicidal wishes are extremely common...among approximately 100 children referred for outpatient treatment to a New York hospital, 33 percent had threatened or attempted suicide. (Studies in the 1960s indicated that no more than 10 percent...showed suicidal behavior.)[27]

Long ago Bahá'u'lláh predicted the disease-stricken state of our world:

Witness how the world is being afflicted with a fresh calamity every day. Its tribulation is continually deepening ...Its sickness is approaching the stage of utter hopelessness, inasmuch as the true Physician is debarred from administering the remedy, whilst unskilled practitioners are regarded with favor, and are accorded full freedom to act.[28]

What about the state of the physical health of the world? In spite of the marvels of science and technology and the vast resources devoted to maintaining health and fitness, a combination of both mental and physical causes is contributing to widespread disease and suffering. Stress, loneliness, despair, fear, and a sense of emptiness and futility, on the one hand, and adverse effects from a polluted environment, dependence on alcohol, tobacco, and drugs of all kinds (both legal and illegal), combined with a sedentary life, the spread of sexually transmitted diseases (the most common infectious diseases next to colds and flu), the consumption of unwholesome foods (often to satisfy spiritual and emotional hunger), and disregard for preventive medicine are all taking their terrible toll, are all adding to the weight of suffering borne by this generation.

Even the earth, which kept her health and vitality for eons, is now diseased and suffering:

According to Worldwatch Institute, about 40 trillion pounds [80 pounds per person] of waste around the globe make their way into the sea each year.[29]

According to Matthew Fox:

> In the ordinary course of events one species disappears about every two thousand years. Currently, however, species are disappearing at the rate of one every twenty-five minutes. At this rate humankind will eliminate ten percent of the remaining species (one million of the remaining earth creatures) in the next ten years. If current rates of destruction continue, within the next one hundred years there will be no living species left on this planet— including humankind, since we are totally interdependent with all these other creatures.[30]

> Why has the land become a dead land...? It is because they forsook my law...   Jeremiah 9:12 NEB

As our life span has increased, so has suffering from sickness. Some authorities maintain that the proportion of people afflicted with chronic diseases (arthritis, allergy, asthma, AIDS, Alzheimer's, alcoholism, diabetes, digestive problems, irregular heart beats, backache, headache, herpes, fatigue, cancer, and countless others) has increased substantially. What can we expect when we pollute our environment, eat processed foods, overfeed our bodies, and then keep them unfit and under stress? What can we expect when 65 percent of the calories we consume comes from fat and sugar?

Let us look at more evidence pertaining to other dimensions of modern life to see if the citizens of our ancient planet have ever before witnessed troubles and tribulations on the scale endured by the people of this age:

• In the 20th century, more people have been killed in wars than in all wars since the dawn of recorded history, a period covering about 6,000 years.

• Similarly, in this century, more people have been killed *by their own government* than in all wars in past centuries. According to an editorial in *The New York Times*, "In no previous age have people shown so great an aptitude, and appetite, for killing millions of other people for reasons of race, religion or class."

• Every 22 minutes someone is maimed or killed by land mines—26,000 a year.

• In the United States alone about 100,000 people are killed by accident *every year*. Every *day* 1,500 people are seriously injured or disabled. The sufferings of survivors who lose their loved ones as well as the pain and anguish borne by millions among the injured are incalculable. One in every six persons suffers from disability. Never before have so many people succumbed to accidental death and injuries as in our time.

In their textbook, *Abnormal Psychology And Modern Life*, Drs. R. Carson, J. Butcher, and J. Coleman state:

On every side we see anxious, unhappy people who miss the realization of their potential because they cannot find adequate solutions or answers to problems that seem beyond them. The hassles of modern life are reflected in the massive amounts of tranquilizing chemicals—alcohol or otherwise, prescription and nonprescription—we as a society consume...

Despite the stressful nature of modern life, *most of us seem to muddle through*, although probably not without at least some psychological scars...*Mental impairments of one sort or another now afflict more people than all physical health problems combined...*

What will be the outcome of this jarring new reality? We do not pretend to know the answer in any comprehensive way, *but prospects for an increasing rate of adaptational failure, particularly in the psychological domain, seem compelling...How shall we cope* [emphasis added]?[31]

How awful that day will be! None will be like it.

Jeremiah 30:7 NIV

> And there shall be a time of trouble, straitness [difficulty, pressure, perplexity, and] distress, such as never was since there was a nation until that time. Daniel 12:1 AB

Oliver Holmes said, "I find the greatest thing in this world not so much in where we stand, as in what directions we are moving." Unless the divine remedy is accepted and applied, nothing indicates that the direction toward which the human race is moving will change. On the contrary, the prevailing trends will continue to intensify. This statement from a Christian publication expresses eloquently not only the mental and spiritual state of our time but also *the need for freedom from the illusion of well-being as well as hopelessness*:

> Things are not as they seem. The thought keeps coming around. Things are not as they seem...not as they seem. Behind the faces, front doors, and casual relationships of our neighborhoods, workplaces, and churches is an underworld of personal pain and embarrassment. Untold stories of alcoholism, anger, anxiety, addiction, abortion, affairs, alienation, and abuse are epidemic. Under the surface we are fast becoming a people like those of Isaiah's day: beaten and bruised in heart, mind, and body, from the top of our heads to the bottom of our feet (Isa. 1:1-6)...The Bible gives us every reason to believe that, yes, it's true: Things are not as they seem. Things are only as God says they are. *Father, don't let us succumb either to the illusion of well-being or to the illusion of hopelessness* [emphasis added].[32]

The scriptural and scientific evidence presented on the state of the world indicates that the people of this age are not enjoying the peace of mind and the spiritual pleasures and blessings that God has designated for them. Their hearts do not rejoice in the heavenly hope; their souls do not exult and glory in God's great blessings and bounties, but suffer and mourn in quiet desperation:

...all the nations of the earth will mourn.

Matthew 24:30 <small>NIV</small>

We can well perceive how the whole human race is encompassed with great, with incalculable afflictions. We see it languishing on its bed of sickness, sore-tried and disillusioned.[33]

Bahá'u'lláh

In our age (since the beginning of 19th century), two major changes have been taking place side by side.

- The light of faith that bestowed eternal hope and gave people the strength and enlightenment to deal with stress and adversity has been steadily growing dimmer.

- Many of the old values, ties, and loyalties that created consistency and certainty in the life of the individual and made him an integral part of his family and community have also been steadily waning and weakening.

Social scientists believe that what ails the people of our time is the loss of a support system. What gave the individual security and strength in the past has itself become a source of stress and distress. Statistics show that most of the violence against people comes from someone they know: a parent, a spouse, a son or daughter, a neighbor, or a friend. An individual is far more likely to be killed or abused by a friend or family member than by a stranger. (The ratio for murder is three to one.) Prophecies predicted this trend:

The godly have been swept from the land...the ruler demands gifts, the judge accepts bribes...the day God visits you...Do not trust a neighbor; put no confidence in a friend. Even with her who lies in your embrace be careful of your words. For a son dishonors his father, a daughter rises up against her mother, a daughter-in-law against her mother-in-law—a man's enemies are the members of his own household. But as for me, I watch in hope for the Lord, I wait for God my Savior...

Micah 7:2-7 <small>NIV</small>

True, material comforts have given many people some peace of mind, but this advantage is counteracted by still another change: the decline in concern for basic physical needs has led to a sharpened awareness of spiritual needs. The end result of the titanic changes of our time has been a steady rise in stress, and a steady decline in strength. The disease carrying invaders have been allowed to advance, while the immune system, which must protect people, has been left to disintegrate and break down.

In His interpretation of "tribulation," Bahá'u'lláh singles out one aspect of the stressful life of the modern age. Suppose a person decides to find a path to God. What confusion must he face! How bewildered will he become! How can he tell which path to pursue?

> Clinging unto idle fancy, they [the interpreters of the word of God] have strayed far from...divine knowledge...Though they recognize in their hearts the Law of God to be one and the same, yet from every direction they issue a new command, and in every season proclaim a fresh decree...

> What "oppression" [tribulation] is greater than that which hath been recounted? What "oppression" is more grievous than that a soul seeking the truth, and wishing to attain unto the knowledge of God, should know not where to go for it and from whom to seek it? For opinions have sorely differed, and the ways unto the attainment of God have multiplied. This "oppression" is the essential feature [at the dawning] of every Revelation. Unless it cometh to pass, the Sun of Truth will not be made manifest.[34]

The following quotations, one a prophecy, the other a statement from a psychology textbook, confirm Bahá'u'lláh's assessment:

> Men wander about like sheep *in distress* for lack of a shepherd. My anger is turned against the shepherds...
>
> Zechariah 10:2-3 NEB

Human beings **need** to believe, even passionately, in things abstract, moral, and "spiritual." But there are so many divergent "moralities" from which to choose today that the choice itself can be a source of confusion.[35]

Abnormal Psychology and Modern Life

These verses further confirm the cloudy confusion the people of our time must face:

...the day God visits...is the time of their confusion (Micah 7:4 NIV). It will be a unique day, without daytime or nighttime—a day known to the Lord (Zechariah 14:7 NIV).

My purpose in showing the "great tribulation" of our time is not to dwell in darkness. ***Distressing news serves no purpose unless it is presented in the light of "good news," unless it is linked to hope and action***. Seeing the stark contrast between the light and the darkness—the dire despair of humanity and the bright and beautiful hand of Heaven—will provide the most potent motivation for action. We stand accountable not only for the avoidable pain and sufferings we endure, but also for much of what others have to bear. Only by offering to God an open and humble heart can we become an instrument in His hand and remain loyal to His trust and our responsibility.

To Summarize

The day of the Lord and the Lord Himself come not only as a thief in the night, but also when the world is filled with clouds and smoke (see Volume IV), and the people are confused and intoxicated. The spirits that keep them intoxicated are these:

• The wonders of modern science and technology

• Materialism

• The spread of theological theories, especially about the way the Master returns

• Severe stress and distress (tribulation) that result from lack of spiritual guidance

These four elements together create a sense of **unawareness**, on the one hand, and **self-satisfaction** and **self-conceit**, on the other. This is what intoxication means.

A veneer of self-satisfaction, complacency, apathy, and denial prevents many from sensing the global pain and suffering endured by the people of our time, from seeing the reality and the urgent need for action. They must arise and raise their voices in prayer and supplication, in seeking help from the Provider:

> Blessed are they that mourn: for they shall be comforted.
>
> Christ (Matthew 5:4)

> They mounted up to the heavens and went down to the depths; in their peril their courage melted away. They reeled and staggered like drunken men; they were at their wits' end. Then they cried out to the Lord in their trouble, and he brought them out of their distress. He stilled the storm to a whisper; the waves of the sea were hushed. They were glad when it grew calm, and he guided them to their desired haven. Let them give thanks to the Lord for his unfailing love and his wonderful deeds for men. Let them exalt him in the assembly of the people and praise him in the council of the elders.
>
> Psalms 107:26-32 NIV

When Jesus cried for Jerusalem, He could clearly see the dark destiny of the people of Israel. He was aware and awake; the Jews were in a state of spiritual drunkenness. Are there not similarities between the state of Israel then and the state of the world now?

> As he approached Jerusalem and saw the city, he wept over it and said, "If you, even you, had only known on this day what would bring you peace—but now it is hidden from your eyes. The days will come upon you when your

enemies will...dash you to the ground...because you did not recognize the time of God's coming to you.

Christ (Luke 19:41-44 NIV)

God's judgment of the people of the end-time is quite un-favorable. People can always conceal their true identity from themselves and others but not from God. At the end of the age, our Creator declares "knowledge shall be increased" (Dan. 12:4), but wisdom will *de*crease: "The wisdom of their wise men shall perish" (Isa. 29:14). Information shall multiply but faithfulness will diminish: "many will turn away from the faith" (Matt. 24:10 NIV). Multitudes go to school to learn yet fail "to acknowledge the truth" (II Tim. 3:2-8 NIV). What appeals to people most is self-love or pursuit of pleasure (II Tim. 3:2-6) with an ***appearance*** of faithfulness. And so they preserve and present "a form of godliness" (II Tim. 3:5) to themselves and others.

The state of their ***mind***, the Predictor declares, follows the state of their ***soul***. Their understanding of the Word of God consists mostly of "a precept of men, learnt by rote," (Isa. 29:13 NEB), of man-made ideas and illusions retained without insight and awareness. In the midst of all this spiritual and mental confusion, they need to decipher the true meaning of God's most mysterious words: prophecies. But how can they? Are they humble enough to accept God's harsh judgment against them, set aside their own personal thoughts and theories, and listen to the revealer of all mysteries?

What are our tendencies and weaknesses? How do our choices and thoughts differ from God's? These are explored in the next chapter.

7

You Judge By
Worldly Standards
John 8:15 NEB

God's Way Versus
the Human Way

Why is there such a disparity between people's expectations and reality, between what *they* want and what *God* gives them? Human expectations are activated mainly by two forces: the desire for a visible display of power and glory, and the wish for instant rewards and remedies. Most people like a positive message, especially if nothing is demanded of them. Literal interpretation of prophecies accomplishes this very purpose. This is the kind of message almost everyone would like to hear:

Think about that day when the Lord Jesus Christ breaks through the eastern sky. Think about it over and over. Let it give you something to live for. Could anything be more exciting to contemplate?

Seeing first a small black cloud. Watching it move nearer and nearer till it becomes white and glorious. A cloud like none you've ever seen before—a cloud of angels, uncounted angels. Hearing a sound like none you've ever heard before—the sound of a trumpet echoing round the world. Then a voice like none you've heard before. It's the voice of our Lord calling the dead to life.

The earth quivers. Tombs burst open. Angels everywhere carry little children to their parents' eager arms. Loved ones long separated by death reunite with shouts of joy, never to part again! And then, together with those resurrected ones, we who have waited through earth's long night are caught up into that angel starship for the trip to our heavenly home.[1]

Imagine the feeling! Defying gravity, we soar through the sky. Without a spacesuit we sail through the stars up to our heavenly home...[2]

Human imagination is stirred and excited by the images of the supernatural. A Christian writer confirms this:

A person can really get excited about seven-headed beasts, mysterious seals, a great red dragon, four ghastly horsemen, vast armies and cosmic destruction. Such dazzling and sensational images cannot help but arouse interest and wonder, especially when in connection with the end of the world.[3]

Those who proclaim the message of the coming of the Master deserve the highest praise (Matt. 24:45-47), for they instill faith, peace, and hope. What they fail to do is to transform this hope from a state of complacency into alertness, into a continuous searching for the Master. This prophecy was undoubtedly spoken concerning the peoples of our time:

For the time will come when men will not put up with sound doctrine. Instead, to suit their own desires, they will gather around them a great number of teachers to say what their itching ears want to hear.   II Timothy 4:3 NIV

People love dramatic spectacles and instant transformation, but God has a different plan and purpose for His creation. He sees things differently:

...how can My way accord with thine?[4]   Bahá'u'lláh

The Lord does not see as man sees; men judge by appearances but the Lord judges by the heart. I Samuel 16:7 NEB

You judge by worldly standards.   Christ (John 8:15 NEB)

...man can never hope to attain unto the knowledge of the All-Glorious...unless and until he ceases to regard the words and deeds of mortal men as a standard for the true understanding and recognition of God and His Prophets.[5]
Bahá'u'lláh

Say: O leaders of religion! Weigh not the Book of God with such standards and sciences as are current amongst you, for the Book itself is the unerring Balance established amongst men. In this most perfect Balance whatsoever the peoples and kindreds of the earth possess must be weighed, while the measure of its weight should be tested according to its own standard, did ye but know it.[6]
Bahá'u'lláh

...human standard of judgment is faulty, finite.[7]
'Abdu'l-Bahá

The Spirit gives life; the flesh counts for nothing. The words I have spoken to you are spirit and they are life.
Christ (John 6:63 NIV)

What is highly valued among men is detestable in God's sight.   Christ (Luke 16:15 NIV)

Has human nature changed since those noble words were spoken? History attests that human judgment has always been at variance with the divine. Jesus predicted that at the time of His return, everything will be the same as it was in the days of Noah. This indicates that the way people think and act will not have changed at all.

God conceals His great power and glory in poverty, suffering, and meekness:

> ...the kingdom of heaven is like unto treasure hid in a field...   Christ (Matthew 13:44)

Our Creator's plan and purpose is that we should search for truth by exercising our freedom of choice, and never be over-whelmed by His transcendent might and majesty. He wants us to acknowledge His Messengers through our own efforts, our own love for truth, our own purity and sincerity. His wish is that we should accept His guidance, and then by patience and persistence create "a new earth and a new heaven." Instead of sending a perfect *city* from heaven, He sends a perfect *plan*. Instant and easy remedies satisfy *our* desire, but not *His*:

> Shall a woman bear a child without pains?...Shall a nation be brought to birth all in a moment?   Isaiah 66:7-8 NEB

> We must go through many hardships to enter the kingdom of God...   Acts 14:22 NIV

Our Creator has made us in His exalted Image, endowing us with His own attributes, among them freedom of choice and creativity. His vision of us is grand and glorious. He wants us to participate in creating the world of our dream. If we use *His* blueprint, the impossible becomes possible, the ideal becomes real.

> ...all things are possible to him that believeth.
>   Christ (Mark 9:23)

> Then the Lord...said, 'Here they are, one people with a single language...henceforward nothing they have a mind to do will be beyond their reach.'   Genesis 11:6 NEB

Flaming Fire

Let us examine one more sign linked to the second Advent. It is predicted that when Jesus returns from heaven, He will be accompanied not only by power and glory but also by *flaming fire*.

> ...the Lord Jesus shall be revealed from **heaven** with His mighty angels, in flaming *fire* taking vengeance on them that know not God, and that obey not the gospel...
>
> II Thessalonians 1:7-8
> See also Matthew 13:41-42

If we take the "coming from heaven" literally, should we not also take the "fire" in the prophecy literally? For the sake of consistency, "fire" must *also* be taken literally. It appears unreasonable to take one part (coming from heaven) of the same prophecy literally, and the other part (fire) symbolically.

Painters through the ages have made majestic drawings of Jesus descending from heaven with grace and glory, power and peace. They have usually blended His image with magnificent clouds touched with the glowing rays of the sun. But they have as a rule left one element out of the scene: the flaming fire. The painters must have instinctively recognized that being seen with fire does not fit the profile of a Man who was the very heart of mercy and forgiveness. They must have sensed that the Exemplar who taught loving one's enemies and blessing one's persecutors (Rom. 12:14), who said to be perfect one must give his wealth to the poor (Matt. 19:21), who was so tender that He wept for Jerusalem, would not return for revenge. They must have known that the Man, who out of His abiding love for people carried the cross and crowned it with His body, who gave His own life to give joy to the world, would not return to *take* life, to bring pain and suffering to the distressed masses of humanity.

Which of these acts fits the profile and the supreme station and mission of a Savior: carrying a torch that burns and destroys, or one that gives light and life to the world? If a child rejects his loving parents, how should they respond to his rejection? Is the natural consequence of his deed— separation from his parents—***not*** in itself a suitable and sufficient punishment for him? God's ways are different, ***but always above—never below—human standards.*** Indeed our Creator is our perfect Model whose lead we are asked to follow:

> I have set you an example that you should do as I have done for you.   Christ (John 13:15 NIV)

> Be perfect, therefore, as your heavenly Father is perfect.
>   Christ (Matthew 5:48 NIV)

God's standards of treating His children have been and always will remain changeless. As Dr. Norman Vincent Peale, the prominent clergyman and author of *The Power of Positive Thinking* notes:

> Do you believe that the God who gives us such precious experiences here [on earth] would suddenly become cruel? Do you believe that God, whose every demonstration here is life and creation, will suddenly change and make every demonstration death and destruction? I have never seen any sign that God is capricious. The orderliness of the universe belies it. The seasons follow one another in absolute regularity. The stars come out in the skies nightly in the same old wonderful pattern. And those that show only periodically return on the stroke of the minute.[8]

God's love for humans always has been and always will be supreme:

> The Lord is...not willing that any should perish, but that all should come to repentance.   II Peter 3:9

Who needs the divine remedy most?

> It is not the healthy that need a doctor, but the sick.
>   Christ (Matthew 9:13 NEB)

Did not Jesus in His first advent express more interest in saving the sinners (Matt. 18:11-12) than the saints who outwardly observed the law? The life and teachings of Jesus testify to His infinite love even for the lowest and meanest of humans (Luke 15:2-10). Would He not show the same compassion again? Traditional expectations, based on literal interpretation of prophecies, have led many Christians to believe otherwise. Consider these examples from several Christian leaders and writers:

> So everyone who is ready to meet Jesus He will take up to heaven. Anyone who is unprepared will remain here dead—and tragically, left on the ground for vultures to consume. No second chance!...If our unsaved friends and relatives don't make their decision before Christ comes, they can never be saved. As God's Word puts it, "Behold, now is the day of salvation!" 2 Corinthians 6:2.[9]

> At the end of the world, instead of the wicked all being converted, they are to be cast into a furnace of fire, where there will be wailing...[10]

> In hell there is never the bliss of annihilation. You'd give anything for annihilation, but it's unavailable, only the conscious continuation of emotional anguish, physical anguish, relational anguish, and spiritual anguish forever.[11]

> Those who have ignored him [Christ], denied him, pretended but never really repented of their sins, shall be consumed with everlasting destruction—in flaming fire.[12]

> All of the non-Christians will be cast into the lake of fire.[13]

We should note that St. Paul's prophecy (II Thess. 1:7-8) includes Christians too. Literal interpretation of his prophecy requires that any Christian who does not practice his beliefs, who "does not obey the Gospel," must also perish.

Both the principle of "no mercy, forgiveness, and repentance" and the idea of "harsh punishment by fire" are the consequences of a strong belief in the literal descent of Jesus from heaven. Those who deny any expression of mercy or forgiveness by Jesus at His second coming do so on this ground: if people saw their Savior coming from the sky with His mighty angels, they would all be moved to repentance. Everyone who saw would wish to escape the fire. In that case there would be no separation between the faithful and the unfaithful. Good and bad would join the Lord. This would obviously be unfair. Further, if people believed that an opportunity for repentance would be offered to them, they would have no incentive for living a good life *before* Christ's coming. Thus, the reasoning goes, at the very instant of the Savior's appearance on the clouds, every opportunity for repentance or restoration must be terminated. As C. S. Lewis notes:

> It will be too late then to choose your side. There is no use saying you choose to lie down when it has become impossible to stand up. That will not be the time for choosing. It will be the time when we discover which side we have really chosen whether we realized it before or not. Now, today, this moment is our chance to choose the right side. God is holding back to give us that chance. It will not last forever. We must take it or leave it.[14]

Aside from being contrary to God's infinite love for humans, *the literal interpretation* of St. Paul's prophetic words suffers from other flaws as well. For instance:

- It allows no provision for lack of opportunities. (People are either taken to heaven or left on earth to die.) This is contrary to the words of Jesus that from those who are given more, more shall be demanded (Luke 12:48).

- It does not take into account the degree of the individual's age or mental maturity. For instance, will children of "the unsaved" also perish? And at what age or level of intelligence are people accountable?

- It does not take into account the infinite variation of character among the believers.

- It does not take into account the infinite variation of faith among the believers.

- It offers no reward to those who are not Christian, but still live by the law of love. Should they receive the same harsh punishment as those who pursue a life of crime and cruelty?

We are asked by our Creator to reason (Isa. 1:18). This is exactly what Paul himself did in proving Jesus to the Jews:

And Paul...reasoned with them out of the scripture...

Acts 17:2

And this is what Peter asked us to do:

Always be prepared to give an answer to everyone who asks you to give the reason for the hope that you have. But do this with gentleness and respect, keeping a clear conscience, so that those who speak maliciously against your good behavior in Christ may be ashamed of their slander. I Peter 3:15-16 NIV

If reason is disregarded or denigrated, then tradition, dogmatism, and emotionalism will fill the vacuum. Tradition is perhaps the most powerful force in society. By itself it can still the voice of reason as readily now as it did at the time of the first advent.

Literal interpretation of divine language sometimes leads to conclusions contrary to the very purpose for which God sends His Messengers and Redeemers. How many have died because they took these verses literally?

And these signs will accompany those who believe...they will pick up snakes with their hands; and when they drink deadly poison, it will not hurt them at all...

Mark 16:17-18 NIV

It is evident **snake** and **poison** symbolize negative forces of the world. True faith safeguards the spiritual life of the believer from the deadly influence of despair and deviation.

Thus, to avoid danger—physical or spiritual—we must decode the divine language, by thinking in *heavenly* terms.

To understand Jesus' heavenly *thoughts*, we must first understand *Him*. His words give us a glimpse of His identity, of His boundless love, mercy, and gentleness:

> Come to me, all whose work is hard, whose load is heavy; and I will give you relief. Bend your necks to my yoke, and learn from me, for I am gentle and humble-hearted; and your souls will find relief. For my yoke is good to bear, my load is light.   Christ (Matthew 11:28-30 NEB)

> Lord, how often am I to forgive my brother?...seventy times seven.   Matthew 18:21 NEB

> How blest are those of a gentle spirit...How blest are those who show mercy...How blest are the peacemakers...
>   Christ (Matthew 5:5-9 NEB)

Would the One who was "gentle and humble-hearted," who blessed the peacemakers, return to bring death to the masses of humanity and destruction to the world? Would the One who was the quintessence of love and forgiveness, who rejoiced in leading one sinner to God, return without mercy? To understand the divine words, we must elevate our thinking to higher horizons, as close to God's as possible. Even Peter, the distinguished disciple, sometimes had difficulty doing so:

> Then Jesus turned and said to Peter...'You think as men think, not as God thinks.'   Matthew 16:23 NEB

Was not Jesus' first advent also engulfed in fire? The Son of God carried no torch save that of knowledge, love, and enlightenment. Yet He said:

> I have come to set fire to the earth...   Luke 12:49 NEB

What did He mean by *setting fire*? Every new Redeemer by His teachings disrupts the old and entrenched order as He uproots false beliefs and traditions. At the time of His coming, people are so consumed with apathy and complacency that only "fire" can move them and set them free.

A divine Redeemer always comes with a crucible filled with flames! He offers people an opportunity to be tested and tried:

> For that day dawns in fire, and the fire will test the worth of each man's work.   I Corinthians 3:13 NEB

> The day comes, glowing like a furnace; all the arrogant and the evildoers shall be chaff, and that day when it comes shall set them ablaze, says the Lord of Hosts...
>   Malachi 4:1 NEB

> ...the hour of trial that is going to come upon the whole world to test those who live on the earth.
>   Christ (Revelation 3:10 NIV)

The testing separates the people:

> When the Son of Man comes in his glory...he will separate the people one from another...   Christ (Matthew 25:31-32 NIV)

People respond to "the fire" in various ways. A few face the challenge: they allow its flames to touch their hearts and souls, to burn *the veils of self and separation from God*. By its power they cleanse and transform themselves into a pure light of love:

> It is the warmth that these Luminaries of God generate, and the undying fires they kindle, which cause the light of the love of God to burn fiercely in the heart of humanity.[15]
>   Bahá'u'lláh

> Love setteth a world aflame...[16]   Bahá'u'lláh

> ...when the fire of the love of Jesus consumed the veils of Jewish limitations...[17]   Bahá'u'lláh

Those whose faith is tested and tried in God's crucible attain riches beyond measure:

> ...buy of me gold tried in the fire, that thou mayest be rich...   Christ (Revelation 3:18)

Taking the heat of the crucible *is **not** easy*:

> We must go through many hardships to enter the kingdom
> of God...   Acts 14:22 NIV

> See how I tested you, not as silver is tested, but in the
> furnace of affliction; there I purified you. Isaiah 48:10 NEB

> Not everyone who says to me, 'Lord, Lord,' will enter the
> kingdom of heaven, but only he who does the will of my
> Father...   Christ (Matthew 7:21 NIV)

Many, however, avoid the challenge of entering or even
approaching the crucible. They stand beyond its reach,
unaware that they too are afflicted by the heat of its raging
flames. They fail to recognize the burning desire of their
souls to attain Truth and Knowledge—one that continues to
smolder into the realms beyond. This fire usually is called
hell-fire, sometimes ***the unquenchable fire*** (Mark 9:44 NEB).

> If anyone's name was not found written in the book of
> life, he was thrown into the lake of fire.
>   Christ (Revelation 20:15 NIV)

No one is spared from the raging flames of tests and trials:

> ...every one shall be salted with fire...   Christ (Mark 9:49)

> For our God is a consuming fire.   Hebrews 12:29
>   See also Deuteronomy 4:24

These verses, clear and conclusive, are a token of the mercy
of thy Lord and a source of guidance for all mankind. They
are a light unto those who believe in them and a fire of
afflictive torment for those who turn away and reject
them.[18]   The Báb

...whatsoever was promised in the sacred Scriptures hath
been fulfilled. This is the Day of great rejoicing. It behoveth
everyone to hasten towards the court of His nearness with
exceeding joy, gladness, exultation and delight and to
deliver himself from the fire of remoteness [from God].[19]
                                              Bahá'u'lláh

The Worm That Does Not Die

In addition to the fire, these verses contain still another symbol:

> ...hell...where their worm does not die, and the fire is not quenched.   Mark 9:44-48 NIV

> Then I myself [the Lord] will come to gather all nations and races, and they shall come and see my glory...as the new heavens and the new earth...shall endure...so shall your race...and they [the people of the new earth and heavens] shall come out and see the dead bodies of those who have rebelled against me; their worm shall not die nor their fire be quenched...   Isaiah 66:18, 22-24 NEB

What does "worm" in the preceding passages imply? A literal or a symbolic reality? Would the loving Creator expose human beings for ages and eons to worms that shall not die? If not, then what does the word symbolize? It symbolizes that which annoys the spirit, that which pesters the conscience. It carries messages such as these: How did I get myself into this predicament? When opportunity knocked, why did I not open my heart? Why did I not love God more? Why did I not live a nobler life? Why did I fail to pursue the truth? Why did I fear to search? Why did I not trust my Lord to protect me from falling? Why did I not take time to investigate the news of the coming of my Master? Why? Why? Why? Since the consequences of our deeds are eternal, the wondering and questioning will likewise be eternal. No analogy or metaphor could more aptly portray or dramatize these concerns and questions than the pestering of human conscience by an ever-living worm.

From the examples provided, it becomes clear that divine language is different from human language, that *traditional expectations are sometimes erroneous*. Therefore we should not begin our search by insisting that a new Redeemer must conform entirely to *our* standards. To understand the prophecies, we must think in heavenly terms, not earthly.

This is difficult to do, because we are used to earthly speech. "He who is from the earth...uses earthly speech" (John 3:31 NEB). History shows that the trap of tradition, designed and maintained by human standards, is always tempting:

> But you have no idea where I come from or where I am going. You judge by human standards...
>
> Christ (John 8:14-15 NIV)

> You neglect the commandment of God, in order to maintain the tradition of men. Christ (Mark 7:8 NEB)

> You have a fine way of setting aside the commands of God in order to observe your own traditions!
>
> Christ (Mark 7:9 NIV)

Comparing the First Century With the Twentieth

> That men do not learn very much from the lessons of history is the most important of all the lessons in history.
>
> Aldous Huxley

A great poet has said "We need to live two lives: to acquire wisdom in the first and apply it in the second." The way to turn this fantasy into reality is to study history. For others have already lived the first life for us.

> Remember the days of old, consider the years of many generations... Deuteronomy 32:7

> ...Days should speak, and multitude of years should teach wisdom. Job 32:7

To get a clear view of our spiritual position today, all we need to do is to look at those who were in our position earlier. Hal Lindsey, a widely read contemporary Christian author, has already done some of the work for us. In his book, *The Promise*, he has attempted to assess the spiritual state of the people of Israel at the time of Jesus. Relevant to our discussion is his analysis of the reasons the Jews, for the most part, rejected their Redeemer, the very Object of their heavenly hope. He asks:

> ...the question that continues to plague me and so many other serious students of the Bible is, "Why wasn't it that obvious to the Jews of that day that this [Christ] was their Messiah?" He continually pointed to the things he did and said and declared that these were fulfillments of their own prophetic Scriptures. Couldn't they have checked this out and seen the truth or error of it?[20]

He calls the response of the people of Israel *The Paradox of Anticipation and Rejection*, and then sets out to resolve the paradox by studying the main causes of the response:

• *Dependence on traditions*. He asks:

> ...why didn't the majority of religious leaders, who knew the prophecies concerning Messiah, give Jesus their support and proclaim him to the people as the Promised One of God?[21]

And then he answers:

> One word sums up what has really held sway over all Judaism since their last Prophet Malachi spoke to them about 400 years before Christ and that word is TRADITION! Tradition about God, tradition about His Laws (Torah), tradition about how to live, eat, work, worship, marry and even die.[22]

• *Dependence on religious leaders*. He states that the interpretation of the Scriptures:

> ...was left primarily in the hands of the religious leaders. The sages, teachers, scholars, rabbis, scribes, or whatever else they were called at any given time in Jewish history, were the ultimate authorities on what God had to say to man.[23]

The religious leaders had made such a hedge around the Word thinking to protect it, and in so doing, made it so that no one could get near the true Word. Isaiah predicted that this would happen. He said the time would come when the people would draw near to God with their words and honor Him with their lips, but their hearts would be far from Him and their reverence would consist of tradition learned by rote (Isaiah 29:13).[24]

• *Total devotion to "minute interpretations of the Law."* He points out that the Jews placed undue emphasis on the letter or outward intent of the Word. They showed concern for "external rituals and outward conformity."

• *Preoccupation with prophecies that pointed to a conquering King, and disregard for those that implied "a suffering Servant."* He states that the people of Israel did not understand that:

> First, Messiah would have to deal with the root of men's problems, a nature and a heart of rebellion and sin, and *then* he could set up a Kingdom where all men would be prepared to live at peace with themselves, their families and their neighbors. But until the first was accomplished, the second could only be a dream, never a reality.[25]

If Mr. Lindsey's analysis is accurate, then it seems history is repeating itself in our time with precision. Today, as in the past:

• Most people still follow tradition, regarding it as *the* authority. Only a few search independently for Truth.

• Much emphasis is still being placed on "external rituals and outward conformity." The division of religions into many denominations is an evidence of this.

• Most people still prefer to leave the interpretation of the Word to their religious leaders.

- Prophecies that point to the Redeemer of our age as a suffering Servant ("first He must suffer") and to His coming in an ordinary or undramatic way ("like a thief in the night"), are given little if any attention. Yet frequent reference is made to an all-powerful Savior who upon His arrival transforms the world instantly.

William Miller, the leader of the Advent Movement in the West, wrote:

> The Jews were looking for a temporal king and kingdom. And are not we looking for a temporal millennium—one in which the Christians will have the rule of the world? Let us see to it that we do not stumble at the same stumbling-stone; possibly we may have carnal notions as well as they. Therefore, let us inquire.[26]

He states that the people of Israel "claimed all the learning, all the wisdom, and all the piety of that day"[27] yet could not "discern the signs of the times."[28] Why?

Even Jesus' disciples, who were the wisest and most enlightened people of their time, could not face the reality of receiving a suffering Savior. Despite their Master's repeated predictions of a dark future, they continued to dream of victory. As Dr. George Ladd, professor of New Testament at Fuller Theological Seminary, notes:

> It is a sound psychological fact that we hear only what we are prepared to hear. Jesus' predictions of his suffering and death fell on deaf ears. The disciples, in spite of his warnings, were unprepared for it...[29]

> This is also why his disciples forsook him when he was taken captive. Their minds were so completely imbued with the idea of a conquering Messiah whose role it was to subdue his enemies that when they saw him broken and bleeding under the scourging, a helpless prisoner in the hands of Pilate, and when they saw him led away,

nailed to a cross to die as a common criminal, all their
messianic hopes for Jesus were shattered.[30]

The disciples were not only endowed with wisdom, but gifted
with the unparalleled blessing of receiving knowledge directly
from their Master. *If they, despite their awareness and
astuteness, preferred to disregard their Master's predictions
of pain and suffering, could not the same frailty that
dimmed their perception of reality, dim ours as well?*

When the residents of a village in Israel refused to welcome
Jesus, the disciples James and John felt that punishment by
a display of their Master's miraculous powers was the
right response. So they suggested:

> 'Lord, do you want us to call fire down from heaven to
> destroy them?' But Jesus turned and rebuked them, and
> they went to another village.   Luke 9:54-56 NIV

Even Peter, who is eulogized by many as Jesus' greatest
disciple, the Rock of His Church, could not reconcile his
thoughts with those of his Master:

> Jesus...rebuked Peter..."you do not have in mind the
> things of God, but the things of men."   Mark 8:33 NIV

Is it possible that the scholars and interpreters of our time
suffer from the same weakness for which James, John, and
Peter were rebuked? Then why do they insist that every
prophecy must be fulfilled in a predetermined way, according to human standards?

The people of Israel expected their Savior to come from "an
unknown place." Nazareth was not good enough to give birth
to such a supreme figure:

> ...can anything good come from Nazareth?   John 1:46 NEB

Most of the people of our age also stumble on the same
stone: they refrain from examining Bahá'u'lláh's claim partly
because of His name and birthplace. If people questioned the
worthiness of Nazareth in ancient times, now they question

the worthiness of the earth itself! They have their eyes and hopes on heaven. Some people's spiritual health is so fragile that the sound of a name or label can break it!

If Jesus appeared among us today, *exactly* as He did among the people of Israel, how many of us would welcome Him? How many would rush to pass judgment on Him, without ever testing His evidence? How would the religious leaders behave? What would our evangelists say? Are the peoples of our time more discerning than those who received Jesus? Are they less bound by tradition?

> [What] if Christ was here, as then?...I have much reason to fear, that many may be found among the learned, the great, and teachers of divine things, who would receive from our divine Master, the same reproof [given to the Jews], were he as then a teacher among us. "Let him that thinketh he standeth take heed, lest he fall" (I Cor. 10:12).[31]
>
> William Miller

Spiritual Monotony

Traditions make up the spiritual atmosphere in which we are born and raised. As we learn to adapt to our physical environment, so do we to our spiritual environment. We are exposed to our beliefs gradually, progressively, almost imperceptibly. To us they do not seem out of place. That is why it is almost certain that a child born to a Muslim family will grow up to be a Muslim, a child born to a Christian, a Buddhist, a Jewish, a Hindu, or an agnostic family will grow up to follow and accept as the truth whatever his parents teach him.

The assumptions we accept, the convictions we defend, even the prejudices we cherish, they all seem natural and right to us:

> Every way of a man is right in his own eyes...
>
> Proverbs 21:2

All the ways of a man are clean in his own eyes...

Proverbs 16:2

...every party rejoices in what is their own.   Qur'án 30:31

The only way to escape from "spiritual monotony"—being exposed only to one set of beliefs—and the danger of being deprived of God's abundant riches is to:

• Venture into *new* spiritual realms

• Learn to look with a *new* eye

Without a *new* eye:

You may look and look, but you will never see.

Acts 28:26 NEB

Part II

Proofs: Time Prophecies

Surely the Sovereign Lord does nothing without revealing his plan to his servants the prophets.   *Amos 3:7 NIV*

...behold, I have foretold you all things.
                                        Christ (Mark 13:23)

Prove all things; hold fast that which is good.
                                        I Thessalonians 5:21

Produce your cause, saith the Lord; bring forth your strong reasons.   *Isaiah 41:21*

Lo! He is come in the sheltering shadow of Testimony, invested with conclusive proof...   *Bahá'u'lláh*

This is the Day in which the testimony of the Lord hath been fulfilled, the Day in which the Word of God hath been made manifest, and His evidence firmly established.
                                        Bahá'u'lláh

All the signs have been revealed; every prophetic allusion hath been manifested. Whatever hath been enshrined in all the Scriptures of the past hath been made evident.
                                        Bahá'u'lláh

8

The Wise
Shall Understand
Daniel 12:10

The mid-19th century witnessed the birth of a worldwide movement unparalleled in history. Hundreds of thousands of Christians, on all continents of the planet, awaited the return of Christ. What prompted so many in so many lands to set their hopes and hearts on heaven? And why did they face the most bitter disillusionment and disappointment of all time?

The "Sprouting" of Time Prophecies

During the first part of the 19th century, many seekers of truth from diverse cultural and religious backgrounds recognized that the time was ripe for the advent of a great Savior. The basic reason for this awakening and revival in so many places was the sudden "sprouting" of a series of time prophecies from the Scriptures of several religions, especially the Judeo-Christian and Muslim Scriptures. These prophecies had remained "sealed" for centuries. Then, like the arrival of spring, the advent of the 19th century imparted a new impetus to the unfolding of their potential, and the dormant buds flowered simultaneously in many a seeking mind around the globe.

The enthusiasm generated by this discovery—so definitive, so decisive—grew beyond measure. People thought that at long last they had found something on which they could depend. The evidence pointing to the exact date was overwhelming. Never before had the time of the advent of a Savior been so explicitly and repeatedly predicted. The number of discovered time prophecies pointing to the date of the advent is remarkable:

	The number of prophecies
• Prophecies in the Old Testament pointing to 1844	5
• Prophecies in the New Testament pointing to 1844	11
• Prophecies from other religions pointing to 1844	9
• Prophecies from the Bible pointing to the time of the advent of Bahá'u'lláh	2
• Prophecies from other religions pointing to the time of the advent of Bahá'u'lláh	11
• Total number of time prophecies	38

How could various religions be in such harmony about the advent? And how could such a mystery have remained "sealed" for so long and been declared at the same time by so many?

The expectation of the advent of Christ in the mid-19th century ranks among the most dramatic episodes in the history of religion, yet it is seldom brought out into the open by religious leaders and scholars. It is veiled and ignored in so many ways as to be reasonably called the most guarded secret in the religious history of the world. It is a secret forgotten, ignored, or hidden by those unable to tell the masses of believers why God's words—so emphatic, so clear—seem to stand unfulfilled.

The Failure to Decode the Symbolic Prophecies

Many of those unaware of the advent of the Báb and Bahá'u'lláh, have asked: how could God make a promise that He knew He would not honor? In the mid-19th century some believers were so uprooted, so puzzled and bewildered, as to abandon their faith. The date—1844—that they had thought would crown their heavenly hope, that would fulfill their fairest dreams, was reduced to a time of bitter disillusionment. They called 1844 "The Year of the Great Disappointment."

A pertinent question that may arise is this: if the Báb and Bahá'u'lláh were indeed the expected Redeemers, then why did so many fail to recognize them? This question requires a thorough examination, as detailed and specific as that provided in Volume V, *In the Clouds of Glory*. Briefly, some of the prophecies predicting the Advent are couched in parables and symbols. Others, such as those pointing to the appointed time, are relatively free from symbolism. Those expecting the second Advent simply failed to decode the first set of prophecies, namely, those veiled by symbols.

The Scriptures signaled the manner and condition of Christ's second advent by two sets of clues. The first set contained words and expressions such as "heaven," "the moon," "the stars," "the angels," "lightning," "heavenly descent," "glory and power," "raging fire," "resurrection," and "trumpet blast"—clues that implied action, triumph, drama, astonishment, upheaval; events or signs that can be perceived by every person, that should claim everyone's attention.

The second set of clues offered in the Scriptures contained words and expressions such as "thief," "night," "darkness," "sleep," "smoke," "clouds," "Noah's days," "unknown," "unaware," "drunk," "negligent," "worldly," "suffering," "mustard seed," and "watch"—clues that implied obscurity, secrecy, rejection, gradualism, and lack of drama. Exactly the opposite of the first set of clues.

Most seekers in the mid-19th century only took note of the first set of clues, and completely disregarded the second. If they had not ignored the second set of clues, they would certainly have been saved from crushing disappointment. Bahá'ís believe that the first set of clues—those pointing to dramatic events—were purely symbolic. Chapter 5—which contains comparative examples from the Christian and Bahá'í Scriptures—presents biblical support for this belief.

The Advent Movement

The Advent Movement of the mid-19th century, which Leroy Froom calls *the Advent Awakening* and *the Great Awakening*, was one of the greatest and most dramatic events in the history of the world. Yet many now prefer to regard it as an unfortunate misjudgment that is best buried or forgotten. To do justice to history we should revive it.

During the first half of the 19th century the expectation of the return of a great Redeemer swept across the world, especially among Christians:

> Like a tidal wave the movement swept over the land. From city to city, from village to village, and into remote country places it went.[1]

The advent movement of 1840-44 was...carried to every mission station in the world, and in some countries there was the greatest religious interest which has been witnessed ...since the Reformation of the sixteenth century.[2]

In Great Britain it was reported that:

...the Advent doctrine is chiefly the talk in this country now...Thousands are now looking for the coming of the Lord, and believe it is at the door.[3]

The chief reason for the widespread expectation was the sudden unfolding of the time prophecies in the Scriptures of several of the great religions. In the Christian world many seekers of truth came to the same or similar conclusions. They found the mid-19th century to be the appointed time of Christ's return.

In *Dieux d'homme, Dictionnaire des Messianismes et Milleranismes,* the French scholar, Henri des Roche, presents brief biographies of more than a thousand seekers who proclaimed the nearness of "the time of the end," and in many cases the exact time of its termination when the promised Redeemer was to come.[4]

Leroy Froom, a Christian scholar and author of one of the most extensive works on the Advent Awakening of the 19th century, writes:

...beginning about 1810, just after the French Revolution... a simultaneous study of the 2300 years and the impending judgment hour broke out in the various countries of Christendom. On both sides of the Atlantic, and in different lands, men were led independently to similar conclusions. Not one or two voices, but a swelling chorus of men... proclaimed the approaching terminus of the 2300 years as the message of prophecy for the hour.[5]

Many prominent figures of that period discovered or proclaimed the exact or approximate "time of the end," when God would "cleanse His Sanctuary" and inaugurate a new era in human history (See Table I). The prevailing view among them was that Christ Himself would appear to lead the believers to the expected millennial kingdom.

Among all the prophecies pointing to the time of the second advent, the prophecy of 2300 days had a special attraction for the seekers in the mid-19th century. It served as the chief guiding force in their discovery of the appointed time. By far the most popular dates selected were 1843, 1844, and 1847. The reason for this variation will be discussed later.

Table I lists some recognized *figures* of the 19th century who discovered or proclaimed the time of the advent. Table II lists some *publications* of that period that predicted the time of the advent.

Table I

Some Prominent Figures Who Discovered or Proclaimed the Time of the Second Advent of Christ or the Cleansing of the Sanctuary✣

Name	Expected Date of Advent
Alfred Addis 1806-?	1843-1844
William Anderson 1799-1873	1843
David Arnold 1805-1889	1844
Joseph Bates 1792-1872	1844
David Bernard	1843
Thomas Birks 1810-1883	1843
Joshua William Brooks 1790-1882	1844
Freeman Brown	1843
John Aquila Brown	1844
Charles Buck 1771-1815	1844
Alexander Campbell 1788-1866	1847
John Cook 1804-1874	1843
William Cuninghame	1843

✣ For specific references, please see Table II in this chapter and *The Prophetic Faith of Our Fathers*, Volumes II, III, and IV.

Table I Continued

Name	Expected Date of Advent
William C. Davis 1760-1831	1843-1847
William Digby 1783-1866	1843+
Henry Drummond 1786-1860	1847
George Duffield 1794-1868	1844-1847
Hiram Edson 1806-1882	1844
Edward B. Elliott 1793-1875	1844
Charles Fitch 1805-1844	1843
Lorenzo Fleming 1808-1867	1843
Calvin French ?-1844	1843
James H. Frere	1847
John Fry 1775-1849	1844
Elon Galusha 1790-1856	1843
Matthew Habershon 1789-1852	1843-1844
Appollos Hale	1843
William W. Hales	1844
Silas Hawley 1815-1888	1843
N. Hervey	1843-1844
Joshua Himes 1805-1895	1843
Edward Hoare 1802-1877	1843
Ph. Homan	1843-1844
John Hooper	1847
Richard Hutchinson	1843
Edward Irving 1792-1834	1847
Henry Jones 1804-1880	1843
L. H. Kelber	1843
Thomas Keyworth 1782-1852	1843
Josiah Litch 1809-1886	1843
Joseph Marsh ?-1863	1843
Archibald Mason	1843
David Millard	1843
William Miller 1782-1849	1843
Alphonse Nicole 1789-1874	1846-1847
William W. Pym 1792-1852	1843-1847
Jahann H. Richter 1799-1847	1847
James Sabine 1774-1845	1843
J. F. E. Sander	1843-1847
Robert Scott 1760-1834	1843-1844
Samuel Snow	1844

Table I Continued

Name	Expected Date of Advent
Nathan Southard ?-1852	1843
George Storrs 1796-1879	1843
Edward Vaughan 1777-1829	1843
Henry Dana Ward 1797-1884	1839-1843
Thomas White	1843-1844
Nathan Whiting 1794-1872	1843-1844
Daniel Wilson 1778-1858	1847
Joseph Wolff 1795-1862	1847

Table II

Some Works of Scholars or Writers of the 19th Century With Publications on the Expected Time of the Advent

Author	Title	Publication Date
Alfred Addis	*Heaven Opened*	1829
	The Theory of Prophecy	1830
William Anderson	*An Apology for Millennial Doctrine; in the Form in Which It Was Entertained by the Primitive Church*	1830
David Bernard	*Letter of David Bernard, on the Second Coming of Christ*	1843
Thomas Birks	*First Elements of Sacred Prophecy*	1843
Joshua W. Brooks	*A Dictionary of Writers on Prophecies*	1835
	Essays on the Advent and Kingdom of Christ	1840
Freeman Brown	*Views and Experiences in Relation to Entire Consecration and the Second Advent*	1843
John Aquila Brown	*The Even-Tide...*	1823

Table II Continued

Author	Title	Publication Date
Charles Buck	*Theological Dictionary*	1811
John Cook	*A Solemn Appeal to Ministers And Churches, Especially to Those of the Baptist Denomination, Relative to the Speedy Coming of Christ*	1843
William Cuninghame	*The Pre-Millennial Advent of Messiah Demonstrated from the Scriptures*	1836
William C. Davis	*The Millennium*	1811
	A Treatise on the Millennium	1827
William Digby	*A Treatise on the 1260 Days of Daniel and St. John*	1831
Henry Drummond	*Introduction to the Study of the Apocalypse*	1830
George Duffield	*Dissertation on the Prophecies Relative to the Second Coming of Jesus Christ*	1842
	Millenarianism Defended	1843
Edward Elliott	*A Commentary on the Apocalypse*	1837
Charles Fitch	*Letter to Rev. J. Litch, on the Second Coming of Christ*	1843
James H. Frere	*A Combined View of the Prophecies of Daniel, Esdras, and St. John*	1815
	Eight Letters on the Prophecies Relating to the Last Times	1831
John Fry	*The Second Advent*	1822
Elon Galusha	*Address of Elder Elon Galusha, With Reasons for Believing Christ's Second Coming...*	1844
Matthew Habershon	*A Dissertation on the Prophetic Scriptures, Chiefly Those of a Chronological Character*	1834
Silas Hawley	*The Second Advent Doctrine Vindicated...*	1843
N. Hervey	*Prophecies of Christ's First and Second Advent*	1843

Table II Continued

Author	Title	Publication Date
Joshua Himes	*Views of the Prophecies and Prophetic Chronology*	1842
John Hooper	*The Doctrine of the Second Advent*	1829
Richard Hutchinson	*The Abrahamic Covenant*	1843
Edward Irving	*The Coming of Messiah in Glory and Majesty*	1827
	Exposition of the Book of Revelation, in a Series of Lectures	1831
Henry Jones	*Principles of Interpreting Prophecies*	1837
	A Scriptural Synopsis of the Doctrine in General, of Christ's Second Advent, "at Hand"	1842
L. H. Kelber	*Das Ende Kommt*	1842
Thomas Keyworth	*A Practical Exposition of the Revelation of St. John*	1828
Josiah Litch	*Prophetic Exposition*	1842
Archibald Mason	*Appendix to an Inquiry Into the Prophetic Numbers Contained in the 1335 Days*	1818
	Two Essays on Daniel's Prophetic Number of Two Thousand Three Hundred Days; and on the Christian's Duty to Inquire Into the Church's Deliverance	1820
William Miller	*Evidence From Scripture and History of the Second Coming of Christ, About the Year 1843*	1836
William Pym	*Thoughts on Millenarianism*	1829
Johann Richter	*Erklarte Haus-Bibel (6 vol.)*	1834-1840
James Sabine	*The Relation of the Present State of Religion to the Expected Millennium*	1823
	The Appearing and Kingdom of Our Lord Jesus Christ...	1842

Table II Continued

Author	Title	Publication Date
J. F. Sander	*Versuch einer Erklarung der Offenbarung Johannis*	1829
Robert Scott	*Free Thoughts on the Millennium*	1834
Edward Vaughan	*The Church's Expectation: A Sermon on the Second Advent of the Lord Jesus Christ*	1828
Henry Dana Ward	*Glad Tidings. "For the Kingdom of Heaven is at Hand"*	1838

The 19th century Advent Awakening embraced a cross-section of almost all Christian denominations, and contained within its ranks some of the most distinguished leaders and scholars of the time. As Froom writes:

> These men were accomplished in Biblical languages, Latin, and history, and were well acquainted with the principles of sound exegesis. They were not inclined to catch up some fanciful or irrational theory. On the contrary, they were rather matter of fact and exacting in their scholarship. They had come to their conclusions on the basis of substantial evidence, after painstaking study consuming years and sometimes decades.[6]

Charles Meister, a modern Christian author, has recently published a book on the events of 1844: *Year of the Lord, A. D. Eighteen Forty Four.* He chose 1844 among all the years in history because he found it unique, *a very special year.* His book contains chapters on both the Advent Movement and the Bahá'í Faith. He writes:

> In 1812 a Catholic priest born in Chile, Manuel de Lacunza, published a book called *The Coming of Messiah in Majesty and Glory.* By 1820 about 300 Anglican and 600 Nonconformist clergymen in England were preaching Christ's

early return...Joseph Wolff spread the advent doctrine to more than twenty countries in the Middle East and Asia between 1831 and 1845. In 1820 Archibald Mason in Scotland predicted that 1844 would be the year of Christ's return. Alexander Campbell, in a famous debate with Robert Owen in 1829, also selected 1844 as the year.[7]

The uniqueness of 1844 motivated still another modern author, Jerome Clarke, a Christian scholar and professor at Southern Missionary College, to write three volumes entitled simply: *1844*.[8]

The year 1844 was also a time of awakening in the East. It is indeed astonishing that when multitudes of Christians were awaiting the advent of Christ, many Muslims were cherishing an identical hope. The Sunni sect (Sunnites), who constitute the majority of Muslims, expect the return of Christ in the last days. Some Muslims expected, independently of the Christians, the advent of their Redeemer in that same year of 1844. John Fry, one of the figures of the Advent Movement in the mid-19th century, in his book on prophecies (published in 1835) states:

> ...the Mohammedans in various parts of the world, have their expectation fixed on the same year, A.D. 1844...[9]

Fry then states that such agreement between the prophecies of Christians and Muslims (who constitute a large portion of humanity) concerning the date of the advent of the expected One should not be taken lightly.

It is indeed remarkable that so many seekers and scholars from so many lands came to such similar conclusions. Minor variations, however, can be noted in their findings. One reason for such variations was a failure to move correctly from B.C. to A.D. Still another reason was an inability to locate and use the same starting point (day or month). It seems evident that if the units of time are years and not months or days, one should expect some margin of error, not exceeding one year below or above the intended figure.

Those who selected 1847 instead of 1843 or 1844 did so because they depended on a manuscript preserved in the Vatican. The manuscript included a copying error that distorted the correct and now accepted prophetic figure of 2300.

As far as is known, no one was able to discover the day (May 23) and the hour (two hours and eleven minutes past sunset) in which, according to Bahá'ís, the appointed time did arrive. As foretold in the Scriptures, the knowledge of the hour remained a mystery until the last instant when, suddenly and unexpectedly, it was disclosed and declared by the Báb.

The dawning of the new day was also declared to people through dreams and visions. The Scriptures prophesied:

> In the last days, God says, I will pour out my Spirit on all people. Your sons and daughters will prophesy, your young men will see visions, your old men will dream dreams. Acts 2:17 NIV
> See also Joel 2:28

In 1842 William Foy, a Baptist preacher, told of two visions he had of Christ's second coming. In 1844 he reported a third vision of three mysterious platforms. Hazen Foss in the fall of 1844 told of a vision he had of the second coming, in which three steps were depicted. Twice more he reported receiving this vision.[10]

(See also William Miller's dreams—one of them cited later in this chapter and another in Appendix II. See also Joseph Wolff's visions, and the remarkable story of the child preachers of the mid-19th century in Chapter 19.)

Although some of those who proclaimed the imminent return of Christ were mocked, harassed, regarded as heretics, and even imprisoned, they succeeded nonetheless in attracting thousands of followers.

This awareness of the dawning of a new age did not come too early, when it would have been of little if any use. Those who discovered or confirmed the time of the advent lived in the late 18th and early 19th century. Only when the people needed to know the date were they able to break the seal of concealment. That is why Daniel, who was inspired to predict the date, was also informed of the need for secrecy:

> But you, Daniel, keep the words secret and seal the book till the time of the end.   Daniel 12:4 NEB

> Go your way, Daniel, for the words are kept secret and sealed till the time of the end.   Daniel 12:9 NEB

> This revelation which has been given of the evenings and the mornings is true; but you must keep the vision secret, for it points to days far ahead.   Daniel 8:26 NEB

Before the ripening of the time, even Daniel could not understand the vision:

> I [Daniel] was perplexed by the revelation and no one could explain it.   Daniel 8:27 NEB

Among those intimately involved in the study of biblical prophecies was Sir Isaac Newton, who believed that "prophecies remain veiled until their time of near fulfillment, and then God raises up a prophet to interpret their meaning." He said, "I seem to gather that God is about to open these mysteries."[11]

Those studying the prophecy of 2300 days, the prophecies of 1260 days (to be examined later), and scores of other clues, were certain that the advent would surely take place as promised. But when the year 1844 came and passed with no sign of the descent of their Savior, they were baffled, bewildered, and disillusioned to find that the explicit prophecies of the Bible had remained unfulfilled. Their disillusionment is well reflected in the title some of them gave to 1844, the year of the "Great Disappointment." Despite the disappointment, some Christian scholars have continued to uphold their belief in the accuracy of the year. They maintain that 1844 marked a turning point in the history of the human race.

The Year of Fulfillment

Bahá'ís believe that 1844 was **not** the time of "Great Disappointment." Instead, 1844 marked the onset of the Age of Fulfillment, because it was in that same year that a new Revelation came into being when the Báb declared Himself as the promised one of all ages and religions.

The Báb, the Herald of Bahá'u'lláh, possessed a station equal to that of all the great Messengers and Redeemers of the past. He declared:

> I am the Primal Point from which have been generated all created things. I am the Countenance of God Whose splendor can never be obscured, the Light of God Whose radiance can never fade.[12]

> I am the Flame of that supernal Light that glowed upon Sinai...and lay concealed in the midst of the Burning Bush.[13]

> Verily He [the Báb] is the One Who holdeth, by Our [God's] leave, the kingdoms of earth and heaven in His grasp...[14]

Therefore, Bahá'ís believe that the advent of the Báb fulfilled all the prophecies pointing to 1844.

The Millerite Movement

Any discussion of the Great Awakening of the 19th century is incomplete without a brief review of the life of the man who was its central figure: William Miller (1782-1849). This man of great vision was by far the best-known pioneer, teacher, and leader among all those discovering and proclaiming the time (1844) of the return of the expected Redeemer. In the United States alone he gained, over a period of 13 years, as many as two hundred thousand followers. They were called Millerites, after his name. The Millerite Movement later gave rise to the Seventh-day Adventist Church and a few other denominations.

Miller was a selfless and dedicated seeker of truth. He devoted all he had to proclaiming the dawn of what he deemed the greatest Day in human history, a Day whose arrival he had discovered after many years of ceaseless search. Miller's integrity and honesty were such that even his enemies acknowledged them. Unlike those who seek leadership for the sake of power, who compromise their beliefs to win favors, Miller taught his views with the utmost humility and devotion. When he found that, according to his expectations, his predictions had not come true, he refused to accept any unreasonable explanations or rationalizations that would have pacified his disappointed and outraged followers.

Miller started his search into prophecies with no specific expectations or preconceived notions. He wrote:

> I commenced their study with no expectation of finding the time of the Saviour's coming, and I could at first hardly believe the result to which I had arrived; but the evidence struck me with such force that I could not resist my convictions. I became nearly settled in my conclusions, and began to wait, and watch, and pray for my Saviour's coming.[15]

After finding the appointed date, Miller decided not to disclose it. He wanted to make sure that it was accurate. On November 4, 1826 he had an unusual dream that gave him a glimpse of his future destiny. In his dream:

> ...he saw the blood of Jesus running from a rail-fence. He saw the cross, with garments drenched in blood. He received a book, which he was told would direct him. When he opened it, his eyes came to Isaiah 48:17: "I lead thee by the way thou shouldst go." He then had a vision of a paradise beyond description, and then he awoke. He began to feel that God could use even a humble farmer to awaken the world to biblical prophecy.[16]

Miller had discovered the date after years of research, and his dream seemed to lend credence to his findings. Yet he could not muster enough confidence to unveil to others his awesome and incredible message.

> One Saturday morning in August 1831 Miller felt the call to tell the world about Christ's imminent return. Still somewhat reticent, he made an apparently safe bargain with God: he promised God that if he was ever called upon to preach, he would preach Christ's second coming. Since he had never had such an invitation, the bargain seemed safe enough. But that very day a young man arrived from nearby Dresden, inviting him to preach the following day. Angry, Miller refused. But his conscience bothered him. His six-year-old daughter Lucy told her mother: "Something's the matter with Daddy." Miller had gone into a grove to pray about the invitation to preach. As Francis Nichol summarized: "He went into the grove a farmer, and came out a preacher." He could not go back on his word to God. So he hitched up his horse, and traveled the sixteen miles to Dresden.[17]

From then on his life was a continual climb. Proclaiming the imminent return of Christ dominated his life. He who had been hesitant to face the crowds and present his urgent message, gained such confidence as to deliver, by 1844, some 4,500 talks to over 500,000 people. As the set time approached, his certainty concerning the advent continued to climb. In August 1834, he said:

> The evidence is so clear, the testimony is so strong, that we live on the eve of the present dispensation, towards the dawn of the Glorious Day, that I wonder why ministers and people do not wake up and trim their lamps.[18]

From the outset Miller's message was controversial. Though some admired him, others attacked him. "On some occasions Miller's message so enraged certain people that they planned to take his life as he left the auditorium."[19]

But threats, ridicule, or censure could not turn him away from the cause to which he devoted his whole life and honor.

In fact, opposition simply strengthened Miller's message of hope. People could ridicule him, but they could not refute his reasoning. Many were so moved by his appeals, so convinced by his evidence on the appointed time of the advent, as to count the remaining days with joyful anticipation and preparation. Some farmers declined to plant their crops in the spring. Others refrained from reaping their harvest in the fall.[20] If taken to heaven, they would need heavenly, not earthly, food.

> Restoration of stolen property and payment of debts became unusually common. A man who identified himself only as a believer in Millerism mailed five dollars in conscience money to the United States Treasury. Another man sent a larger sum to a New York insurance company with a note saying, "The Lord is at hand. This was unlawfully taken from you, and I ask forgiveness, for the Lord has forgiven me much." Even the editor of the Midnight Cry, to be sure that every obligation was taken care of, placed this notice above his signature: "If any human being has a just pecuniary claim against me, he is requested to inform me instantly."[21]

Jesus had prophesied that before His coming the stars of heaven would fall (Matt. 24:29). During the years of Miller's teaching, two heavenly events of the greatest magnitude did occur. Dr. Robert Gale writes:

> Few things did more to attract attention to the fulfillment of Bible prophecy and thus to give impetus to Miller's cause than two astronomical phenomena that occurred during the 1830's and 1840's...

> In the early morning hours of November 13, 1833, an unusually large meteoric shower covered much of North America...This was the most extensive and wonderful display of fallen stars that has ever been recorded. Thousands of people viewed this event as a direct fulfillment

of Bible prophecy, a sign of the nearness of the second coming of Christ.

The second phenomenon occurred about ten years later, when from February 28 to April 1, 1843, the night sky was lighted with the most brilliant comet to appear in the nineteenth century.[22]

Miller expressed his views with confidence and devotion. He totally depended on the Scriptures as his guide and inspiration. Here is a summary of his main beliefs in his own words with the biblical references on which they rest:

I believe God has revealed the time. (Isa. 44:7,8; Dan. 12:10; Amos 3:7; I Thess. 5:4.)

I believe many who are professors and preachers will never believe or know the time until it comes upon them. (Jer. 8:7; Matt. 24:50; Jer. 25:34-37.)

I believe the wise, they who are to shine as the brightness of the firmament, Dan. 12:3, will understand the time. (Eccl. 8:5; Dan. 12:10; Matt. 24:43-45; 25:6-10; I Thess. 5:4; I Peter 1:9-13.)

I believe the time can be known by all who desire to understand and to be ready for his coming. And I am fully convinced that some time between March 21st, 1843, and March 21st, 1844, according to the Jewish mode of computation of time, Christ will come, and bring all his saints with him; and that then he will award every man as his works shall be (Matt. 16:27; Rev. 22:12).[23]

Based on the Jewish computation of time, the revelation of the Báb occurred on May 23, 1843, ten months before the closing of Miller's deadline. Based on the Christian calendar, His revelation occurred on May 23, 1844. (More about this later.)

Miller discovered the appointed time by making extensive studies of prophecies throughout the whole Bible, from Leviticus to Revelation, and they all pointed to the same date.

The Great Disappointment

Miller had been the object of rejection and ridicule for 13 years. He had endured the most severe trials all for the reward of seeing his Lord and of awakening others. Only the hope of meeting his Lord could give him the strength and the courage to continue. In his own words:

> What then will be my feelings, when faith will end in sight, and hope in fruition?...No more a stranger in this giddy world...no more to meet the scoffs of friends or foes...My soul rejoices when I think a few more days, at most, and all these scenes will be forgotten in the eternal sunshine of his glory. Why not begin the song of everlasting gratitude to God for this blessed hope.[24]

This is how the Millerites approached the hour of their expectation:

> Those who truly believed Christ was going to come had made a heart preparation for the event that they expected to be theirs throughout all eternity. Their worldly cares were largely forgotten during the weeks immediately preceding the expected Advent, and they examined closely every thought and emotion as if it were to be their last.

> According to Miller's reckoning, March 21, 1844, was the last day of the prophetic period within which Christ must come. At last the great day arrived! The Lord could come during the early-morning hours. But the sun crossed the meridian, the morning passed, and He did not come. Only the afternoon remained. It too passed. The evening came, and still the believers waited—waited and hoped and prayed. He *must* come before midnight! But, alas, midnight too passed. The next morning came, and still Christ had not come.

> The bitterness—the galling bitterness—of that disappointment can be fully appreciated only by those who experienced it. To the disappointment of not being able to greet

their Lord was added the ridiculing and scoffing of the unbelievers who now reveled in their seeming triumph.[25]

What of Miller? "Few men have been called to endure so great an amount of reproach...and few could have endured it as he did."[26] But Miller's disappointment had not yet reached its climax. The galling, climactic disappointment came a few months later, on October 22. After his first disappointment, Miller reluctantly consented to move his deadline a few months forward to October 22, 1844. Again to his utter astonishment, the heavenly descent of the expected Savior did not materialize.

> Early on the morning of October 22, 1844, most Millerites gathered in their churches to await the Advent. In communities where there were no church buildings the people met in the homes of various believers...Many Adventists gathered in the large auditorium in Cincinnati...there were 1,200 inside the building, with another 300 outside. The people were "very orderly," and there was "less excitement" than the reporter had expected. The minister...preached ...his last warning to a sinful world. The meeting was closed before nine o'clock, and the people were advised to go to their homes, there to await the expected Advent that many felt would occur at midnight.[27]

What was the drama in store for the remaining hours of that unforgettable day? Would the adored Redeemer at last descend from behind the clouds of glory?

> ...the sun passed its zenith, and declined toward its setting. The cloud of shining glory for which they strained their eyes, and which they believed would bring their Lord, did not appear. No lightning rent the sky, no earthquake shook the land, no trumpet smote the ear. The westering sun went down silently but relentlessly upon their disappearing hopes. Darkness covered the land, and gloom— irrepressible gloom—settled down upon the waiting, watching host. Grief and despair overwhelmed them all.

Men and women wept unashamedly, for their Lord had not come.[28]

After the Disappointment, Hiram Edson, who had constantly proclaimed "the year of the Lord," expressed the overwhelming despondency and sadness of the people in these words:

> Our fondest hopes and expectations were blasted, and such a spirit of weeping came over us as I never experienced before. It seemed that the loss of all earthly friends could have been no comparison. We wept, and wept.[29]

Then he asked:

> If this, the richest and brightest of all my Christian experiences, had proved a failure, what was the rest of my Christian experience worth? Has the Bible proved a failure? Is there no God, no heaven, no paradise? Is all this but a cunningly devised fable?[30]

Another Adventist, Washington Morse, described that unforgettable day in these terms:

> That day came and passed, and the darkness of another night closed in upon the world. But with that darkness came a pang of disappointment to the Advent believers that can find a parallel only in the sorrow of the disciples after the crucifixion of their Lord. The passing of the time was a bitter disappointment...And now, to turn again to the cares, perplexities, and dangers of life, in full view of jeering and reviling unbelievers who scoffed as never before, was a terrible trial of faith and patience.[31]

Explanation for the Disappointment

After the disappointment, people tried to reexamine the prophecies. They could have erred, they thought, in two ways:

- By miscalculating the date
- By misjudging the event

First they reexamined their calculations and could find no error:

> ...they could detect no error in their reckoning of the prophetic periods. The ablest of their opponents had not succeeded in overthrowing their system of prophetic interpretation. They could not consent, without Bible evidence, to renounce positions which had been reached through earnest, prayerful study of the Scriptures...positions which had withstood the most searching criticism and the most bitter opposition of popular religious teachers...[32]

Then they reexamined the prophecies to see if they could have erred in judging the event. Here they found themselves divided. Some of them lost their faith and hope altogether. They could not believe in a God whose promises could fail:

> In a letter to a friend, Miller said that on the day after the Disappointment it seemed as though all the demons in the bottomless pit had been turned loose upon the believers. Some, who had been begging for mercy two days before, were now mixing with the rabble, mocking and scoffing in a most blasphemous way.[33]

Others found the belief in an invisible return most plausible. So they said that Christ did come as promised, but no one was able to see Him. But if no one could see Him, people wondered, for what purpose did He come?

Still others—perhaps the largest group—supported Hiram Edson's view that the advent was heavenly, not earthly. They claimed that in 1844 Christ entered "the most Holy place of the Heavenly Sanctuary to carry on His work as high priest."

Edson's explanation left many questions unanswered (see Chapter 10, and Appendix I), but it served a vital purpose in saving many believers from rejecting their faith. It bestowed hope on those who could ***not*** deny the accuracy of the date. The Seventh-day Adventist Church is a living proof of that hope. By accepting this new interpretation, they could still set their faith in the Scriptures and their eyes on heaven. After "the Great Disappointment," the Adventists kept alight the lamp of hope, but unfortunately quenched the flaming fire of search. The Seventh-day Adventists have continued to believe to this day that 1844 marked the earliest time that Christ could have come.[34]

Many did not accept Edson's explanation, including Miller. To the end he believed that all the date-prophecies, including the prophecy of 2300 days, point to the physical return of Christ to our planet. Fifteen reasons are presented in Appendix I to prove Miller's sound judgment.

Miller never gave up the hope of seeing Christ return. In spite of the Disappointment, he continued to teach the imminent advent of the Lord. He never wavered in his beliefs, because he had full confidence in God's promises. Towards the end of his life he wrote:

> Were I to live my life over again, with the same evidence that I then had, to be honest with God and man I should have to do as I have done.[35]

And again:

> Although I have been twice disappointed, I am not yet cast down or discouraged...My hope in the coming of Christ is as strong as ever. I have done only what, after years of solemn consideration, I felt it my solemn duty to do. If I have erred, it has been on the side of charity, love, to my fellow men, and conviction of duty to God.[36]

Miller's final admonition was:

> Avoid everything that shall cause offenses. Let your lives be models of goodness and propriety. Avoid unnecessary controversy. God will raise up those to whom He will commit the direction of His cause.[37]

In the spring of 1845, he wrote:

> I have reckoned all the time I can. I must now wait and watch until he is graciously pleased to answer the 10,000 prayers that daily and nightly ascend his holy hill, 'Come, Lord Jesus, come quickly.'[38]

Again he wrote:

> The fatigue of body and mind has almost unnerved this old frame, and unfitted me to endure the burdens which Providence calls upon me to bear...this frail life will soon be over. My Master will soon call me home, and soon the scoffer and I shall be in another world to render our account before a righteous tribunal.[39]

Four years after the Disappointment, Miller's sight failed and his health took a sharp decline. Still full of hope that he might see his adored Redeemer, he died in 1849, at the age of 68. The inscription on his gravestone reads: "At the time appointed the end shall be."

Why did Miller and the multitude of his followers ultimately fail in their search for Truth? They failed primarily because of their extreme literalism. Had they *not* taken literally the prophetic passages that point to the heavenly descent of their Savior, they would have kept their minds open to other possibilities, well supported in the Scriptures. For instance, possibilities conveyed by prophecies such as:

> That is the day when I come like a thief! Happy the man who stays awake and keeps on his clothes...
>
> Revelation 16:15 NEB

> Be dressed ready for service and keep your lamps burning...
>
> Luke 12:35 NIV

> ...the day of the Lord will come like a thief in the night.
>
> I Thessalonians 5:2 NIV

"Keeping one's clothes on" and "being dressed" symbolize qualities that adorn and elevate our spirit and prepare us to see and recognize the truth, qualities such as: sincerity, open-mindedness, purity of heart, patience, persistence, self-sacrifice, self-confidence, thirst for truth, justice, courage, faith, humility, and trust in God.

If hundreds of thousands expected the Redeemer's advent on a given day, and He appeared literally with earthly glory, how would a prophecy like the following be fulfilled?

> But understand this: If the owner of the house had known at what hour the thief was coming, he would not have let his house be broken into. You also must be ready, because the Son of Man will come at an hour when you do not expect him.   Luke 12:39-40 NIV

Many Christians have kept their hopes aflame. Some of them are getting impatient as they instinctively sense a delay in the return of their Lord. They see the crops of faith and hope becoming overripe and perishing, and wonder why they are not being harvested. A few of them explain the delay this way: the Harvester wants to give His servants more time to repent, to grant them further opportunities for escape from unbelief.

> God's delay of this event [the second Advent] is for the purpose of giving people a chance to escape...[40]
>
>   Dr. Ray Stedman

> God is holding back to give us that chance. It will not last forever.[41]   C. S. Lewis

George Vandeman, perhaps the best-known contemporary spokesman in the Seventh-day Adventist church, states:

> ...so far as any time prophecy is concerned, Jesus could have returned to this earth any time after 1844. He is not waiting for any prophetic time period to end. No time prophecy is holding Him back. Then why hasn't He returned? For nearly two hundred years we have been living in the time of the end. Why isn't He here?[42]

Then he responds:

Our wonderful Lord, our compassionate, loving Saviour, doesn't want anyone to be lost. And so He holds up the final flight of time, He slows the march of history— because some have not yet made a decision. And He doesn't want one to be lost![43]

Is such a view supported by the Scriptures? Both the Old and the New Testaments teach otherwise. They declare that the time is fixed and unchangeable, and delay is impossible. (For details see Chapter 17.)

The Subtle and Sealed Language of Prophecy

Most of those who declared that 1844 was the appointed time of Christ's advent came to that conclusion on the basis of Daniel's prophecy of 2300 days. They remained unaware of the meaning of many other time prophecies, not only in Daniel but in the Book of Revelation as well. Had they known the true meaning of those other prophecies, their anticipation and their disappointment would have reached almost unbearable proportions; therefore, their ignorance saved them from an even greater agony. The meaning of the other time prophecies was destined to be unveiled decades later by Bahá'u'lláh's son, 'Abdu'l-Bahá.

Further, if more information had been unveiled to the people before the arrival of the appointed time, it could have led to several other consequences. First, it would have incited many false claims to divine Revelation. Second, it would have interfered with people's freedom of choice. Many would be forced to accept their Redeemer out of fear, and the insincere would have forcefully claimed faith and fidelity.

God in His Wisdom gives us as much evidence as He knows we need to make a decision; no more, no less. This is one reason why in spite of its clarity, Daniel's vision appears partly in the garment of signs and symbols. Instead of prophesying that after 2300 years the Redeemer shall come, it simply says that after this period "the sanctuary shall be cleansed."

> Verily the Hour is coming—My design is to keep it hidden—for every soul to receive its reward by the measure of its endeavor.   Qur'án, 20:15 Y

We see the veil of symbolism clothing other prophecies (those not related to time) as well. ***One reason the Gospel pointed to the heavenly descent of Christ was to discourage false claims at the appointed time.***

What would happen if it were known that Christ would come in an ordinary way? Many people among both the devout and the deniers would try to fulfill the prophecies in their own or their children's lives; some of them with the intention of invalidating the prophecies, others with the hope of playing a decisive role in the divine drama of the advent. It is conceivable that some parents and grandparents would try to have their offspring be born at the right time, in the right place, and with the right name. Many mockers would advance their claims at the designated date. Countless impostors and false prophets would emerge at the appointed time. Many sincere seekers of truth would be bewildered as they would not know to whom they should turn. Prophecies would lose their guiding power and indeed serve the opposite purpose for which they are intended.

We see an application of this same principle in the first advent of Christ. If the Jews knew what was meant by "king," some of them would try to compete with Jesus in fulfilling the Old Testament prophecies. Again the guiding power of those prophecies would diminish.

People were sure—and still are—that if Christ ever came, it would be "on" the clouds. They knew that His miraculous descent from heaven was a feat no one else could copy. Therefore, when the appointed Hour dawned, no one except a humble young Man in Persia—the Báb—claimed to be the

Promised One of all ages, even though hundreds of thousands were well aware of the date. Once the date passed, the Mystery gradually became known. After the appointed year, deceivers could not misuse the time prophecies. For there was—and there will always be—only one 1844 A.D.

This is an astonishing achievement in God's kingdom, one that a human mind never could have conceived. In each of the two advents, two monumental goals were attained by one word. In the first advent, that word was "king"; in the second, that word was "heaven." By each of them, not only did God protect the prophecies from misuse, He tested the hearts of His servants as well. In the first advent, that word loomed so large as to conceal Jesus, the light of the world, from the literal-minded Jews. Today another magical word is presenting Christians with a challenge of a similar magnitude.

9

Cause Thy Face to Shine
Upon Thy Sanctuary

Daniel 9:17

Time Prophecies of the
First Advent

The most remarkable time prophecy in the Bible is found in the Book of Daniel. It is a prophecy without peer: it predicts the times of both the first and second advents of Christ, under the same continuing vision. In order to study the relevance of this vision to the time of the second advent, we need to study its fulfillment by the first.

The Jews have been blessed with a succession of prophets who have enriched their Scriptures with an abundance of prophecies, among them those that point to the advent of their Redeemer, Jesus. It seems improbable that they would be informed by their prophets of some of the most detailed accounts of future events, yet be denied the knowledge of the most critical event in their history: the time of the advent of their Messiah:

> Surely the Sovereign Lord does nothing without revealing his plan to his servants the prophets.   Amos 3:7 NIV

The Scriptures indicate that Jesus often appealed to Old Testament prophecies to substantiate His claim:

> Then he [Jesus] began with Moses and all the prophets, and explained to them [the Jews] the passages which referred to himself in every part of the scriptures.
>   Luke 24:27 NEB

> If you believed Moses, you would believe me, for he wrote about me.   Christ (John 5:46 NIV)

> These are the Scriptures that testify about me, yet you refuse to come to me to have life. Christ (John 5:39-40 NIV)
>   See also Acts 28:23

Daniel's time prophecy of the first advent stands out clearly among all those pointing to the advent of Christ. Dr. and Mrs. Guinness in their book on chronological prophecy describe it as:

> ...a prophecy which is perhaps more fundamental than any other in the Bible, as evidence that Jesus of Nazareth was the promised Messiah of Israel.[1]

Dr. Gleason Archer in *Encyclopedia of Bible Difficulties* writes:

> The prophecy of the Seventy Weeks in Daniel 9:24-27 is one of the most remarkable long-range predictions in the entire Bible. It is by all odds one of the most widely discussed by students and scholars of every persuasion within the spectrum of the Christian church. And yet when it is carefully examined in the light of all the relevant data

of history and the information available from other parts of Scriptures, it is quite clearly an accurate prediction of the time of Christ's coming advent and a preview of the thrilling final act of the drama of human history before that advent.[2]

Only God could have predicted the coming of His Son with such amazing precision; it defies all rationalistic explanation.[3]

Declaring Daniel's prophecy a clear evidence of the validity of Jesus' claim is not new. Its relevance to the promised Messiah of the people of Israel has been verified by countless Christian scholars and writers, some of them as classic as Sir Isaac Newton, others as contemporary as Hal Lindsey.

In the first half of the 19th century, a conference was held in New York city between Christian and Jewish leaders and scholars. One of the prophecies presented by Christians in that conference to prove that Christ was indeed the expected Savior of the people of Israel was Daniel's time prophecy. According to William Miller, the Christian scholars "explained the 70 weeks...and asked the Jews how they could avoid the conclusion." The Jewish leaders and scholars could not refute their argument.[4]

Daniel's Prophecy of 69 Weeks

The time prophecy of the first advent is revealed in a vision to Daniel in four consecutive verses (9:24-27). Let us begin with verse 25:

> Know therefore and understand, that from the going forth of the commandment to restore and to build Jerusalem unto the Messiah the Prince shall be seven weeks, and three score and two weeks $[7 + 62 = 69]$: the street shall be built again, and the wall, even in troublous times.✢

✢ The figures in the first part of this chapter are based on the traditional dates of the ministry and crucifixion of Jesus; the figures in the latter part on the revised dates.

Since **Messiah** and **Christ** have the same meaning (anointed), we could reword the prophecy this way: "From the time the commandment concerning the restoration and rebuilding of Jerusalem is issued until Christ the Prince, there shall be 7 weeks and 62 weeks" (a total of 69). Why is 69 *not* given as a whole number, but divided into parts? This is done for a definite purpose, to be examined later. **Prince** is also one of Christ's titles:

> Him hath God exalted...to be a Prince and a Savior...
>
> Acts 5:31

To decode Daniel's vision, we need to resolve two questions:

- The length of the 69 prophetic weeks.
- Their starting point.

How long is 69 prophetic weeks? Sixty-nine weeks equals 483 days, which in Biblical prophecies equals 483 years, for in the Scriptures each "prophetic day" equals a year:

> I have appointed thee each day for a year.   Ezekiel 4:6
> See also Num. 14:34; Gen. 29:27-28

As Adam Clarke, a noted scholar states:

> The Jews had Sabbatical years, Lev. xxv: 8, by which their years were divided into weeks of years...each week containing seven years.[5]

> Count off seven sabbaths of years—seven times seven years—so that the seven sabbaths of years amount to a period of forty-nine years.   Leviticus 25:8 NIV

Dr. Gleason Archer in *Encyclopedia of Bible Difficulties* writes:

> The word for week is "sabu," which is derived from "seba," the word for "seven"...There is no doubt that in this case we are presented with seventy sevens of years rather than days. This leads to a total of 490 years.[6]

William Biederwolf in *The Second Coming Bible Commentary* writes:

It is conceded by all [commentators] that these are weeks of years...[7]

Leroy Froom, a Christian writer, points out that the principle of "weeks of years" was "discerned by the Jews, at least by the third century B.C.E. [before Common, or Christian, Era].[8] He then adds:

This principle of a day for a year was tenaciously held by the Jews in the succeeding centuries, and came to be well-nigh universally accepted by Christian expositors.[9]

Froom provides many historical references showing the universal application of "the year-day principle" to time prophecies by Bible scholars since biblical times. See *The Prophetic Faith of Our Fathers*, Volume 4, pp. 204-207.

In translating the preceding prophecy from Daniel, *The Amplified Bible* actually adds the word **years** to the verse, but in brackets:

Know therefore and understand that from the going forth of the commandment to restore and to build Jerusalem until [the coming of] the anointed one, a prince, shall be seven weeks [of years], and sixty-two weeks [of years]...

Daniel 9:25 AB

The second question: when is the starting point for the prophecy? The starting point corresponds to the time when the decree for the rebuilding of Jerusalem was issued. But since four such decrees were issued, we must first determine which of the four was meant by Daniel's prophecy. Uriah Smith, a Christian scholar, in his commentary on the book of Daniel introduces the four decrees:

• First decree: issued 536 B.C. by Cyrus. (Ez. 1:1-4).

• Second decree: issued 519 B.C. by Darius. (Ez. 6:1-12).

• Third decree: issued 457 B.C. by Artaxerexes. (Ez. 7).

• Fourth decree: issued 444 B.C. by Artaxerexes. (Neh. 2).[10]

Concerning Daniel's prophecy of 69 weeks, Uriah Smith states:

> The command [referred to in the prophecy] was to include more than mere building. There was to be restoration; by which we must understand all the forms and regulations of civil, political, and judicial society. When did such a command go forth?[11]

Then he explains that the first two decrees:

> ...had reference principally to the restoration of the temple and the temple-worship of the Jews, and not to the restoration of their civil state and polity, all of which must be included in the expression, "to *restore* and build Jerusalem." These made a commencement of the work. They were preliminary to what was afterward accomplished. But of themselves they are altogether insufficient...[12]

Uriah Smith then presents several reasons to show that the edict intended by the prophecy was the third, granted to Ezra; not the fourth, granted to Nehemiah. (The third and the fourth edicts were issued by the same king within the span of 13 years.) These are two of the reasons he cites:

- The grant to Nehemiah cannot be called a decree. It was necessary that a Persian decree should be put in writing, and signed by the king (Dan. 6:8). Such was the document given to Ezra; but Nehemiah had nothing of the kind, his commission being only verbal...

- There was nothing granted to Nehemiah, which was not embraced in the decree to Ezra; while the latter had all the forms and conditions of a decree, and was vastly more ample in its provisions.[13]

George Vandeman, a noted Christian writer and orator states:

> This date [457] has been confirmed by modern discoveries in archaeology, a fact recognized by many Bible scholars. The widely-acclaimed *Encyclopedia of Bible Difficulties*,

for example, endorses the year 457 B.C. as the date for the fulfillment of Daniel 9.[14]

Zondervan NIV Bible Commentary also confirms 457 as the most likely date:

> The most likely fulfillment is the decree issued to Ezra in the seventh year of Artaxerxes I (i.e., 457 B.C.)...[15]

Aside from the reasons given, we can find a special clue in the wording of the prophecy, pointing to the intended edict. The restoration and building of Jerusalem, as the result of the third edict, lasted 49 years,* or seven weeks of years. We find the prophetic figure pointing to the advent of Jesus to be divided in such a way as to correspond to this period:

> Know therefore and understand, that from the going forth of the commandment to restore and to build Jerusalem unto the Messiah the Prince shall be seven weeks [49 years], and threescore and two weeks [434 years]...

We may ask: why was the prophetic figure divided, and at the precise point? Now if we take as the starting point the time when the third decree was issued, we find that the promised period of 69 weeks or 483 years culminates in the year 27 A.D., which corresponds to about the beginning of the last prophetic week (seven years) of Christ's life. Here are the calculations:

457 B.C. The third decree is issued

457 + 26 = 483 years

1 A.D. = 27 A.D.

Twenty-six years from 1 A.D. brings us to the year 27, and not 26 A.D. For details, refer to the next chapter.

---

* See *Some Answered Questions*, 1981 ed., p. 41, *Encyclopedia of Bible Difficulties*, 1982 ed., p. 291, and *The Second Coming Bible Commentary*, p. 219.

The Prophecy of 70 Weeks

In addition to the 69 weeks already discussed, Daniel's vision contains other figures:

> Seventy weeks are determined upon thy people and upon thy holy city, to finish the transgression, and to make an end of sins, and to make reconciliation for iniquity, and to bring in everlasting righteousness, and to seal up the vision and prophecy, and to anoint the most Holy.
>
> Daniel 9:24

The preceding prophecy provides us with two definitive clues: *to anoint*, and *the most Holy*. The word *Christ* comes from the Greek *christos*, meaning *anointed* (the Anointed One). Similarly, *Messiah* in Hebrew means *anointed*. Thus this prophecy not only refers to the date of the advent of Jesus, but also to His title *Christ*. Jesus fulfilled the prophecy both literally when He was baptized (anointed) by water, and symbolically when baptized by the Holy Spirit. Moreover, He confirmed the fulfillment of the preceding prophecy in His own advent: "The spirit of the Lord is upon me because He has anointed me..." (Luke 4:18 NEB; Isaiah 61:1-2).

Still another clue: in Daniel's prophecy, the *anointed One* is also called *the most Holy*. Who else but the divine Redeemer is deserving of such an exalted title and honor?

What do the words *seal up* imply? A seal is a sign of confirmation or approval. Two of the modern translations of the Bible use other substitutes for this word. *The New American Bible* uses *ratify*, *the Modern Language Bible* uses *confirm*. The following verse further clarifies the point: "He that hath received his testimony hath set to his seal that God is true" (John 3:33).

The prophecy of 69 weeks points to the beginning of the time of redemption; the prophecy of 70 weeks designates the end of that opportunity. The prophecy of 70 weeks reminds

Daniel's people (called "thy people") that God allows them a specific period of grace during which they must put an end to their transgressions, make amends for their wrongs, and thus be able to attain everlasting righteousness. They were given a designated amount of time to prove themselves by "sealing up the vision," that is, by accepting its message. The sign of acceptance was the anointing of the One called the most Holy, entitled the Messiah, the Christ, or the Anointed One.

According to the prophecy of 70 weeks and several others expressing the same theme, the Jews could prevent self-punishment by avoiding "the abominable acts or transgressions that cause desolation." They could attain peace and prosperity by following God's commandments and accepting their promised Savior. The allotted time was to continue until the advent of the Messiah; His appearance at the appointed time would constitute the crowning of all the hopes and aspirations of the chosen people. If they failed to take advantage of the opportunity accorded them, they would have to face the consequences. The allotted time reached its last moment when Christ was crucified.

Now, if we again take as the starting point of the prophecy the time when the third decree was issued, we find the full realization of the prophecy in Christ's crucifixion, believed to have occurred in the 33rd year of His life, corresponding to 34 A.D. For according to verse 24, the time allotted to the Jews was to last seventy prophetic weeks or 490 years. And this is what happened; after about 490 years, Christ was crucified:

457 B.C.   457   +   33 = 490 years

The third decree is issued   ⟵⟶   1 A.D. ⟵⟶

= 34 A.D.
Approximate date of crucifixion

Here is how William Miller discovered the beginning point of Daniel's prophecy. He knew that Christ was crucified at age 33. He subtracted 33 from 490, and got 457. To his surprise, he found that 457 B.C. was the exact year in which a decree for the rebuilding of Jerusalem has been issued.

Both dates (69 and 70), however interpreted, bring us remarkably to the exact time of Christ—the last prophetic week or seven years of His life. If we do *not* acknowledge the fulfillment of Daniel's prophecy in the advent of Jesus, then:

- We must search for someone other than the Son of God who would *deserve* the unsurpassed and exalted title of *the Most Holy* as well as the honor of being called *the Anointed* or *the Messiah*.

- We must search for a figure who laid claim to these titles. The time of the coming of this figure must have been either less than two years (490 days) after the edict for the rebuilding of Jerusalem was issued, or at the exact time of the advent of Christ. Since such a figure does not exist, denying the relevance of this prophecy to Jesus undermines the very purpose and meaning of Daniel's vision.

The remaining verses of Daniel's time prophecies present us with a further indication of their fulfillment in the advent of Jesus. They predict that the last, or 70th, week will be very special. During that week the Messiah will confirm God's covenant with His people. "And he [the Messiah] shall confirm the covenant with many for one week" (Daniel 9:27).

Confirming God's Covenant With People

What is God's covenant? It consists of a solemn agreement between God and humanity. It describes what the Creator does for people, and what they must do in return. A Biblical term that shares an identical meaning with *covenant* is *testament*. Thus the New Testament was a renewal of God's Old Testament or Covenant with His people. In the Bible we can find many references to a covenant between God and His creation.

> I have set my rainbow in the clouds, and it will be the sign of the covenant between me and the earth. Whenever I bring clouds over the earth and the rainbow appears in the clouds, I will remember my covenant between me and you and all living creatures of every kind.
>
> Genesis 9:13-15 NIV

One term of God's covenant is that He will always provide His children with guidance:

> He sent and redeemed his people; he decreed that his covenant should always endure. Psalms 111:9 NEB

Since humans evolve, the guidance that they need must also evolve. In the Old Testament, the people of Israel were told that God would renew His old covenant with them:

> Behold, the days come, saith the Lord, that I will make a new covenant with the house of Israel... Jeremiah 31:31

The coming of Jesus was based on a covenant, confirmed by an oath; this is called the Divine covenant.

> The Lord swore to David an oath which he will not break: 'A prince of your own line will I set upon your throne.'
>
> Psalms 132:11 NEB

When a new Messenger comes, He always mediates a *new* covenant:

> ...Jesus the mediator of a new covenant...
>
> Hebrews 12:24 NIV

What happens when a *new* covenant or testament goes into effect?

> By calling this covenant [New Testament] "new," he [Jesus] has made the first one obsolete... Hebrews 8:13 NIV

What became obsolete were nonessential laws and rituals, such as forbidden foods, burial rites, or the ritual of making sacrifices at the altar. Spiritual laws—love, forgiveness, and honesty—never become obsolete.

Another reason for renewing the covenant is the increasing capacity and curiosity of humans for new knowledge. Our Creator's response to our increased capacity is called: the progressive revelation of truth. God in His wisdom selects for us the spiritual food we can best digest and assimilate.

> I gave you milk, not solid food, for you were not yet ready for it.   I Corinthians 3:2 NIV

Jesus knew far more than He revealed, and He promised that more knowledge and truth would be disclosed in the future:

> I have much more to say to you, more than you can now bear. But when he, the Spirit of truth, comes, he will guide you into all truth.   John 16:12-13 NIV

The next prophecy also speaks of mysteries that will be unveiled:

> Therefore, judge nothing before the appointed time; wait till the Lord comes. He will bring to light what is hidden in darkness and will expose the motives of men's hearts.
> I Corinthians 4:5 NIV
> See also Isa. 28:9-10

The preceding verses clearly point to a new covenant that will bring to light new truths.

A covenant, like a contract, has more than one side. The receivers of guidance are always expected to honor the terms of the agreement:

> Then he [Moses] took the book of covenant and read it aloud for all the people to hear. They said, 'We will obey, and do all that the Lord has said.'   Exodus 24:7 NEB
> See also Genesis 9:12-17; 17:1-14

Every Messenger and Redeemer promises and predicts the renewal of God's covenant in the future:

The Lord of the universe hath never raised up a prophet nor hath He sent down a Book unless He hath established His covenant with all men, calling for their acceptance of the next Revelation and of the next Book...[16]   The Báb

Bahá'u'lláh asks us to be loyal to God's covenant:

...violate not the Covenant of God, nor break your pledge to Him.[17]   Bahá'u'lláh

We should now be able to decode Daniel's prophecy:

And he [the Messiah] shall confirm the covenant with many for one week...   Daniel 9:27

As we noted in verse 24, the people of Israel were given 70 weeks to "seal up" or "confirm" the vision. That pointed to *their* side of the covenant or contract. Verse 27 points to the other side. According to this verse, the last week of the 70 weeks is the interval during which the Messiah confirms or fulfills God's side of the covenant. (In reference to both sides of the covenant, words with similar meanings are used: "seal up," and "confirm.") And this is exactly what happened: during the last week, John the Baptist and Jesus appeared to fulfill or confirm God's side of the covenant. Since John the Baptist was Jesus' forerunner, He confirmed the covenant during the *first* part of the 70th week. The second part of the verse declares the middle of the 70th week to be a critical juncture:

...and in the midst of the week he [the Messiah] shall cause the sacrifice and the oblation [offering] to cease...
                                              Daniel 9:27

The Symbolism of Sacrifice and Oblation

What do the prophetic words "causing the sacrifice and oblation [offering] to cease" signify? The rise of a Redeemer signals the advent of a new Age in the spiritual evolution of humanity. It constitutes the dawning of a new dispensation with a new Sun (Redeemer) through whose radiance the stars (temporary laws, rites, and rituals) of the previous Faith disappear, to rise again in a new cycle, and with a new splendor.

Among the Jews, the ceremonies of the sanctuary constituted the basis of all their rituals. They provided a fitting symbol to signal the dawning of a new age and the need for a new covenant. For although every divine Teacher reaffirms the moral-spiritual laws (love, honesty, etc.) of previous Teachers, He alters some of their temporary laws and practices (ways or days of worship, forbidden foods, baptism, etc.). Thus the advent of Jesus signaled the abrogation of previous rites and rituals, including the making of sacrifices or offerings in the sanctuary.

The prophecy indicated that "in the midst of the week" the Messiah "shall cause the sacrifice and oblation to cease." The advent of Jesus during the last week (the 70th week) caused the Jewish ceremonial practices to lose their luster, to become empty rituals.

Although Jesus by His advent symbolically terminated *the sacrifice and oblation*, the literal fulfillment of the prophecy did not come until sometime later—about 36 years after His crucifixion when the Romans attacked and destroyed the temple. The ceremonies of the sanctuary seemingly continued, but as mere enactments deprived of the spirit.

There is as yet another meaning to the symbol of "causing the sacrifice and oblation to cease." The perfect sacrifice made by the Messiah (His crucifixion) eliminated the need of making other sacrifices at the altar. (See Heb. 10:12-14.)

Thus we can see that the last, or 70th week, was a unique interval, replete with many momentous events: first the reaffirmation and fulfillment of God's covenant; second the offering of an opportunity to the people of Israel to end their transgression, to attain everlasting righteousness and to anoint or consecrate their Savior; third the abrogation of Jewish rituals in the midst of the week (signaling the birth of a new Day); and finally, at the end of the week, the crucifixion of Jesus, the literal and perfect sacrifice of the Messiah.

The crucifixion of Jesus was the consummation of the prophecy, an event that signaled the termination of the opportunity granted to Daniel's people, their last chance to turn to God's gift of guidance, to acknowledge the Anointed One.

When Christ uttered His last words on the cross: "It is finished" (John 19:30), He meant not only the closing of His earthly life and the fulfillment of His Mission, but also the end of opportunity for those who had awaited and anticipated His advent, but failed to awaken from their fantasies. The words declared the culmination of the 70th week. For Jesus, death was not the end, but the beginning of a far more abundant life in paradise. What was "finished" was not His life, but the opportunity for Daniel's people.

Other Time prophecies of the First Advent

Daniel's vision of 69-70 weeks contains two other closely interrelated predictions. In verse 26, immediately after referring to the martyrdom of the Messiah, the vision points to "the people of the prince" who shall come and destroy the city and the sanctuary. Following this the vision describes further wars and desolations pouring upon the holy city.

Although the allotted time assigned to the people of Israel expired at the end of the last or 70th week, the outward consequences of their denial did not immediately ensue. They received further respite to end "their transgressions and to bring everlasting righteousness upon themselves." But they refused, and because of this, desolations poured upon them one after the other. The first desolation was wrought by the forces of Titus (70 A.D.) and then later by Hadrian (125

A. D.). They invaded Jerusalem and destroyed the sanctuary, literally fulfilling Daniel's prophecy by putting an end to the ritual of oblation or daily sacrifice.

The last two verses of Daniel's vision indicate that wars and desolations will continue until the end of the age. For He who revealed the prophecy to Daniel knew that the Jews would not welcome their Savior and therefore would have to face the consequences. Such a dire and dark destiny for the people of Israel was also distinctly foretold by Moses.

> But if you will not listen to me and...you reject my decrees...I will bring upon you sudden terror...If after all this you will not listen to me, I will punish you for your sins seven times over. I will break down your stubborn pride...I will turn your cities into ruins and lay waste your sanctuaries...I will scatter you among the nations...
>
> Leviticus 26:14-33 NIV

The same destiny for the people of Israel was also foretold by Jesus:

> They will fall by the sword and will be taken as prisoners to all the nations. Jerusalem will be trampled on by the Gentiles until the times of the Gentiles are fulfilled.
>
> Luke 21:24 NIV

Time Prophecies of the First Advent Based on the Revised Dates

The calculations offered so far on Daniel's vision of 69-70 weeks are based on the conventional dates of the birth, ministry, and crucifixion of Jesus. The exact time of the advent is believed to have been a few years earlier than commonly assumed, but has not been definitely determined. Let us see how the vision proves itself against the revised or corrected dates.

The variations brought about by revised dates do not in any way diminish the accuracy of the prophecy. The reason is that Daniel's prophetic dates are stated in units of "seven-year-periods" (weeks), rather than years. Hence even if we set the date of the birth, ministry, and crucifixion a few years earlier than conventionally assumed, the predictions are still valid because they undoubtedly correspond to the last seven years (week) of Jesus' life.

If we base our calculations, for instance, on one of the most commonly accepted dates of birth and crucifixion, namely, 4 B.C. and 29* A.D., we find the beginning of Jesus' ministry to have coincided with 26 A.D.✝ (at age 30), nearly three years before the crucifixion. Now if we add 457 (the starting point of the 69-week period) to 26, we get the exact predicted figure of 483, equaling precisely 69 weeks:

$$457 + 26 = 483$$
$$69 \times 7 = 483$$

The above calculation places the crucifixion somewhere within the 70th week, exactly as foretold.

The relationships between the figures resulting from Daniel's prophecy of 69-70 weeks appear quite astounding. For if we base our calculations on *conventional* dates, the prophecy of 70 weeks brings us to the exact year of crucifixion and the exact week (seven-year period) of the ministry. But, if we base our calculations on the *revised* dates, the prophecy of 69 weeks brings us to the exact beginning point of the ministry and the exact week (seven-year period) of the crucifixion.

This may be one reason the prophecies, in this instance, are stated in units of weeks rather than days. Had they **not** been stated in week intervals, they could have confused those unaware of the revised dates. For they could not have seen the exact fulfillment of the prophecy of 69 weeks.

---

* Although not as yet settled, 4 B.C. and 29 A.D. are among the dates most commonly confirmed by the scholars.

✝ *Encyclopedia Britannica* sets the date at 26 or 27 A.D.

The Prophecy of 62 Weeks

So far, Daniel's prophetic dates seem to have corresponded with the events of the advent of the Messiah with marvelous precision. But Daniel, in addition to 69 and 70 weeks, refers also to another prophetic figure:

> And after threescore and two weeks [62 weeks] shall Messiah be cut off...   Daniel 9:26

The verse states that after 62 weeks, the Messiah's physical connection with the world shall be cut off (He shall be crucified). The following prophecy from Isaiah links the meaning of *cut off* to *death*:

> ...how he was cut off from the world of living men, stricken to the death for my people's transgression?
> Isaiah 53:8 NEB

The relationship between the prophecy of 62 weeks and the previous ones (69-70 weeks) appears quite puzzling. The figures 69 and 70 work hand in hand with remarkable precision. What about the figure of 62? 'Abdu'l-Bahá explains:

> The second period, which is found in the twenty-sixth verse, means that after the termination of the rebuilding of Jerusalem until the ascension of Christ, there will be sixty-two weeks: the seven weeks are the duration of the rebuilding of Jerusalem, which took forty-nine years. When you add these seven weeks to the sixty-two weeks, it makes sixty-nine weeks, and in the last week (69-70) the ascension of Christ took place. These seventy weeks are thus completed, and there is no contradiction.[18]

In other words, the first two verses refer to the beginning date of the construction of the sanctuary, the last one to the termination date of the construction. If viewed this way, verse 27 confirms both of the preceding verses (25 and 26), and as 'Abdu'l-Bahá states, no contradiction arises. For, as the prophecy foretold, after the termination of 69 weeks (namely in the 70th week) the Messiah's earthly connection with the world was cut off.

We can find, with a little scrutiny, a clue in verse 26 confirming the accuracy of this interpretation. In verse 26, the figure 69 is given in two parts (62 and 7). This implies that it is a composite figure pointing to two separate events or facts; otherwise, one might ask, why was it given in two segments, and divided at that precise point?

Still another way to decode the mysterious use of 62 in Daniel's vision is to see it in its relationship to, and in the context of, the previous verse:

Verse 25:

> Know therefore and understand, that from the going forth of the commandment to restore and to build Jerusalem unto the Messiah the Prince shall be seven weeks, and threescore and two weeks...

Verse 26:

> After threescore and two weeks shall Messiah be cut off...

What verse 26 is communicating is that after the designated period of ***threescore and two weeks*** (referred to before) has passed, the Messiah will be crucified. In other words, the figure 62 (threescore and two) in verse 26 should not be regarded as standing alone. It is the repetition of the figure 62 in the preceding verse, which itself is assumed to start after the termination of a 49-year (seven weeks) period. From this perspective, all the segments of the vision stand in perfect accord not only with each other but with the life of the Messiah (Jesus) as well.

If we add "the" before the phrase "threescore and two weeks" in verse 25, the meaning becomes clearer. Let us review these two verses as translated in *New American Standard*, with the added ***the***:

So you are to know and discern that from the issuing of a decree to restore and rebuild Jerusalem until Messiah the Prince there will be seven weeks and sixty-two weeks. Then after the sixty-two weeks the Messiah will be cut off.

The Amplified Bible uses a similar translation:

And after the sixty-two weeks [of years] shall the anointed one be cut off *or* killed...[brackets as in source].

The Coded Language of Prophecy

The use of *seemingly* inconsistent figures and the selection of signs or clues for signaling the time of the first advent are quite instructive. They hold the key to the decoding of other prophecies, especially those pointing to the time of the *second* advent. They exemplify the intricacy and complexity of prophetic language. They indicate how the decoding of prophecies bears likeness to the solving of complicated puzzles or the deciphering of ancient and forgotten scripts, requiring both sustained efforts and a vision free and unhampered.

If it were in harmony with divine Wisdom, Daniel could have plainly revealed the precise moment of the advent of Christ in such a way that no one could have entertained the slightest doubt regarding the event and the circumstances surrounding it. But as can be noted from the language used in the vision, divine Wisdom ordained that the bare facts be clothed with signs and symbols. To review two of the major functions of symbolic language:

• The armor of symbolism safeguards one of God's choicest gifts to His children: their freedom of choice. Those unbound by selfish motives or desires can see through the mists of signs and figures, discerning with awe and wonder the beauty of the Beloved. Those bound by tradition stand veiled within their own desires, unable to rise above the clouds of suppositions. Thus if they choose to reject, they have the choice—the freedom—to bow to their own desires, a "reason" to exalt their own fantasies.

At the dawning of every dispensation, people are put to the test, are given a chance to "expose the motives of their hearts," thereby receiving their deserved and due share of divine bounties:

> Therefore, judge nothing before the appointed time; wait till the Lord comes. He will bring to light what is hidden in darkness and will expose the motives of men's hearts.   I Corinthians 4:5 NIV

- Symbolism protects the prophecies from misuse. Had the time of the advent of Jesus been plainly foretold, how many false saviors, one wonders, would have appeared on the exact appointed day and hour, all claiming divine inspiration; and how difficult it would have been for the sincere seekers to benefit from the time prophecies.

As we shall see later, with the exception of the "fruits" of the divine Messengers, namely their noble words and deeds and their transforming influence on the world, no proof can stand fully on its own. Prophecies play a supportive role; they reinforce other proofs. No one can be expected to acknowledge a Messenger by two or three prophetic dates that may have come true. Prophecies should always be viewed and judged in the context of the *whole* panorama of proofs.

Of course, the greater the number of prophetic dates given for an event, the greater their persuasive power. Had there been ten other references confirming the appointed time of the advent of Jesus, the strength of the prophecy would have been enormously increased.

If reason and justice dominated the human mind, the recognition of a Redeemer would be a simple task indeed. Because a Savior sent by God stands so far above others in so many ways that He cannot be misjudged or mistaken. But alas, the clouds of misjudgment often obscure the human vision. This is why the radiant Sun of righteousness—the glorious Son— in spite of His transcendent splendor, remained unrecognized save by a handful of sensitive and devoted disciples to whom He confided:

> For this people's heart has become calloused; they hardly hear with their ears, and they have closed their eyes. Otherwise they might see with their eyes, hear with their ears, understand with their hearts and turn, and I would heal them. But blessed are your eyes because they see, and your ears because they hear.   Matthew 13:15-16 NIV

10

Unto Two Thousand and Three Hundred Days

Daniel 8:14

Part I

The Date of the Second Advent in Relation to the First

The chief advantage of *time* prophecies over other prophecies is their precision. Numbers constitute clear or fixed entities, least subject to disagreement or misjudgment. For instance, it is prophesied that during the last days "evil shall abound." Such a sign simply points to the character of the age and cannot constitute a conclusive proof, for the rise and fall of evil often follows a curve—subtly, imperceptibly. To refute such evidence, the skeptic can argue that there has always been evil in the world, and there always will be. But numbers are not subject to such objections. They stand on their own. Furthermore, since time is a passing entity, once a certain date has passed, it can never return. Hence, an unfulfilled time prophecy will forever be unfulfilled. The skeptic cannot explain away the evidence by saying that there have always been 1844's, and there always will be.

We must first establish beyond any doubt that God made a firm covenant with His people that He would send His Chosen One, Christ, in 1844. If He did, then we face two alternatives: either He *did* send Him (even though undetected by the masses); or He failed to honor His covenant. It is clear and certain that God fulfills His covenant with us. Hence, the second alternative is impossible and we are left to consider only the first. That God fulfills His covenant is a fact clear and certain:

> Heaven and earth will pass away; my words will never pass away.   Christ (Luke 21:33 NEB)
> Also Mark 13:31

> He who is coming will come and will not delay.
> Hebrews 10:37 NIV

Once it is established that the advent is inevitable, our next step is to seek and identify those who have actually made the claim at the appointed time. If several are found to have made the claim, then we must test them by other proofs as well. And if, from among those tested, one is found to meet, in addition to the requirement of time, all the other proofs, then, to be true to God's covenant and our own convictions, we have no choice but to acknowledge Him.

Fortunately, our task is made easy for us. The only person known to have declared Himself the Promised One of all religions, at the appointed time of 1844, was the Inaugurator of the New Age, the Báb.

In addition to meeting the prophetic signs (the time, the place, etc.), Bahá'ís believe the Báb and Bahá'u'lláh have also met, to the fullest extent, all the other requirements as well. If this is true, then, denying their Word and their Mission means denying the Word of God and ultimately God Himself.

This chapter provides the first link in the long chain of time prophecies on the second advent. No one is asked to judge the Báb or Bahá'u'lláh on the basis of a few pieces of evidence. What matters ultimately is the *overall* picture of the prophetic Profile, consisting of hundreds of facts and figures that fit with marvelous precision.

Because of the number of codes involved in this and the next chapter, greater effort and patience are needed in examining their contents. An understanding of these codes provides a background for the points covered later in the text.

The Significance of Daniel's Time Prophecies

Among time prophecies, those of Daniel stand as the most remarkable in all history. First, they reveal not only the exact time of the first advent, but that of the second as well. Second, he is the only biblical prophet to predict the precise year of the coming of *both the Báb and Bahá'u'lláh*. Third, he reveals the time of the second advent in relation to two great religions—Christianity and Islam.

The focus of the present chapter is on a time prophecy linking the first advent to the second. Daniel's other prophecies, namely those based on the Islamic calendar and history, will be covered in succeeding chapters.

A distinct feature of Daniel's time prophecies of the second advent is their unusual frequency: they appoint the time not once, but at least five times. Hebrew Scriptures contain fewer references to the time of the advent of the Promised One of the people of Israel (Christ's first coming) than to the time of the advent of the Promised One of our age. Likewise the Book of Revelation contains fewer prophecies concerning the advent of Islam (next in time to Christianity) than the advent of the Bahá'í Revelation.

Such a practice holds true of all the other sacred Scriptures. They all seem to point to a particular Era, and a particular Messenger—a world Teacher and Savior who brings a new order and establishes an everlasting peace.

The Prophecy of 2300 Days

As we noted, many people expected the return of Christ to occur around 1844. Daniel's prophecy of "abomination of desolation" (specifically confirmed by Jesus) was their chief guide to the discovery of the date. Daniel's was the prophecy that initiated the Great Awakening of the mid-19th century, that moved tens of thousands around the globe to anticipate the return of their Redeemer. No prophetic message has ever stirred such excitement, displayed such power, and moved so many to set their hearts and hopes on heaven. No prophecy has ever resulted in such high anticipation and bitter disappointment, brought so many tears of joy and grief, inspired such visions of glory and instilled such fear of gloom in the hearts of so many. To know what convinced so many people—among them some of the most conservative and well-established members of society—to risk their livelihood, their careers, their reputation, and even their faith, is as fascinating as it is instructive in understanding history. This chapter demonstrates whether those who undertook a risk of such magnitude were stirred by fantasy or moved by reason; whether their hope was merely a fond dream or the fruit of years of scholarly and inspired search.

The Cleansing of the Sanctuary

The tabernacle symbolizes all that is holy in religion. It is the very heart and home of divine revelation, where the Spirit of God abides. The Jews were often told that by their transgressions they defiled and desecrated the seat of God's presence among His people:

> By your many sins and dishonest trade you have desecrated your sanctuaries.   Ezekiel 28:18 NIV

> Therefore as surely as I live, declares the Sovereign Lord, because you have defiled my sanctuary with all your vile images and detestable practices, I myself will withdraw my favor; I will not look on you with pity or spare you.
> Ezekiel 5:11 NIV
> See also 23:39

> Her priests profane the sanctuary and do violence to the law.   Zephaniah 3:4 NIV

The Jews were also told that at the appointed time their Redeemer would come to cleanse them of all their transgressions:

> I will make them one nation in the land upon the mountains of Israel...Neither shall they defile themselves any more... with any of their transgressions: but I will save them...and will cleanse them: so shall they be my people, and I will be their God...and they all shall have one shepherd...
> Ezekiel 37:22-24

Expressions such as "they shall be my people, and I will be their God" appear several times in both the Old and New Testaments in relation to the advent of the Redeemer of our time. The following prophecy, which relates to our time, indicates that God comes with His tabernacle to dwell among His people. He cleanses or restores His tabernacle by bringing a new one:

> And I heard a great voice out of heaven saying, Behold, the tabernacle of God is with men, and he will dwell with them, and they shall be his people, and God himself shall be with them, and be their God...the former things are passed away...I make all things new...   Revelation 21:3-5

...he who sits on the throne [the Redeemer] will spread his tent [tabernacle] over them [the believers]...the Lamb at the center of the throne will be their shepherd...

Revelation 7:15,17 NIV

When Shall These Things Be?

When Jesus was on the Mount of Olives, He spoke of the dark future, of the desolation of the temple or sanctuary. The disciples recognized their Master's intent, so they asked Him about both the time and the signs of His return. In response to their question, Jesus offered many instructions, among them two clues to the time of His advent. This chapter will examine one of them. Here is the question asked by the disciples:

And as he sat upon the mount of Olives, the disciples came unto him privately, saying, Tell us, when shall these things be? And what shall be the sign of thy coming, and of the end of the world [the end of the age]?   Matthew 24:3

To this Jesus responded:

When ye therefore shall see the abomination of desolation, spoken of by Daniel the prophet, stand in the holy place, (whoso readeth, let him understand)...   Matthew 24:15
See also Mark 13:14

There are two prophecies in Daniel that not only contain the key expression *the abomination of desolation* used by Jesus, but also a prophetic number. One of them is the prophecy of 1290 days (to be examined in Chapter 17); the other is the prophecy of 2300 days. The latter is the subject of this chapter:

Then I heard one saint speaking, and another saint said unto that certain saint which spake, How long shall be the vision concerning the daily sacrifice, and the transgression of desolation, to give both the sanctuary and the host to be trodden under foot? And he said unto me, Unto two thousand and three hundred days; then shall the sanctuary be cleansed...So he came near where I stood: and when he came, I was afraid, and fell upon my face: but he said unto me, Understand, O son of man: for at the time of the end shall be the vision.   Daniel 8:13, 14, 17

This prophecy is so critical we should see it in another translation:

Then I heard a holy one speaking, and another holy one said to him, "How long will it take for the vision to be fulfilled—the vision concerning the daily sacrifice, the rebellion that causes desolation, and the surrender of the sanctuary and of the host that will be trampled underfoot?" He said to me, "It will take 2300 evenings and mornings; then the sanctuary will be reconsecrated [cleansed *and* restored* AB]"..."Son of man," he said to me, "understand that the vision concerns the time of the end."

Daniel 8:13, 14, 17 NIV

The prophecy concerns the destiny of the people of Israel. By the time Daniel had his vision, the Jews had been suffering humiliation for many centuries. Their sanctuary, which symbolized their glory, had been made desolate. The loss of their glory came about because they broke their covenant with God; they transgressed against His Commandments.

The saint was concerned about the desecration and pollution of the sanctuary and wanted to know when they would end. He was also concerned about the adversities and humiliations the people of Israel had been enduring, and he wanted to give them some knowledge of their bright future. He, therefore, asked: how long will "the transgression that causes desolation" continue? "How long will this misfortune, this ruin, this abasement and degradation last?"[1] How long will the sanctuary (the symbol of God's presence among His people and of spiritual honor and survival of the Jews) and those who protect and serve it (the host) receive humiliation and "be trampled under foot?" The other saint responded that the desolation and pollution and dishonoring of the sanctuary will last for 2300 days. After that period, it will be cleansed and made holy.

The overall message of the prophecy is simple, yet it is concealed in codes. It contains these coded expressions:

- The daily sacrifice.
- The rebellion or transgression that causes desolation (abomination of desolation).
- The humiliation of the sanctuary and its host (being trampled under foot).
- 2300 days.
- The cleansing of the sanctuary.

Two of the preceding codes have already been deciphered. To repeat:

- The daily sacrifice symbolizes the setting and the dawning of religious cycles. (See the preceding chapter.)
- "Abomination of desolation" points to the abominable acts or transgressions performed by the people of Israel; acts that led to desolation of the sanctuary and the humiliation of its host (the Jews).

Three codes remain to be clarified: (1) the cleansing of the sanctuary, (2) the beginning point of 2300 days, and (3) the length of the 2300 days.

What does *the cleansing of the sanctuary* symbolize? This question is so critical, it will be examined later in great depth. Briefly, it symbolizes any or all of the following:

- Rebuilding and reviving the desolate centers of worship; purifying them from human innovations and deviations
- Restoring the divine power to the world
- Reviving and cleansing the very heart and home of religion
- Preparing the ground for the seat of God's Kingdom

• Cleansing the "temples" of the human heart
• Restoring spiritual health to the distressed spirit of humanity

Note this promise from Jesus:

> I will not leave you desolate; I will come to you.
>
> John 14:18 RSV

To simplify the interpretation of the vision, it seems best to study this symbol first quite briefly and then examine it in greater depth later in the chapter. As we noted, the prophecy of the first advent declared that the Jews' first opportunity to restore themselves spiritually would arrive after 69 prophetic weeks and terminate at the end of the 70th week (490 years). This knowledge was revealed in response to Daniel's prayer for the restoration of God's holy place, Jerusalem, and its sanctuary:

> ...O Lord, make thy face shine upon thy desolate sanctuary...and look upon our desolation and upon the city that bears thy name [Jerusalem]... Daniel 9:17-18 NEB

The segment of Daniel's vision we are now studying gave the people of Israel the tidings of a second opportunity, which would arrive after 2300 prophetic days (years). If they refused their first opportunity, the vision predicted, if they failed to anoint their first Messiah, they would have to wait for a second time. This knowledge was revealed after an angel expressed concern about the fate of the Holy Place:

> ...how long will...impiety cause desolation, and both the Holy Place and the fairest of all lands [Jerusalem] be given over to be trodden down? Daniel 8:13 NEB

As in the prophecy of the first advent, the response given concerned the restoration of the Holy Place:

> For two thousand three hundred evenings and mornings; then the Holy Place shall emerge victorious. Daniel 8:14 NEB

...then the sanctuary shall be cleansed and restored.

The Amplified Bible

In both parts of Daniel's vision, which deal with the first and second Advents, the beginning of the timetable given is linked to the physical restoration of Jerusalem, and its termination to its spiritual restoration. This was a key code through which the prophecy was concealed. Since *the cleansing of the sanctuary* plays perhaps the most critical role in the prophecy, it is explored in great depth in Appendix I. *It presents fifteen reasons, based on scriptural evidence, to prove conclusively that the phrase points to the coming of the expected Redeemer of the world.*

Next we should decode the date. What is the starting point of the prophecy? The starting point of the prophecy of 2300 days is the same as that of 69-70 weeks. Why? First, both of the prophetic figures, namely 69-70 weeks and 2300 days, are parts of the *same* continuing vision. (See the section entitled *The Similarities Between Daniel's Vision of the First and Second Advents*, later in this chapter.) Second, when Jesus referred the seekers to Daniel's vision of *abomination*, He said:

...whoso readeth, let him understand...   Matthew 24:15

If it were not possible to identify all the essential facts for the decoding of the vision, Jesus would not have made such a statement. Both the vision and Jesus' confirmation of the vision would have been totally useless. Third, we find hundreds of seekers and scholars from many cultures using the same starting point and arriving at almost the same conclusion. These seekers were so sure of their findings that even after they failed to find their Redeemer in the clouds, they still maintained that their calculations were correct. For instance, William Miller, the greatest figure in the Advent Movement wrote:

Were I to live my life over again, with the same evidence that I then had, to be honest with God and man I should have to do as I have done.[2]

Fourth, the prophecy of 2300 days is only one of at least 16 biblical prophecies (see chapters 11 through 17) pointing to the year 1844. Therefore, we have 15 others that confirm this one to the exact year.

As we noted in the preceding chapter, the beginning of the time period for Daniel's vision dates back to 457 B.C., when the third edict for the rebuilding of Jerusalem was issued. That figure was the beginning point for determining the time of the first advent. To discover the intended date of the second advent we need to find two intervals of time on both sides of 1 A.D. that would add up to 2300. We already know the interval that precedes the birth of Jesus, namely, 457. The other figure is 1843.

$$457 + 1843 = 2300$$

Since the Christian calendar began with the year one instead of zero, whenever we move from B.C. to A.D., we need to make a correction, otherwise we will have one uncounted extra year. An example will clarify the point. When a baby is born, we do not say he is one year old. Yet this is exactly what happened to Christianity. It was considered one year old at its birth. Thus 1844 A.D., when the Báb declared His Mission, was *in fact* 1843 A.D.!

Daniel's vision points to two time intervals:

- 69-70 weeks, which ended with the crucifixion of Jesus.
- 2300 days, which ended in 1844.

Its numerical message is that there will be two prophetic periods: a long stretch of time (2300 years), and a short one (490 years), which would be "determined" or cut off from the 2300 years. According to a Christian source:

The Hebrew word for determined is "chathak" and literally means "cut out" or "marked off"...Therefore, what God is saying in Dan. 9:24 is that 70 weeks of time or 490 years is cut out or marked off for the Jewish people until the beginning of the Millennium.[3]*

The first part of the 2300-year period (which was to last 490 years) ended in 34 A.D., the conventional date when Christ was crucified at the age of 33.✣ (Thirty-three years beyond 1 A.D. brings us to 34 A.D.) The second part of the 2300-year period should therefore begin in 34 A.D. and continue for 1810 more years, which would bring us to 1844 A.D. That was the second appointed time for the restoration of the sanctuary, when the expected Savior was promised to come.

Tables I and II portray the prophecies predicting the dates of Christ's first and second comings together.

To summarize the calculations:

- The duration of both prophetic periods = 2300 years.

- The duration of the first prophetic period = 70 prophetic weeks, or 490 years (ending in 34 A.D.).

- The duration of the second prophetic period (or the remainder of 2300 years) = 2300 - 490 = 1810.

- The year in which the 2300-year period terminated = 1810 + 34 = 1844.

If we use the prophecy of 69 weeks, we will come once again to the same conclusion:

- The duration of the first prophetic period = 69 prophetic weeks, or 483 years (ending in 27 A.D.).

---

* Leroy Froom writes: "the 70 weeks are the first segment of the 2300 days. And Gabriel was instructed to make plain *the vision*, from which the 70 weeks were determined, or *cut off*. No Hebrew scholar has denied it; the best scholars admit it should read 'cut off'—the remaining years extending beyond the 490." *The Prophetic Faith of Our Fathers*, Vol. 4, p. 873.

✣ The dates of the birth and crucifixion of Christ do not affect the length of time between 457 B.C. and 1844 A.D. More about this later.

- The duration of the second prophetic period (or the remainder of 2300 years) = 2300 - 483 = 1817.

- The year in which the 2300-year period terminated =
  1817 + 27 = 1844 A.D.

Table I

70 Weeks and 2300 Days

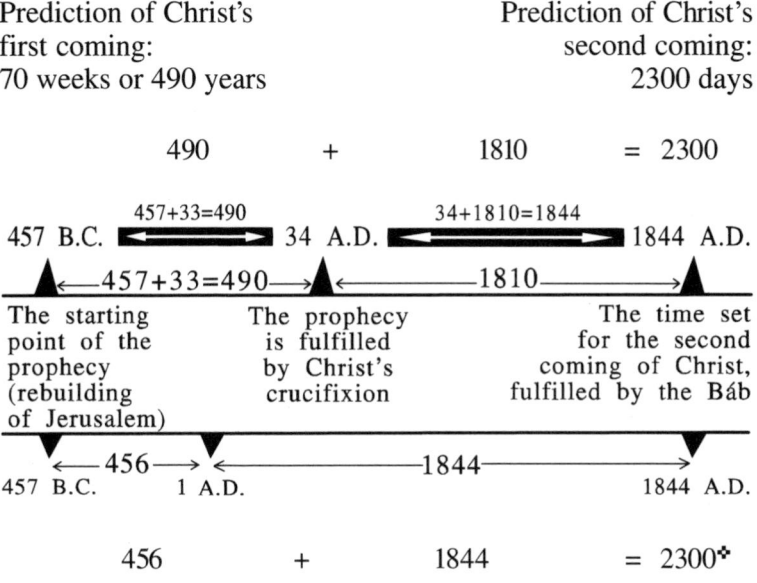

Prediction of Christ's first coming: 70 weeks or 490 years

Prediction of Christ's second coming: 2300 days

| 490 | + | 1810 | = 2300 |

457+33=490

34+1810=1844

457 B.C. ◄════► 34 A.D. ◄════► 1844 A.D.

◄—457+33=490—► ◄————1810————►

| The starting point of the prophecy (rebuilding of Jerusalem) | The prophecy is fulfilled by Christ's crucifixion | The time set for the second coming of Christ, fulfilled by the Báb |

◄—456—► ◄————————1844————————►

457 B.C.   1 A.D.   1844 A.D.

| 456 | + | 1844 | = 2300✣ |

✣ 2300 years beyond 457 B.C. brings us to 1844 A.D., and not 1843.

Table II

69 Weeks and 2300 Days

The first prophetic period: the length of time between the rebuilding of Jerusalem and the beginning of Christ's first advent: 69 weeks or 483 years

The second prophetic period: the length of time between the first and second advents

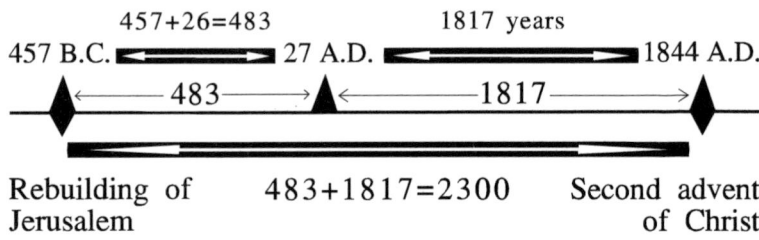

Rebuilding of Jerusalem   483+1817=2300   Second advent of Christ

The length of time between the rebuilding of Jerusalem and the second coming of Christ: 2300 years

The figure 1817 coincides with the year in which Bahá'u'lláh was born; in other words, the length of time between the first advent and second advent of Christ equals the birth-date of Bahá'u'lláh.

Beyond the date, the prophecy offers two other clues. First, the edict for rebuilding the Holy City was issued in Persia, the same country where 2300 years later the promised Redeemer was to appear. Second, Daniel received his vision of 2300 days in Elam, an area near Shíráz, the city in which the Báb was born and then declared His Mission in the appointed year (1844)—precisely 2300 years after the issuing of the third edict to rebuild the Holy City. Here is the part of Daniel's vision where Elam is mentioned:

> ...while I was in Susa the capital city of the province of Elam, a vision appeared to me, Daniel, similar to my former vision.
>
> Daniel 8:1-2 NEB

Another prophecy designates Elam as the place where God's Throne—a symbol of His Kingdom—will be set:

> I will set my throne in Elam...
>
> Jeremiah 49:38

This verse links *throne* with *sanctuary*:

> A glorious throne [throne of glory, NEB], exalted from the beginning, is the place of our [God's] sanctuary.
>
> Jeremiah 17:12 NIV

And finally, the decree to rebuild Jerusalem was issued in the spring of 457 B.C., the same season in which the Báb declared His Mission (May 23). Once again we see how precisely the prophecy is fulfilled. For from the spring of 457 B.C. to the spring of 1844 A.D. there are exactly 2300 years.

Perhaps when Jesus used a parable to show that the seekers could tell *the season* of His return (Matt. 24:32), He enclosed a literal message in the parable. Both the Báb and Bahá'u'lláh declared their Mission in Spring, a time coinciding with the renewal of nature.

The Law of Double Fulfillment

Hal Lindsey, a widely-read Christian author, writes:

> A principle that's absolutely necessary to understand in interpreting prophecy is a law called "The law of double fulfillment." Simply stated, this involves any two or more predicted events widely separated in times as far as their fulfillment is concerned, but they are brought together within the scope of one prophecy. The first, *partial* fulfillment, becomes a further assurance of the second, more complete fulfillment.[4]

Uriah Smith, a Christian scholar, confirms the relevance of
the preceding principle to Daniel's prophecy:

> By the events given to transpire in the seventy weeks, the
> prophecy is tested. By this the application of the whole
> vision is determined. If the events of this period are
> accurately fulfilled, the prophecy is of God, and will all
> be accomplished; and if these seventy weeks are fulfilled
> as weeks of years, then the 2300 days of which these are
> a part, are so many years. Thus the events of the seventy
> weeks furnish a key to the whole vision.[5]

That was the key that inspired William Hales, a Christian
writer, to declare:

> ...there is no other number in the Bible, whose genuine-
> ness is better ascertained than that of 2300 days.[6]

That was the key that led the seekers in various parts of
the globe to discover the same date. In the words of Leroy
Froom:

> It was this grand clue—of the seventy weeks as the first
> segment of the 2300 years, cut off for the Jews and cli-
> maxing with the Messiah—that burst simultaneously upon
> the minds of men in Europe and America, and even in
> Asia and Africa. This was the great advance truth that led
> to the emphasis upon the 2300 years from 457 B.C. to
> A.D. 1843 or 1844 which we have surveyed. Clearer and
> clearer became the perception in the first four decades
> of the nineteenth century, until it reached its peak in
> America in the summer and autumn of 1844, contempo-
> raneously with the predicted time of the prophecy.[7]

That was the clue that convinced William Miller, the leader
of the Advent Movement in the West, of his discovery:

> Therefore the death of Christ would make Daniel's vision
> sure; for if a part of the vision should be exactly fulfilled,

as to time and manner, then the remainder of the vision would be accomplished in manner and time, as literally as the seventy weeks had been.[8]

And again:

I then begged the privilege, and do now, for any person to show me any failure of proof on this point, or where, possibly, according to Scripture, there may be a failure in the calculation I have made on this vision. I have not yet, by seventeen years study, been able to discover where I might fail.[9]

To Conclude

Daniel's prophetic dream of 2300 days is only one of at least 16 biblical prophecies designating the exact year of the second advent of Christ. Since it predicts both advents in the context of *the same* continuing vision, it occupies a position of preeminence among all the other time prophecies. Not only that, it receives Jesus' own seal of approval, for He directed His inquisitive disciples to this vision, admonishing them as well as other seekers to use discernment in unraveling its meaning:

...let the reader understand...   Matthew 24:15 NEB

...let the reader take notice *and* ponder *and* consider *and* heed [this]...   The Amplified Bible

For these reasons, it may be timely, even at such an early stage of our search into time prophecies, to pause and ponder. Would God in His infinite wisdom, only partially fulfill His covenant with us by sending His promised Redeemer at the *first* appointed time, but not at the *second*? After all the assurances that God gives us through His chosen one Daniel, with Jesus' own confirmation of the time predicted in the vision, and in spite of the undeniable fulfillment of one segment of the vision (that designates the time of the first advent and by its realization confirms the remaining segment), can we still doubt the divine words?

My covenant will I not break, nor alter the thing that is gone out of my lips.   Psalms 89:34

11

Unto Two Thousand and Three Hundred Days
Daniel 8:14

Part II

The Tarrying Time

The difference between 2300 and 457 is 1843. Therefore, it *appears* that Jesus should have come in 1843, and not 1844. But as mentioned, there is a problem with this calculation. The Christian calendar began with year one, instead of year zero. There never was a year zero. This caused a discrepancy of one year between the actual time intervals and the calendar. The calendar, as adopted, is one year ahead of time. Failure to take this point into account caused some seekers to set the date at 1843.

God in His infinite wisdom encouraged all seekers not to give up hope too soon. They were told that "even if it delays, wait for it:"

> Then the Lord made answer: Write down the vision, inscribe it on tablets, ready for a herald to carry it with speed; for there is still a vision for the appointed time. At the destined hour it will come in breathless haste, it will not fail. If it delays [seems to tarry NRSV], wait for it; for when it comes [there] will be no time to linger.
>
> Habakkuk 2:2-3 NEB

> So do not throw away your confidence; it will be richly rewarded. You need to persevere so that when you have done the will of God, you will receive what he has promised. For in just a very little while, "He who is coming will come and will not delay."   Hebrews 10:35-37 NIV

The Exact Time Never Revealed

God in His wisdom ordains that the exact time—the day or the hour—of the dawning of His revelations remains concealed. He clothes even the year of their appearance with mystery until its appointed time approaches. Jesus said that He was sent to proclaim "the acceptable year of the Lord" (Luke 4:18-19), yet He refrained from specifying the exact time:

> No one knows about that day or hour, not even the angels in heaven, nor the Son, but only the Father. Be on guard! Be alert! You do not know when that time will come. It's like a man going away: He leaves his house in charge of his servants, each with his assigned task, and tells the one at the door to keep watch. Therefore keep watch because you do not know when the owner of the house will come back—whether in the evening, or at midnight, or when the rooster crows, or at dawn. If he comes suddenly, do not let him find you sleeping. What I say to you, I say to everyone: 'Watch!'   Mark 13:32-37 NIV

From this verse alone the seekers in the mid-19th century should have discovered that the advent was not to be a literal descent from heaven. Otherwise, why would they need to stay awake? They would know anyway.

Another passage relevant to the present theme is this:

> So when they met together, they asked him, "Lord, are you at this time going to restore the kingdom to Israel?" He said to them: "It is not for you to know the times or dates the Father has set by his own authority. But you will receive power when the Holy Spirit comes on you..."
>
> Acts 1:6-8 NIV

Again we see Jesus declining to give more information than that which was already destined to be known. He stated that it served them no purpose to know the date of the advent, and that in due time the Holy Spirit would give the people the power to unseal the mystery.

We find the same rule followed in the Qur'án. The exact year (1844) of the return of Christ—as we shall see in Volume IV—is specified at least four times in the Qur'án. Yet when people asked about the time, they received an answer almost identical with that given by Jesus:

> They will ask thee of the Hour...Say [thus sayeth the Lord]: The knowledge of it is only with my Lord; none shall manifest it in its time but He; it is the burden of the Heavens and of the Earth...on a sudden will it come on you.
>
> Qur'án 7:186
> See also Qur'án 33:63*

The same rule also holds true in relation to the first advent of Christ. In that case, the question was even more complicated. For from Daniel's time prophecy alone even the

---

* Selections from the Qur'án are mostly from Rodwell's translation. Two other translations used are those of Yúsuf 'Alí, identified as "Y" and A. J. Arberry, identified as "A". The numbering of the verses of the Qur'án varies from translation to translation.

year of Jesus' advent could not be calculated with certainty.
People could have wondered: "Which of the last two decrees
should serve as the starting point of the prophecy?" (The first
two were already outdated.) Once again we see that the people
were given the time, but not the *exact* time.

Proclaiming the Year of the Lord

Those who believe that the knowledge of *the year* of the advent
of Christ is a well-kept secret, unknown and unknowable,
should ponder these points:

- Jesus said "no one knows about that day or hour" (Matt.
  24:36 NIV). He did *not* say that "No one *will* know," or
  that in due time "God *will not* inspire the wise to know."

- As we just noted (Acts 1:6-8), Jesus told His disciples that
  they did not need to know the date of the expected kingdom, but that in due time they *will* receive power to gain
  such a knowledge.

- Daniel confirmed the same fact by pointing to the unseal-
  ing of the Book in *the future*, namely at the time of the
  end (Daniel 12:4; 12:9; 8:26-27). Daniel received several
  time prophecies whose meaning he could not understand.
  He was then told that they will remain sealed until "the
  time of the end."

  The verse quoted earlier from the Qur'án (7:186) confirms
  both the Old and the New Testaments. When people asked
  about "the Hour," they were told "none shall manifest it
  in its time but He." And again:

  > To every prophecy is its set time, and bye-and-bye ye
  > shall know it!   Qur'án 6:66

- Just before saying that "no one knows about that day or
  hour," Jesus used an analogy (Matt. 24:32-33) to imply
  that from His prophecies (some of which point to the year
  of His return) the seekers will be able to discover "the
  season" of His return, even as they would detect the

approach of the summer from the new leaves. Like "day or hour," season is a time word, but it is less precise.

- If the date-prophecies were not to be unsealed *in due time*, what purpose would they serve? The chief purpose of prophecy is to prepare the seekers of truth.

- Jesus declared that He had come to preach the acceptable year of the Lord; "to proclaim the year of the Lord's favor" (Luke 4:19 NIV).

> Surely the Sovereign Lord does nothing without revealing his plan to his servants the prophets.   Amos 3:7 NIV
>
> ...behold, I have foretold you all things.
>
> Christ (Mark 13:23)

- Our purpose now is to prove that the advent *has* taken place. We are no longer referring to the future.

- We are asked not to "despise prophetic utterances, but bring them all to the test" (I Thess. 5:20-21 NEB). To ignore the time prophecies is to despise them.

- The date of the advent forms only a part of the proofs. It should be viewed in the context of *all* proofs.

Whether we seek earthly or heavenly food, to produce a crop, we must persist. How many millions, through the ages, were deprived of the heavenly harvest of Jesus because they disregarded this divine law—that without effort and patience nothing great can be accomplished, that *the honor of knowing the truth is bestowed only on those who strive with hope, faith, and courage*. As Bahá'u'lláh suggests, constantly ask yourself: why did so many Jews—scholars and laymen alike—deny the very Messiah for whose Advent they were praying day and night?

> But the seed in good soil represents those who bring a good and honest heart to the hearing of the word, hold it fast, and by their perseverance yield a harvest.
>
> Christ (Luke 8:15 NEB)
See also Heb. 10:36; Matt. 24:13

Similarities Between Daniel's Vision of the First and Second Advents

Sometimes the prophecies of the first and second advents are intertwined. Sir Isaac Newton recognized this link:

> There is scarcely a prophecy of the Messiah in the Old Testament which does not to some extent at least refer to His second coming.[1]

The similarities and relationships between the two segments of Daniel's visions—namely the one designating the time of Christ's first advent (69-70 weeks) and the one specifying the time of His second advent (2300 days)—are remarkable. Both constitute part of a *continuing* vision dreamed by Daniel and recorded in succession in two consecutive chapters of his book (8 and 9). Both refer to the illumination, restoration, or purification, and both speak of the termination of the daily sacrifice or offering. In both parts of the dream Daniel experiences astonishment and wonder as to the meaning or significance of his spiritual encounters, and in both cases the same angel, Gabriel, comes to his aid. In one case he hears someone saying: "Gabriel, make this man [Daniel] to understand the vision" (Dan. 8:16). In another instance he hears Gabriel himself speaking: "O Daniel, I am now come forth to give thee skill and understanding" (Dan. 9:22).

Verse 21 clearly indicates the continuity of the dream and the inseparable link between the two time intervals. Let us review this verse along with the three interrelated verses following it:

> ...while I was still in prayer, Gabriel, the man I had seen in the earlier vision, came to me in swift flight about the time of the evening sacrifice. He instructed me and said to me, "Daniel, I have now come to give you insight and understanding. As soon as you began to pray, an answer was given, which I have come to tell you, for you are highly esteemed. Therefore, consider the message and

> understand the vision: Seventy 'sevens' are decreed for your people and your holy city to finish transgression, to put an end to sin, to atone for wickedness, to bring in everlasting righteousness, to seal up vision and prophecy and to anoint the most holy." Daniel 9:21-24 NIV

When Daniel states: "Gabriel, the man I had seen in the earlier vision," he is indeed referring to his vision of 2300 days (which had immediately preceded that of the 70 weeks). For it was Gabriel himself who had, a short while earlier, appeared to him and informed him of the 2300-day interval. And since Daniel could not fully comprehend what 2300 days signified, Gabriel came to his aid by offering him further facts: that far in advance of 2300 days, his people would have another opportunity to restore or redeem themselves. If they refused to turn to their expected Savior at the first appointed time, then they would have to wait for the time of the end, the dawn of the promised Kingdom, which would arrive centuries later.

The similarities between the two parts of Daniel's vision are remarkable. Yet in spite of their many common elements, they differ in one significant way. The part of the vision concerning the first advent makes no mention of "the time of the end"; but the part concerning the second advent points to "the time of the end" in different ways:

> "Son of man," he said to me, "understand that the vision concerns the time of the end." Daniel 8:17 NIV

> ...the vision concerns the appointed time of the end. Daniel 8:19 NIV

So that no one will doubt the truth of the divine testament and the realization of God's eternal and unswerving covenant with man, Daniel, in the course of the dream, is assured that:

> *The vision* of the evenings and mornings that has been given you *is true*, but seal up the vision, for *it concerns the distant future* [emphasis added]. Daniel 8:26 NIV

And this is precisely what happened; the vision remained sealed. For over two millennia no one was allowed to unseal its mysteries, until the dawn of the advent of the Báb and Bahá'u'lláh drew near.

The phrase "distant future" presents us with one more evidence that the days intended in the vision are "prophetic," not literal. Literally, 2300 days equals about six years and four months, an interval well within the life span of Daniel and his contemporaries.

Stand in the Holy Place

One more code remains to be deciphered. When Jesus referred His disciples to Daniel's prophecy, He said:

> When ye therefore shall see the abomination of desolation, spoken of by Daniel the prophet, *stand in the holy place*, (whoso readeth, let him understand) [emphasis added].
>
> Matthew 24:15

What does "stand in the holy place" imply? It carries a clue or coded message that holds the key to understanding the purpose of Daniel's prophecy. The clue can be decoded by these prophetic verses that pertain to our time:

> Who may go up the mountain of the Lord [Mt. Carmel]? And who may *stand in his holy place*? He who has clean hands and a pure heart, who has not set his mind on falsehood, and has not committed perjury. He shall receive a blessing from the Lord, and justice from God his savior. Such is the fortune of those who seek him, who seek the face of the God of Jacob [emphasis added].
>
> Psalms 24:3-6 NEB

As we shall see, these verses as well as those that follow them point specifically to the advent of the Báb and Bahá'u'lláh. They also contain the key that unlocks Jesus' intention in using the critical passage. He asks those who wish to understand Daniel's prophecy to "stand in the holy place." How can we do this? As the Psalmist declares, we can do this by purifying our hearts and deeds (hands) from that which stands between us and our Creator—the veils of separation.* Our efforts in this spiritual venture, as the Psalmist declares, will cause the outpourings of divine blessings and bounties.

The following verses also declare the same message:

> Lord, who may dwell in your sanctuary? Who may live on your holy hill? He whose walk is blameless and who does what is righteous...   Psalms 15:1-2 NIV

Our experience as well as the Scriptures testify that knowledge does not always in itself result in a change of heart, habits, or attitudes. Examples are many. Millions regard prejudice as an evil, yet they practice it. Millions with sound minds and full knowledge of the consequences of habits harmful to their health, continue to disregard this knowledge even though their very lives may be at stake. Wars have been waged and cruelties inflicted on the innocent by some of the best educated societies.

For most people it is the heart—not the mind—that decides what they should believe. For instance, after 2,000 years of missionary work, Christians are still a minority on our planet. Dr. James Kennedy notes:

> The Bible never calls us to blind faith but always to a faith in that which has been established by evidence. The evidence for Jesus Christ is absolutely overwhelming. No one disbelieves in Christ because of a lack of evidence... For those who are honest seekers after the truth there is abundant evidence.[2]

---

* Most new translations of the Bible use the phrase, "standing in the holy place" instead of "stand in the holy place." In this case, the verse would imply that, "when you see desolation is standing in, or occupying, the holy place." Both meanings are possible.

Knowledge in itself is not, *as it may seem*, the key that can open the heart to truth. The heart commands powers and conceives schemes of which the mind knows nothing.

When the Psalmist asks: "Who may go up the mountain of the Lord? And who may stand in his holy place?" What does he mean by "the mountain of the Lord"? He means Mt. Carmel (see Volume II). That is where Bahá'u'lláh pitched the tabernacle of Glory. And what does he mean by "his holy place"? He means the domain of the new Redeemer's sanctuary, the tabernacle of His Glory. The third message in the following verse also declares purity of heart to be the light that reveals the Master's identity:

> That is the day when I come like a thief! Happy the man who stays awake and keeps on his clothes...
>
> Revelation 16:15 NEB

What does Jesus mean by "keeps on his clothes"? It is evident He refers to the person who protects and adorns his heart with heavenly virtues, among them purity:

> Fine linen stands for the righteous acts of the saints.
>
> Revelation 19:8 NIV

By saying "when you see the abomination of desolation spoken by Daniel, *stand in the holy place*," Jesus communicates these messages:

- When you see the time has come for the fulfillment of Daniel's prophecy in which the key phrase "abomination of desolation" is used, strive to stand in the new sanctuary that has been raised, cleansed, and consecrated by the new Redeemer.

- Purity of heart and mind is the only standing from which you can enter the new sanctuary. If you approach that holy and hallowed place with a mind set by tradition, a heart stained by preconceived notions or personal desires, and with hands attached to the world, you cannot enter therein.

O SON OF SPIRIT!

My first counsel is this: Possess a pure, kindly and radiant heart, that thine may be a sovereignty ancient, imperishable and everlasting.[3]   Bahá'u'lláh

Blessed are the poor in spirit, for theirs is the kingdom of heaven...Blessed are the pure in heart, for they will see God.   Christ (Matthew 5:3,8 NIV)

What does Jesus mean by "the poor in spirit"? To attain the presence of God, the soul must travel through seven stages or "valleys." The final stage is:

The valley of true poverty and absolute nothingness. This station is the dying from self and the living in God, the being poor in self and rich in the Desired One. Poverty as here referred to signifieth being poor in the things of the created world, rich in the things of God's world.[4]

Bahá'u'lláh

The evidence presented in this chapter clearly indicates that "the cleansing of the sanctuary" in Daniel's prophecy signifies nothing short of the advent of the divine Redeemer; nothing short of the coming of the One in whose hands lies the power to purify the defiled "temples" of the human spirit, and to restore the glory of God and the power of faith to the Centers of Worship.

Restore us, O God, and make thy face shine upon us that we may be saved. O Lord God of Hosts, how long wilt thou resist thy people's prayer?   Psalms 80:3-4 NEB

...do not withdraw from the sanctuary of His presence, for, by the righteousness of the One true God, He is none other than the sovereign Truth from God...[5]   The Báb

Do not be stubborn as your forefathers were; submit yourselves to the Lord and enter his sanctuary...

II Chronicles 30:8 NEB

O thou who art waiting, tarry no longer, for He is come. Behold His Tabernacle and His Glory dwelling therein. It is the Ancient Glory, with a new Manifestation.[6]

Bahá'u'lláh

12

The Times of the Gentiles
Luke 21:24

The Bible foretells the advent of a religion between Christ's first and second comings, referring to its followers as the Gentiles (non-Jews). The biblical prophecies on this faith find their fulfillment in Islam, the only independent religion born between the rise of Christianity and 1844 A.D.

It is intriguing that the voice of prophecy should have specified the date of Christ's second coming not only in relation to the date of His first coming, but also in relation to the calendar of the next religion, Islam, destined to appear about 600 years after Christ's first coming and 1200 years before His second coming. This might have been done for a number of reasons. First, the promised Savior was to appear among the Muslims, and therefore their calendar could not be ignored. Second,

Islam was the only independent religion to appear between the first and the second advents, a religion destined to establish a great civilization, and to gain over the course of its history many millions of followers. How could a religion of such stature remain out of the scope of biblical prophecy? As we shall note in this chapter, the Book of Revelation predicts not only the advent of the Báb and Bahá'u'lláh but that of Muhammad as well.

The Times of the Gentiles

A prophecy from the Gospel (Luke 21:7, 24, 27) links the time of the advent to "the times of the Gentiles." As stated, when Jesus was on the Mount of Olives, He spoke of the desolation of the temple and the dark future in store for the Jews. The disciples discerned the intent of their Master, and so they asked about both the *signs* and the *time* of His return:

> 'Tell us,' they said, 'when will this happen? And what will be the signal for your coming and the end of the age?'   Matthew 24:3 NEB

The same question is recorded in Luke but with minor variations:

> 'Master,' they asked, 'when will it all come about? What will be the sign when it is due to happen?'   Luke 21:7 NEB

Jesus responded to both questions. (His response to the second question, namely the *signs* of the time, will be covered in Volumes II and III.) As for the *time*, He made two references. The first reference He made was to "the abomination of desolation spoken of by Daniel." (This prophecy was examined in detail in the preceding chapter.) The other reference He made was to "the fulfillment or completion of the times of the Gentiles:"

> ...and Jerusalem shall be trodden down of the Gentiles, until the times of the Gentiles be fulfilled.   Luke 21:24

To enhance clarity, let us review the question and Jesus' response in two modern translations:

> And they asked Him, Teacher, when will this happen, and what sign will there be when this is about to occur? And He said...Jerusalem will be trodden down by the Gentiles until the times of the Gentiles are fulfilled—completed... And then they will see the Son of man coming...
>
> Luke 21:7, 8, 24, 27 AB

> 'Master,' they asked, 'when will it all come about? What will be the sign when it is due to happen?' He said... Jerusalem will be trampled down by foreigners until their day has run its course...And then they will see the Son of Man coming...
>
> Luke 21:7, 8, 24, 27 NEB

The key phrase in Jesus' prophetic words is: "until the times of the Gentiles are fulfilled," or *completed*. The questions we should now turn to are these: what did Jesus mean by "when the times of the Gentiles are completed?" And how and when were they completed?

The history of the Holy Land shows that the Gentiles, or non-Jews, attacked, destroyed, and trampled on Jerusalem and its holiest center, the Sanctuary, several times and over many centuries. Therefore, Jesus' words, "Jerusalem will be trampled on by the Gentiles until the times of the Gentiles are fulfilled" (NIV), point to the various periods in history when non-Jews (Romans, Christians, and Muslims) dominated Jerusalem, humiliated it, dispersed the Jews, or prevented them from returning to their holy and beloved city.

The most critical "trampling of Jerusalem by the Gentiles" occurred in 637 A.D. by the Arabs, under 'Umar, an ambitious leader who had usurped power from Muhammad's lawful successor, 'Alí, known as the Commander of the Faithful. As a result of 'Umar's conquest, the people of Israel lost almost all contact with their beloved city for many centuries.

The following Hebrew prophecy, as translated in *The New King James Version*, also links "the times of the Gentiles" to the day of the Lord:

> Son of man, prophesy and say, 'Thus says the Lord God:' Wail, 'Woe to the day!' For the day is near, Even the day of the Lord is near; It will be a day of clouds, the time of the Gentiles.   Ezekiel 30:2-3 NKJ

A Call for the Creation of Israel

The advent of great Messengers is like the coming of spring. It creates a spiritual environment that stimulates change. Their dawning releases new and mysterious powers that pervade the entire planet. New ideas begin to germinate everywhere, even though we may be unaware of their original source. The spiritual springs always set in motion profound changes in human history, and little by little they lead to the birth of new civilizations. The story of the world's great religions confirms this.

As we noted earlier, the mid-1800's served as a pivotal point for the birth of new ideas and social transformations. As evidence of this, refer to the three-volume series entitled simply *1844*, by Christian scholar Jerome Clarke, from Southern Missionary College.

An example of the social transformation in the new age is the gradual replacement of dictatorships by democracies, and an awareness of human rights and freedoms everywhere on our planet.

Of special interest to us in this chapter are the recognition of human rights in general and the efforts and reformations that culminated in the conception and birth of the State of Israel. The birth of Israel has a long history. "Orthodox Jews had traditionally invoked the return to Zion in their daily prayers. In 1799 Napoleon had thought of establishing a Jewish state in the ancient lands of Israel."[1]

The dawning of the 19th century stirred the idea of the birth of Israel as a nation in many minds and many places more intensely than ever before. *The Encyclopedia Britannica* refers to social and religious conditions that set in motion the conception of the idea of a Jewish state in the 18th and the 19th century. It singles out *1844* as a critical year:

> The age of the Enlightenment in the second half of the 18th century, with its growth of religious toleration and universal and liberal ideals, laid the foundation in western Europe and North America for the emancipation of the Jews and their participation as citizens in the life of the nations in the midst of which they lived and whose members they became...For reasons of religious piety, a small number of Jews, supported by donations from outside, settled in Palestine.

> The interest in a return of the Jews to Palestine was kept alive in the first part of the 19th century more by Christian millenarians, especially in Great Britain, than by Jews themselves. Among the few Jews pleading then for a Jewish settlement or state was the American Mordecai Manuel Noah (1785-1851), who in 1813 became U.S. consul in Tunis and later high sheriff and surveyor of the port of New York. In 1825 he acquired Grand Island in the Niagara River and invited the Jews of the whole world to create a Jewish state...*In 1844 he pleaded with the Christian world in* Discourse on the Restoration of the Jews *to help the Jews resettle in Palestine* [emphasis added throughout].[2]

The mid-19th century marked a critical point in the shift of the Jewish destiny. Noah's call is a prime example of this shift. In his preface to his discourse delivered in 1844, he declared:

> In the political, as well as the religious world, there are singular commotions which point to the East as the

theatre of approaching revolutions of great and absorbing interests....

I confidently believe in the restoration of the Jews, and in the coming of the Messiah; and believing that political events are daily assuming a shape which may finally lead to that great advent.[3]

For his great adventure, Noah had the moral support of such distinguished figures as Thomas Jefferson and John Adams, who had in earlier years served as United States presidents. In a letter to him, Adams wrote:

I wish your nation may be admitted to all the privileges of citizens in every part of the world. This country has done much; I wish it may do more...Let the wits joke, the philosophers sneer! What then? It has pleased the Providence of the "first cause," the universal cause, that Abraham should give religion not only to the Hebrews, but to Christians and Mohammedans, the greatest part of the modern civilized world...I really wish the Jews again in Judea, an independent nation...your Jehovah is our Jehovah, and your God of Abraham, Isaac, and Jacob is our God.[4]

Here is a passage from Noah's appeal made before thousands of "the most distinguished [American] citizens and the highest dignitaries of the Church."[5] Note how skillfully he blends reason and emotion to touch the hearts of his audience:

I have long desired, my friends and countrymen, for an opportunity to appear before you in behalf of a venerable people, whose history, whose sufferings, and whose extraordinary destiny have, for a period of 4000 years, filled the world with awe and astonishment, a people at once the most favored and the most neglected, the most beloved, and yet the most persecuted; a people under whose salutary laws all the civilized nations of the earth now repose; a people whose origin may date from the cradle of creation, and who are likely to be preserved to the last moment of recorded time.

I have been anxious to appeal to you, citizens and Christians, in behalf of the chosen and beloved people of Almighty God, to ask you to...feel for their sufferings and woes, to extend to them your powerful protection and undivided support in accomplishing the fulfillment of their destiny, and...to restore them to the land of their forefathers and the possession of their ancient heritage. *It is, I acknowledge, a novel...appeal...for the first time to Christians since the advent of Christianity*; but the period I believe has arrived for this appeal: Extraordinary events shadow forth results long expected, long prophesied, long ordained...and the political events in Syria, Egypt, Turkey, and Russia indicate the approach of great and important revolutions which may facilitate the return of the Jews to Jerusalem, and the organization of a powerful government in Judea, and [will] lead to that millennium which we all look for, all hope for, all pray for.[6]

After referring to America's support of several nations and peoples to gain independence, Noah concludes:

...If these nations were entitled to our sympathies, how much more powerful and irrepressible are the claims of that beloved people before whom the Almighty walked like a cloud by day and a pillar of fire by night; who spoke to them words of comfort and salvation, of promise, of hope, of consolation, and protection; who swore they should be *his* people and he would be their God; who, for their special protection and final restoration, dispersed them among the nations of the earth...[7]

Noah shows his audience the first step toward an independent Israel:

The tree must be planted...The first step is to solicit from the Sultan of Turkey permission for the Jews to purchase and hold land, to build houses, and to follow any occupation they may desire, without molestation and in perfect security. There is no difficulty in securing this privilege for them. The moment the Christian powers feel an interest in behalf of the Jewish people, the Turkish government will secure and carry out their views, for it must always be remembered that the one hundred and twenty millions of Mussulmen [Muslims] are also the descendants of Abraham.[8]

Like William Miller, who stirred interest in the second advent, Noah's efforts awakened the dormant dreams of an independent Israel in many receptive minds.

The English statesman Benjamin Disraeli, a Jew, [wrote] a Zionist novel, *Tancred*. Moses Hess, a friend and co-worker of Karl Marx, published an important book, *Rom und Jerusalem* (1862), in which he declared the restoration of a Jewish state a necessity both for the Jews and for the rest of humanity. Among the Jews of Russia and eastern Europe, a number of groups were engaged in trying to settle emigrants in agricultural colonies in Palestine.[9]

Another noteworthy figure influenced by Noah was Laurence Oliphant, who in 1882 moved to the Holy Land and settled in Haifa:

In 1878 he proposed to Disraeli and Robert Cecil, 3rd marquess of Salisbury, a plan for the Jewish colonization of Palestine (he was not Jewish himself). The plan was well received by Salisbury and by eastern European Jews but was refused by the sultan of Turkey, ruler of Palestine.[10]

Still another prominent figure who followed the example of Noah was:

Theodore Herzl, founder of the political form of Zionism, a movement to establish a Jewish homeland. His pamphlet

The Jewish State (1896) proposed that the Jewish question was a political question to be settled by a world council of nations. He organized a world congress of Zionists that met in Basel, Switz, in August 1897 and became first president of the World Zionist Organization, established by the congress...He negotiated unsuccessfully with the Sultan of Turkey to the grant of a charter that would allow Jewish mass settlement in Palestine on an autonomous basis. He then turned to Great Britain...[11]

The efforts put forth by Noah and his supporters in the mid-19th century did not lead immediately to the birth of a nation, but they served their purpose. They created a momentum that culminated a century later in that birth. They signaled a new beginning for the scattered and persecuted people of Israel. They symbolized the dawning of a new day in their destiny. As Anthony Robbins notes:

In pursuit of our goals, we often set in motion far-reaching consequences. Does the honeybee deliberate on how to propagate flowers? No, but in the process of seeking sweet nectar, the bee unknowingly gathers pollen on its legs, flies to the next flower, and sets in motion a wondrous chain reaction that results in a hillside awash in color.[12]

*The Edicts of Submission**

The stirrings of the recognition of human rights and freedom in the 19th century spread gradually from the West to the East. A nation that could not withstand the winds of change was the Ottoman Empire, the very heart of the Islamic world—the nation that ruled over the Holy Land.

---

* These edicts have been called the *Edicts of Toleration*, but the word "submission" seems more appropriate. The dictionary defines "toleration" as "willingness to allow freedom of thought and action to others, and the practice of allowing such freedom especially in religion." As the evidence shows, the edicts represented only a symbolic act of submission—out of desperation—to greater powers, rather than noble acts of toleration, understanding, and compassion.

In the mid-19th century, a few Sultans of the Ottoman Empire were forced to issue several edicts of reformation and toleration. Among them were *Noble Edict of Rose Chamber* (November 3, 1839), and *The Imperial Edict* (February 18, 1856). These edicts were aimed at creating a new social order for all citizens of the Empire, including minorities. But the prime motive behind them was political:

> To the Ottomans...the purpose of reform was to preserve the Ottoman state. Although the Ottomans found it necessary to make some concessions to European powers and to their own non-Muslim subjects, and although some Tanzimat [Reformation] statesmen did consider equality to be an ultimate goal, it was the desire to preserve the state that brought about the mobilization of resources for modernization.[13]

Among the many seeds of awareness sprouting in the 19th century was the birth of documents through collaboration between the two powerful empires of the time. As a result of the persecution of Christian subjects under the Ottoman Empire, the nations of Europe, especially the British, forced the Ottomans to make a pledge of tolerance by signing documents, which may best be called **Edicts of Submission**, for they were not given for the good of the world but for self-interest and as an act of submission of the Turks to greater European powers.

Here is the copy of the Edict issued on March 21, 1844, and confirmed again on March 23:

> Official Declaration of the Sublime Porte [the chief office of the Ottomon Empire], relinquishing the practice of Executions for Apostasy. It is the special and constant intention of His Highness the Sultan that his cordial relations with the High Powers [Christian nations] be preserved, and that a perfect reciprocal friendship be maintained, and increased. The Sublime Porte engages to take effectual measures to prevent henceforward the execution

and putting to death of the Christian who is an apostate. March 21, 1844.[14]

Declaration of His Highness the Sultan to Sir Stratford Canning at his Audience on the 23rd of March, 1844. Henceforward neither shall Christianity be insulted in my dominion, nor shall Christians be in any way persecuted for their religion.[15]

Like the call issued by Mordecai Noah and others, the *Edicts of Submission* did not result in immediate or significant changes in the lives of the Jews. They only symbolized a new direction for a sovereign Islamic Empire and the divine destiny of a persecuted minority under its rule. They were the first critical cracks in a mighty structure. They signaled the fall and disintegration of a vast Empire that had dominated the world and endured for many centuries. *The Edicts symbolized a shift of power, the submission of one of the most powerful nations the world has ever known to newer and greater Christian powers.* They pointed to the dawning of a new age of tolerance, independence, and recognition of human rights and freedoms for all people.

Some Christian authors have recognized the Messianic message implied in these Edicts in the unfoldment of God's prophetic and progressive plan for humankind. Distinguished scholars Dr. and Mrs. Guinness* in their book *Light for the Last Days* have emphasized their symbolic significance in the destiny of the Jews. Here they refer to the edict issued on March 21:

In 1844 the Porte was compelled by the Christian nations of Europe to issue an edict of religious toleration...[16]

This year [1844] brought no military defeat, but one of a far more important character, both as marking [symbolizing] the loss of the independence of the Porte, and the

---

* Leroy Froom in his classic work, *The Prophetic Faith of Our Fathers*, describes Dr. Guinness "as one of the most outstanding among all modern expositors" and a biblical scholar without peer among those in Britain.[17]

274 I Shall Come Again

liberation of its Jewish and Christian subjects...This decree
was published in the 1260th year of the Hegira. *It is
dated March 21st, 1844*. This date is the first of Nisan in
the Jewish year, and *is exactly to a day twenty-three
centuries from the first of Nisan, B. C. 457, the day on
which Ezra states that he left Babylon in compliance
with the decree given in the seventh year of the reign
of Artaxerxes.*[18]

The 1844 decree did not carry any military significance. It
did not allow the Jews to return to the Holy Land. It rather
symbolized "the day of trouble and dismemberment" for a
mighty Empire and the shift of power from the East to the
West.

In his discourse, delivered in the United States in 1844,
Mordecai Noah confirmed this shift of power:

Within the last twenty-five years great revolutions have
occurred in the East, affecting in a peculiar manner the
future destiny of the followers of Mohammad, and *distinctly marking the gradual advancement of the Christian
power*.[19]

The Turkish governments cannot be insensible to the fact
that clouds are gathering around them, and destiny, in
which they wholly confide, teaches them to await *the day
of trouble and dismemberment*. It is their interest to draw
around them the friendly aid and cooperation of the
Jewish people throughout the world, by conferring these
reasonable and just privileges upon them...[20]

What points to the symbolic significance of the preceding
Edict is not only the *year 1844*, but the *day* on which it was
signed. One figure coincides with the *first year* of the Bahá'í
Era (1844), the other coincides with the *first day* of the Bahá'í
year (March 21). Could this be a coincidence? It could be if
we ignore the grand jigsaw puzzle of prophetic profile. Otherwise, it serves as one more piece of that gigantic puzzle.

The Principle of
"the Critical Domino"

According to this principle, the long-term consequences of an act or event are both unpredictable and sometimes radically out of proportion to the act or event.

Sometimes small changes of direction or little acts of justice and kindness set in motion changes far beyond expectation. When Rosa Parks refused to sit in the back of a bus, could anyone have detected the stirrings of the Civil Rights Movement in her seemingly little act of courage and defiance? In one of his talks, King Duncan, author and orator, traces and finds a seemingly impossible link between Rosa Parks and the collapse of hard-line communists! To defeat Gorbachev, he states, Yeltsin mounted a tank to rally the Russian people in Red Square. Later someone asked him, "What caused you to take the stand that helped defeat communism?" Yeltsin said, "I guess it was Lech Walesa, that electrician in Gdansk who took a stand and helped Poland overthrow communism in that country."

Someone asked Walesa, "What was the pivotal event that caused you to stand against communists?" He answered, "I guess it was reading about Dr. Martin Luther King Jr. and the Civil Rights activists in the United States."

Someone asked Dr. King, "What was the pivotal event in your life that caused you to take the stand against racism?" He answered, "I guess it was reading about Rosa Parks. That little lady in Birmingham who refused to go to the back of the bus." Mr. Duncan then asks, "Is it possible that international communism was brought down by one little Afro-American lady who took a stand?"

Noah's call for freedom and independence and the Edicts of Submission may have seemed insignificant at the time, yet they may have served as "the critical domino" that set in motion the gradual but persistent downfall of walls of separation and prejudice. They may have symbolized the dawning of a new age, especially for the people of Israel, who have been the prime targets of persecution for centuries.

Prophecies are sometimes first fulfilled *symbolically*, just like a seed that first germinates, but only *later* bears fruits. When Jesus entered Jerusalem on a donkey, He fulfilled *symbolically* the prophecies that pointed to a king. His literal kingdom emerged centuries later. In his book *The Master Plan*, Christian scholar Dr. David Reagan offers several examples of this principle concerning prophecies of the first advent, and then concludes:

> ...prophecy is often pre-filled in *symbolic type* before it is completely fulfilled.[21]

We can find another example of the preceding principle in the fulfillment of the following prophecy, covered in Chapter 14:

> The dragon stood in front of the woman *that he might devour her child the moment it was born*. She gave birth to a son...   Revelation 12:4-5 NIV

The preceding prophecy was fulfilled *symbolically* long before "the child" (the Báb) was born. Its literal fulfillment came about later. (See *Some Answered Questions*, Chapter 13.)

The state of Israel was officially born in 1948, but a birth is always preceded by a conception. The call issued in the West by the statesman Mordecai Noah in 1844 to the Christian world to acknowledge the rights of the Jews and to recognize the advent of the appointed time for planting the Seed of the State of Israel, on the one hand, and the submission of the Ottoman Empire—which ruled over the Holy Land with absolute authority—to western nations to sign the Edicts of Submission in that same year, on the other, marked the conception of a new day of freedom and independence for all nations, especially the Jews. By that year, "the times of the

Gentiles" had run their course and come to an end, not only symbolically—which was marked at least by two historical events—but also spiritually. The advent of a new Messenger (the Báb) had signaled the End of the Age for *all* nations and religions, including the Jews and the Gentiles.

In the early years of the 20th century (1904-1906), some forty years before the birth of the state of Israel, while 'Abdu'l-Bahá Himself was confined in 'Akká in the Holy Land, He spoke of the coming together of the children of Israel:

> ...in this cycle Israel will be gathered in the Holy Land, and...the Jewish people who are scattered to the East and West, South and North, will be assembled together.[22]

Many biblical and historical references are cited in the succeeding volumes to prove that gradualism is a universal law, and that nothing of great consequence can come without effort, patience, persistence, and sacrifice.

Comparing the Prophecies of the First and Second Advents

A comparison of the three major time prophecies examined so far shows the perfect harmony that binds together all the prophecies.

• Daniel's prayer concerning the first advent:

> O Lord, make thy face shine upon thy desolate sanctuary...and look upon our desolation and upon the city that bears thy name [Jerusalem]...   Daniel 9:17-18 NEB

The answer to this prayer: after 69 weeks, the Anointed One (the Messiah) will come to anoint "the Most Holy Place" (Daniel 9:24 NEB).

• Daniel's prayer concerning the second advent:

...how long will impiety cause desolation, and both the
Holy Place and the fairest of all lands [Jerusalem] be
given over to be trodden down?   Daniel 8:13 NEB

The answer to this prayer: after 2300 days the sanctuary
or the Holy Place will be restored (Daniel 8:14).

• The disciples' question concerning the second advent:

'Master,' they asked, 'when will it all come about?'
                                        Luke 21:7 NEB

Jesus' answer: Jerusalem will be trampled down by foreigners until their day has run its course (Luke 21:24 NEB).

All the preceding prophecies pertain to the destiny of Jerusalem
or its temple. This indeed seems a great mystery. Why should
the life history of a city and its temple be singled out so
frequently as the point of reference for such a momentous
event?

In the following verses Jesus also links the destiny of
Jerusalem and its temple to the advent of divine Messengers.
Since the people of Israel rejected their Redeemer, Jesus said
that their sanctuary would remain forsaken until the advent
of the Lord at the end of the age.

O Jerusalem, Jerusalem, the city that murders the prophets
and stones the messengers sent to her! How often have I
longed to gather your children, as a hen gathers her
brood under her wings; but you would not let me. Look,
look! there is your temple, forsaken by God. And I tell
you, you shall never see me until the time comes when
you say, "Blessings on him who comes in the name of the
Lord!"   Luke 13:34-35 NEB

Similarly, Isaiah 40:12 implores the Lord to come down
from heaven to restore His sanctuary and gain its deserved
freedom from those who have trampled it.

"The Times of the Gentiles" and "That Day"

The fulfillment of "the times of the Gentiles" has still another meaning. The advent of the Báb and Bahá'u'lláh fulfilled not only the Jewish prophecies but also prophecies from other scriptures as well. As we shall see later, many religions have designated 1844 as a time marking the termination of their spiritual cycle. The end of "the time of the Gentiles" signaled the dawning of a new day not just for the people of Israel, but for *all peoples*.

The expression commonly used in the Scriptures to signal the termination of all previous dispensations are: *that day, the latter days, the last days, harvest-time, the end of the age,* and *the time of the end.* Here *the age of prophecy* ends and *the day of fulfillment* dawns. It is a most blessed time in history, for its arrival signals the coming of the promised Kingdom, when one universal faith guides and inspires all humanity.

Evidence of the change from promise to fulfillment is that past Scriptures contain an abundance of prophecies, while the Bahá'í Scriptures do not:

> The Prophetic Cycle hath, verily, ended. The Eternal Truth is now come.[23]
> Bahá'u'lláh

It is helpful to note that the divine Messengers have stated, in similar terms, that the duration of their dispensation is limited. Daniel was told, "Seventy weeks are determined upon thy people." Christ used a similar language, "Until the times of the Gentiles be fulfilled," that is, until the times allotted to them come to an end. Muhammad also confirms this:

> To each age its Book. What God pleaseth He will abrogate or confirm...
> Qur'án 13:38-39

> Neither too soon, nor too late, shall a people [body of believers] reach its appointed time...
> Qur'án 23:45

The life cycle of a religion is like that of a plant. It begins at some point in history and then passes through the various stages of development until its allotted "time" comes to an end. At that point the divine Gardener takes a Seed from the previous Plant and puts it once again into the vineyard of the world.

To conclude: Jesus linked the time of His return to the completion of the times of the Gentiles. His prophecy was fulfilled symbolically by at least two historical events: a call in 1844 for the formation of the State of Israel, and the signing of an Edict of Submission issued on March 21, 1844. The year and the day correspond to the *first year* of the Bahá'í Era, and the *first day* of the Bahá'í New Year. As we noted, it is also the day on which the third edict for the rebuilding of Jerusalem was issued. Once again we see an example of the precise fulfillment of prophecies. For from the day on which the third edict concerning the rebuilding of Jerusalem was issued until the day on which an Edict of Submission was signed, there is an interval of exactly 2300 years. There is not even one day of discrepancy. The two edicts (the Third Edict, and the Edict of Submission), the two prophecies (the prophecy of 2300 days, and the words of Jesus about the times of the Gentiles) all point to the same sacred surroundings: Jerusalem or the Holy Land.

13

The Spirit That Acknowledges Jesus Christ
I John 4:2

An Introduction to Islam

Islam is sometimes called the Misunderstood Religion. To appreciate and decode the remaining time prophecies, we need to take a closer look at the only independent major religion born between the first and second advents—Islam. Islam is the link between Christianity and the Bahá'í Faith. Some knowledge of Islam is essential to enhance our understanding of the Bahá'í Faith, even as Judaism is to Christianity. To appreciate the grand design of the Supreme Architect, we must look at His whole plan. Islam is part of this plan.

The subject is so vast and vital that a separate volume has been devoted to it. Volume IV of this work compares the teachings and prophecies of the Bible and the Qur'án and demonstrates the astonishing similarity between them. This chapter properly belongs to that volume, but is presented here because many time prophecies of the Bible concerning the advent of the Redeemer of our age are linked to the advent of Islam. With a more realistic perception of the teachings of the Qur'án we will be in a better position to appreciate those prophecies.

Christian scholars believe that the Bible has influenced the world more than all other books combined; that it has shaped human life more than all the philosophers, politicians, and rulers who have ever lived. Muslim scholars can say the same about the Qur'án. Is it not fitting to study and understand a book of such stature? All the sacred Scriptures emphasize the need for true knowledge:

> ...through knowledge shall the just be delivered.
>
> Proverbs 11:9

> My people are destroyed from lack of knowledge.
>
> Hosea 4:6 NIV

Listening to new ideas is considered a sign of wisdom:

> A wise man will hear, and will increase learning...
>
> Proverbs 1:5

> ...let the wise listen and add to their learning...
>
> Proverbs 1:5 NIV

> ...the ear of the wise seeketh knowledge.   Proverbs 18:15

Unfortunately true knowledge about Islam is lacking, especially in the West, and this is not a new problem:

> ...most of them have no knowledge.   Qur'án 31:24

> ...the greater part of people know it [Islam] not...
>
> Qur'án 30:29

Scholars believe that Islam gave rise to one of the greatest civilizations the world has ever known. This positive dimension of Islam has seldom received due credit, especially in the West. Stanwood Cobb in *Islamic Contributions to Civilization* writes:

> Even in this modern age of enlightenment few people are aware of the significant contributions made by the Islamic world to the progress of humanity. Yet for more than five centuries, that civilization not only led the world in science, but was the only portion of mankind actively engaged in the systematic pursuit of knowledge.[1]

Many reasons have contributed to a lack of true knowledge about Islam. Among them are:

- Islam is often believed to be antagonistic to Christianity.

- Western writers, as a whole, have paid little attention to the contributions of Islam to world culture.

- The Qur'án is seldom studied seriously.

- Those leaders and followers of Islam who have been least faithful to its teachings have attracted more than their fair share of attention.

- What Muslims do is often equated with what Islam teaches.

Let us begin with the last point. As a result of the wars waged by Muslims, many Westerners assume that Islam enjoins force as a means of spreading its beliefs. Every religion has been misused and exploited. We should judge Islam by the Qur'án, not by the actions of its leaders or followers. Freedom of conscience is one of the most fundamental and emphatic themes of the Qur'án:

> To proclaim a clear message is our [God's] only duty...
>
> Qur'án 36:16
>
> Of God it is to point out "the Way."   Qur'án 16:9

Let him then who will, take the way to his Lord.

Qur'án 73:19

Say: O ye unbelievers!...I shall never worship that which ye worship, neither will ye worship that which I worship. To you be your religion; to me my religion.

Qur'án 109:1-6

But if thy Lord had pleased, verily all who are in the earth would have believed together. What! wilt thou compel men to become believers?   Qur'án 10:99

Let there be no compulsion in religion.   Qur'án 2:257

The Qur'án does not allow harsh words or arguments:

Of the mercy of God thou hast spoken to them [the unbelievers] in gentle terms.   Qur'án 3:153

Speak ye to him with gentle speech...   Qur'án 20:46

Enjoin My [God's] servants to speak in kindly sort...

Qur'án 17:55

And the servants of the God of Mercy are they who walk upon the earth softly; and when the ignorant address them, they reply, "Peace!"   Qur'án 25:64

...speak with well-guided speech...   Qur'án 33:70

And woe...to those...who plunged...into vain disputes...

Qur'án 52:11-12

Happy...the believers, who...keep aloof from vain words.

Qur'án 23:1,3

If force and harsh words are forbidden, how then should Islam be taught?

Summon thou to the way of thy Lord with wisdom and with kindly warning...   Qur'án 16:126

...speak words that may penetrate their souls. Qur'án 4:66

These gentle and kind words were spoken to primitive people whose major occupation was war. It is hard to conceive of a society more violent than the tribes of Arabia prior to the advent of Islam.

The Qur'án even illustrates how Muslims should teach their faith to Jews and Christians:

> And say ye, "We believe in what hath been sent down to us [Qur'án] and hath been sent down to you [the Torah or the Gospel]. Our God and your God is one, and to him are we self-surrendered." Qur'án 29:45

Imposing faith or belief is not only against the teachings of the Qur'án but against those of all the other sacred Scriptures as well. They all teach that truth must be sought and received with gratitude. It is God's glorious gift:

> And whoso maketh efforts for us [God], in our ways will we guide them... Qur'án 29:69

The best test of Islam is Muhammad's own example in implementing the teachings of the Qur'án. Muhammad's standards of justice are clearly exemplified in a charter He "granted to the Christians in general and to the monks of the monastery of St. Catherine, near Mount Sinai, in particular, the actual document itself having been faithfully preserved down the centuries by the annalists of Islam."[2] As George Townshend points out, according to this charter, the Muslims were supposed to:

> ...protect the Christians, to defend their churches, the residences of their priests, and to guard them from all injuries. They were not to be unfairly taxed; no bishop was to be driven out of his bishopric; no Christian was to be forced to reject his religion; no monk was to be expelled from his monastery; no pilgrim was to be detained from his pilgrimage. Nor were the Christian churches to be pulled down for the sake of building mosques or houses for the Muslims. Christian women married to Muslims were to enjoy their own religion, and not to be subjected to compulsion or annoyance of any kind on that account. If Christians should stand in need of assistance for the repair

of their churches or monasteries, or any other matter pertaining to their religion, the Muslims were to assist them.[3]

To understand Islam, we must look at what Muhammad Himself taught and accomplished, rather than what others did in His name. For after His death, the history of Islam took a new turn. Those hungry for power did not even wait for the Prophet to be buried. Through political plots they usurped the leadership of Islam from Muhammad's lawful successor 'Alí. The history of Islam following Muhammad's death is one of struggle, division, and deviation. Notable among those who usurped both the political and spiritual powers of Islam were the rulers of the dynasty of the Umayyads who, in the name of Islam, committed many atrocities. They even massacred some of the closest and most beloved descendants of the Prophet.

In the following passage, the Báb asks Muslims not to treat Him the way they treated Husayn, the third Imám, grandson of Muhammad, known as the Prince of Martyrs:

> O peoples of the earth! Inflict not upon the Most Great Remembrance [the Báb] what the Umayyads cruelly inflicted upon Husayn...[4]

Not all Muslims, however, came under the domination of such atrocious leaders. There were many who acknowledged the inspired leaders—Imáms—and practiced the teachings of the Qur'án. Islam, as taught by the Prophet, was to expand by the power of the tongue; Islam, as practiced by many of its misguided leaders, was spread by the sword. One can see in the entire history of Islam two forces moving in opposition—the forces of light and the forces of darkness.

The deviation of some Muslim leaders from the original teachings of their Faith, however, should in no way obscure or belittle the overall influence of Islam on the advancement of civilization. All religions have been misused, to some extent or other, by misguided leaders. We should always look at the original Gem bestowed by the divine Jeweller, not at the crushed and polluted pieces. It should also be noted that when we refer to deviation from the original teachings of Islam, we do not intend to single out a given sect, or imply that those who followed Muhammad's lawful successor—'Alí— necessarily lived a more exemplary life.

The Spirit That Acknowledges Jesus Christ

> This is how you can recognize the Spirit of God: Every spirit that acknowledges that Jesus Christ has come in the flesh is from God...   I John 4:2 NIV

Many Christians are unaware of the great love Muhammad had for Christ, and of the praise He bestowed on Him. Muhammad called Christ *the Spirit of God*, a title that has been widely used by Muslims since the dawn of Islam. *The Spirit of God* (Rúh'u'lláh) and *Mary* (Maryam) are used frequently as names by Muslims, just as *Joshua* and *Sarah* are used by Christians. Dr. G. Parrinder of the University of London quotes this passage from the sayings of Muhammad:

> I bear witness that Jesus Son of Mary is the spirit of God and His word which He cast to Mary the virgin.[5]

Similarly, this verse from the Qur'án points to Christ as *the Spirit of God*:

> We [God] breathed into her [Mary] of Our Spirit [the Spirit of God], and We made her and her son [Jesus] a Sign [of God] for all peoples.   Qur'án 21:91 Y

According to a prophecy from Muhammad:

> Even if no more than one day remains in the world, God will make it long enough until in it will appear My progeny Mahdí* [the Báb], and then descend the Spirit of God, Jesus Son of Mary...and the earth will shine with the light of her Lord...[6]

---

* Literally *the One* [divinely] *guided*. The Báb was a descendant of Muhammad.

We find a similar prophecy in the Book of Revelation:

> After this I saw another angel coming down from heaven...
> and the earth was illuminated by his splendor.
>
> Revelation 18:1 NIV

It appears that the verse "Every spirit that acknowledges
Jesus Christ..." points specifically to Muhammad, the Báb,
and Bahá'u'lláh. They all have used those same titles (*the
Spirit*, and *the Spirit of God*) to refer to Christ. In one
passage Bahá'u'lláh declares that He is the One who once
came in the name of *the Spirit*, namely Christ.

> By God! This is He Who hath at one time appeared in the
> name of the Spirit...[7]

In another passage, Bahá'u'lláh refers to Christ as *the Spirit
of God*:

> If ye be intent on crucifying once again *Jesus, the Spirit
> of God*, put Me to death, for He hath once more, in My
> person, been made manifest unto you. Deal with Me as ye
> wish, for I have vowed to lay down My life in the path
> of God.[8]

Bahá'u'lláh calls Christ "the Lord of all being:"

> ...the Spirit of God, the Lord of all being.[9]

He also calls Him "the Spirit:"

> Say, O followers of the Son! Have you shut out yourselves
> from Me by reason of My Name?...Consider those who
> rejected the Spirit [Christ] when He came...[10]

Christ assumed the title of the Spirit when He declared
that the Spirit of the Lord was upon Him (Luke 4:18). As the
Gospel testifies, after Christ's baptism, "the Spirit of God"
descended and alighted upon Him (Matt. 3:16). Further,
Christ's conception was by the power of the Holy Spirit
(Matt. 1:18; Luke 1:35), which is the Spirit of God.

Another title bestowed on Christ in the Gospel, as well as the Islamic traditions, and the Qur'án is *the Word* or *the Word of God*:

> The Word became flesh and lived for a while among us.
>
> John 1:14 NIV

> I bear witness that Jesus...is the Spirit of God and His Word...[11]
>
> Muhammad

> ...the angel said, "O Mary! Verily God announceth to thee the Word from Him [the Word of God]: His name shall be, Messiah Jesus...
>
> Qur'án 3:40

> ...an angel of the Lord...said...She will give birth to a son, and you are to give him the name Jesus...
>
> Matthew 1:20-21 NIV

Compared to the Gospel, how does the Qur'án portray Mary? According to the Gospel, Mary's glory lies in being the mother of Jesus. Concerning her status as described in the Scriptural record, *Nelson's Illustrated Bible Dictionary* states:

> That Mary 'found favor with God' and was allowed to give birth to His child indicates that she must have been of high character and faith.[12]

Of her position as portrayed in the Gospel, *Unger's Bible Dictionary*, published by Moody Bible Institute, states:

> In a word, so far as Mary is portrayed to us in Scripture, she is, as we should have expected, the most tender, the most faithful, humble, patient, and loving woman, but a *woman* still.[13]

Harper's Bible Dictionary states that:

> She is negatively portrayed in Mark, less so in Matthew, and positively in Luke.[14]

What would happen if Christians recognized the great station the Qur'án bestows on Mary, the mother of the Son of God—

a station much higher than that granted her in the Gospel?
What would they think if they saw this verse from the
Qur'án?

> ...the angels said, "O Mary! Verily hath God...*chosen thee*
> *above the women of the worlds* [emphasis added].
>
> Qur'án 3:37

Could a station or an honor greater than this—standing
above every woman in the 'worlds'—be conceived for a
human being, especially one about whom the world knows
very little? Please notice the word *worlds*, used in the plural.
In one of His sayings, Muhammad further glorifies Mary's
status by placing her above His own daughter, Fátimih, who
is the noblest and most exalted woman in Islam.

Knowledge of this kind leads to understanding and peace, to
love and fellowship not only between Christians and Muslims,
but among all nations and religions. Such understanding has
the power to lift the hearts and fuse them in harmony, yet
the power has remained untapped for fourteen centuries. If
Christians had a true knowledge of Islam, if they had known
Muhammad's glorification of Jesus and Mary, would they
have engaged in the Crusades? How much would our world
change, if these facts were proclaimed, especially among
Christians, who as a whole have a negative attitude toward
Islam?

Among the doctrines of the Christian faith is the virgin
birth of Jesus. This is a doctrine that cannot be proven. Only
the power of faith can lead one to acceptance. Even some
Christians hesitate to embrace it, yet the Qur'án clearly
confirms it. Christians need not ask for more evidence
concerning Muhammad's love and respect for Jesus than this
confirmation of one of their most fundamental beliefs:

> ...said the angel...'It is by the Holy Spirit that she has
> conceived this child...'   Matthew 1:20 NEB

We [God] sent our spirit [the Holy Spirit] to her...He [the Spirit] said: "I am only a messenger of thy Lord, that I may bestow on thee a holy son."   Qur'án 19:17-21

We [God] breathed into her of Our Spirit, and We made her and her son, a Sign [of God] for all peoples.
                                                        Qur'án 21:91 Y

The Qur'án contains chapters titled Noah, Abraham, Joseph, Jonah, Mary, and Imrán (Moses' father). It gives a special prominence to the stories of Moses, John the Baptist and Jesus. It confirms the divine mission of the Hebrew prophets.

The Jews have suffered cruel humiliation and lived with persistent prejudice directed against them by many nations. Most of them are unaware that the Qur'án reaffirms God's deep love for them as declared in their own Scripture:

...you are a people holy...the Lord your God chose you out of all nations on earth to be his special possession.
                                                        Deuteronomy 7:6 NEB

And We [God] chose them [the people of Israel]...above all peoples.   Qur'án 44:31

One God, One Race, One Religion

Among the most fundamental teachings of great religions are these: one God rules the universe; all divine religions express His purpose; all humans are His creation, and all of them receive His favors, blessings, and bounties.

...the peoples of the world, of whatever race or religion, derive their inspiration from one heavenly Source, and are the subjects of one God.[15]   Bahá'u'lláh

I am the first and I am the last; apart from me there is no God. Who then is like me? Let him proclaim it.
                                                        Isaiah 44:6-7 NIV

God...hath made of one blood all nations of men...
Acts 17:24, 26

Have we not all one father? Did not one God create us? Why do we violate the covenant of our forefathers by being faithless to one another?   Malachi 2:10 NEB

And truly this your religion is the one [eternal] religion; and I am your Lord.   Qur'án 23:54

...the one and indivisible religion of God...[16]   The Báb

Say: In whatsoever Books God hath sent down do I [Muhammad] believe...God is your Lord and our Lord... between us [Muslims] and you [those of other faiths] let there be no strife; God will make us all one; and to Him shall we return.   Qur'án 42:14

To gain a global picture of the oneness of peoples and religions, we must first clarify the historical perspective. Jews, Christians, and Muslims are close relatives. As confirmed in Hebrew Scriptures, the peoples of these faiths belong to the same family: Abraham is their father. The Jews believe they are the descendants of Isaac, Abraham's second son; the Arabs believe they are the descendants of Ishmael, Abraham's eldest son. As *The Zondervan Bible Dictionary* notes, the descendants of Ishmael, whose wife was an Egyptian, settled "in camps in the desert of Northern Arabia."[17] The racial bond between Ishmael and the Arabs is well recognized. For instance, *Unger's Bible Dictionary* writes: "we may fairly regard the Arabs as essentially an Ishmaelite race."[18]

People make great efforts to find a lost brother or sister. And when they find him or her, they sense an indescribable joy and peace. Why, then, does the knowledge of having the same father (Abraham), of being brothers and sisters, not move Jews, Christians, and Muslims to jubilation?

People may lose their sense of fellowship with one another; *the divine Messengers* never do. Every religion confirms the past religions and predicts the coming of future revelations. Both the Old and New Testaments predict the advent of Islam. The following prophecies, often quoted by Muslims, demonstrate such predictions:

> Do not be afraid: God has heard the child [Ishmael] crying where you laid him. Get to your feet, lift the child up and hold him in your arms, because I will make of him a great nation...God was with the child, and he grew up and lived in the wilderness of Paran. Genesis 21:17-21 NEB

And again:

> I [God] have heard your [Abraham's] prayer for Ishmael. I have blessed him and will make him fruitful. I will multiply his descendants; he shall be father of twelve princes, and I will raise a great nation from him.
> Genesis 17:20 NEB

This prophecy was fulfilled in the fullest sense. Ishmael indeed became fruitful—from him descended the vast majority of Muslims who now number about one sixth of the earth's population. From a small beginning in the desert of Arabia, Islam grew into a great nation, governing a large portion of the globe for centuries. In fact, there has never been a religious polity as vast as the Islamic empire; its embrace extended from western China to Spain.

The promise of "twelve princes" attained double fulfillment: Ishmael was blessed with twelve sons, some of whom became rulers. Thus he "became the progenitor of twelve tribes of desert nomads."[19]

The promise of "twelve princes" attained fulfillment once again in the appearance of the twelve Imáms under the Islamic dispensation. The last of these twelve princes was the Báb, who also descended from Ishmael. As we shall see later, John the Revelator saw these twelve princes as "twelve stars" on a crown (Rev. 12:1-2). To deny Islam is to deny a religion whose followers have received all the blessings of God.

Christians and Jews revere their own ancestor Isaac above
Ishmael, yet both brothers were blessed by God. Concerning
Ishmael, *Harper's Bible Dictionary* writes:

> He is especially celebrated in the Priestly source as one
> whom God would bless, multiply, and make fruitful...
> (Gen. 17:20). Also in the Yahwistic and Elohistic sources,
> Ishmael is favored of God. The angel of the Lord who
> guarded Isaac...Lot...and...Joseph, also protected Ishmael's
> mother in pregnancy...and then protected both Hagar and
> Ishmael (Gen. 21:15-21). These sources reiterate that God
> will make Ishmael "a great nation" (Gen. 21:18).[20]

The New Testament too confirms God's favor for the descendants of Ishmael. The Book of Revelation contains clear and
significant prophecies about Islam. (Some of them will be
examined in succeeding chapters.)

The more we study the sacred Scriptures, the clearer becomes
our perception of their oneness; we see them as pieces of a
magnificent painting revealed progressively by the grand
Designer.

14

They Will Prophesy for 1260 Days

Revelation 11:3 NIV

Prophecies From the Book of Revelation

The Revelation of John is a most marvelous book, containing countless signs and prophecies. It was revealed solely to prepare people, especially Christians, for the Object of their desire, the Redeemer of our age. It begins with these words:

> The revelation of Jesus Christ, which God gave him to show his servants what must soon take place...Blessed is the one who reads the words of this prophecy, and blessed are those who hear it and take to heart what is written...
>
> Revelation 1:1-3 NIV

The last chapter of Revelation once again reminds the seekers of truth of the invaluable prophetic knowledge it contains:

> Happy is the man who heeds the words of prophecy contained in this book...I, Jesus, have sent my angel to you with this testimony for the churches.
>
> Revelation 22:7, 16 NEB

Chapters 11 and 12 of the Book of Revelation contain some of the most specific prophecies concerning the advents of both Islam and the Bahá'í Faith. The Muslims for the most part have been unaware of the relevance of these prophecies to Islam. Intertwined with the prophecies is a message that does not appeal to them. That message is this: at the appointed time, the Islamic dispensation will come to an end. This message undermines the Muslims' most dearly cherished—yet unfounded—doctrine: Islam will never be followed by another religion.

The Two Witnesses Who Will Prophesy 1260 Days

Before examining the time prophecies of the Book of Revelation, we need to know a few facts about the Islamic calendar:

- The Islamic calendar dates from the migration (Hegira) of Muhammad from Mecca to Medina. The year of this migration was 622 A.D. The abbreviation used to identify Islamic dates is "A.H." (Anno Hejirae), in the year of Hegira.

- The Muslims count their calendar according to a lunar— not a solar—year.*

- The year 1844 in the Christian calendar corresponds to the year 1260 in the Islamic calendar.

---

* A lunar month is "the period of complete revolution of the moon around the earth...equal to 29.531 days." The Islamic year consists of 12 such months, or 354 days in total.

Chapter 11 of Revelation makes three references to the time of the advent. Verse 3 involves little if any symbolism:*

> And I will give power to my two witnesses, and they will prophesy for 1260 days, clothed in sackcloth.
>
> Revelation 11:3 NIV

The prophecies of Revelation, like those of the book of Daniel, are revealed to John in a vision; and like all visions they wear the veil of symbolism. At first glance we may have difficulty recognizing the underlying meanings of the symbols. But once the veil is lifted, the meanings become so apparent and so closely interrelated with all the other segments of the prophetic profile that we would have difficulty ***not*** recognizing them.

Those who receive power from God to testify for Him must also be divine. This is the extent of their powers:

> These men [two witnesses] have power to shut up the sky [the heaven of divine revelation] so that it will not rain [revelation] during the time they are prophesying [the prophetic dispensation, which ends the age of prophecy]...
>
> Revelation 11:6 NIV

Having power and serving as God's witness are honors bestowed only on divine Messengers and their apostles. Jesus declared that all power was given Him (Matt. 28:18), and that He will return with great power. He was also called "the faithful witness" (Rev. 1:5). Similarly, apostles "bore witness with great power from God" (Acts 4:33 NEB). The prophecy indicates that the two witnesses "were clothed in sackcloth" implying that they

> ...were to be clothed in old raiment, not in new raiment; in other words, in the beginning they would possess no splendor in the eyes of the people, nor would their Cause appear new...[1]
>
> 'Abdu'l-Bahá

---

* This interpretation of prophecies from the Book of Revelation is based mainly on those given by 'Abdu'l-Bahá. See *Some Answered Questions*, Chapters 11 and 13.

God promises to grant divine power to two witnesses. Who are these two witnesses? And for what purpose do they prophesy? According to 'Abdu'l-Bahá, the two witnesses referred to in this verse are Muhammad and His successor 'Alí, who were related to each other both spiritually and physically (Muhammad being 'Alí's cousin and father-in-law).

As we proceed to examine other facts about the two witnesses, the validity of 'Abdu'l-Bahá's words will become more evident.

As John's vision reveals, God promises to send two witnesses who will have the authority to prophesy in His Name. This same chapter (Rev. 11:10) calls the two witnesses *the prophets.* Both of these titles were bestowed on Muhammad. For He was called not only a prophet—"the seal of prophets"—but a witness as well:

> Surely We [God] have sent thee [Muhammad] as a witness, good tidings [of the coming of the Kingdom] to bear, and warning...   Qur'án 48:8 A

Who was 'Alí, the other witness? 'Alí had the honor of being the first man to accept Islam and was appointed the successor to Muhammad. In one passage from Islamic traditions Muhammad hails him by saying:

> I and 'Alí are the Father of this [the Islamic] people [body of believers].[2]

'Abdu'l-Bahá compares 'Alí to Joshua, for as Joshua assisted Moses in His life and served as His successor after His death, so did 'Alí for Muhammad.

The prophecy indicated that the two witnesses or prophets would prophesy for 1260 days. (As stated, 1260 in the Islamic calendar corresponds to 1844 in the Christian calendar.) For what purpose would the two prophets prophesy? All the past Messengers have predicted the coming of God's Kingdom upon the earth. They have been the heralds of the Good News. Hundreds of references in the Bible and the Qur'án

point to the coming of the Kingdom and the advent of the
Lord. The time up to the advent of the Báb is called *the
prophetic age*, or *the prophetic cycle*:

> The prophetic Cycle hath, verily, ended. The Eternal Truth
> is now come.[3]   Bahá'u'lláh

During the prophetic age, all the Messengers and Prophets of
God prophesied and prepared the people for the dawning of
the age of fulfillment, the coming of God's Kingdom on
earth as it is in heaven:

> ...We [God] have indeed sent tidings unto every Prophet
> concerning the Cause of Our Remembrance [the Báb]...[4]
> The Báb

In addition to prophesying, past Messengers and Redeemers
have also served as God's Witnesses, for they have delivered
His Message and warned humanity of the consequences of
unbelief. Both the Gospel and the Qur'án indicate that their
Revelators or Revealers (Jesus and Muhammad) were sent to
serve as the Heralds of the New Age, to give the good news
of the Kingdom. Compare the words of Jesus with those of
Muhammad:

> I [Jesus] must give the good news of the kingdom of
> God...for that is what I was sent to do.   Luke 4:43 NEB

> Surely we [God] have sent thee [Muhammad] as a witness,
> good tidings [of the coming of the Kingdom] to bear, and
> warning...   Qur'án 48:8

One more question requires clarification. How long is 1260
days? As we noted in Chapter 9 concerning the prophecies
of the first advent (69-70 weeks), in the prophetic language
a day equals a year.

Let us review two more references from Christian sources:

> ...each 'day' mentioned by the seer represents a year
> (Guinness, 1880, p. 295ff). The key to this is seen in

Ezekiel 4:6 where God tells Ezekiel that He has assigned him 'a day for each year.' Hence, 1260 days means 1260 years and so on. Guinness compares this to a cartographer who draws a map to a scale where, for example, one inch represents 100 miles (1880, p. 299). With the correct scale, we can then correctly interpret all the time measurements in the prophetic Scriptures.[5]

The period mentioned is 1260 days, which in this place prophetically refers to 1260 years according to the "day for a year" principle found in Numbers 14:34 and Ezekiel 4:5.[6]

Now we should be able to interpret the prophecy:

And I will give power to my two witnesses, and they will prophesy for 1260 days...   Revelation 11:3 NIV

God promises to select two prophets or witnesses who will serve as instruments of His Will, who will continue to prophesy and proclaim the coming of the Kingdom until the end of their dispensation. The end arrives in the year 1260. They also stand as God's Witnesses, testifying that the tidings and the warnings were conveyed.

This is exactly what they did. They prophesied the advent and warned of the consequences of unbelief. The period of their prophesying, the prophetic cycle, lasted until the year 1260 (1844 A.D.), when the Báb proclaimed that by His coming the previous dispensation had come to an end and that the time allotted to the spiritual rulers of Islam had terminated.

Apart from the many other clues or signs revealed throughout the Bible, the preceding verse (Rev. 11:3) may appear somewhat puzzling. But when viewed from a broader perspective and compared with many other facts and figures, its meaning becomes quite clear.

The Gentiles Will Trample the Holy City 42 Months

The end of the Islamic dispensation is also predicted in units of months rather than days:

> They [the Gentiles] will trample on the holy city for 42 months.   Revelation 11:2 NIV

Forty-two months converted into days equals 1260 days:

$$42 \times 30 = 1260$$

At first thought, the exact conversion of months into days may seem impossible, for "a month," as we know it, is a variable entity (28, 29, 30, or 31). Not so when we consider biblical times or the language of prophecy. Both the Egyptians and Babylonians used calendars based on 12 months, each month consisting of 30 days. Hugh Schonfield writes:

> In ancient Egypt the year consisted of 12 months, each of 30 days, making 360 days. To bring this into line with the solar year of 365 days, five year-end days were added associated with the birthdays of the divinities.[7]

Christian writer, A. J. McClaim, states:

> There is conclusive evidence to show that the prophetic year of Scriptures is composed of 360 days, or twelve months of 30 days.[8]

In Chapter 12 we discussed "the times of the Gentiles." We demonstrated that the appointed "times" ended with Mordecai Noah's Declaration of 1844, and by the Edicts of Submission issued in 1844 of the Christian calendar and 1260 of the Islamic calendar. Once again we see the confirmation of that prophecy in similar wording from another book in the Bible. Here in this prophecy we are directed to the same historic year 1844 A.D. or 1260 A.H.

The Symbolism of "the Trampling of Jerusalem"

"The trampling of Jerusalem by the Gentiles" carries two meanings: spiritual and literal. Literally it points to the last conquest of Jerusalem by the Gentiles (Muslims), and the conclusion of this period (of the persecution of the Jews) by the birth of two documents: the Declaration of Mordecai Noah in the West, and the Edicts of Submission in the East. Both of these documents were issued in 1260 A.H., a figure prophetically equal to 42 months. Spiritually, the expression refers to the disintegration or completion of the old cycle, paving the way for the rising of the new. For, as stated, the advent of every new faith terminates the old dispensation and inaugurates a new one. Therefore, "42 months" (or 1260 days) points to the completion of the Islamic dispensation, the only independent major religion to appear between the advent of Jesus and the advent of the Promised One of all ages and religions, an event known to Christians as the return of Christ in the glory of His Father. In the year 1260 A.H. when the Báb declared His Mission, the Islamic dispensation came to an end.

As the prophecy of 70 weeks (Daniel 9:24-27) was fulfilled first spiritually and then literally after the crucifixion, so was the prophecy of 42 months. As stated previously, the advent of Jesus removed the need for making any offering. The spiritual fulfillment was then followed by a literal fulfillment, when the sanctuary, the place of offering, was completely destroyed by the Romans. First occurred the spiritual conquest of Jerusalem (a city symbolic of divine Laws) by Muhammad Himself, and later the literal conquest of Jerusalem by His followers soon after His death. (The span of time between the death of Jesus and the conquest of Jerusalem by the Romans was, according to the conventional calendar, about 36 years. The span of time between Muhammad's death and the conquest of Jerusalem by the Muslims was about 5 years.)

Once again the absolute harmony between the sacred words from two sources separated by centuries (the Book of Daniel* and the Book of Revelation) is demonstrated. These books link the desolation of the human spirit and the inception of the era of spiritual renewal and purification (the cleansing of the sanctuary) to an identical period in human history, despite using entirely different starting points. They also harmonize with Jesus' prophecies by linking the time of His return, on the one hand, to Daniel's prophecy of "the abomination of desolation" and, on the other, to the treading down of Jerusalem by the Gentiles until their time came to an end. Again the termination of this period was shown to correspond to 1260 A. H. or 1844 A. D., when the Báb inaugurated a new dispensation (spiritual fulfillment), and when Noah's Declaration and the Edicts of Submission were issued (literal fulfillment).

Compare the prophetic words of Jesus about His return as recorded in Luke and again as decoded by Him in the Book of Revelation:

> "Teacher," they asked, "when will these things happen?"
> "...Jerusalem will be trampled on by the Gentiles until the times of the Gentiles are fulfilled [completed]."
> Luke 21:7, 24 NIV

> They [the Gentiles] will trample on the holy city [Jerusalem] for 42 months.
> Revelation 11:2 NIV

In the first passage Jesus links His return to the completion or fulfillment of "the time of the Gentiles." In the second passage, He clearly specifies "the times of the Gentiles." Since the last group of Gentiles to dominate Jerusalem were the Muslims, it seems reasonable to assume that the figure given refers to the Muslims, whose reign completed or brought to an end the domination of Jerusalem by the Gentiles. After being exposed to its last humiliation, Jerusalem eventually came under the control of the state of Israel, the seeds of

---

* See Daniel's prophecy of 2300 days discussed earlier.

whose birth were planted in the year 1260 (equal to 42 months) by two historical declarations.

The Two Witnesses Who Lie Unburied for Three and a Half Days

In the prophecies that follow, the veil of symbolism in the vision begins to darken somewhat, as if the Revealer has resolved to test the depths of human vision. Here the story becomes more challenging, for its meaning remains sealed or incomprehensible unless the seeker resolves to tread patiently through the dark and deep valleys of search.

The succeeding verses of Revelation (Chapter 11) deal with the struggle between the positive and negative forces in Islam. In sum, the two Witnesses (likened to two olive trees or "two candlesticks standing before the God of the earth") shall enjoy divine protection and shall be endowed with great powers to perform wondrous things. And when they have completed their work—"finished their testimony"—the beast (symbolic of the Umayyads,[9] who usurped the leadership from the lawful successors) shall "ascend out of the bottomless pit," that is, from the depths of ignorance and shame, and "shall make war against them, and shall overcome them, and kill them" (Rev. 11:7), that is, destroy the spirit of their Faith.

The spirit they kill, but the body or skeleton they expose "in the street," that is, they reduce religion to a social or political skeleton; preserving its name, its institutions, and its dogmas, but destroying its inspirational or spiritual powers. The faith that was meant to be centered on the Spirit is gradually altered into a public show or museum, where lifeless bodies are stored and displayed. (For the Islamic prophecies pointing to the spiritual state of the Muslims in the last days, please refer to Volume IV).

The prophecy concerning the two Witnesses continues:

> For three and a half days men from every people, tribe, language and nation will gaze on their bodies and refuse them burial. Revelation 11:9 NIV

The symbolism in the preceding verse should by now have become quite clear. Simply, the dead body of religion is not allowed to be buried, that is, to disappear from the eyes of the people. It is rather kept in sight for three and a half days.

How long is "three and a half days"? It equals the same prophetic periods of 42 months, or 1260 days, to which we have already referred. Here are the calculations: since each day is equal to a year, three and a half days means three and a half years, which equals 42 months or 1260 days.

$$3\frac{1}{2} \times 12 \text{ months} = 42 \text{ months}$$
$$42 \times 30 = 1260 \text{ days}$$

As you may have noted, the conversion of the figure "3½" is carried not once, but twice. Are we justified in doing so? First, as stated, in the prophetic language no one piece of evidence, no single fact or figure, can by itself be binding. Each bit of the evidence must be assessed in relation to the whole panorama of proofs.

Second, unlike Daniel's single vision designating the time of Christ's first coming, here we have not one, but many references from many sources, all pointing to the appointed time.

Third, as mentioned, the language of prophecy is a language of signs, shrouded in mystery, otherwise facts would not remain sealed or guarded until the appointed time. The mist of symbolism seems to increase in proportion to the frequency with which a given prophetic figure is repeated. The biblical prophecies foretell the appointed time of the second advent in four different ways: (1) 1260 days, (2) 42 months, (3) three and a half days, (4) time, times, and half a time. This may be one reason why Daniel's vision on the first advent also comprised different or *seemingly* different dates: 62, 69, and 70 weeks.

Fourth, the figure 3½ (or its equivalent "a time, times, and half a time") is used synonymously with the other two figures (1260 days, and 42 months). Therefore the context of the vision reaffirms the accuracy and necessity of the conversion of the figure 3½. For instance, it is prophesied that:

> The woman fled into the desert to a place prepared for her by God, where *she might be taken care of for 1260 days*.
>   Revelation 12:6 NIV

And soon thereafter (verse 14) it is said that:

> The woman was given the two wings of a great eagle, so that she might fly to the place prepared for her in the desert, where *she would be taken care of for a time, times and half a time*, out of the serpent's reach.
>   Revelation 12:14 NIV

(The symbolism contained in the preceding verses will be decoded later in this chapter.)

Fifth, in the context of the prophecies, we can find the same relation between 42 months and 1260 days as we do between "a time, times and half a time," and "1260 days." In some translations such as *The New English Bible* and *The New American Bible* their identical meaning is more evident. A review of two of the time prophecies previously quoted will prove this point.

> ...they [the Gentiles] will trample the Holy City underfoot *for forty-two months*. And I have two witnesses, whom I will appoint to prophesy, dressed in sackcloth, *all through those twelve hundred and sixty days*.   Revelation 11:2-3 NEB

What does the phrase "all through those twelve hundred and sixty days" refer to? Obviously it refers to the preceding figure, namely, "forty-two months."

The above two verses once again confirm what was already stated about the duration of the prophetic month. If 1260 days and 42 months are equal, then the length of a prophetic month must be:

$$1260 \div 42 = 30$$

In fact the identity of the four figures (1260 days, 42 months, 3½ days, and "time, times and a half time") is so well established that *The Amplified Bible* in translating any one of them often adds their equivalents in brackets to emphasize their unity. (See any of the quoted verses in *The Amplified Bible*.) Many of the new versions of the Book of Revelation drop "time, times, and half a time" altogether. They replace it with "three years and a half." (See for instance: *The New English Bible, Today's English Version of the New Testament, The Amplified Bible,* or *The New American Bible*.)

Sixth, many Christian scholars, who have puzzled over these mysterious figures, have at least recognized the identical interval they represent. (See *The Major Prophetic Eras*, Chapter 16.) As we shall see later, the mysterious figure "time, times, and a half time" was also revealed to Daniel, in the same context (the destiny of the people of Israel) and in relation to the same advent.

Here is a reference from a Christian source confirming such a view:

> ...in Revelation, each group of 360 days is called a 'time' (12:6, 14). If each day in turn becomes a year, then each 'time,' in fact, represents 360 years. (This is all based on a lunar year, of course). So the seven 'times' mentioned in Leviticus 26:28 as a period of punishment for Israel are seen as a total period of 2520 years...[10]

The Resurrection of
the Two Witnesses

So far, in St. John's vision, the dead bodies of the two Witnesses are not allowed to be buried. What about the reaction of the nations antagonistic to these two Prophets or Witnesses? The vision reveals that these nations shall rejoice over the dead bodies and "shall send gifts one to another." The prophecy then continues:

> But after the three and a half days a breath of life from God entered them, and they stood on their feet, and terror struck those who saw them.   Revelation 11:11 NIV

Each preceding passage makes the meaning of the succeeding ones a little more clear. The dead bodies of the two Witnesses or the two Prophets have been lying in the open. Then after three and a half days—1260 years—the spirit of life vivifies them; that is, in the year 1260, the Spirit of God once again enters the skeleton of their faith to endow it with a new life. Many are terrified to hear this news.

The prophecy of the two Witnesses was fulfilled not only symbolically but literally as well. As stated, the two Witnesses "whose bodies had been lying in the open for 1260 years" were Muhammad and His greatest apostle 'Alí. As it happens, the names of the other two Witnesses who fulfilled the prophecy by appearing after the appointed time of 1260 days (thereby empowering the dead body of religion with a new Spirit) contained the same two names: 'Alí and Muhammad.

The first and the greater of the two Witnesses to receive the power of the Holy Spirit in the year 1260 was the Báb, with the given name of 'Alí-Muhammad. The Báb was, further-more, a direct descendant of both Muhammad and 'Alí, who, as mentioned, were spiritually and physically related to each other. The other Witness to receive a portion of the Holy Spirit and "to stand upon his feet" was Quddús—meaning Holy or Blessed—the greatest apostle of the Báb, who embraced the new faith in that same eventful year: 1260 (corresponding to 1844 A. D.). Quddús' given name consisted of a combination of the same two names but in the reverse order: Muhammad-'Alí. Bahá'u'lláh has conferred great honors on Quddús. He indicates that the Qur'án refers to him as a Messenger or Prophet.[11] That is the exact title the Book of Revelation bestows on him (11:10).*

The Woman With the Child and the Seven-headed Dragon

A similar story, but one clothed in a somewhat different symbolism, is repeated in Chapter 12 of Revelation. Here we find not only the time of the advent of the Promised One of all Faiths, but also a major part of the history of Islam, the faith prophesied to appear between Christ's first and second comings.

To appreciate the prophecies that follow, we need to review some of the history of Islam. As stated, soon after Muhammad's death, the Muslims lost the unity they had enjoyed during their Messenger's ministry. A major cause of division among them was the question of succession. The group that followed Muhammad's lawful successor 'Alí, the first Imám—as well as the other ten Imáms who succeeded him—is called Shí'ah or Shí'i. The duration of inspiration in Islam lasted as long as these eleven spiritual leaders or Imáms continued (in spite of severe opposition from other sects) to assume the leadership of the minority of the Muslims who followed them. This period ended in the year 260 A. H., when the eleventh Imám—Imám Hasan-i-'Askarí—died and left no heir.

---

* Quddús was not an independent Messenger with a new Revelation. He simply received an honorary title. Similarly, divine Messengers are not God, yet God honors them with that very title.

But according to the Islamic prophecies, there were to appear not eleven, but twelve Imáms—the twelfth one to come and lead the people in the last days, referred to in Islamic Scripture as "the end of time." The Báb, the Inaugurator of the New Age, claimed to be not only an independent Messenger but also the twelfth Imám prophesied in Islamic Scriptures. The time span between the death of the eleventh Imám (in the year 260) and the proclamation of the Báb was one thousand lunar years.

Among those deviating from the true spirit of Islam were a group of Muslims headed by a succession of leaders who established a dynasty—or Caliphate—called the Umayyads. The Umayyads were extremely hostile to the descendants of Muhammad and massacred many of them. There were 14 rulers in this dynasty with 10 different names. (Several of them had exactly the same names.) Let us now proceed with the prophecies.

Chapter 12 of Revelation contains John's marvelous and mysterious vision of the next two religions, those of Muhammad and the Báb:

> A great and wondrous sign appeared in heaven: a woman clothed with the sun, with the moon under her feet and a crown of twelve stars on her head. She was pregnant and cried out in pain as she was about to give birth.
>
> Revelation 12:1-2 NIV

To interpret the preceding verses we need to decode several symbols:

- In the Scriptures, religion is likened to heaven, and the Law of God to an adorned bride, or a woman (see Volume V). So the woman coming from heaven is the same as the Law of God or divine truths coming from religion.

- Among the kingdoms coming under the Law of Islam were the two neighboring countries of Persia, whose national emblem contains an image of the sun, and Turkey, whose national emblem contains an image of the moon.

Now we should be able to interpret the passage quite readily. The Law of God (the woman) dawned in the heaven of religion and spread to the neighboring countries of Persia and Turkey, which are represented by their national emblems, the sun and the moon. In the heaven of this faith also dawned twelve Imáms likened to twelve stars. The faith bore a baby (the Báb) and had difficulty delivering Him because of the opposition of the heedless people.

The Báb, although an independent Manifestation, was "born from the Law of Muhammad." He was a descendant of Muhammad and the last of His twelve Imáms. The other eleven Imáms followed each other without interruption. But the Báb appeared a thousand years later. The vision continues:

> Then another sign appeared in heaven: an enormous red dragon with seven heads and ten horns and seven crowns on his heads. Revelation 12:3 NIV

Interpretation: This dragon (that appeared in the heaven of Islam) represents the succession of the Umayyad dynasty, which swallowed country after country. It wore the crowns of seven dominions—Damascus, Persia, Arabia, Egypt, Africa (consisting of Tunisia, Morocco, and Algeria), Andalusia (Spain), and Turkestan. The ten horns of the dragon represent the ten names of the rulers of the dynasty.

Verse 4:

> His tail swept a third of the stars out of the sky and flung them to the earth. The dragon stood in front of the woman who was about to give birth, so that he might devour her child the moment it was born.
> Revelation 12:4 NIV

Interpretation: As 'Abdu'l-Bahá states, the Umayyad dynasty massacred a "third part of the holy and saintly people of the lineage of Muhammad who were like the stars of heaven."[12] The Umayyads "were always waiting to get possession of the Promised One [the twelfth Imám], who was to come from the line of Muhammad." They wished "to destroy and annihilate Him."[13]

Herod conceived and carried out the same scheme and met the same failure. He tried to get possession of the Promised One of the people of Israel:

> Jesus was born in Bethlehem during the reign of Herod the Great. The wise men came asking, "Where is he that is born King of the Jews?" This aroused Herod's jealous spirit. According to Matthew's account, Herod tried to eliminate Jesus by having all the male infants of the Bethlehem region put to death (Matt. 2:13-16). But this despicable act failed. Joseph and Mary were warned by God in a dream to take their child and flee to Egypt. Here they hid safely until Herod died (Matt. 2:13-15).[14]

Verse 5:

> She gave birth to a son, a male child, who will rule all the nations with an iron scepter. And her child was snatched up to God and to his throne.*   Revelation 12:5 NIV

Interpretation: The Faith of Islam (the woman) gives birth to a "man child" (the Báb) who is to be the King of the nations. (The Kingdom of the past Messengers was spiritual, that of the Báb and Bahá'u'lláh is both literal and spiritual, "the Kingdom of God on earth as it is in Heaven.") The child then offers his life and ascends to the divine Kingdom ("was snatched up to God"). The martyrdom of the Báb was the fulfillment of this prophecy.

Verse 6:

> The woman fled into the desert to a place prepared for her by God, where she might be taken care of for 1260 days.
>   Revelation 12:6 NIV

---

* 'Abdu'l-Bahá explains that "the man child," the Báb, existed in the worlds of God before His birth. The Book of Revelation confirms the eternal destiny of the Báb. It refers to the Báb as, "the Lamb that was slain from the creation of the world" (Rev. 13:8 NIV).

Interpretation: The woman or the Law of God, which first appeared in heaven moves to the wilderness (Arabia), where God had chosen to nourish her for 1260 years. This is exactly what happened; Arabia became the center of the Law of God. The Law received nourishment from God until it reached the end of its cycle in 1260 A. H.—the year in which the Báb inaugurated a New Age.

In verse 14 of this same chapter (12) it is again repeated that the woman goes into the wilderness and receives nourishment "for a time, times, and half a time," or three years and a half, already shown to equal 1260 prophetic days.

"The beast with seven heads and ten horns" emerges again (Rev. 13:1), wielding power and authority and drawing the admiration and acclamation of the masses. Again the duration of the beast's authority is prophesied:

> The dragon gave the beast his power and his throne and great authority...The beast was given a mouth to utter proud words and blasphemies and to exercise his authority for forty-two months.   Revelation 13:2,5 NIV

As stated, the Islamic dispensation was marred by many deviant leaders (the beast) who were guided not by the divine teachings, but by their own selfish or satanic desires, symbolically called *the dragon*. Again, as the preceding verse predicts, the time allotted to the beast is prophesied to endure 42 months or 1260 days.

It is astounding how these prophecies agree with one another. As 'Abdu'l-Bahá reminds every seeker of truth:

> There are no clearer proofs than this in the Holy Books for any Manifestation.* For him who is just, the agreement of the times indicated by the tongues of the Great Ones is the most conclusive proof. There is no other possible

---

* As stated, in the Old Testament there are only three verses (Daniel's vision of 62, 69, and 70 weeks) designating the time of Christ's first coming.

explanation of these prophecies. Blessed are the just souls who seek the truth.[15]

Other Explanations

Christian commentators have tried to accomplish what 'Abdu'l-Bahá has declared impossible. Let us see if they have succeeded. Failing to find any event that would relate the prophecies of 1260 days, 42 months, etc. to the year 1260 in the Christian calendar, some of them have tried to find events *at any two points* in history separated by a span of 1260 years. Since this too has proved impossible, as a last resort, they have tried to find an *approximate* fulfillment for these prophecies by events that coincide closely with the figure 1260. In this case, these interpreters have not considered *the precise* fulfillment of time prophecies essential.

The bewilderment of Bible interpreters in understanding Revelation's time prophecies and the events associated with them is reflected clearly in an assessment presented by the Christian scholar, William Biederwolf, who carried out one of the most exhaustive searches into biblical prophecy in search for common, consistent, and reasonable elements in the works of recognized Bible interpreters. He spent "by far the largest part of ten years of his time" reviewing and summarizing the works and views of "some five hundred or more authorities."[16] He found several schools of thought, each with a unique perspective, for virtually all biblical prophecies.

To illustrate the bewilderment of interpreters, let us take the views of only *one* of the schools—perhaps the most popular one.

The supporters of this school have tried to find links between the time prophecies of the Book of Revelation and the historical events associated with "Papal Rome in its political and ecclesiastical character, that is, the empire and the Hierarchy of the Papacy."[17] As we noted, Revelation contains seven prophecies relating to 1260. One of them is found in

Chapter 13 of that Book. Even if we ignore the events of other chapters, we find many difficulties in associating Papal Rome with the events or facts contained in that one chapter alone. Biederwolf lists in this connection seven discrepancies or difficulties. Here are three of them, quoted in his own words, from his monumental work *The Second Coming Bible Commentary*:

- No one has ever found the ten-fold division of the empire. Twenty-eight different commentators have named sixty-five different lists. What would it be if all the commentators were consulted!

- Even if the 1260 days mean "years" none of them [scholars] have been able to agree as to when they begin or when they end; whether they have already ended or whether the saints are yet in the power of the beast: and the saints themselves do not seem to know!

- This class of interpreters has as many different interpretations of 666 as there are interpreters.[18]*

Thus we see that the difficulties of relating even one chapter of Revelation to historical events other than those declared by 'Abdu'l-Bahá are enormous. The probability of finding the fulfillment of these prophecies by "trial and error" or chance is a virtual impossibility.

As we have noted, the Bahá'í interpretation shows the fulfillment of two events in the precise designated year (1260). One was the declaration of the Báb, who proclaimed the dawning of a new Age for humankind. The other was the declaration of Mordecai Noah, whose efforts signaled the dawning of a new age for the people of Israel. Furthermore, it shows an absolute harmony between the prophecy of 2300 days (which is totally *in*dependent of the Islamic calendar), and the prophecy of 1260 days (which is totally *de*pendent on

---

* For the fulfillment of the figure 666 by the Umayyad dynasty, see *The Apocalypse Unsealed*, by Robert F. Riggs, Chapter 13. The three discrepancies listed here are exact quotations.

the Islamic calendar). As we have noted, the "2300-days" of Daniel ended in 1844 A.D., which was 1260 in the Islamic calendar. In addition, the Bahá'í interpretation demonstrates the fulfillment of all the other events not associated with dates.

The Context of the Prophetic Figures

Before concluding our examination of Revelation's prophetic puzzle, let us make one last observation. The Book of Revelation contains seven time prophecies on the second advent. These prophecies are expressed in four seemingly different forms: 42 months, 1260 days, three days and a half (all of them used twice), and three times and a half (used only once). But there is a pattern in the way these four forms of prophetic figures are used.

1. The figure "42 months" in both cases is used in relation to the *worldly* powers in Islam. One of the "42" figures relates to "the beast," which symbolizes the worldly kingdom, and the other to those who trample the Holy City, namely *the forces* of the worldly kingdom.

2. The figure 1260 is used in both cases in relation to the *spiritual* powers in Islam. One of the "1260" figures relates to the Founders of Islam (the two Witnesses), and the other, to the religion itself (the woman).

3. The figure "three and a half days" is used in both cases in relation to the dead body of Islam, which symbolizes the outward observance of religion, such as attending and building magnificent mosques or shrines, praying and fasting especially in public, wearing veils, calling to prayer, building and attending seminary, carrying and reading the Holy Book just for the sake of reading, wearing priestly costumes, celebrating the Holy Days with fanfare, etc.

4. Finally the last coded figure "three times and a half" is used (like 1260) in relation to the woman, which symbolizes the spiritual forces in religion.

The Prophecy of the Four Angels

The Book of Revelation contains still another time prophecy pointing to 1844:

> "Release the four angels who are bound at the great river Euphrates." And the four angels who had been kept ready for this very *hour* and *day* and *month* and *year* were released to kill a third of mankind [emphasis added].
>
> Revelation 9:14-15 NIV

Let us first decode the main symbolism contained in the prophecy and then study its fulfillment:

Codes	*Meaning*
The four angels bound at the Euphrates River	Secularly, the Islamic empire. Spiritually, the four existing religions born in the Middle East
Killing* a third of mankind	Secularly, cutting off, conquering, or controlling a third of Christendom. Spiritually, directing or controlling a third of mankind
hour	one hour (the Hour)
1 day	1 year
1 month	30 years
1 year	360 years
	391 years

---

* "Killing" sometimes symbolizes self-control or self-sacrifice. We are asked repeatedly to destroy our ego, to sacrifice our earthly pleasures, and to "die in the Lord."

Perhaps the first writer or scholar to gain a glimpse of the inner meanings of this prophecy and decode its timing was Charles Buck (1771-1815). He wrote:

> This period, in the language of prophecy, makes 391 years, which being added to the year when the four angels were loosed (prepared), will bring us down to 1844, or thereabouts, for the final destruction of the Mahometan [Muhammadan] empire.[19]

What helped Charles Buck find the date was his realization that on May 30, 1453, Constantinople and Eastern Christendom had fallen to the Turks, namely the Islamic empire. He took that date as the beginning point of the prophecy. He then computed the period assigned to the four angels, namely, the time interval for which they had been prepared to rule. This, as we noted, totals 391 years. To get the final date, he added the two figures: the span of time assigned to the angels, and the beginning point of the prophecy (the date the angels were let loose):

$$391^* + 1453 = 1844$$

Besides its literal or temporal meaning, the prophecy seems to contain a spiritual message as well. The four angels bound at the Euphrates River represent the four existing religions that originated in the Middle East, in the same geographical zone where the Euphrates flows. The four religions are: **Judaism, Zoroastrianism, Christianity**, and **Islam**. Although Islam was the dominant force, all four religions were granted 391 more years to control a third of mankind. Then at the end of the 391 years (1844) their reign was terminated, by another angel that appeared in the same region.

---

* "The hour" is discounted. It is frequently used by Christ to refer to the exact point of His advent. As author Robert Riggs indicates, that is probably what it symbolizes here. Even if we add an extra "hour" (which is the equivalent of 15 days) to our time span, the final year (1844) derived from the prophecy still stands untouched.

These are the same four religions Bahá'u'lláh specifically names in the public proclamation of His Message:

> At one time We address the people of the Torah [the Jews] and summon them unto Him...At another We address the people of the Evangel [the Christians]...At still another, We address the people of the Qur'án [the Muslims]...Know thou, moreover, that We have [also] addressed to the Magians [the Zoroastrians] Our Tablets.[20]

What Charles Buck discovered early in the 19th century has been accepted and its accuracy confirmed by hundreds of Christian writers and scholars, who for the most part were unaware of the advent of the Bahá'í Revelation in 1844.

The prophecy of the four angels is so precise as to designate not only the year (1844) but the season (spring) in which the past dispensations ended and the new age dawned. The span of time assigned to the four angels began and ended in spring: May 30, when the angels were let loose; and May 23, when the Báb declared His Mission. The Báb's advent signalized the closing of all past dispensations.

> The Prophetic Cycle hath, verily, ended. The Eternal Truth is now come.[21]
> Bahá'u'lláh

Other Prophecies from the Book of Revelation

The Book of Revelation contains, in addition to the time prophecies, many other references to the return of Christ. Like the Book of Daniel, it refers to the rise of Michael—whose name means *"Who is like God?"*—and calls Him the Archangel. Daniel referred to this same angel as "Michael...the great Prince which standeth for the children of thy [Daniel's] people" (Daniel 12:1). Then, after giving the time of the advent, the Book of Revelation predicts the triumph of this

heavenly spirit over the dragon and other negative forces.
And then it goes on to declare:

> Now have come the salvation and the power and the king-
> dom of our God, and the authority of his Christ...
>
> Revelation 12:10 NIV

In subsequent chapters, the apocalypse declares the descending of the city of God (Jerusalem) from heaven:

> I saw the Holy City, the new Jerusalem, coming down out
> of heaven from God, prepared as a bride beautifully
> dressed for her husband.   Revelation 21:2 NIV

As has been stated, the desolation of Jerusalem and the
sanctuary is symbolic of deprivation from the restoring power
of the divine Spirit. Similarly, the restoration or cleansing
of Jerusalem and the sanctuary is symbolic of the dawning
of divine Power over the desolate and despairing centers of
faith. Once again we see the very symbol revealed to Daniel
is also used in the Book of Revelation with an identical
meaning.

The descent of Jerusalem signifies the descent of divine Law
or divine Revelation. Indeed this is one meaning of the
descent of Christ from heaven. Christ's Spirit (the Bridegroom) descended from the heaven of divine Knowledge
adorned with the Robe of divine Revelation (the Bride).

As every city needs a source of light, so does the Holy City;
it shines with *the Glory of God*, the meaning of the title
Bahá'u'lláh:

> The city does not need the sun or the moon to shine on
> it, for *the glory of God* gives it light, and the Lamb is its
> lamp.   Revelation 21:23 NIV

The *Lamb*, which symbolizes *sacrifice*, refers not only to
Jesus, but also to the Báb. They both offered their youthful
lives for the life of the world. (See Volume II.)

And again:

And he...showed me the Holy City, Jerusalem, coming down out of heaven from God. It [Jerusalem] shone with *the glory of God* [Bahá'u'lláh]...   Revelation 21:10-11 NIV

The Book of Revelation refers also to the advent of the Báb, an independent Messenger as well as the Forerunner of Bahá'u'lláh:

Blessed are those who wash their robes, that they may have the right to the tree of life and may go through *the gates* into the city.   Revelation 22:14 NIV

The word "Báb" in Arabic means "Gate." The Báb proclaimed repeatedly that He was a Gate to the Revelation of Bahá'u'lláh, a portal through whom the seekers of truth could enter the City of God and partake of the tree of life. Likewise, one of the most distinguished disciples of the Báb and the first to recognize Him was named Bábu'l-Báb, meaning "*the gate of the Gate*." The two seers, who predicted the advent of the Báb, were also called "the Gates:"

O ye peoples of the earth! During the time of My absence I sent down the Gates unto you. However the believers, except for a handful, obeyed them not...What hath befallen you, O people of the Book? Will ye not fear the One true God, He Who is your Lord, the Ancient of Days?...O ye who profess belief in God! I adjure you by Him Who is the Eternal Truth, have ye discerned among the precepts of these Gates anything inconsistent with the commandments of God as set forth in this Book? Hath your learning deluded you by reason of your impiety? Take ye heed then, for verily your God, the Lord of Eternal Truth, is with you and in very truth is watchful over you...[22]   The Báb

The Book of Revelation is rich not only in prophecy but also in offering counsels and warnings to seekers of truth, lest they ignore or underestimate their responsibility. God in His justice never punishes people without giving them ample warning in advance:

Behold, I am coming soon! My reward is with me, and I will give to everyone according to what he has done... Blessed are those who wash their robes, that they may have the right to the tree of life and may go through the gates into the city. Outside are...the sexually immoral, the murderers, the idolaters and everyone who loves and practices falsehood.   Revelation 22:12-15 NIV

A great portion of the Book of Revelation concerns the advent of the Bahá'í Faith and to a lesser extent that of Islam. To examine all the prophecies of Revelation that have been fulfilled by the Báb and Bahá'u'lláh requires a separate volume. This is exactly what *The Apocalypse Unsealed* by Robert Riggs accomplishes.[23]

15

The Great Prince
Daniel 12:1

Prophecies From Daniel

Michael, the Great Prince

Daniel's last and briefest chapter contains one of the most remarkable prophetic visions in all the Scriptures. In less than a page, it presents a distinct, unmistakable, and readily recognizable profile of "the time" and "the signs of the time." These are the opening words of Daniel's vision:

> And at that time [of the end] shall Michael stand up, the great prince which standeth for the children of thy people...   Daniel 12:1

Obviously by Michael is meant the adored and the exalted Savior of the Jews, destined to stand as the symbol and embodiment of their fairest hopes and dreams. The literal meaning of Michael, "Who is like God?" provides us with the first clue. Who, we might ask, deserves such an exalted honor—*like God*—save the Son coming in the Glory of the Father, a Manifestation reflecting the fullest Image of divine Perfections?

Dr. Ray Stedman in *Waiting for the Second Coming* writes:

> The only angel in the Bible called an archangel is Michael. Though Gabriel is a great angel, he is never referred to as an archangel.[1]

Still another clue comes from the perfect harmony between the Books of Daniel and Revelation. It is intriguing to note that *the same* chapter (12) in both Books (each consisting of about a page) refers to the coming of *the same* divine Being, Michael, (verse 1 in Daniel, verse 7 in Revelation), then uses *the same* prophetic figure "time, times and half a time" to identify the time of His advent.

Both of these chapters also provide us with a decoded figure. Chapter 12 of Revelation refers to 1260, the time of the advent of the Báb; and Chapter 12 of Daniel points to 1290 (as we shall see later), the time of the advent of Bahá'u'lláh.

Daniel introduces Michael as the great prince. Here we find one more clue. As we noted earlier, Daniel in his vision of the first advent also referred to Jesus as the Messiah, the Prince:

> Know therefore and understand, that from the going forth of the commandment to restore and to build Jerusalem unto the Messiah the Prince shall be seven weeks...
>
> Daniel 9:25

"The Prince of Peace" is among the best-known titles of the Redeemer of our age. Bahá'u'lláh fulfilled the designation "great Prince" both symbolically, by bringing a plan of peace; and literally, by being a descendant of ancient Persian kings.

Beyond the title bestowed upon the Prince of the last days, other signs and clues, linking the prophecy to the advent of the Lord, abound throughout the vision.

After referring to the coming of Michael, the great prince, Daniel points to the darkness of the time and the abundance and triumph of evil (a common prophetic theme appearing in all the Scriptures). Then he alludes to the acceptance of the Redeemer by some and the denial or rejection of Him by others. Following this, the vision begins to become increasingly more specific as to the time and the signs of the time.

Increase in Knowledge and Travel

Daniel's vision of the time of the end offers two striking signs that signal the ripening of the Age and the dawning of the new Day: an increase in knowledge, and an abundance of travel. Here are the words of the vision:

> But thou, O Daniel, shut up the words, and seal the book, even to the time of the end: many shall run to and fro, and knowledge shall be increased.   Daniel 12:4

The history of civilization shows that for thousands of years humans moved at an extremely slow pace along the path of progress until the end of the 18th century when there occurred a sudden and dramatic acceleration of knowledge. It is believed that the changes brought about in the last two centuries far exceed all those recorded in the entire previous history of civilization. An example of this dramatic change has occurred in the mode and speed of travel. Alvin Toffler in *Future Shock* portrays the phenomenal increase in the speed of travel since the mid-19th century:

> ...in 6000 B.C. the fastest transportation available to man over long distances was the camel caravan, averaging eight miles an hour...when the first mail coach began operating in England in 1784, it averaged a mere ten mph.

The first steam locomotive, introduced in 1825, could muster a top speed of only thirteen mph, and the great sailing ships of the time labored along at less than half that speed. It was probably not until the 1880's that man, with the help of a more advanced locomotive, managed to reach a speed of one hundred mph. It took the human race millions of years to attain that record. [Less than a century later (1960's)]...men in space capsules were circling the earth at 18,000 mph.[2]

Toffler then goes on to explain:

Whether we examine distances traveled, altitudes reached, minerals mined, or explosive power harnessed, the same accelerative trend is obvious. The pattern, here and in a thousand other statistical series, is absolutely clear and unmistakable. Millennia or centuries go by, and then, in our own times, a sudden bursting of the limits, a fantastic spurt forward.[3]

From 6000 years before the advent of Christ up to eighteen and a half centuries after His advent (a total of 78 centuries), the speed of traveling remained quite constant. Why, then, did the change happen around the appointed time of Christ's return, namely 1844? Was this simply a coincidence?

Dr. Harold Bernard writes:

It has been conjectured that if all the knowledge mankind had accumulated up to the time of Christ could have been compressed into one volume, it would have taken until 1750 to double that knowledge. But instead of another 1750 years to double knowledge again, it took only 150 years. The postulation of acceleration of knowledge looks like this:

        Year 1 - one volume
        1750 - two volumes
        1900 - four volumes
        1950 - eight volumes
        1960 - sixteen volumes
        1967 - thirty-two volumes[4]

Since the dawn of history up to the middle of the 18th century, the rate of the accumulation of knowledge was about one volume every three thousand years. From the middle of the 18th century up to 1967, it climbed to about one volume every seven years. This is an increase in the acceleration rate equal to at least 428 times.

The following chart indicates that the greatest acceleration in creativity—measured by the number of patents issued per capita—occurred around 1850 and continued unabated until around 1890, a period that roughly covers the years from the beginning of the ministry of the Báb to the end of the ministry of Bahá'u'lláh (1844-1892):

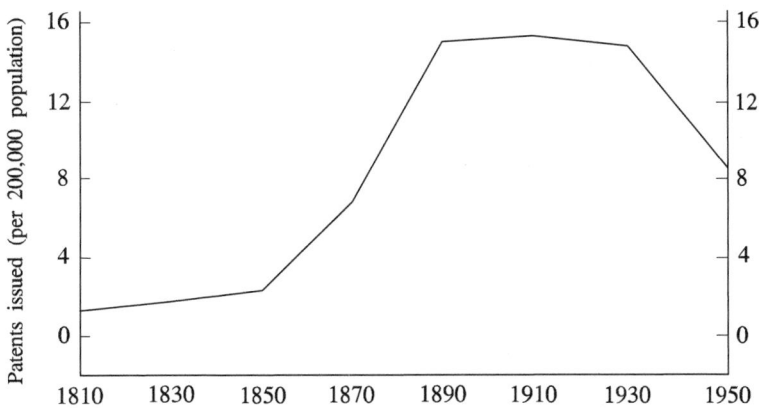

Source: Journal of Abnormal and Social Psychology, 1962. (Quoted in *Child, Family, Community*, 1989, p. 298.) Reprinted with permission from the American Psychological Association.

Charles Meister, a Christian writer who wrote *Year of the Lord*, a book devoted entirely to the events of 1844 asks: "Why did so many earth-shaking events occur in the year 1844?"[5] One major scientific achievement in 1844 was the operation of the first telegraph service. The first message was sent about one day after the Báb had declared His Message:*

---

* The Báb declared His Mission on the evening of May 22nd. But as the Bahá'í day begins at sunset, and not at midnight as in the West, the Báb's declaration is celebrated on 23rd of May.

The telegram inaugurating commercial service was sent May 24, 1844, by Professor Samuel Finley Breese Morse... The message, "What hath God wrought," was selected from the 23rd verse of the 23rd chapter of Numbers.[6]

Another source confirming the dawning of a new civilization in the mid-19th century is a three-volume series called *1844*, by Christian scholar Jerome Clarke, professor of history at Southern Missionary College. The author introduces his work in these words:

The 1830's and 1840's were a time of religious, social, cultural, and political reforms so widespread and intensive that historians have termed this the period of the Benevolent Empire. In this period, 1844 was a pivotal year, during which many of the movements had their beginning, experienced a severe crisis, or reached their climax, or high point.[7]

And again:

Seldom has an awakening sense of social consciousness wrought such changes as did these which had their rise in the 1830's and 1840's. Reforms arose in politics, dress, health, temperance, medicine, and education, and in prisons and insane asylums. Peace, antislavery, and women's rights movements gained momentum. Socialism in the form of organized experimental communities flourished.[8]

Mr. Clarke describes the contents of his three volumes (named *1844)* as:

Selected religious, humanitarian, social, cultural, and intellectual movements prominent in 1844 are covered. Volume I is concerned with topics having a religious orientation; Volume II deals with areas whose emphasis is on man's physical and/or mental development; Volume III covers movements having a philosophical, cultural, or social focus.[9]

Surprisingly, Mr. Clarke does not mention the Bahá'í Faith in any of his three volumes!

A passage from a book published in 1881 (some 37 years after the Advent of the Báb) confirms the fulfillment of Daniel's prophecy:

> Look at the marvelous achievements of the human mind, and the cunning works of men's hands, rivaling the magician's wildest dreams, which have been accomplished within the last fifty years. It was recently stated in the *Scientific American* that more advancement had been made in all scientific attainments, and more progress in all that tends to domestic comfort, the rapid transaction of business among men, and the transmission of intelligence from one to another, than all that was done for three thousand years previous, put together. Or, on the other hand, look at the wonderful light which, within the past thirty years, has shone upon the Scriptures. The fulfillment of prophecy has been shown in the light of history. Applications are made which are beyond dispute, showing that the end of all things is near. Truly the seal has been taken from the book, and knowledge respecting what God has revealed in his word, is wonderfully increased.[10]

The increase in knowledge is one more evidence of the uniqueness of our age. It is a reflection of the release of the heavenly power, a gleam of the Glory of God.

The Time of the Advent of the Great Prince

After giving the two specific signs of the approach of the new Age—an increase in knowledge and travel—Daniel goes on to designate the exact time of the advent of the Prince. In his vision he observes two men standing on the opposite sides of a river. One of the two asks the other: "How long shall it be to the end of these wonders?" (Verse 6). That is, when shall these prophecies be fulfilled? A question to which the other man responds by raising his hands towards heaven and swearing:

...by him that liveth for ever that it shall be for a time, times, and an half; and when he shall have accomplished to scatter the power of the holy people, all these things shall be finished.   Daniel 12:7

Most new translations use the familiar but coded figure "time, times, and half a time." Some of the new translations, such as *The New American Bible*, are more specific; they decode the figures. Others, such as *The Amplified Bible* and *The New International Version* place the decoded figure (three and a half years) in the footnote, or add it to the text in brackets. The passage appears in *The New American Bible* this way:

...by him who lives forever that it should be for a year, two years, a half-year; and that, when the power of the destroyer of the holy people was brought to an end, all these things should end.   Daniel 12:7

In the brief passage cited, the vision designates the date in two different but by now familiar ways. First, by the phrase "a time, times, and half a time," an exact prophetic figure revealed to John many centuries later* (Rev. 12:14); and then by linking the date to the time when the scattering of the power of the holy people, the Jews, has been accomplished. This is again in perfect accord with the prophetic words of Jesus to His inquisitive disciples wishing to know the time of His return. It is also in accord with the testimony given in Revelation.

There are still other clues that link Daniel's prophecy of three years and a half to Jesus' own words about His return. Due to their special significance, let us review the verses we just studied, in the context of a few additional verses:

---

* As stated, this important prophetic figure was revealed to John in four different ways: *a time, times, and half a time* (Rev. 12:14), *three days and a half* (Rev. 11:11; 11:9), *forty two months* (Rev. 13:5; 11:2), and *1260 days* (Rev. 11:3; 12:6).

> At that time Michael, the great prince who protects your people, will arise. There will be a time of distress such as has not happened from the beginning of nations until then..."How long will it be before these astonishing things are fulfilled?"...It will be for a time, times and a half.
>
> Daniel 12:1,6,7 NIV

Besides the clarity with which the preceding prophecy conveys its chief message, it provides us with one more clue that has an exact counterpart in the New Testament. The clue is: "There will be a time of distress such as has not happened from the beginning of nations until then."

The preceding passage from Daniel is in perfect harmony with what Jesus told His disciples on the Mt. of Olives about His return:

> For then [at the time of the advent] there will be great distress, unequaled from the beginning of the world until now—and never to be equaled again.   Matthew 24:21 NIV

Just six verses before uttering these words (Matt. 24:15), Jesus had asked those who wished to know the time of His return to refer to the Book of Daniel, where, He knew, the rich treasures of these time prophecies were deposited.

Daniel's prophecy declares that "when he shall have accomplished to scatter the power of the holy people, all these things shall be finished" (Dan. 12:7). Because the holy people transgressed the divine laws, God inactivated or "scattered" the power that joined them together. The winds of destiny dispersed them to the farthest reaches of the earth.

The prophecy declares that when the goal of scattering is accomplished, when the holy people are no longer being dispersed, all "these things should be finished." Among "these things" is the promise of the coming of Michael. By then that promise must have *already* been fulfilled.

The force that had been scattering the people of Israel for 26 centuries turned *visibly and dramatically* at the appointed

time into a unifying power. The appointed time was 1948.*
Since then Israel has once again become an independent
nation. The motherland has called and continues to gather her
scattered children. Then, where is Michael? The house has
been built. Where is its Master? Will the Bridegroom be late
for His banquet? Has not God's purpose of scattering been
accomplished? Then, where is the great Prince?

Daniel's Second Prophecy of "Three Times and a Half"

Daniel's remarkable prophecies of the last days reveal further
detail. In still another vision, he refers to the rise of several
kingdoms that are followed by the rise of a last king (kingdom), one that "will speak against the Most High, oppress
his saints, and try to change the set times and the laws."
Then Daniel's vision predicts the exact time allotted to this
king or kingdom:

> The saints will be handed over to him for a time, times
> and half a time.   Daniel 7:25 NIV

As mentioned, the last religious kingdom (Islamic) was
dominated by rulers who disregarded some of the divine
laws and introduced their own. Soon after Muhammad's
death, rivalry and division broke out among the Muslims and
continued throughout the Islamic dispensation. The Umayyad
dynasty was the first to take power away from the lawful
successors of Muhammad, to oppress the saints, and to try to
change the laws to its own favor. Other leaders followed suit.
We know too well how often throughout history people have
used religion as a weapon to win selfish ends.

---

* This was preceded by Noah's call in 1844 A.D. to establish the State of Israel
and the signing of the Edicts of Submission that symbolized the weakening and
the ultimate downfall of the Ottoman Empire, which ruled the Holy Land.

It is essential to note that the prophecy does not concern religion; it only points to rulers or kingdoms. Although many of the Islamic governments deviated from the divine Laws, we should in no way disregard or belittle the Islamic contributions to both the spiritual and secular development of civilization. We should also note that Islam was not the only religion to be misused by religious leaders, though it will be the last. We will soon learn why.

Harmony Among the Prophecies

Earlier we noted some remarkable similarities between Daniel's and St. John's visions of the last days. There are also similar parallels between Daniel's preceding vision of "time, times, and half a time" (7:25) and Jesus' words on His own return. For example, the Book of Daniel states:

> In my vision at night I looked, and there before me was one like a son of man, coming with the clouds of heaven. He approached the Ancient of Days and was led into his presence. He was given authority, glory and sovereign power; all peoples, nations and men of every language worshiped him. His dominion is an everlasting dominion that will not pass away, and his kingdom is one that will never be destroyed.   Daniel 7:13-14 NIV

This prophecy is confirmed by Jesus. Such expressions as *a son of man, coming with the clouds of heaven,* and *glory and sovereign power* are almost identical with Jesus' words on His own return:

> ...they shall see the Son of man coming in the clouds of heaven with power and great glory.   Matthew 24:30

The phrase *one like a Son of man* is particularly enlightening, for it fully accords with the Bahá'í view of "return." Neither the Báb nor Bahá'u'lláh claimed to have possessed or embodied the same identical soul as Jesus. Instead they declare themselves to be separate creations, but endowed with powers and attributes similar to those possessed by the Son. (See the explanation offered in Volume V on the return of Elijah as John the Baptist.)

Further, the prophecy refers to two Beings: one *like a son of man* (the Báb), and the other *the Ancient of Days* (Bahá'u'lláh). *The Ancient of Days* is a title assumed by Bahá'u'lláh. Here are His words:

> God is my witness! He, the Ancient of everlasting days is come, girded with majesty and power.[11]

There is an amazing similarity between Jesus and the Báb. Volume II offers over 86 specific parallels between their lives.

The more we examine and compare the prophetic passages, the more we see their similarity and common purpose. Before concluding this chapter, let us make one more comparison. At the beginning of his vision of 2300 days, Daniel states that:

> ...a vision appeared to me, Daniel, similar to my former vision.   Daniel 8:1-2 NEB

"The former vision" Daniel is referring to is the vision of "three times and a half" we have just examined. Here we can see one more evidence of harmony and relationship between the intent of two seemingly different visions, one based on Jewish history, the other on Islamic history.*

---

* Those interested in continuing their study of Daniel's visions may wish to refer to *The Quest for Eden* by E. M. Marsella, Philosophical Library, 1966, pp. 207-218.

16

The Seven Times
Leviticus 26:18

Prophecies from the
Books of Moses

Moses' Prophecy of
the Seven Times

Before concluding our examination of time prophecies pointing to 1844 or 1260, let us examine one more piece of the grand puzzle concealed in Hebrew Scriptures. A special time prophecy in the books of Moses covers the second longest prophetic period recorded in the Bible. It is called the prophecy of the *seven times*. Knowing it will help us gain a broad perspective on major prophetic eras of the Scriptures:

But if you will not listen to me...and if you reject my
decrees...I will punish you for your sins seven times over.
Leviticus 26:14, 15, 18 NIV

If in spite of these things you do not accept my correction
but continue to be hostile toward me, I...will afflict you
for your sins seven times over...I will turn your cities into
ruins and lay waste your sanctuaries, and I will take no
delight in the pleasing aroma of your offerings. I will lay
waste the land...I will scatter you among the nations...
Leviticus 26:23, 24, 31, 33 NIV

These coded prophecies, many Christian scholars have
maintained, point to the interval or the era during which the
Jews were deprived of the temporal power and glory they had
once enjoyed. Those who decoded the prophecies calculated
the intended era in this way: since in prophetic language *a
time* equals a year of 360 days, *seven times* must equal
$7 \times 360 = 2520$. They called these twenty-five centuries the
times of the Gentile rule. They believed this period extended
from the latter part of the 7th century B.C.—perhaps the most
critical period in the disintegration of Jewish independence—
to the mid-19th century A.D.

The scholars knew that since the fall of the Jews from power
was gradual, their rise to power must also be gradual; therefore, they did not expect a single date or event to mark the
closing of the twenty five centuries. In spite of this, they
found so much evidence as to be convinced that a closing
date could be set.

They were aware of the biblical prophecies linking 1260—
which is one half of 2520—to the end of "the times of the
Gentiles." To them the prophecy of the *seven times* seemed to
carry a similar message, linked to an earlier starting point.
And they found a turning point—a historical milestone—in
the lives of Jewish people that confirmed their observations.
Before examining their findings, we should look briefly at
both their successes and failures in decoding the prophecies.

The Meteor that Lighted the World

The astuteness, enthusiasm, and persistence exemplified by the seekers of the mid-19th century in unraveling the prophecies were remarkable. Their zeal and dedication led them to many discoveries. Like a brilliant meteor they lighted the world, but sadly their light did not endure. What narrowed their horizons and the range of their influence was a strong inclination to expect a literal fulfillment of all the prophecies.

Surprisingly, this handicap worked in opposite ways. It sharpened their understanding of *time* prophecies, but dulled their perception of *other* prophecies.

It is evident that dates involve numbers, and numbers constitute literal—not symbolic—entities. A *literal* mind detects specific facts and relationships, and delights in traditional thinking; a *liberal* mind, like an eagle, soars beyond conventional beliefs and traditions to gain a global vision of reality.

Those seekers, like many Christians of today, acknowledged being literal in interpreting the Bible and were proud of it. The assumption was and still is that the more literal a believer, the closer he or she will be to the reality of God's words. William Miller, the leader of the Advent Movement, was characterized by one of his close associates, Joshua Himes, as

> ...a great stickler for literal interpretation; never admitting the figurative, unless absolutely required to make correct sense...[1]

Miller described his standards in interpreting the Scriptures this way:

> I believe the Bible is the revealed will of God to man... and that it is to be understood as literal as it can be and make good sense...[2]

The problem with the preceding statement is this: what makes good sense to us may have no place in God's grand scheme of creation. The expectation that God would send a Savior to restore a literal kingdom to the Jews—who had suffered for so long and prayed so hard—made perfect sense to every Jew at the time of Jesus. But their "perfect sense" turned out to be flawed—distorted by human desire for earthly power and glory:

> ...the Lord seeth not as man seeth; for man looketh on the outward appearance, but the Lord looketh on the heart.
>
> I Samuel 16:7

> Ye judge after the flesh...   John 8:15

The idea of receiving a King-Messiah was so logical and defensible that even Jesus' disciples—who were the most enlightened people of their time—expected and cherished it. They were quite disappointed by the reality of God's wisdom and ways of doing things:

> When Jesus was crucified, all his disciples, except John, left him, discouraged and heartbroken, partly because their dreams for the Kingdom of God on earth were now shattered.[3]

In addition to suffering from extreme literalness, the seekers of the mid-19th century suffered from still another handicap: their unquestioned rejection of Islam. To solve a puzzle, all the facts must be accepted and integrated without any pre-conceived notions. Those seekers for the most part either ignored or distorted the prophecies that seemed to give credibility to a religion they considered to be false. They were severely handicapped by their inability to liberate themselves from a deeply rooted tradition, one that is still present among Christians. They rejected Muhammad even as an atheist would reject Jesus without ever examining His evidence. The forces of tradition command awesome powers. They have obscured the identity of every Messenger God has ever sent.

The seekers of the mid-19th century knew that the year 1260 of the Islamic Era coincided with the year 1844 of the Christian Era. But this knowledge would not prompt them to make an impartial search into the Islamic Scriptures. They displayed marvelous ingenuity and made grand discoveries, but because of their "Islamic handicap," they could not detect some simple connections. They could not see that the figure 1260 (and its counterparts) specified the duration of the Islamic dispensation, that it pointed to the interval during which "God's two Witnesses or Prophets" (Rev. 11:3; see Chapter 14) guided the people to the path of the coming Kingdom. This handicap thwarted their efforts and diminished their insight. Had they viewed Islam with an open mind, they could have deciphered many more mysteries in the grand jigsaw puzzle of prophecies.

There was one more piece of the puzzle they did not notice. They failed to realize the significance of Mordecai Noah's call to the western nations for the establishment of the State of Israel. Noah's call, like the advent of spring, awakened and nourished the seed-idea of an independent nation for the Jews. It activated the dormant dreams of nationalism among the people of Israel. They were also unaware of the weakening and downfall of an Empire that ruled the Holy Land. Had the seekers of the mid-19th century known that such glimmers of hope and fulfillment were on the horizon, their expectation would have turned into utter ecstasy.

The Link Between Two Critical Events

Let us now see if we can discern a closer link between two significant landmarks in Jewish history: 1844 A.D. and the year when they lost their independence, twenty-five centuries earlier. As mentioned, the decline of the Jews was gradual and sporadic. Yet we can find a turning point in their history

from which they never recovered, the point at which began
a succession of declines.

As Jeremiah declares and history confirms, the Jews reached
that critical point during the reign of Manasseh, characterized
as the most abominable ruler during the Jewish dispensation.
And the lowest point during his long reign was reached when
he was taken captive by Esarhaddon, the powerful king of
Assyria. This marked "the first captivity of the tribe of Judah,
the inhabitants of Jerusalem."[4]

Here is what Jeremiah was inspired to say:

"I will make them abhorrent to all the kingdoms of the
earth because of what Manasseh son of Hezekiah king of
Judah did in Jerusalem. Who will have pity on you, O
Jerusalem? Who will mourn for you? Who will stop to
ask how you are? You have rejected me," declares the
Lord. "You keep on backsliding. So I will lay hands on
you and destroy you; I can no longer show compassion.
I will winnow them with a winnowing fork at the city
gates of the land. I will bring bereavement and destruction on my people, for they have not changed their ways."
Jeremiah 15:4-7 NIV

It is said that Manasseh "possessed a profound knowledge of
the Torah and could interpret Leviticus in 55 different ways,"[5]
yet he loved and adored idols so much as to burn his own
son as an offering. This is an example from amongst his cruel
acts as described in a Jewish encyclopedia:

After his father's death, Manasseh began to worship idols.
He destroyed the altar and set up an idol with four faces,
copied from the four figures on the divine throne of
Ezekiel, so that from whatever direction a man entered the
Temple he saw a face of the idol. Manasseh also made
another idolatrous image so heavy that it required 1,000
men to carry it. New bearers were employed daily because
the king had each group executed at the end of the day's
work. He expunged the name of God from the Scriptures,

and delivered public lectures whose sole purpose was to
ridicule the Torah.[6]

During Manasseh's reign "Every faith was tolerated but the
old faith of Israel. This was abandoned and proscribed."[7] He
sought to destroy all the copies of the Mosaic Law because
they condemned the very abominable acts he was pursuing,
among them offering children as sacrifice to pagan gods.
Fortunately he failed.

Among his many abominable acts was the murder of his own
grandfather, Isaiah, the great Jewish prophet, who was sawed
in half. A Christian encyclopedia describes Manasseh this
way: "His abominations were cited by the prophets as the
climactic cause for God's sealing the judgment of Judah by
captivity (II Kings 21:10-15)."[8] The preceding statement is
confirmed by many other scholars who believe that Manasseh's
captivity marked the end of the independence of the Jews as
a nation.* The long cycle of "abomination that causes
desolation" was set in motion by his evil acts and those of
his cohorts.

All these historical and scriptural evidences establish a link
between the prediction in Leviticus and the onset of the
fulfillment of that prediction during Manasseh's reign.✝

William Miller wrote:

> We have the same cause assigned by Jeremiah as was
> given by Moses, and the same judgments denounced
> against his people, and the time is here, clearly specified
> when these judgments began, "in the days of Manasseh."
> And we find in 2 Chron. xxxiii:9-11, that for this same

---

* According to *Harper's Bible Dictionary*, on the whole: "Jerusalem under the
succeeding kings of Judah did not continue its trust in God as it had under
Hezekiah (Manasseh's father)." See page 467, first edition. According to the
same source: The story of Manasseh's repentance "is evidently historical fiction."
(See page 600.)

✝ In 605 B.C., 38 years after the death of Manasseh, Nebuchadnezzar, king of
Babylon, appeared on the scene.

crime they were scattered. "Wherefore the Lord spake of
Manasseh and to his people, but they would not hearken.
Wherefore the Lord brought upon them the captains of the
host of the kings of Assyria, which took Manasseh among
the thorns, and bound him with fetters and carried him to
Babylon." Here then began the "power (their king) of the
holy people to be scattered."[9]

We should note that God's wrath did not, nor will it ever,
come as a consequence of the evil acts of one man. The king
was but a symbol and embodiment of the ingratitude and
corruption of the kingdom he ruled.

This abandonment of Israel's law was not limited to the
royal court; through Manasseh's example, idolatry spread
abroad to the people of Judah and Jerusalem (2 Kings
21:9).[10]

Transforming the Codes into Dates

According to *The Encyclopedia Judaica*, Manasseh ascended
the throne at the age of 12 and reigned for 55 years; 698-
643 B.C. He was taken captive in the 22nd year of his reign,
namely 677-676 B.C.[11]* If we use the captivity of Manasseh
and the tribe of Judah as the critical starting point in the
decline of the Jews as a nation, we arrive at the grand
terminal point of the *seven times*: $677 + 1843 = 2520$.

What Moses predicted was fulfilled with precision. The
termination of the *seven times* that the Jews were granted
arrived in 1843 B.C.E. (Before Common, or Christian,
Era), which corresponds to 1844 A.D. As stated in Chapter
10, since the Christian calendar began with the year one
instead of zero, whenever we move from B.C. to A.D., we
need to make a correction, otherwise we will have an extra
year. Thus 1844 A.D., when the Báb declared His Mission,
was actually the 1843rd year of the Christian Era.

---

* After his captivity, Manasseh was released and allowed to continue his reign in
  subjugation.

Before concluding our examination of the prophecy of the *seven times*, we should examine two more examples from among the works of the many Christian scholars of the mid-19th century who proclaimed and promoted it. Perhaps the first seeker to decode the prophecy was William Miller, who made his discovery before the advent of the Báb. He states:

> From a further study of the Scriptures, I concluded that the seven times of Gentile supremacy must commence when the Jews ceased to be an independent nation, at the captivity of Manasseh, *which the best chronologers assigned to B. C. 677.*[12]

> The seven times are 2520; take 677 from it, and it leaves 1843 after Christ, when "all these things will be finished."[13]

And again:

> ...[in] B.C. 677, Esarhaddon, king of Assyria and Babylon, came with a large army into the land of Israel and Judah, carried away the last remnant of Israel, and they have not been a nation since. Then he also made war against Jerusalem, took Manasseh and carried him to Babylon; which begins the "seven times" Judah was to be in bondage to the kings of the earth, and also the "seven years" Israel should be a captive, robbed and spoiled people; both beginning and ending at one time, 2520 years, beginning B.C. 677, ending A.D. 1843. To 1843 add 677, and the sum equals 2520.[14]

Matthew Habershon was another early pioneer to examine this prophecy. In his works, he lists the dates 677-676 B.C. as the commencement of "the times of the Gentiles" or 2520 years. He states that in 677-676 B.C. Esarhaddon "carried away the small remnant of Israel...and thus totally and finally destroyed the kingdom of Israel from being a nation."[15] He then adds that both prophetic areas of "2520-years" and "2300-years" have a common ending:

The final termination of the 'seven times' was proved to correspond exactly to this year—that is, 2520 years, reckoned from 677 B.C., the date of Israel's final ruin; and 2300 years, reckoned from Ezra's commission in 457 B.C., both terminate in the year 1843.[16]*

A Unique Prophetic Figure

Surprisingly, the figure 2520 also appears prophetically in Islamic literature. Ibn-i-'Arabí (Shaykh Ibnu'l-'Arabí, known as Muhyi'd-Dín, 1165-1240 A.D.)—one of the most eminent scholars of the East and author of some two hundred volumes—reveals the time of the advent of the Redeemer of our time in this puzzle:

> The time of the advent of Mahdí [the Promised One of the Muslims] is equal to half of the smallest number divisible by the numbers 1 through 9.[17]

This number is 2520, and half of it is 1260. Perhaps because of his great discernment, Ibn-i-'Arabí found the figure from Islamic prophecies and then enclosed it in a puzzle.

Dr. Guinness, a distinguished Christian scholar from the West, on the basis of his studies of biblical prophecies, discerned the significance of the figure 2520 as Ibn-i-'Arabí had done centuries earlier. Dr. Guinness began publishing his works (nine volumes) "after twenty years of intensive, independent study of the Scripture prophecy and the second advent." As Dr. Guinness notes:

> ...2520 is arithmetically a most remarkable number; a number as distinct from all other numbers as the circle is from all other forms. It is not a number that could possibly have been selected by chance...Its selection in preference

---

* For a list of other Christian writers or scholars who selected 677 B.C. as the beginning point of the prophecy of the *seven times*, please refer to *The Prophetic Faith of Our Fathers*, Volume 4, p. 847.

to all other numbers is an indication of intelligent design ...The omniscient God has deliberately passed by all other conceivable numbers...that He might select...a number which is *sui generis*, altogether unique, one which stands forth by its very nature as a king among other numbers...*2520 is the least common multiple of the first ten numbers*; in other words, it is the first in the entire series of numbers, that is exactly divisible by all the first ten numerals.

1 is contained in it	2520	times without remainder
2	"	1260	"
3	"	840	"
4	"	630	"
5	"	504	"
6	"	420	"
7	"	360	"
8	"	315	"
9	"	280	"
10	"	252	" 18

Also if we add the figures contained in 2520, we get 9, which is the numerical value of *Bahá*. *Nine* symbolizes the divine attributes of perfection and oneness. It is the highest one-digit number that also encompasses all the primary numbers.

The Major Prophetic Eras

Looking at the major prophetic eras will help us see more clearly not only the main stages of the social and spiritual evolution of humanity, but also the cycles of God's promises and their fulfillment at the appointed intervals.

These are the main Prophetic Eras found in the Bible:

• The Grand Gentile Era of 25 centuries (seven times).
• The Gentile Era of 12 centuries (three and a half times).

- The Grand Sanctuary Era of 23 centuries (2300 days).
- The Sanctuary Era of 5 centuries (69-70 weeks).

Dr. and Mrs. Guinness present this analysis of the two Gentile Eras:

> The great "Seven Times" is divided into two halves, and the predictions respecting the *second half* of the week are far more numerous than those respecting the whole period. Bisect a week, and you have three and a half days. Bisect seven times, and you have three and a half times. Bisect 2520 years, and you have 1260 years.

> Now *this* last period is more frequently used in prophecy to measure historic episodes than any other. It is mentioned under various names, all conveying the same interval of time; it is sometimes called "forty and two months"; sometimes "1260 days"; sometimes "time, times, and a half"— *some* mysterious designation being always employed instead of the clear statement 1260 years, in order that a veil might rest for a time over the period, and that its true scale might only become clear in the light of its fulfillment.[19]

The Relationship Between Heavenly and Earthly "Jerusalem and Sanctuary"

This section is a summary of the time prophecies we have studied and a comparative examination of the codes by which they were concealed. Seeing the prophecies in close succession will give us a clearer perspective of their harmonious relationships.

The prophecy of the *seven times* carries an ultimatum to the people of Israel: obey God or face the consequences.

> If...you still do not listen to me...I will turn your cities into ruins and lay waste your sanctuaries...I will scatter you among the nations...   Leviticus 26:27,31,33 NIV

This prophecy supports all the others examined earlier. And it offers the same clues they do to convey the same message. Here are the clues:

- The transgression or rebellion against God and His commandments, which leads to...
- The desolation of the sanctuary
- The desolation of Jewish cities (including Jerusalem)
- The dispersion of the Jewish people among the nations

As we noted in Chapter 10, Daniel had this vision:

> "How long will it take for the vision to be fulfilled—the vision concerning the daily sacrifice, the rebellion that causes desolation, and the surrender of the sanctuary and of the host that will be trampled underfoot?" He said to me, "It will take 2300 evenings and mornings; then the sanctuary will be reconsecrated.".…"Son of man," he said to me, "understand that the vision concerns the time of the end."   Daniel 8:13,14,17 NIV

The clues offered in Daniel's vision are identical with those revealed to Moses. They consist of:

- The surrender of the sanctuary, and its humiliation and desolation ("trampling under foot").
- The surrender, humiliation, and desolation of the host of the sanctuary—those who protect and serve it—namely the Jews.
- The impact of these events on one of the ceremonies of the sanctuary, namely the daily sacrifice.

When the disciples asked Jesus about His return, He cited some of these same clues:

'Master,' they asked, 'when will it all come about?'...They will fall at the sword's point; they will be carried captive into all countries; and Jerusalem will be trampled down by foreigners [Gentiles] until their day has run its course... And then they shall see the Son of Man coming...

> Luke 21:7, 24, 27 NEB

On still another occasion, Jesus linked one of these clues—the destroying of Jerusalem and its sanctuary—to the advent of the Lord, namely His own return:

O Jerusalem, Jerusalem, the city that murders the prophets and stones the Messengers sent to her!* How often I have longed to gather your children, as a hen gathers her brood under her wings; but you would not let me. Look, Look! there is your temple, forsaken [left to you desolate, NIV] by God. And I tell you, you shall never see me until the time comes when you say, "Blessings on him who comes in the name of the Lord!"

> Luke 13:34-35 NEB

This same sign was revealed also in the Book of Revelation:

I saw the Holy City, the new Jerusalem, coming down out of heaven from God...The city does not need the sun or the moon to shine on it, for the glory of God [Bahá'u'lláh] gives it light, and the Lamb [the Báb] is its lamp.

> Revelation 21:2, 23 NIV
> See also verses 10-11

Here Jerusalem symbolizes *the divine Revelation*. When people cease to live in the City of God, when its light turns into darkness, God sends a *new* Jerusalem, a *new* City illumined with His infinite light and glory.

According to *The Zondervan Bible Dictionary*, "There is no doubt about it that even in the Old Testament, Jerusalem,

---

* An allusion to Jesus' own crucifixion in Jerusalem, and the dawning and reappearance of His divine Power in the name of the Lord.

especially when referred to as Zion, sometimes was used to express spiritual rather than geographical or historical ideas."[20] It then quotes this verse as an evidence:

> You have not come to a mountain that can be touched... you have come to Mount Zion, to the heavenly Jerusalem, the city of the living God.   Hebrews 12:18, 22 NIV[*]

The symbol of "Jerusalem" appears again in the Book of Revelation with additional facts. As we noted, Jesus linked His return to the time when the trampling of Jerusalem by the Gentiles "has run its course." (Luke 21:24 NEB). In the following prophecy He specifies the time when that event will have been accomplished:

> ...and they [the Gentiles] will trample the Holy City [Jerusalem] underfoot for forty-two months.
>
>   Revelation 11:2 NEB

The next verse is preceded and confirmed by still other prophecies from Daniel:

> But you Daniel, keep the words secret and seal the book till the time of the end...'How long will it be before these portents cease?...' 'It shall be for a time, times, and a half. When the power of the holy people ceases to be dispersed, all these things shall come to an end.'
>
>   Daniel 12:4-7 NEB

---

[*] In addition to "the city that descends from heaven" (divine Revelation), Zion and Jerusalem sometimes symbolize the heart of the Holy Land, the spirit of Israel. For instance, when Jesus declared "O Jerusalem, Jerusalem, the city that murders the prophets...How often have I longed to gather your children" (Luke 13:34 NEB), it is certain He was not pointing to a specific city in Israel, but to the people of that blessed Land, whose heart is Jerusalem. Similarly, some of the prophecies that declare Zion to be the dawning-place of the divine Kingdom do not refer to a specific location but rather to what Zion stands for: the blessed land of the people of Israel:

> ...from the heart of Zion [Israel] there cometh the cry: "The promise of all ages is now fulfilled."[21]   Bahá'u'lláh

There is a clear link between the preceding prophecies (Jesus' and Daniel's) and the prophecy of the *seven times*. For Moses predicted that:

- The Jewish people will be scattered among nations.
- The scattering will continue for seven times.

Daniel's vision contains the same expression and predictions:

- The scattering or disintegration of the temporal power or sovereignty of the holy people, namely the Jews, will continue. (By Daniel's time, the disintegration had already started.)

- The scattering of that power will cease after three and a half times.

Jesus referred to the same time interval by the figure 42 months, instead of 3½ times. To help His followers gain more knowledge about the time of His return, Jesus asked them specifically to search into Daniel's prophecies that speak of *desolation*:

> Tell us, when shall these things be? and what shall be the sign of thy coming?...When ye therefore shall see the abomination of desolation spoken of by Daniel...(whoso readeth, let him understand).   Matthew 24:3, 15

These were but a few segments of a grand prophetic profile put together piece by piece by the Prophets and Messengers over an interval of about fifteen centuries, from the time of Moses to Jesus.

To Conclude

The prophecy of the seven times specified the exact interval between two critical points in the fall and the rise of the Jewish people as citizens of both the earthly and the heavenly Jerusalem.

During the reign of Manasseh they completely abandoned the *heavenly* Jerusalem, and thus God's time of grace for them ran out (Jeremiah 15:4-7). The chosen people, who were adored and cherished, fell from favor.

> If only you will now listen to me and keep my covenant, then out of all peoples you shall become my special possession... Exodus 19:5 NEB

During the reign of the same sovereign, namely in 677 B.C., as the result of the first captivity of the tribe of Judah and of Manasseh—the sovereign of Jerusalem—the dominoes of their earthly splendor also began to fall and crumble. The loss of the heavenly splendor of Jerusalem for the Jews was followed by the loss of its earthly splendor.

Their dominoes continued to fall for 2520 years. (By rejecting Jesus, they had already lost an earlier opportunity for redemption.)

Then at the end of this long interval, they were presented once again with a new opportunity to restore themselves. Once again they could find favor with God by welcoming their new Redeemer, and once again they could build the kingdom they had lost. The key to the earthly Jerusalem was presented to them in 1844 when Mordecai Noah called the western nations to establish a homeland for Jewish people. The gate to the heavenly Jerusalem was opened to them, and to all humanity, in that same year—1844—when the Báb declared the dawning of the new age.

As stated in this and the preceding chapters, the time prophecies covered a period of about 25 centuries, and all of them— the seven times, 2300 days, three and a half times, and its equivalents, 42 months, and 1260 days—converged on one point: 1844.

17

The Ancient of Days
Daniel 7:9 NIV

Prophecies Concerning the Time of the Advent of Bahá'u'lláh

The Prophecy of 1290 Days

As I looked, thrones were set in place, and the Ancient of Days took his seat.   Daniel 7:9 NIV

The Ancient of Days is come in His great glory.[1]

Bahá'u'lláh

God is my witness! He, the Ancient of everlasting days is come, girded with majesty and power.[2]   Bahá'u'lláh

Daniel's visions of the appointed "time of the end" seem inexhaustible. After referring repeatedly to the time of the dawning of the new Day in 1844 or 1260, the prophecies finally point to the time of the rising of its "Sun," namely Bahá'u'lláh.

As stated earlier, Daniel was told that Michael, the great Prince, would come. He then asked about the time, and was told that "It shall be for a time, times, and half a time." Daniel could not interpret the meaning of this figure, so he asked for further explanation. In response, he received further clues that helped him recognize that the vision pertained to the time of the end. After all these, he was given still another figure:

> From the time when the regular offering is abolished and "the abomination of desolation" is set up, there shall be an interval of one thousand two hundred and ninety days.
>
> Daniel 12:11 NEB

The compass of prophetic utterances seems to have been drawn primarily toward the beginning point of the new Age (1260 A.H. or 1844 A.D.) and seldom toward the time of Bahá'u'lláh's advent (1280 A.H. or 1863 A.D.), Daniel's prophecy is one of the few exceptions.

According to 'Abdu'l-Bahá, the prophetic figure "1290 days" refers to the time lapse between the public ministry of Muhammad and the public ministry of Bahá'u'lláh. According to the Islamic calendar, Bahá'u'lláh proclaimed His Mission publicly in 1280, and Muhammad had proclaimed His Mission publicly ten years prior to His departure from Mecca to Medina, the event that marked the beginning of the Islamic Era.[*]

Thus the time period between the inauguration of the public ministries of Muhammad and Bahá'u'lláh was 1290 prophetic

---

[*] As stated, all the prophetic dates linked to the advent of Islam are based on the lunar year, the time interval used by the Muslims.

days. Again, this one fact cannot and should not by itself be regarded as conclusive evidence; it should rather be viewed as one more fact fitting into the whole profile.

We can also find the ten-year difference by comparing the distance between the advent of Muhammad and the advent of the Báb. Even though the Báb proclaimed His Mission in the year 1260 of the Islamic Calendar, the length of time between the onset of the revelation of His holy Book, the Bayán, and that of Muhammad, the Qur'án, was 1270 years. The Báb frequently refers to this interval:

> Indeed, if any living creature were to pause to meditate he would undoubtedly realize that these verses are not the work of man, but are solely to be ascribed unto God, the One, the Peerless...Had human beings been able to accomplish this deed surely someone would have brought forth at least one verse during the period of twelve hundred and seventy years which hath elapsed since the revelation of the Qur'án until that of the Bayán [the Báb's Holy Book].[3]

Daniel's prophecy also carries two symbols. We noted that when Jesus was on the Mount of Olives, His disciples asked Him about the time of His return, and He gave them two clues. One had to do with the fulfillment of *the times of the Gentiles*, whereas the other pointed to *the abomination of desolation* spoken of by Daniel. (The abominable acts that caused the desolation of the spiritual and temporal civilization of the Jews, transgressions that "scattered" their unifying powers.) We also noted that the Book of Daniel carries two prophecies in which the abomination of desolation is used along with a number. The first prophecy was that of 2300 days, already demonstrated to end in 1844, the time of the declaration of the Báb. The second prophecy to contain the same symbolic expression, along with a number, is the prophecy of 1290 we are now examining. Here is once again the question raised by the disciples:

> 'Tell us,' they said, 'when will this happen? And what
> will be the signal for your coming and the end of the
> age?'
>   Matthew 24:3 NEB

After referring to the *signs* of the time of His return, Jesus
referred to the *time itself*:

> When ye therefore shall see the abomination of desolation,
> spoken of by Daniel the prophet, stand in the holy place,
> (whoso readeth, let him understand)...   Matthew 24:15

Thus Jesus has specifically referred us to the prophecy of
1290 days we are now examining.

We should now return to Daniel's prophecy of 1290 days to
decode its symbols. The two symbols it carries are: *the taking
away (or cessation) of daily sacrifice*, and *the abomination
of desolation*. The first symbol, namely *the cessation of
daily sacrifice* (explained in Chapter 9) is used prophetically
to signal the change of the age. This same symbol was also
revealed in Daniel's vision of 70 weeks to signal the beginning of the public ministry of Jesus (see Daniel 9:27). The
advents of Christianity and Islam signaled a change of the age
and the dawning of a new day, which is always accompanied
by change in social laws such as: ways of worship, daily
sacrifice, marriage, divorce, forbidden foods, holy days, etc.
The advent of both of these religions was followed by the
literal cessation of daily sacrifice. Less than forty years after
the crucifixion of Jesus, Titus caused the daily sacrifice
among the Jews to cease. 'Umar did the same, five years
after the death of Muhammad when he conquered the Holy
Land. Once again we see the same symbol used to convey
the same message in relation to both the first and second
advents of Christ.

What does *the abomination of desolation* imply? Titus and
'Umar stopped the daily sacrifice and deprived the Jews of
any access to their beloved Jerusalem. The holy people were
pushed out of their beloved city and dispersed among other
nations. This was indeed an abominable desolation for the

Jews. It was also an outward expression of a spiritual desolation, which always ensues as a result of the denial of the new Messengers.

In addition to the specific signs of the time, Daniel's remarkable vision also includes counsels, admonitions, and warnings, lest any one fall into complacency and take the Word of God in vain. A compassionate Creator can only offer advice and encouragement and warn of the consequences of disobedience and denial. He would not force His Will upon His children.

> But at that time your people—everyone whose name is found written in the book [the book of faith and affirmation]—will be delivered. Multitudes who sleep in the dust of the earth will awake: some to everlasting life, others to shame and everlasting contempt. Those who are wise will shine like the brightness of the heavens, and those who lead many to righteousness, like the stars for ever and ever. Daniel 12:1-3 NIV

The Biblical Sources of Time Prophecies

Before completing the discussion of the time prophecies from the Bible, let us pause for a moment and view their origin. The time prophecies in the Old and the New Testaments are not scattered as if by chance throughout the many books of the Bible. First, the time of the second advent was predicted by both Moses and Jesus. Second, in the Old Testament, the honor of offering time prophecies on both of Christ's advents was bestowed mainly upon Daniel. For he alone predicted the time of the first advent, and he alone offered at least four time prophecies pointing clearly to the second advent. No wonder Jesus cited Daniel's book as the source of the appointed time of His return. And third, in the New Testament, the honor of offering time prophecies was conferred mainly upon St. John the Revelator. For out of 16 time prophecies in the Bible, 8 were revealed through him.

The prophecies—such as 1260 or 1290 days—whose beginning coincide with the advent of Islam are all expressed in *lunar units*, namely the calendar the Muslims use. But the prophecies—such as 2300 days, 69-70 weeks, or 7 times—whose beginnings coincide with major events in Judaism or Christianity are all expressed in *solar units*. Clearly, it is not chance that governs the units of time enclosed in the prophecies.

The Báb's Prophecies Concerning Bahá'u'lláh

Bahá'u'lláh first declared His Mission to a few of His fellow-prisoners in 1852, about nine years after the Báb had declared His Mission. The Báb repeatedly predicted that the advent of the next Redeemer would take place in the year nine, or in the 9th year from the onset of His Revelation. The ninth year was the period from May 1852 to May 1853. Shoghi Effendi has collected and translated some of these prophecies:

> In the year nine ye will attain unto the Presence of God.[4]

> In the year nine, ye shall attain unto all good.[5]

> Ere nine will have elapsed from the inception of this [the Báb's] Cause, the realities of created things will not be made manifest...Be patient until thou beholdest a new creation.[6]

> Wait thou until nine will have elapsed from the time of the Bayán [the Báb's Holy Book]. Then exclaim: "Blessed, therefore, be God, the most excellent of Makers!"[7]

By using gematria, the Báb also predicts the time of *the public* declaration of Bahá'u'lláh, which took place 19 years after His own declaration: $1844 + 19 = 1863$.

The Lord of the Day of Reckoning will be manifested at the end of Váhid (19) and the beginning of eighty (1280 A. H.).[8]

Be attentive from the inception of Revelation till the number of Váhid (19).[9]

In Arabic, each letter has a specific numerical value. For instance A=1, B=2, J=3, D=4. Thus, a letter, a word, or a combination of words (a meaningful sentence) can be used as a code for a given number. The same procedure is followed in some other languages:

For example, Roman numerals correspond to certain letters in Latin. "I" becomes one, "V" becomes five, "X" becomes ten, "L" becomes fifty, "C" becomes one hundred, etc. In a similar fashion, Hebrew numbers are taken from their alphabet. The first ten letters become 1 through 10. The eleventh letter becomes 20, the twelfth becomes 30, etc. A special procedure is used by which Hebrew letters are turned into numbers.[10]

Summer Is Near

Repetition always strengthens a prophecy. For instance, about "the year of the Lord" we have numerous references, all confirming each other. The prophecies that follow do not enjoy this status. Thus they cannot be placed on a par with those with multiple references.

Since this volume is about time prophecies, it should not exclude the following two references. The first gives us a hint as to *the season* in which "the tree" begins to blossom and bear fruits:

Now learn this lesson from the fig tree: As soon as its twigs get tender and its leaves come out, you know that summer is near. Even so, when you see all these things, you know that it is near, right at the door.

Matthew 24:32-33 NIV

Christian scholars have speculated about the symbolism of "the fig tree" and whether Jesus specified intentionally the time of its germination. Do His words contain codes that may be broken? We cannot be absolutely sure, but curiosity demands that we explore such a possibility.

> Alford says that as the withered fig tree, which the Lord cursed, represented the Jewish race in their unfruitfulness, so this fig tree represents the reviviscence [revival] of that race.[11]

Biederwolf in his commentary states that the fig tree puts forth its leaves "about Passover season, near the last of March. The fruit of the fig tree accompanies the mature leaf."[12] It happens that the Báb and Bahá'u'lláh declared their Missions in the months following March: April and May. The symbolism may be this: once the spring arrives and the leaves break out, we know the "harvest time of fruit"[13] is nigh. Similarly, once the fig tree puts forth its leaves (around the end of March), we should recognize that "the harvest reward in the Messianic kingdom"[14] is approaching; it is "right at the door" (Matt. 24:33 NIV). Is the use of "the door" (the meaning of the word "the Báb") also intentional? Some prophecies seem to confirm this:

> Blessed are those who wash their robes, that they may have the right to the tree of life and may go through the gates into the city.   Revelation 22:14 NIV

> O ye peoples of the earth! Hearken unto My call...Enter ye, one and all, through this Gate...[15]   The Báb

> ...there stands the Judge, at the door.   James 5:9 NEB

Some translations of the prophecy in which Jesus speaks about "the fig tree" (Matt. 24:32-33) read with a slight difference. They use "he" in place of "it." For instance, *The American Revised Version* reads:

...[when the fig tree] puts forth its leaves, ye know that the summer is nigh; even so...know ye that *he* is nigh [emphasis added].

We should note that Jesus uttered the prophecy in response to the disciples' inquiry about the onset of the parousia (His coming and presence) and the end of the age.

The following verses may also contain a prophetic message. They may refer to the advent of the Báb and Bahá'u'lláh and the failure of the masses to receive their blessings in due season.

Listen to the cry of my people from a land far away: "Is the Lord [the Báb] not in Zion [the Holy Land]? Is her King [Bahá'u'lláh] no longer there?...The harvest is past, the summer has ended, and we are not saved."

Jeremiah 8:19-20 NIV

The "harvest" may symbolize the advent of the Báb, and the "summer" the advent of Bahá'u'lláh. As we just noted, Jesus referred to His second coming as the approaching of the "summer." Jeremiah declares that the "summer" has come and gone and people are still waiting. Most of them have not yet been harvested. The harvest-time coincides with the closing of one age and the beginning of another. When a new Messenger comes, people must spread the news of His coming so that the ripe ones are harvested. Those who spread His mighty message are called the angels.

...gather the clusters of the vine of the earth; for her grapes are fully ripe (Rev. 14:18)...open your eyes and look at the fields! They are ripe for harvest. (John 4:35 NIV). The harvest is the end of time. The reapers are angels (Matt. 13:39 NEB).

The next prophecy also pertains to time. It seems to give us a hint concerning the part of the day when the new light would dawn:

No one knows about that day or hour, not even the angels in heaven, nor the Son, but only the Father. Be on guard! Be alert! You do not know when that time will come. It's like a man going away: He leaves his house in charge of his servants, each with his assigned task, and tells the one at the door to keep watch. Therefore keep watch because you do not know when the owner of the house will come back—whether *in the evening*, or *at midnight*, or *when the rooster crows*, or *at dawn*. If he comes suddenly, do not let him find you sleeping. What I say to you, I say to everyone: 'Watch!' [Emphasis added.]

Mark 13:32-37 NIV

William Biederwolf, a Christian scholar, in *The Second Coming Bible Commentary* writes:

By "even" is meant 9:00 P.M.; by "midnight," 12:00; by "cockcrowing," 3:00 A.M., and by "morning," 6:00 A.M. "These periods," says Lange, "may denote the same unexpectedness:—the evening, the evening of the old world (Matt. 20:8); the midnight, the frame of mind of the slumbering Church (Matt. 25:6); the cockcrow, the voice of the watchers (Isa. 21:11); the morning, the dawn of Christ's appearing, the breaking into day of the new world (Mal. 4:2)." (See Matt. 14:24.)...*The coming, which is to be unexpected and sudden, is pictured as taking place in the night between 9:00 P.M. and 6:00 A.M.* [Emphasis added.][16]

The Báb declared His message on May 22, 1844, two hours and eleven minutes after sunset to a lone stranger in search of his Master. The Báb's conversation with this stranger (who attained the honor of being His first disciple) continued in His home throughout the evening and night and into the early morning of the next day.

The hours match Biederwolf's expectation that the advent takes place between 9:00 p.m. and 6:00 a.m. This is how this first disciple, one of the most distinguished scholars of his time, whose title is *the gate of the Gate*, recalled his encounter with the Báb on that night:

> I sat spellbound by His utterance, oblivious of time and of those who awaited me...All the delights, all the ineffable glories, which the Almighty has recounted in His Book as the priceless possessions of the people of Paradise, these I seemed to be experiencing that night.
>
> Sleep had departed from me that night. I was enthralled by the music of that voice which rose and fell as He chanted...[17]

And again:

> This Revelation, so suddenly and impetuously thrust upon me, came as a thunderbolt which, for a time, seemed to have benumbed my faculties. I was blinded by its dazzling splendor and overwhelmed by its crushing force. Excitement, joy, awe, and wonder stirred the depths of my soul. Predominant among these emotions was a sense of gladness and strength which seemed to have transfigured me. How feeble and impotent, how dejected and timid, I had felt previously! Then I could neither write nor walk, so tremulous were my hands and feet. Now, however, the knowledge of His Revelation had galvanized my being. I felt possessed of such courage and power that were the world, all its people and its potentates, to rise against me, I would, alone and undaunted, withstand their onslaught. The universe seemed but a handful of dust in my grasp. I seemed to be the Voice of Gabriel personified, calling unto all mankind:
>
> "Awake, for, lo! the morning Light has broken. Arise, for His Cause is made manifest. The portal of His grace is open wide; enter therein, O peoples of the world! For He Who is your Promised One is come!"[18]

The Báb asked this first disciple to keep the new message secret for a short while:

O thou who art the first to believe in Me! Verily I say, I
am the Báb, the Gate of God, and thou art the Bábu'l-
Báb, the gate of that Gate. Eighteen souls must, in the
beginning, spontaneously and of their own accord, accept
Me and recognize the truth of My Revelation. Unwarned
and uninvited each of these must seek independently to
find Me.[19]

Similarly, Bahá'u'lláh first declared His Mission privately to
a few of the Báb's disciples. This took place when He, along
with a few of the Báb's followers, were imprisoned in a pitch
dark dungeon known as the Black Pit. Here is how Bahá'u'lláh
describes the first intimation of His Revelation there:

One night, in a dream, these exalted words were heard on
every side: "Verily, We shall render Thee victorious by
Thyself and by Thy Pen. Grieve Thou not for that which
hath befallen Thee, neither be Thou afraid, for Thou art
in safety. Erelong will God raise up the treasures of the
earth—men who will aid Thee through Thyself and through
Thy Name, wherewith God hath revived the hearts of
such as have recognized Him."[20]

Unlike the initial declaration of His Mission to one humble
seeker of truth, the Báb later had an opportunity to announce
His Mission publicly to an official assemblage organized and
attended by crown prince Násiri'd-Dín and some of the most
prominent and powerful religious and political leaders of
the time. The Báb repeated His claim three times to make
sure His audience would not ignore or underestimate its
magnitude.

I am, I am, I am the promised One! I am the One Whose
name you have for a thousand years invoked, at Whose
mention you have risen, Whose advent you have longed
to witness, and the hour of Whose Revelation you have
prayed God to hasten.[21]

Bahá'u'lláh, too, announced His message a second time
during a 12-day-festival attended by many people. Still later,

He proclaimed His message in Epistles addressed to common people in general and to the political and religious leaders of the earth in particular.

As we shall see in greater depth in succeeding volumes, these declarations fulfilled both the prophecies that compare Jesus' parousia to the coming and presence of "a thief in the night" and the prophecies that compare His parousia to "the lightning" that flashes forth from the east (Matt. 24:27). The following prophecy should clarify or decode the meaning of "the lightning" in passages that declare the universal and open expression of God's glory to all people:

> The Lord reigns, let the earth be glad; let the distant shores rejoice. Clouds and thick darkness surround him...His lightning lights up the world; the earth sees and trembles.
>
> Psalms 97:1, 2, 4 NIV

What manner or kind of "earth" sees, rejoices, and trembles? The hearts of the people.

What clouds surround the Redeemer? The thick and dark clouds of illusions, misunderstandings, superstitions, and fears; the vapors that rise from people's hearts and souls; the elements that create the night of concealment.

What lightning enlightens the world? The lightning of the Lord's presence, of His spiritual splendor, the resplendent glory of His word, which every "eye" can see.

> O people! Verily, the Day is come, and My Lord hath made Me to shine forth with a light whose splendor hath eclipsed the suns of utterance. Fear ye the Merciful, and be not of them that have gone astray.[22]   Bahá'u'lláh

> ...the Word which is uttered by God shineth and flasheth as the sun amidst the books of men. Happy the man that hath discovered it, and recognized it, and said: "Praised be Thou, Who art the Desire of the world..."[23]   Bahá'u'lláh

The Sun of Truth shineth resplendently, at the bidding of the Lord of the kingdom of utterance...and ten thousand hosts arrayed against it were powerless to withhold it from shining.[24]   Bahá'u'lláh

He...is come in the clouds of light, that He may...unify the world, and gather all men around this Table which hath been sent down from heaven. Beware that ye deny not the favor of God...Better is this for you than that which ye possess; for that which is yours perisheth, whilst that which is with God endureth.[25]   Bahá'u'lláh

Would the Master Be Late?

As we noted earlier, some Christian scholars and writers indicate that the Master has delayed His return. They state that the signs of the time indicate that He could have come sooner, as early as 1844. George Vandeman, perhaps the best known spokesman for Seventh-day Adventists, declares:

...so far as any time prophecy is concerned, Jesus could have returned to this earth any time after 1844. He is not waiting for any prophetic time period to end. No time prophecy is holding Him back. Then why hasn't He returned? For nearly two hundred years we have been living in the time of the end. Why isn't He here? Scripture provides the answer. "The Lord is not slow in keeping his promise, as some understand slowness. He is patient with you, not wanting anyone to perish, but everyone to come to repentance." 2 Peter 3:9 NIV.

Do you see the reason for the delay? Our wonderful Lord, our compassionate, loving Saviour, doesn't want anyone to be lost. And so He holds up the final flight of time, He slows the march of history—because some have not yet made a decision. And He doesn't want one to be lost![26]

C.E. Lewis confirms the same message:

God is holding back to give us that chance [to repent].[27]

The world trends do not support the idea that the passage of time will make the sinners any more repentful than they have been in the past. Many believe that in this century people have become even less spiritual, less repentant. In a book called *The Return*, Christian scholar, Dr. Barry Chant states:

> William Booth [founder of the Salvation Army] pointed out a century ago that the greatest dangers of the 20th century would be religion without the Holy Spirit, Heaven without Hell, faith without repentance, salvation without Lordship, and Christianity without Christ.[28]

As time goes on and the Lord does not come, the unbelievers and sinners keep multiplying and losing their chance for repentance. Delay only *increases* the total number of sinners and sufferers.

> ...evil men and imposters will go from bad to worse...
>
> II Timothy 3:13 NIV

Dr. John White in *Re-entry* writes:

> But truth is truth and the Church is currently in a state of decline. No one grieved more than our Lord that the Church would fall into appalling decay prior to His coming. Indeed this is the primary reason for His coming.[29]

Jesus issued stern warnings to those servants who say the Master will be late (Matt. 24:48-51). The book of Hebrews also confirms the firm promise of no delay:

> He who is coming will come and will not delay.
>
> Hebrews 10:37 NIV

The verse quoted from II Peter 3:9 states clearly that "the Lord is not slow in keeping his promise." Peter implies that the advent will happen neither later nor sooner than planned. God keeps a *perfect timing*. If He sends His Harvester too early, He meets with an *unripe* crop; if He sends Him too

late, He meets with a ***perishing*** crop. Waiting eighteen and
a half centuries can point to God's patience. If most of the
people of our planet would not repent in that long period,
would the respite of another century make much difference?

Whether too soon or too late, the evidences of His effulgent
glory are now actually manifest. It behoveth you to ascertain whether or not such a light hath appeared. It is neither
within your power nor mine to set the time at which it
should be made manifest. God's inscrutable Wisdom hath
fixed its hour beforehand. Be content, O people, with that
which God hath desired for you and predestined unto
you...Had it been in my power, I would have, under no
circumstances, consented to distinguish myself amongst
men...And whenever I chose to hold my peace and be
still, lo, the voice of the Holy Ghost, standing on my
right hand, aroused me, and the Supreme Spirit appeared
before my face, and Gabriel overshadowed me, and the
Spirit of Glory stirred within my bosom, bidding me arise
and break my silence.[30]   Bahá'u'lláh

18

The Times Spoken of by All Holy Prophets

Acts 3:21

A Summary of Prophetic Dates

The times of refreshing shall come from the presence of the Lord; And he shall send Jesus Christ...Whom the heaven must receive until the times of restitution of all things, which God hath spoken by the mouth of all his holy prophets since the world began.   Acts 3:19-21

Our Lord! Grant us what Thou didst promise unto us through Thy Messengers...   Qur'án 3:194 Y

Zoroastrian and Native American
Time Prophecies

The Zoroastrian Scriptures point to the dawning of a new age
in the mid-19th century. The following prophecy attributed to
Zoroaster refers to the gradual decay and disintegration of
Islam during its first millennium, and by implication the
expiration of its cycle and the dawning of a new one:

> When a thousand years have passed from the Arabian
> Faith, such will be its condition, due to division and disunity,
> that even if presented to its Founder, He won't recognize it.[1]

The Zoroastrian Scriptures contain another prophetic figure,
more specific than the preceding:

> When one thousand two hundred-odd years have elapsed
> from the Arabian Faith, Húshídar will be raised to
> prophethood.[2]

"The Arabian Faith" obviously refers to Islam and Húshídar
to the Báb, who appeared about 1200 years after the birth of
Islam.

Furthermore, the name **Húshídar** provides us with more clues,
for it consists of two Persian words: **húsh** meaning **understanding** and **wisdom**, and **dar** meaning **door** or **gate**. (The
pronunciation of **dar** and **door** is so similar as to indicate a
common origin.) The Báb, meaning **the Gate**, serves **as the
Gate of Wisdom and Understanding** through whom the
seekers of truth and tranquility can gain access to the City
of God.

> Happy he who has found wisdom, and the man who has
> acquired understanding...   Proverbs 3:13 NEB

> Teach us to order our days rightly, that we may enter the
> gate of wisdom.   Psalms 90:12 NEB

Another prophecy with a similar message from the Zoroastrian
Scriptures:

When a thousand two hundred and some years have passed from the inception of the religion of the Arabian and the overthrow of the Kingdom of Iran and the degradation of the followers of My religion, a descendent of the Iranian kings will be raised up as a Prophet.[3]

This prophecy refers to Bahá'u'lláh because He too appeared "1200 and some years" (1280 A.H.[*]) after the inception of the Arabian Faith. Further, He was a descendant of Iranian kings, namely, the Sásáníyán Dynasty, which was overthrown by Islamic armies; a defeat that in turn led to the dispersion and degradation of the Zoroastrians. In this prophecy alone there are five basic elements, all of which were fulfilled to the letter.

Haarb, a German scholar, in his translation of the book of Dínkird (attributed to Zoroaster) includes this clear prophecy, which contains many elements of Bahá'í history, and a few of Islamic:

When 1260 years have passed from the Arabian Faith, it will be in such a state that if it is shown to its Messenger, He will not recognize it. At this time, Húshídar will appear and the land of Iran will again become the land of Faith, to lead the world...[then] the Iranians will kill Him [Húshídar]...[4]

The same prophecy also predicts the coming of Bahá'u'lláh with astonishing details. It points to "the appearance of the Glory of God in Iran," His universal Mission "to lead the world to God," and the next two locations in which He would live.

This brief prophecy contains as many as eleven points or predictions, all of which have come true, with marvelous precision, in the Islamic, the Bábí, and the Bahá'í Revelations.

The prophecies listed here are by no means complete. Others will be discovered in the future.

---

[*] 1280 A.H., or 1290 years after the public declaration of Muhammad. As mentioned, all the figures associated with Islam are based on the lunar calendar.

The time of the advent can also be found in some of the American Indian prophecies. These prophecies, as Olin Karch has recently discovered, designate the 13th Toltec Era—extending from 1844 A.D. to 1896 A.D.—as the time of the dawning of a Savior from the East, One who is to inaugurate "a reign of peace" and "a new spiritual order."[5] This is similar to the prophecy from Revelation indicating that "the old order of things has passed away" (Rev. 21:4 NIV).

The Native American prophecies also refer to the advent of another "great Spiritual Being" predicted to appear in "the twelfth tun," namely between 1862-1863 A.D.[6] This prophecy was fulfilled by the public declaration of Bahá'u'lláh in Baghdad, which took place in the spring of 1863.

Prophecies Pointing to 1844 or 1260

The following is a list of 25 prophecies designating the year 1844 or 1260 as the time of the advent of the Redeemer of our age. As mentioned, 1844 and 1260 refer to the same year, because 1844 of the Christian calendar corresponds to 1260 of the Muslim calendar.

From Hebrew Prophecies

1. Moses' prophecy of seven times	1844 A.D.	Leviticus 26:18, 23, 24, 28
2. Daniel's vision of 2300 days	1844 A.D.	Daniel 8:14
3. Daniel's vision of three and a half times	1260 A.H.	Daniel 7:25
4. Daniel's vision of three and a half times	1260 A.H.	Daniel 12:7

5. Daniel's vision pointing to the completion of the scattering of the holy people, fulfilled by Noah's call   1844 A.D.   Daniel 12:7

From Christian Prophecies

6. Christ's confirmation of 2300 days	1844 A.D.	Matthew 24:15
7. Christ's words on the termination of the times of the Gentiles	1844 A.D.	Luke 21:24
8. John's vision of 42 months	1260 A.H.	Revelation 11:2
9. John's vision of 1260 days	1260 A.H.	Revelation 11:3
10. John's vision of three days and a half	1260 A.H.	Revelation 11:9
11. John's vision of three days and a half	1260 A.H.	Revelation 11:11
12. John's vision of 1260 days	1260 A.H.	Revelation 12:6
13. John's vision of three and a half times	1260 A.H.	Revelation 12:14
14. John's vision of 42 months	1260 A.H.	Revelation 13:5
15. John's vision of the four angels bound at the Euphrates	1844 A.D.	Revelation 9:14-15
16. Peter's prediction of the length of the Last Day (covered in Volume IV)	1260 A.H.	II Peter 3:8

From Zoroastrian and Native American Prophecies

17. Zoroaster's prophecy pointing to Húshídar — 1200 + some more years — *Glad Tidings of Sacred Scriptures*, p. 94

18. Zoroaster's prophecy of 1260 years from the Arabian Faith — 1260 A.H. — *Glad Tidings of Sacred Scriptures*, p. 61

19. The Native American Prophecies designating the earliest time of the coming of the Promised One — 1844 A.D. — *Four Remarkable Indian Prophecies*, p. 8

Islamic Prophecies Pointing to 1260, Covered in Volume IV

20. Islamic prophecy of a day of a thousand years + the period of Revelation, which ended in 260 A.H. — 1260 A.H. — Qur'án 32:4

21. Another prophecy confirming the preceding prophecy of 1000 + 260 = 1260 — 1260 A.H. — *Glad Tidings of Sacred Scriptures*, p. 85

22. The prophecy of the numerical value of **ghars** — 1260 A.H. — *Glad Tidings of Sacred Scriptures*, p. 93

23. The prophecy giving the last two figures of the date — ? + 60 — *Glad Tidings of Sacred Scriptures*, p. 93

24. The coming of the day of judgment or chastisement after the lapse of a thousand years. 260 + 1000 = 1260 — 1260 A.H. — Qur'án 34:25-29

25. The coming of the day of chastisement after the lapse of a thousand years. 260+1000=1260	1260 A.H.	Qur'án 22:46, 49, 50

Prophecies Pointing to 1852-1853 and 1863

The following is a list of 13 prophecies designating 1852-1853 and 1863 as the time of the advent of a Great Message. As stated, Bahá'u'lláh received the first intimations of His Message near the end of 1852 (1269 A.H.), and declared it publicly in 1863 (1280 A.H.).*

Prophecies Pointing to the Public Declaration of Bahá'u'lláh

1. Daniel's prophecy of 1290 days, from the proclamation of Muhammad's Mission	1863 A.D.	Daniel 12:11
2. Christ's confirmation of the preceding prophecy	1863 A.D.	Matthew 24:15
3. The Indian prophecy pointing to the years between	1862-1863 A.D.	*Four Remarkable Indian Prophecies*, p. 8
4. Zoroaster's prophecy pointing to a descendent of Iranian kings	1200+ some more years	*All Things Made New*, p. 171
5. Zoroaster's prophecy pointing to the coming of the Glory of God 19 years after Húshídar. 1844+19=1863	1863 A.D.	*Glad Tidings of Sacred Scriptures*, p. 61

---

* "The Declaration of the Báb took place in 1260 A.H. Year nine was therefore 1269 A.H., which began in the middle of October when Bahá'u'lláh had been in prison for about two months." [7]

| 6. The Báb's prophecy pointing to the year 19 (two prophecies quoted) | 1863 A.D. | *God Passes By*, p. 29 |

The Qur'án's Prophecy Pointing to the First Declaration of Bahá'u'lláh Covered in Volume IV

| 7. Qur'ánic prophecy pointing to the year "after Hín," or 69 A.H. | 1852-1853 A.D. | Qur'án 38:88 |

The Báb's Prophecies Pointing to the First Declaration of Bahá'u'lláh

| 8. The Báb's prophecy pointing to the year 9 (four prophecies quoted) | 1852-1853 A.D. | *God Passes By*, p. 29 |
| 9. The Báb's prophecy confirming the Qur'án's prophecy pointing to "after Hín," or 69 | 1852-1853 A.D. | *God Passes By*, p. 29 |

The Evidence is Established

I bear witness, O friends! that the favor is complete...the proof manifest and the evidence established.[8]   Bahá'u'lláh

To ask if the Báb and Bahá'u'lláh fulfilled the time prophecies is superfluous, for it is evident that they did. What we should ask is this: did any Messenger ever appear with such an overwhelming array of evidence pointing to the exact time of His advent?

Have not all the prophets spoken about the dawning of such a glorious day? Have not all the great Messengers foretold a new age, when all things are made new (Rev. 21:5)? Have they not predicted the coming of "the time of refreshing" and "restitution of all things" when the Lord "shall send Jesus Christ," the times "spoken by the mouth of all holy prophets since the world began" (Acts 3:19-21)?

> ...Thou didst enter into a Covenant, concerning me, with all that hath been created in Thy realm.[9]   Bahá'u'lláh

> With each and every Prophet Whom We have sent down in the past, We have established a separate Covenant concerning the Remembrance of God [the Báb] and His Day.[10]   The Báb

The total number of the prophetic dates cited here from the Scriptures of such diverse peoples as the American Indians, the Christians, the Jews, the Zoroastrians, and the Muslims all pointing to the same year (1844) reaches 25. It seems most incredible and unjust to think that God would keep His two or three promises of the date concerning Christ's first coming (Daniel's vision of 69-70 weeks), and yet He would not honor His more than twenty promises—spoken over several thousand years by so many Messengers— concerning Christ's second coming.

Is it merely a matter of chance that out of thousands of probable dates only one should emerge and stand out so many times from such seemingly diverse and unrelated sources? Is this not clear evidence in itself that these sources all spring from one single Source?

What is the probability that all these prophecies just "happened" to point to the same date? Let us assume that out of hundreds of possibilities, the chance of each time prophecy pointing to the same date, by chance alone, is one in a hundred. Then according to the laws of chance, the probability that all the 16 *biblical* prophecies, pointing to 1844 or 1260, could appear by chance alone is equal to: 10^{32}.

To have a better understanding of the preceding number, consider this. A sextillion is equal to 10^{21}. The figure 10^{32} is hundred billion times larger than a sextillion.

If we include all the 38 prophecies from various Scriptures that point to the times of the coming of **both** the Báb and Bahá'u'lláh, our probability figure rises to 10^{76}. A number of this magnitude can best be understood when it is compared with the number of elementary particles (protons, neutrons, and electrons) in the known universe—estimated at 10^{80}. (More about this in Volume II.)

The preceding probability figure (10^{76}) pertains only to **the time** of the advent of the Báb and Bahá'u'lláh. If we include the fulfilled prophecies that pertain to other aspects of the new Revelation (to be covered in the next two volumes), our probability figure will rise many times higher. In fact, it will reach a point of practical impossibility!

Of God it is to point out "the Way."

Muhammad (Qur'án 16:9)

Let him who wisheth turn unto Him, and him who wisheth turn aside. Our Lord, the Merciful, is verily the All-Sufficing, the All-Praised.[11]   Bahá'u'lláh

By God! If ye do well, to your own behoof will ye do well; and if ye deny God and His signs, We, in very truth, having God, can well dispense with all creatures and all earthly dominion.[12]   The Báb

Come forward, you who are thirsty; accept the water of life, a free gift to all who desire it.

Christ (Revelation 22:17 NEB)

He Will Not Be Late
Hebrews 10:37

This investigation raises many questions—questions to which the Scriptures have already responded.

Are we not asked to reason and to put everything to the test?

> Come now, and let us reason together, saith the Lord...
> Isaiah 1:18

Test everything. I Thessalonians 5:21 NIV

Can we disregard all these clear and conclusive time prophecies?

> ...do not despise prophetic utterances, but bring them all
> to the test... I Thessalonians 5:20 NEB

Did Jesus not appeal to prophecies to substantiate His claim?

> Then he [Jesus] began with Moses and all the prophets,
> and explained to them the passages which referred to him-
> self in every part of the scriptures. Luke 24:27 NEB

> If you believed Moses, you would believe me, for he
> wrote about me. John 5:46 NIV

> These are the Scriptures that testify about me, yet you
> refuse to come to me to have life. John 5:39-40 NIV

Is it possible that God would not honor His firm covenant
to send His Messenger to humanity?

> Heaven and earth will pass away; my words will never
> pass away. Luke 21:33 NEB
> Also Mark 13:31

> Does he speak and then not act? Does he promise and not
> fulfill? Numbers 23:19 NIV

Would God abandon His children at such an hour of darkness?

> Never will I leave you; never will I forsake you.
> Hebrews 13:5 NIV

Is not the earth's crop ripe to be harvested?

> Stretch out your sickle and reap; for harvest-time has
> come, and earth's crop is over-ripe. Revelation 14:15 NEB

Have not **the times of the refreshing** and **restitution of all
things** come?

...the times of refreshing shall come from the presence of the Lord; And he shall send Jesus Christ...Whom the heaven must receive until the times of restitution of all things...
Acts 3:19-21

Should we not stand awake in the day of darkness, so that we may not be overtaken by "the thief"?

But you, my friends, are not in the dark, that the day [of advent] should overtake you like a thief.
I Thessalonians 5:4 NEB

Would God delay the fulfillment of His promises?

The Lord is not slow in keeping his promise...
II Peter 3:9 NIV

He who is coming will come and will not delay.
Hebrews 10:37 NIV

What about those who do not heed the prophecies? What about those who say "My master is staying away a long time"?

The master of that servant will come on a day when he does not expect him and at an hour he is not aware of. He will...assign him a place with the hypocrites, where there will be weeping and gnashing of teeth [anger].
Christ (Matt. 24:50-51 NIV)

Shake off, O heedless ones, the slumber of negligence, that ye may behold the radiance which His glory hath spread through the world. How foolish are those who murmur against the premature birth of His light...Whether too soon or too late, the evidences of His effulgent glory are now actually manifest. It behoveth you to ascertain whether or not such a light hath appeared. It is neither within your power nor mine to set the time at which it should be made manifest. God's inscrutable Wisdom hath fixed its hour beforehand. Be content, O people, with that which God hath desired for you and predestined unto you...Had it been in my power, I would have, under no circumstances, consented to distinguish myself amongst men...And whenever I chose to hold my peace and be still, lo, the voice of the Holy Ghost, standing on my right hand, aroused me, and the Supreme Spirit appeared before my face, and Gabriel overshadowed me, and the Spirit of Glory stirred within my bosom, bidding me arise and break my silence.[13]

Bahá'u'lláh

The Three Stages of the Social and Spiritual Evolution of Humanity

The scriptural prophecies portray a clear picture of human history, with the following distinct outline: civilization goes through three stages of growth and evolution, each preparing it for the next.

First is the period of trial and error, when government is left to humans. This is an era of struggle, conflict, and war in which there are many encounters between the forces of good and evil, with the forces of evil winning most of the time. This stage is well exemplified in Daniel's time prophecy quoted earlier (Daniel 7:25). As we noted, the last kingdom, mentioned in the vision, spoke against the Most High, oppressed His saints, and tried to change the set times and the laws. This first stage of human evolution ended with the advent of the Báb (1844 A.D., 1260 A.H.).

Humanity's second stage of evolution, as the prophecies reveal, is that of purification or transition. The old and decayed institutions and ideologies (nationalism, racism, communism, sectarianism, etc.) are judged and toppled, the dominion of the forces of darkness destroyed, and the world is gradually prepared for the establishment of the divine Kingdom. This stage began with the advent of the Báb in 1844 and will continue to an hour as yet undisclosed. In terms of time, this is by far the shortest stage. This stage is often called *the time of the end, the latter days, the last days, the end of the age,* or *that day.*

Daniel's vision of the latter days, after referring to the last kingdom and its allotted period of three and a half times, characterizes this second stage in these words:

> But the court will sit, and his [last kingdom's] power will be taken away and completely destroyed forever.
>
> Daniel 7:26 NIV

Jesus' parable of *the Lord of the vineyard* (Matt. 21:33-41) also confirms God's progressive plan for humanity. The parable indicates that God sent many Messengers, but people mistreated them throughout the ages. At last the Owner of the Vineyard Himself comes to put an end to their transgressions. From then on, the Owner takes charge by establishing His own Kingdom.

> For our Lord God Almighty reigns. Let us rejoice and be glad and give him glory!   Revelation 19:6-7 NIV

Another passage in Daniel's vision provides further details about the coming of *the Ancient of Days* (Bahá'u'lláh) and His Role as a Judge:

> As I looked, thrones were set in place, and the Ancient of Days took his seat...The court was seated, and the books were opened.   Daniel 7:9-10 NIV

> The Book shall be set...and judgment shall be given between them with equity...   Qur'án 39:69

Ours is this second stage, *the Day of Judgment*, when the divine Court is established. We are given the tools and asked to accomplish the goal of preparing the ground. The old order is crumbling and in its place is rising a new order destined to give rise to a Kingdom imperishable and everlasting.

After the judgment and purification, the third stage dawns— an age characterized by the triumph of the forces of light over the hosts of darkness and decay; the era of the Kingdom, when peace prevails, love abounds, and righteousness reigns. We are now at the dawning of this Golden Millennium of Enlightenment. Here in the following verse Daniel completes his description of the three stages:

> Then the sovereignty, power and greatness of the kingdoms under the whole heaven will be handed over to the saints, the people of the Most High. His kingdom will be an everlasting kingdom, and all rulers will worship and obey him.   Daniel 7:27 NIV

In the following passage, Shoghi Effendi, the Guardian of the Bahá'í Faith, refers briefly to the connecting link—the cleansing stage—between the first and the third stage, which as testified by Bahá'u'lláh, is destined to give rise to the fruits of the Kingdom:

> We stand on the threshold of an age whose convulsions proclaim alike the death-pangs of the old order and the birth-pangs of the new. Through the generating influence of the Faith announced by Bahá'u'lláh this New World Order may be said to have been conceived. We can, at the present moment, experience its stirrings in the womb of a travailing age—an age waiting for the appointed hour at which it can cast its burden and yield its fairest fruit.[14]

19

And This Gospel of the Kingdom Will be Proclaimed

Matthew 24:14 NEB

T o make people aware of the dawning of the Kingdom, Christ promised that *the good news* of its coming would be preached among all nations, so that God's testimony to His people would be complete.

> And this gospel [good news] of the Kingdom will be proclaimed throughout the earth as a testimony to all nations; and then the end will come.   Matthew 24:14 NEB

The fulfillment of this prophecy and promise has been so dramatic as to deserve further study. In the spiritual history of the world, the mid-19th century stands out conspicuously.

The intensity of the desire of the people of that age to meet their Savior and their fervor and dedication in preaching and proclaiming the dawning of His kingdom are without parallel in all history. Never before had so many so fervently set their hopes on heaven—a hope that within a few decades embraced the whole planet.

A Christian scholar who has done much research on the Advent Awakening of the mid-19th century writes:

> Nothing like it had ever been proclaimed before. Simultaneously, in England, Scotland, Ireland, Germany, France, Switzerland, Scandinavia, America, India, Northern Africa, and the Near East, a growing chorus of voices were heard, springing up independently but proclaiming the same message and prophetic time period. It bore all the earmarks of a true advance in contemporary recognition of a currently fulfilling epoch in the grand prophetic outline.[1]

According to one authority, as many as a thousand scholars and seekers around the world were proclaiming and preaching the millennial message. Himes announced that in the United States, "by May 1844...5,000,000 copies of Adventist publications had been distributed."[2]

The events of the 1840s seemed so impressive to a Christian scholar—Jerome Clarke, professor of history at Southern Missionary College—as to prompt him to write three volumes on the subject and entitle them by the date: *1844*. Each volume covers certain aspects of reform (social, religious, political, and educational) instituted in the mid-19th century. The Bahá'í Faith does not appear in any of the three volumes. In his preface, the author indicates that an atmosphere of reform permeated the mid-19th century. He then adds:

> Such an atmosphere made people receptive to change and provided the attitude of mind which made the widespread dissemination of new ideas possible. Surely it was in the providence of God that the "great Second Advent Movement" arose at such a time.[3]

The Child Preachers of the
Mid-19th Century

Sometimes a goal is achieved through some unusual or dramatic means. Jesus said:

> I tell you, if my disciples keep silence the stones will shout aloud.   Luke 19:40 NEB

As historical records reveal, in one country the torch of the dawning of the new age was carried aloft by children and youth, some of them as young as ten and twelve. This drama unfolded in Sweden and caused a stir in that land:

> The nineteenth-century Advent Awakening penetrated Scandinavia in the early forties, but by a means markedly different from that employed in any other country of the Old World or the New. In Sweden, preaching contrary to that of the established church was forbidden. The clergy of the state church opposed emphasis upon the soon coming of Christ. Their refusal to speak was met by the amazing spectacle of children and youth in the homes of humble cottagers—some of whom had not yet learned to read—proclaiming the impending judgment hour and imminent advent, and giving expositions of prophecy.[4]

The records of this incredible event, the opposition of the priests to these "child preachers," and the response of the population "permeated the Swedish press for two or three years—particularly in 1842 and 1843."[5] First, let us see an unfriendly report from a paper published in Stockholm (February 23, 1842):

> They [the child preachers] claimed to have received their revelations directly through the Holy Spirit and claim to have visited heaven and hell...A general superstition has taken hold of the people, who refute the warnings and instructions of the priests, and in multitudes ranging from 2,000 to 3,000 go to listen to those who claim to be the chosen messengers of heaven.[6]

Another record from another paper is somewhat neutral to this unusual phenomenon (March 4, 1842):

> From far and near hundreds of persons come daily to listen to these girls. The girl from Swenarum, daughter of a poor peasant, preached twice a day, and had always two or three hundred listeners daily...The common people either believe the girls to be God's [messengers], as they themselves claim, or they do not know what to think. Few are they who do not see in this something marvelous, or feel this to be the voice of God to man. Almost everyone believes or trembles.[7]

As we would expect, people's perceptions of these young preachers varied. Many were inspired and transformed by their childish purity and sincerity; others considered them pawns of the devil; and still others viewed them as "the sick ones." Some of the participants in the drama advocated severe punishment as the best cure for a rampant disease. On one occasion, two of the young preachers were arrested and tried in court. Years later, one of them recalled:

> When we were brought before the governor for examination, he demanded by what authority we were sent to preach. We referred him to Joel 2 and Rev. 14:6-8, and told him further that the Spirit of God came upon us with such power that we could not resist it.[8]

The prophecies from *Joel* quoted by the youths before the governor were these:

> Thereafter the day shall come when I will pour out my spirit on all mankind; your sons and your daughters shall prophesy, your old men shall dream dreams and your young men see visions...   Joel 2:28 NEB

Then Joel adds that such events will happen "before the great and terrible day of the Lord comes" (Joel 2:31 NEB). The prophecies from *Revelation* were these:

> Then I saw an angel flying in mid-heaven, with an eternal gospel to proclaim to those on earth, to every nation and

tribe, language and people. He cried in a loud voice, 'Fear God and pay him homage; for the hour of his judgment has come!'   Revelation 14:6-7 NEB

Apparently, the biblical argument did not convince the governor. He decided that the best remedy for such a "contagious disease" was punishment:

> After being beaten they were taken to the hospital for mental examination by physicians. Their heads were shaved, with the exception of two strips of hair left in the form of a cross. Then they were imprisoned and tortured by powerful streams of cold water. Finally they were released, only to keep on preaching until 1844.[9]

We should note that in the first advent children also played a role:

> When the young children of Jerusalem joined the crowd at the temple, proclaiming Jesus as the Messiah, the "son of David," they fulfilled the Old Testament promise that "babes" would give praise to God. The religious leaders were outraged at this outburst of faith from these mere "children" and demanded they be silenced. Yet, Jesus knew that these words had been placed in the mouths of these children by God Almighty, Himself.[10]

Joseph Wolff, the Hero of the Advent Movement

This discussion of the fulfillment of Jesus' prophecy, that before His advent the Gospel will be preached in all the world, would be incomplete without a brief reference to Joseph Wolff (1795-1862), who spread the Good News (Gospel) more than anyone else in the 19th century.

If William Miller was the herald of the Advent Movement in the West, its hero must undoubtedly be Joseph Wolff. (In the East, too, there appeared two bright "stars" that heralded the dawning of the new day: Shaykh Ahmad and Siyyid Kázim.)

Joseph Wolff was a brilliant orator "of Jewish birth, Catholic education, and Protestant persuasion." His zeal, courage, devotion, sacrifice, and adventures are all legendary. John Quincy Adams called him "one of the most remarkable men living on earth at this time."

Joseph Wolff was born to a strict Jewish family and received Hebrew training from the age of four. To make him impervious to the influence of Christians, his parents frightened him with dire warnings. They told him that Christians worship wooden crosses. To teach him German, his ambitious but unwary parents sent him to a Christian school, where he learned much more than German: he also learned about Jesus and recognized Him as the expected Messiah of the Jews. He professed his faith to the Lutheran minister, but fearing his father, who was a rabbi, he concealed his love for the beloved Messiah until the age of seventeen, when his father died.

Because of his many distinctions, Joseph Wolff received the full support of British royalty and even joined them by marrying a member of the royal family. But the ease and comfort did not satisfy his spiritual hunger. He left the security of his surroundings for adventures that immortalized him. For almost two decades, he was on the move, often traveling under the most trying conditions, carrying the news of an imminent advent to the farthest reaches of the earth, "from the Thames to the Oxus, the Ganges, the wilderness of Arabia, and the mountains of Abyssinia."[11]

He called himself "Missionary to all the Nations." Joshua Brooks, one of the leaders of the Advent Movement, said: "no individual has perhaps given greater publicity to the doctrine of the *second coming*."[12] Wolff declared that "an invisible power" continually moved him "from land to land, and from sea to sea to preach the tidings of salvation, and the second coming of our Lord in glory and majesty."[13]

To succeed in his endeavors, Wolff learned 14 languages, among them Persian, Chaldean, Arabic, Hebrew, Greek, and Latin. He carried the message of the imminent advent of Christ to all, from peasants to pashas and princes, from bishops and priests to kings and American presidents. He even addressed the assembled Congress of the United States. The hardships he endured for the purpose of fulfilling Jesus' predictions—that before "the end," the Gospel shall be preached as a testimony to all nations—is beyond the scope of this book. But a brief reference to his tenacity and resilience is in order. In a letter addressed to Sir Thomas Barring, he states that he had:

> ...traversed the most barbarous countries for eighteen years, without protection of any European authority whatsoever, and...[had] been sold as a slave, thrice condemned to death, attacked with cholera and typhus fever and almost every Asiatic fever in existence, and bastinadoed and starved.[14]

Perhaps the most intriguing part of his adventures occurred in 1843-1845, while he was travelling through Persian territory. This was the interval during which the Báb declared His Mission. It was during that trip that "the Persian banditti of the Khán of Khorásán made him a slave." They planned to sell him to a Turkoman chief, but changed their minds, treated him as a guest, and sent the Arabic Bibles he had brought them to their religious leaders. While he was in Mashhad— a city that a few years later became a rallying point for the followers of the Báb—he announced the imminent advent of the Redeemer of the world. He believed the date was 1847. About his activities in Mashhad, he wrote:

> I fixed on their tents public proclamations, announcing to them the second coming of Christ in Glory and Majesty, called on them to repent of their evil doings, and especially exhorted them to give up the practice of making slaves of the Persians.[15]

Like William Miller, he too was sustained in his hope by
visions. While in Bukhárá, depressed and despondent because
of the obstacles he was facing:

> ...suddenly a splendor covered the room, and the voice
> 'Jesus enters!' thundered in my ears. I saw suddenly
> Jesus standing upon a throne surrounded by little children,
> mercifully and kindly looking at them. I fell down, and
> worshipped, and the vision disappeared.[16]

Again, while in Malta and "very much cast down:"

> ...suddenly my room was transfigured and I believe I was
> in New Jerusalem. Jesus Christ, surrounded by Abraham,
> Isaac, and Jacob, and the Apostles, walked about the street.[17]

Due to his courage, persistence, and dedication, Joseph Wolff,
unlike many others in his time, became an immortal "star"
shining "like the brightness of the heavens" (Daniel 12:2-3),
not only in our kingdom but in the kingdom of heaven as
well. How many millions will be inspired by his selfless
example, in centuries to come? Had he been pleased "with
the ease of a passing day," he would have been soon forgotten.

> **O OFFSPRING OF DUST!**
> Be not content with the ease of a passing day, and deprive
> not thyself of everlasting rest. Barter not the garden of
> eternal delight for the dust-heap of a mortal world. Up
> from thy prison ascend unto the glorious meads above,
> and from thy mortal cage wing thy flight unto the paradise
> of the Placeless.[18]   Bahá'u'lláh

> Praise be to God that He hath enabled us to become
> cognizant of Him Whom God shall make manifest
> [Bahá'u'lláh] in the Day of Resurrection, so that we may
> derive benefit from the fruit of our existence and be not
> deprived of attaining the presence of God. For indeed
> this is the object of our creation and the sole purpose
> underlying every virtuous deed we may perform. Such is
> the bounty which God hath conferred upon us; verily He
> is the All-Bountiful, the Gracious.[19]   The Báb

Part III

God's Covenant With Humanity

*The remaining chapters do not deal directly with proofs.
They offer some insight into these two questions:*

- *Why has the Bahá'í Faith not been acknowledged by the
  majority of humanity, and why have religious leaders not
  seriously investigated Bahá'u'lláh's claim? (Chapter 20).*

- *What are the four main elements of God's covenant
  with humanity? (Chapters 21 and 22).*

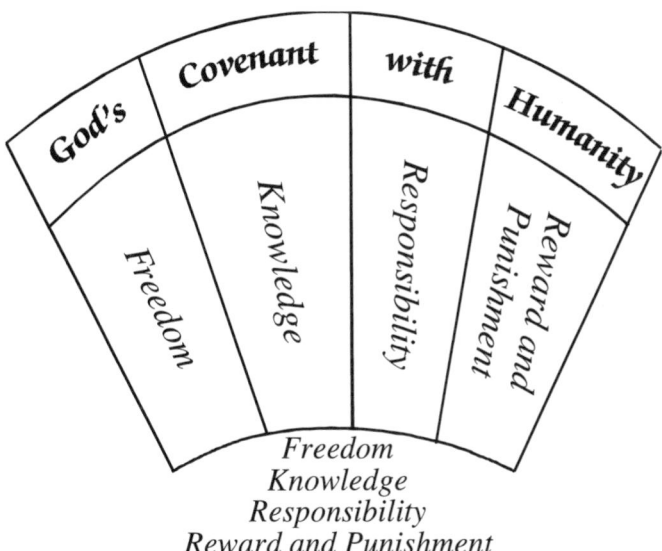

Freedom
Knowledge
Responsibility
Reward and Punishment

*The first three elements of God's covenant with humanity
(freedom, knowledge, and responsibility) are covered here.
The fourth element (reward and punishment) is covered in
Volume III.*

20

My People Perish for Want of Knowledge

Hosea 4:6 NAB

Why Haven't I Heard About this Faith Before?

Many of those who hear the message of the new revelation for the first time wonder why they haven't heard of it before. They say: "Bahá'u'lláh presents the greatest claim and the most awesome challenge. Why hasn't such a mighty message spread more widely?" The reasons are many and varied. They stem both from the means or methods the Bahá'ís use to teach their Faith, and from the lack of receptivity on the part of most people.

The Gentle Method of Teaching

Let us begin with an examination of the Bahá'í ways of teaching. Bahá'u'lláh admonishes His followers to teach His Faith with the utmost dignity and care, expressing the deepest reverence for the seeker's freedom to follow the dictates of his own conscience. It is His Command that His followers should not proselytize, lest they encroach upon anyone's freedom of choice. This is how Bahá'u'lláh describes the accepted way of teaching:

> O people of Bahá! Ye are the dawning-places of the love of God...Set forth that which ye possess. If it be favorably received, your end is attained; if not, to protest is vain. Leave that soul to himself and turn unto the Lord...Be not the cause of grief, much less of discord and strife.[1]

And again:

> Consort with all men, O people of Bahá, in a spirit of friendliness and fellowship. If ye be aware of a certain truth, if ye possess a jewel, of which others are deprived, share it with them in a language of utmost kindliness and good-will. If it be accepted, if it fulfill its purpose, your object is attained. If anyone should refuse it, leave him unto himself, and beseech God to guide him. Beware lest ye deal unkindly with him.[2]

Because of such admonitions, the Bahá'ís have been cautious—sometimes too cautious—in declaring Bahá'u'lláh's Message with the zeal and boldness it deserves. Some Bahá'ís are extremely concerned about imposing their beliefs on others, lest their Faith be identified with those denominations that use aggressive and undignified means to gain converts. Others hesitate to share their beliefs because of a lack of self-confidence, insufficient knowledge of the Bahá'í teachings, or an inadequate understanding of their spiritual responsibility.

But we should remember that what matters are the long-range—not the short-range—consequences. The gentle method of teaching may not bring immediate results, but it does bring enduring ones. Although coercion may enjoy a quick and crushing triumph, a lasting victory can come only from gentleness and loving-kindness.

Yet in spite of the caution and the care, the spread of the Bahá'í Message has been phenomenal. For within the span of a century and a half, it has encircled the earth, touching the hearts and minds of many followers in over 200 countries and territories, encompassing over 110,000 centers around the globe.

Mistrust of the Non-traditional And Unfamiliar

Among the obstacles hampering the spread of the Bahá'í Faith is a prevailing suspicion and mistrust among many people toward any outsiders trying to teach them something about religion. This mistrust and suspicion is a defense against all those who have misused religion, who in the name of preserving the pearl of faith have pursued their own prejudices, their own selfish ends, who have demeaned the nobility and distinction of the divine Words by teaching dogmatism and fanaticism, by rejecting reason, by exaggerating minute theological questions to further their own causes.

Since fanaticism and dogmatism do not thrive on freedom of choice and reason, other means must be devised to sustain them. The obvious solution is to employ pressure to subdue freedom and to apply emotionalism to dull reason. This is exactly what has happened. These are the means some of the preachers and churches have used, and are using, in search of converts.

Such unjustified methods of spreading beliefs have succeeded in stirring the masses, but they have proved costly to the dignity and nobility of religion. They have alienated the educated and the enlightened segments of society. They have also strengthened and sensitized people's suspicion to such an extent that they are alarmed by even the most subtle and innocent attempts at an exchange of ideas.

From their own experience and that of their family and friends, people have learned to be on their guard against intruders, to be armed with apathy, to tune out the loud and varied voices of a myriad of preachers, all trying to convert them, to make them to be born again quickly and painlessly by uttering a few simple words.

The spread of strange cults with weird and dangerous beliefs and the influence of propaganda (political, commercial, and religious) through the mass media have further intensified suspicion to such a degree that people refuse even to do the most elementary research into a claim as awesome as that of the Báb and Bahá'u'lláh. They have heard so many half-truths and have been lied to so often that, even faced with the truth, they would fail to see it. Their spiritual senses have grown so dull through repeated misuse as to become inoperative. No wonder the Scriptures declare that when the Redeemer comes "the world neither sees nor knows him" (John 14:17 NEB). If we do not muster up the courage to break the bonds of suspicion and apathy, we will remain deprived of this glorious gift.

> For the Lord hath poured out upon you the spirit of deep sleep, and hath closed your eyes...   Isaiah 29:10
> See also Jer. 5:21; Isa. 42:20; Mark 8:18

> Go to this people and say: You may hear and hear, but you will never understand; you may look and look, but you will never see. For this people's mind has become gross; their ears are dulled, and their eyes are closed.
> Acts 28:26-27 NEB

The Excessive Fear of Falsehood

The combined effects of the infamy of cults, as well as the misuse of the mass media in general and of religion in particular, have caused excessive fear of falsehood at the expense of love for truth. Most people do not fear the consequences of denying truth as much as they fear the danger of being deceived. The force of fear has caused undue apathy, doubt, and despair; it has led to a feeling that "Everyone claims to know the truth, but no real truth may be found anywhere."

This fear of falsehood gains strength—and becomes contagious—especially among family and friends. It causes well-wishing individuals to discourage their spouses from searching. It leads caring parents to deprive their mature children of their right to freedom of conscience. Friends, peers, and priests join their powers of persuasion with those of parents and partners to stifle inquiry. Thus those endowed with the least courage and afflicted with the most apathy, suspicion, and conformity not only refuse to pursue their own independent search for truth, but also use their influence to discourage others. They become, in the words of Jesus, stumbling-blocks to the seekers of truth. They forget the words of Jesus addressed to their forebears who had done the same:

> As for the man who is a cause of stumbling to one of these little ones who have faith, it would be better for him to be thrown into the sea with a millstone round his neck. If your hand is your undoing, cut it off; it is better for you to enter into life maimed than to keep both hands and go to hell and the unquenchable fire.   Mark 9:42-44 NAB

> Causes of stumbling are bound to arise; but woe betide the man through whom they come.   Luke 17:1 NEB
> See also Matt. 18:7

Many people assume that any religion with an unfamiliar name must be the work of deceivers. Others lack self-confidence. When they hear the call of their conscience to search, they respond by thinking: "How would I know someone is right or wrong? I am not good enough to make a judgment. At least I have something to hold on to. Why not play it safe? Why take chances?"

Then there are other seekers who trust their spiritual instincts. These seekers do not fear falsehood, they know they cannot be fooled, they know man's words can *never* be disguised as God's Words. They have trust in their insight; they know their insight is illuminated by divine injunctions. They remember the words of the Scriptures to "test the spirits, to see whether they are from God" (I John 4:1 NEB); whether they are divine or deceptive. The words of Paul, "test everything" (I Thess. 5:21 NIV), constantly ring in their conscience, stirring them to action, to search. They know that the Creator would never fail in His promise to guide their search. They know that He who has commanded His children saying *ye shall seek* and *ye shall knock*, has promised *ye shall find*, and *it shall be opened unto you* (Matt. 7:7-8). These seekers also know that by *not* searching they put their fears above God's assurances, casting a vote of *no confidence* in His covenant, in His promises.

Preoccupation With Worldly Concerns

Still another obstacle in people's way is the world—preoccupation with surviving or making a living. People are too busy earning their daily bread to have time for spiritual enrichment. It seems a great sacrifice to them to spend their precious time for something that fails to bring immediate and tangible rewards. Of course, this is exactly what the prophecies predicted would happen. For we are told that the promised Redeemer will walk among the masses like those to whom Noah was sent:

> As things were in Noah's days, so will they be when the Son of Man comes. In the days before the flood they ate and drank and married, until the day that Noah went into the ark, and they knew nothing until the flood came and swept them all away. That is how it will be when the Son of Man comes.   Matthew 24:37-39 NEB
> See also Luke 17:26-30

Lack of Knowledge,
the Common Denominator

Almost all the reasons cited so far seem to converge at one point: a lack of recognition results to a large extent from not knowing the claim advanced by the Báb and Bahá'u'lláh nor the proofs that sustain their claim.

...my people are destroyed from lack of knowledge.

Hosea 4:6 NIV

If people became well informed, they would not reject the truth. Indeed, after gaining full knowledge, the new Bahá'ís ask the same question they asked before, but with an opposite intent. Before knowing the claim of Bahá'u'lláh, many of them would say to themselves, "If the expected Redeemer ever comes, it will be impossible for me not to know about it." After gaining full knowledge of Bahá'u'lláh's claim, they ask, "How could I *not* have known about such an awesome event? Why is it that the world cannot see? Why don't the majority of people even try to test Bahá'u'lláh's claim?"

These are the kinds of questions the Bahá'ís keep asking, always wondering why others do not see what *they* see. They forget that before becoming well informed of the Bahá'í Revelation, they too had the same problem, they too were handicapped by the same obstacles. To give a simple analogy, let us assume that near you there is a most exquisite and enchanting garden, but it is hidden by walls. You pass by the garden many times without even considering the possibility of seeing anything but wild grass and weeds. Then perhaps by chance, perhaps by the word of a friend, you raise your vantage point and you suddenly see what startles your imagination, what awakens a vision of undreamed-of ecstasy and splendor. This is exactly what happens to those who change their perspective on Bahá'u'lláh's Revelation. They see a glory and splendor that only the grand Designer could have planned and implemented. Alas, the celestial Scene is concealed behind many veils and walls.

Let us go back once more to the original questions: If Bahá'u'lláh is indeed the promised Redeemer, why haven't I heard about Him? And why has the world **not** known Him? The answer is simple and brief, and it is given by Jesus Himself. First He predicts, "The world cannot receive him" (John 14:17 NEB), and then He adds: "because the world neither sees nor knows him" (John 14:17 NEB). Thus lack of true knowledge of the new Messenger is the main reason the world has not as yet received Him.

God has fulfilled His promises. He has sent His Messenger exactly as He had promised: "as a thief in the night." He has also asked us to stay awake and aware, to make the effort to be informed, to gain knowledge of the truth. God does not want to force anyone into belief, to offer the water of life to those who are not thirsty, to those who would rather sleep than search for truth.

Among all the major reasons that Bahá'u'lláh's Message has not as yet shaken the world, there exists one more that overshadows and influences all the others. That reason, as suspected, has to do with the religious leaders.

The Role of Religious Leaders

These questions often arise: "The masses may not know about Bahá'u'lláh's claim, but what about the religious leaders? Is it not **they** who are responsible for people's spiritual guidance? Should not **they** be the first to wish to know? And if they do know, why haven't they guided us? If Bahá'u'lláh is indeed the world Savior and Teacher, the return of the Son in the Glory of the Father, then the religious leaders would be—and should be—the first to find Him, follow Him, and adore Him." This seems a very logical assumption to make, but the prophecies predict otherwise. They foresee apathy and lack of discernment on the part of these leaders:

All prophetic vision has become for you like a sealed book...Then the Lord said: Because this people approach me with their mouths and honor me with their lips while their hearts are far from me, and their religion is but a precept of men, learnt by rote, therefore I will yet again shock this people, adding shock to shock: the wisdom of their wise men shall vanish and the discernment of the discerning shall be lost.   Isaiah 29:11-14 NEB

One of the most prominent Christian leaders and scholars to accept Bahá'u'lláh was George Townshend, formerly Archdeacon of Clonfert and Canon of St. Patrick's Cathedral in Dublin, Ireland. In his works he addressed the religious leaders of Christendom again and again, urging them to examine the claim of Bahá'u'lláh. The concluding words of his book *Christ and Bahá'u'lláh*, composed shortly before his death, were:

The Bahá'í Faith today presents the Christian Churches with the most tremendous challenge ever offered them in their long history: a challenge, and an opportunity. It is the plain duty of every earnest Christian in this illumined Age to investigate for himself with an open and fearless mind the purpose and the teachings of this Faith and to determine whether the collective center for all the constructive forces of this time be not the Messenger from God, Bahá'u'lláh, He and no other; and whether the way to a better, kinder, happier world will not lie open as soon as we accept the Announcement our rulers rejected...O, Christian believers! for your own sakes and for the sake of the Churches, for the sake of all mankind, for the sake of the Kingdom, cast away your conflicting dogmas and interpretations which have caused such disunity and led us to the verge of wholesale self-destruction. Recognize the age of Truth. Recognize Christ in the glory and power of the Father and, heart and soul, throw yourselves into His Cause.[3]

Bahá'u'lláh had made the same plea repeatedly to the leaders of all religions. He had addressed them in the most definitive and emphatic terms. Did they listen? Did they try to test the new Revelation? The mass of religious leaders have so far preferred to ignore Bahá'u'lláh's claim as the bearer of a divine Revelation. They have preferred to remain detached from the new Faith.

To those spiritual leaders whose character and conduct conform to their confession, Bahá'u'lláh accords the highest honor:

> The divine [the religious leader] whose conduct is upright, and the sage who is just, are as the spirit unto the body of the world. Well is it with that divine whose head is attired with the crown of justice, and whose temple is adorned with the ornament of equity.[4]

The most trying time for religious leaders is the dawn of a new dispensation. Most of them stand so veiled by centuries of man-made traditions and doctrines, and so engulfed by the prevailing views as to be unable to discern the Day-Star of Truth. They allow human knowledge to become a veil between them and the One Who is the Object and the Source of all knowledge.

> The denials...of these leaders of religion have, in the main, been due to their lack of knowledge and understanding.[5]
>
> Bahá'u'lláh

What has held many religious leaders back from examining the claim of Bahá'u'lláh is their supposition that all the scriptural prophecies are literal. They still maintain that the Redeemer must come from heaven on the clouds. Some of them even go so far as to say that Jesus must return bearing the scars inflicted on His body during the crucifixion.

They fail to heed the warnings of the Scriptures, to recognize that they should not insist on their own interpretation; that symbolic language is used abundantly throughout the Bible.

Their negligence in insisting on literal interpretation of the prophecies has allowed a simple word such as *cloud* (signifying misconception and misjudgment) to become truly a cloud that obscures the glory of the One who is the Light of the world (John 8:12). Countless references in the Scriptures prove beyond any doubt that expressions such as *coming from heaven* or *on the clouds* are simple metaphors. Some religious leaders fail to realize sufficiently that expectations based on literal interpretation of prophecies also prevailed during the first advent of Christ. The literal-minded Jews of that time were deprived of the light of their Redeemer for the same reason.

Bahá'u'lláh repeatedly asks us to look back and try to learn from the example of those who have lived at the dawning of earlier revelations. Here are some of His words about the conduct of the religious leaders during the time of the advent of previous Messengers:

> Consider the former generations. Witness how every time the Day Star of Divine bounty hath shed the light of His Revelation upon the world, the people of His Day have arisen against Him, and repudiated His truth. They who were regarded as the leaders of men have invariably striven to hinder their followers from turning unto Him Who is the Ocean of God's limitless bounty.

> Behold how the people, as a result of the verdict pronounced by the divines [religious leaders] of His age, have cast Abraham, the friend of God, into fire; how Moses, He Who held converse with the Almighty, was denounced as liar and slanderer. Reflect how Jesus, the Spirit of God, was, notwithstanding His extreme meekness and perfect tender-heartedness, treated by His enemies. So fierce was the opposition which He, the Essence of Being and Lord of the visible and invisible, had to face, that He had nowhere to lay His head. He wandered continually from place to place, deprived of a permanent abode.[6]

To conclude, the recognition of Truth requires purity, open-mindedness, and detachment from traditions, from one's ego, and from worldly concerns. It does not require knowledge of Greek, or Hebrew, or theology. Far be it from divine justice to make the truth accessible or recognizable only to those with a degree in divinity.

Wisdom and knowledge based on human standards sometimes create pride and self-satisfaction.

> Your wisdom [and knowledge, KJV] betrayed you, omni-scient as you were, and you said to yourself, 'I am, and who but I?'   Isaiah 47:10 NEB

Therefore, let your judgment be dependent on *yourself*, and yourself on Him who gave you the gift of life, *not anyone else*! If the attitude of self-dependency is *not* assumed and maintained, there can be little hope of finding the truth. At the beginning of *The Book of Certitude*, Bahá'u'lláh writes:

> The essence of these words is this: they that tread the path of faith...must cleanse themselves of all that is earthly— their ears from idle talk, their minds from vain imaginings, their hearts from worldly affections, their eyes from that which perisheth. They should put their trust in God, and, holding fast unto Him, follow in His way. Then will they be made worthy of the effulgent glories of the sun of divine knowledge and understanding, and become the recipients of a grace that is infinite and unseen, inasmuch as man can never hope to attain unto the knowledge of the All-Glorious, can never quaff from the stream of divine knowledge and wisdom, can never enter the abode of immortality, nor partake of the cup of divine nearness and favor, unless and until he ceases to regard the words and deeds of mortal men as a standard for the true understand-ing and recognition of God and His Prophets.[7]

As stated, not all religious leaders have ignored or rejected the new Messenger. A few have indeed acknowledged Him, and others have admired His teachings. But neither their acceptance nor their rejection should make any difference to you in meeting your spiritual responsibility to pursue *your own* independent search. Even if all the religious leaders and all those who follow them unanimously acknowledged Bahá'u'lláh, you should still decline to take their word for granted and their judgment for truth until you have carried out your own independent investigation of truth.

> Thus on the Day of Resurrection God will ask everyone of his understanding and not of his following in the footsteps of others. How often a person, having inclined his ears to the holy verses, would bow down in humility and would embrace the Truth, while his leader would not do so. Thus every individual must bear his own responsibility, rather than someone else bearing it for him...How often the most insignificant of men have acknowledged the truth, while the most learned have remained wrapt in veils. Thus in every Dispensation a number of souls enter the fire by reason of their following in the footsteps of others.[8]   The Báb

This work offers the leaders of all faiths an opportunity to honor their spiritual obligation, to put Bahá'u'lláh's claim to the test, and to decide if this Savior is divine or deceptive. Such a search must rank first among all their worthy endeavors, and first in their hearts and their minds, above every other responsibility they may ever encounter as the guardians of faith.

In the meantime no one should wait for his religious leaders to make the first move. The records of history, the voice of reason, and the testimony of the Scriptures all declare that it is unwise indeed to wait for them to rise first. There have been many in the past who have waited and waited, with no end in sight. Among them are millions and millions of Jews, who have been waiting for twenty centuries for their religious leaders to bring them the glad-tidings of the coming of the Messiah. They are *still* waiting and praying for His advent!

21

I Have Set My Rainbow in the Clouds

Genesis 9:13 NIV

God's Eternal Covenant
With Humanity

A covenant defines the relationship between God and man. It may be broad or specific. It is always mutual:

> ...be true to your covenant with me; I will be true to my covenant with you...   Qur'án 2:38

According to a Christian source:

> The concept of covenant between God and His people is one of the most important theological truths of the Bible.

By making a covenant with Abraham, God promised to bless His descendants and to make them His special people. Abraham, in return, was to remain faithful to God and to serve as a channel through which God's blessings could flow to the rest of the world (Gen. 12:1-3)...Another famous covenant was between God and David, in which David and his descendants were established as the royal heirs to the throne of the nations of Israel (II Sam. 7:12; 22:51). This covenant agreement reached its highest fulfillment when Jesus the Messiah, a descendant of the line of David, was born in Bethlehem about a thousand years after God made this promise to David the king.[1]

But the striking thing about God's covenant with His people is that God is holy, all-knowing, and all powerful; but He consents to enter into covenant with man, who is weak, sinful, and imperfect.[2]

Every Messenger mediates a new covenant or testament between God and humanity:

> ...Christ is the mediator of a new covenant [testament]...
>
> Hebrews 9:15 NIV

One of the most vital terms of the covenant concerns the coming of a new mediator, who comes to fulfill the previous covenant and establish a new one. For instance, as the New Testament confirms, this prophecy from Moses predicted the advent of Jesus:

> The Lord your God will raise up for you a prophet like me [Moses] from among your own brothers. You must listen to him.   Deuteronomy 18:15 NIV

> I will raise up for them a prophet like you from among their brothers; I will put my words in his mouth, and he will tell them everything I command him. If anyone does not listen to my words that the prophet speaks in my name, I myself will call him to account.
>
> Deuteronomy 18:18-19 NIV
> See also John 1:45; Acts 3:22; 7:37

Muhammad, too, predicted the advent of other Messengers:

> O children of Adam! There shall come to you Apostles [Messengers] from among yourselves, rehearsing my signs to you; and whoso shall fear God and do good works, no fear shall be upon them, neither shall they be put to grief. But they who charge our signs with falsehood, and turn away from them in their pride, shall be inmates of fire: for ever shall they abide therein.   Qur'án 7:33-34

There is no exception to this rule:

> The Lord of the universe hath never raised up a prophet nor hath He sent down a Book unless He hath established His covenant with all men, calling for their acceptance of the next Revelation and the next Book...[3]   The Báb

> He...redeemed his people; he decreed that his covenant should always endure.   Psalms 111:9 NEB

> When God entered into covenant with the prophets, he said, "This is the Book and the Wisdom which I give you. Hereafter shall a prophet come unto you to confirm the Scriptures already with you. Ye shall surely believe on him, and ye shall surely aid him. Are ye resolved?" said he, "and do ye accept the covenant on these terms?" They said, "We are resolved"; "Be ye then the witnesses," said he, "and I will be a witness as well as you. And whoever turneth back after this, these are surely the perverse."   Qur'án 3:75-76

All great Messengers have also made a covenant with their followers concerning the Redeemer of our time—the Desire of ages. They have **all** foretold His coming. This is called **the Greater Covenant**:*

---

* See *God Passes By*, p. 27, 1957 edition. **The Greater Covenant** is also used in Bahá'í literature in a broader sense to denote the Covenant which every Messenger of God makes with His followers, promising that a new Messenger will, at a time decreed by God, appear among humanity.

...Thou [God] didst enter into a Covenant, concerning me, with all that hath been created in thy realm.[4] Bahá'u'lláh

...We [God] have taken a covenant from every created thing...concerning the Remembrance of God [the Báb]...[5]

The Báb

Another covenant seeks to preserve the unity and indicate the line of authority in a given faith. When Jesus called Peter "the rock" (Matt. 16:18), or the foundation of His church, that was His covenant with Christians.

Perhaps the most fundamental of all covenants is *God's Eternal Covenant*, symbolized by rainbow:

I have set my rainbow in the clouds, and it will be the sign of the covenant between me and the earth. Whenever I bring clouds over the earth and the rainbow appears in the clouds, I will remember my covenant between me and you and all living creatures of every kind.

Genesis 9:13-15 NIV

Then I saw another mighty angel [Bahá'u'lláh] coming down from heaven. He was robed in a cloud, with a rainbow above his head...A rainbow...encircled the throne.

Revelation 10:1; 4:3 NIV

This covenant pertains to the spiritual laws that govern our relationships with God. The terms of this covenant *never* change. They are as fixed and unchangeable as the laws of nature:

His works are truth and justice; his precepts all stand on firm foundations, strongly based to endure for ever, their fabric goodness and truth. He sent and redeemed his people; he decreed that his covenant should always endure.   Psalms 111:7-9 NEB

The way of God is that which has been in the past, and you shall never see any change in God's way.   Qur'án 48:23

Translated by the author

See also 33:62; 30:29

This is why the sacred Scriptures ask us to study history to learn how people behaved and what was God's role in human affairs.

> There is, in their stories, instruction for men endued with understanding... Qur'án 12:111 Y

In *The Book of Certitude*, Bahá'u'lláh draws the reader's attention to the past and asks him repeatedly to ponder this question: why did people, throughout all ages, reject the very Redeemers for whose advent they prayed day and night? He uses expressions such as these again and again:

- Consider the past...
- Ponder for a moment...
- Reflect a moment...
- Meditate profoundly...
- Reflect what could have been the motive for such deeds?
- What could have prompted such behavior?

Since the people of our age are not much different from the people of past ages the conclusion must be:

> Whatever in days gone by hath been the cause of the denial and opposition of those people hath now led to the perversity of the people of this age.[6] Bahá'u'lláh

The history of past religions displays the basic and unchanging elements of human nature as well as the unchanging ways in which God's wisdom operates. Just as scientists learn from the experiments of other scientists, so can we learn from the "experiments" of history. Unfortunately, most people do not look to the past as a guide for the future. They are not touched by the "tests and trials" of past generations. One reason is that humans learn best from *direct* experience. For instance, those who have been touched by the ravages of war, often have strong feelings against war. They know war is real. For others, war is a fantasy, they can only imagine it.

Sometimes they cannot even believe it. So it is and has always been. This is how humans think and behave.

Thus, the better we understand human nature, the better we can be guided to the ways of divine wisdom. The spiritual history of the world is perhaps the richest source of this wisdom. Understanding history helps us understand the basic elements of God's Covenant. Knowing the Covenant also helps us understand history. The basic elements of **God's Eternal Covenant** are these:

- Freedom of choice is granted to humans by God.

- Spiritual guidance is provided by God through His Mediators, according to people's capacity, so that they may learn about their Creator, their purpose in living, and the difference between good and evil.

- Each individual has the responsibility and duty to avoid evil and pursue that which is good.

- Reward and punishment are provided according to one's abilities, motives, and deeds.

The Gift of Freedom

A most precious and generous gift God has granted us is freedom to pursue, within our potential and possibilities, the spiritual path we prefer. In His wisdom, He has allowed us an infinite range of choices—good, evil, and a myriad of stages in between—so that each of us may attain his or her due position in the scheme of spiritual evolution.

Freedom is a distinctive mark of our nature, of our nobility, of our humanity. It is so fundamental and essential to our nature that if we were ever to lose it, we would be reduced to the state of mere animals.

> Behold, I have set before thee an open door, and no man can shut it...
>   Revelation 3:8

> This day I call heaven and earth as witnesses...that I have set before you life and death...Now choose life...the Lord is your life...
>   Deuteronomy 30:19-20 NIV

Any major alteration in the everlasting laws would permanently destroy human freedom. It would violate God's own eternal covenant with His creation. It would be as if the law of gravity were made void. The literal descent of Jesus from heaven with power and glory, and with flaming fire to "punish those who do not know God and do not obey the gospel" (II Thess. 1:8 NIV), is a clear example of such an alteration.

God accomplishes His goals through the instruments He has already created. Otherwise:

> If He so pleased, He could blot you out and bring in a new creation (Qur'án 35:16 Y). Had God pleased, He could have made you one people (Qur'án 16:95). Had He pleased, He had guided you all aright (Qur'án 16:9).

> Should it be Our wish, it is in Our power to compel, through the agency of but one letter of Our Revelation, the world and all that is therein to recognize, in less than the twinkling of an eye, the truth of Our Cause...[7]   The Báb

The law of cause and effect is as binding in the spiritual world as in the material:

> All things must needs have a cause, a motive power, an animating principle.[8]   Bahá'u'lláh

God is all-powerful. "His arm is not too short" to save all humanity, to make them see His great glory. This He has never done. Why? He wants humans to use *their own power* to discern His glory. To succeed, they must first remove the veils of the world. He hides His face from all those who worship their own desire:

> Surely the arm of the Lord is not too short to save, nor his ear too dull to hear. But your iniquities have separated you from your God; your sins have hidden his face from you...
>   Isaiah 59:1-2 NIV

The next prayer was revealed for our time. First, the passage contains the expression "that day," used frequently in the Bible and the Qur'án to refer to our time; and second, its message resembles that of the Lord's prayer, a prayer about the coming of the kingdom. Jesus asked Christians to pray for protection from temptations. Muhammad asked Muslims to pray for protection from evil.

> O our Lord!...keep them from evil, for on him hast thou mercy whom on that day [of the Advent] thou shalt keep from evil...   Qur'án 40:8-9

God's Plan is that we should grow under the shadow of tests and trials, the unknown and the unknowable, so that our freedom is preserved, so that our worthiness may bloom out of our endeavors:

> Verily the Hour is coming—My design is to keep it hidden— for every soul to receive its reward by the measure of its endeavor.   Qur'án 20:15 Y

Human freedom to choose good or evil can be maintained only in the darkness of concealment, and the twilight of mysteries. The greater the darkness, the greater the freedom. If people saw the light of God, they could do nothing but His will. All humans would turn into perfect robots forever.

> Were I to remove the veil, all would recognize Me as their Best Beloved, and no one would deny Me.[9]   The Báb

> **O SON OF MY HANDMAID!**
> Didst thou behold immortal sovereignty, thou wouldst strive to pass from this fleeting world. But to conceal the one from thee and to reveal the other is a mystery which none but the pure in heart can comprehend.[10]   Bahá'u'lláh

This is why the Son of God came as the son of a carpenter, poor and homeless. This is why the One greater than Solomon (Matt. 12:42) was wrapped in meekness. He who influenced the world more than all the kings and philosophers who have ever lived, chose the cross for His throne, thorns for His crown, and suffering as His glory. This is why He declared that His identity will be wrapped again in "clouds" and "darkness" (see Chapter 2).

Recently a blackout occurred in the business section of a major city. Many ordinary people, the news media reported, took advantage of the darkness by carrying away what they considered their fair share of goods from the stores. So many were involved that the police could not keep up with them. The veil of darkness granted people a freedom they had not enjoyed before. It allowed their hidden desires and motives to bloom.

> For there is nothing hidden that will not become public, nothing under cover that will not be made known and brought into the open.   Christ (Luke 8:17 NEB)

> ...the hour of trial that is going to come upon the whole world to test those who live on the earth.   Revelation 3:10 NIV

> Blessed be He...Who hath created death and life to prove [test] which of you will be most righteous in deed...
>   Qur'án 67:1-2

> That which is on earth we have made but as a glittering show...in order that we test them—as to which of them are best in conduct.   Qur'án 18:7 Y

Among all those who seek to educate humankind, the divine Teachers rank first in teaching and honoring human freedom. They admonish us to seek and adore the truth, without ever imposing their will on us. They reveal laws, indicate the consequences of obedience and disobedience, and then leave us to decide for ourselves how to live.

> We send not our Sent Ones but to announce [the most great news] and to warn* (Qur'án 18:54). Come forward, you who are thirsty; accept the water of life, a free gift to all who desire it (Rev. 22:17 NEB). If a man is thirsty, let him come to me and drink (John 7:37 NIV). Come, all you who are thirsty, come to the waters (Isa. 55:1 NIV).

---

* For references that confirm this, see Volume IV.

He satisfieth the longing soul, and filleth the hungry soul with goodness (Ps. 107:9).

Come to me, all whose work is hard, whose load is heavy; and I will give you relief. Bend your necks to my yoke, and learn from me, for I am gentle and humble-hearted; and your souls will find relief. For my yoke is good to bear, my load is light.   Matthew 11:28-30 NEB

Blessed are they which are called unto the marriage supper of the Lamb [the Báb].   Revelation 19:9

Come and gather yourselves together unto the supper of the great God [Bahá'u'lláh]...   Revelation 19:17

Only those who thirst for truth, who seek and desire the water of life, are invited. "Hear, you who have ears to hear" (Rev. 13:9 NEB).

Bahá'u'lláh echoes the same message:

Let him who wisheth turn unto Him, and him who wisheth turn aside. Our Lord, the Merciful, is verily the All-Sufficing, the All-Praised.[11]

Let him who will, acknowledge the truth of My words; and as to him that willeth not, let him turn aside. My sole duty is to remind you of your failure in duty towards the Cause of God, if perchance ye may be of them that heed My warning. Wherefore...return ye to God and repent, that He, through His grace, may have mercy upon you, may wash away your sins, and forgive your trespasses.[12]

Similarly, the teachings of Islam, as declared in the Qur'án, uphold religious freedom:

To proclaim a clear message is our only duty (Qur'án 36:16). Verily, thy [Muhammad's] work is preaching only, and ours [God's] to take account (Qur'án 13:40). Let there be no compulsion in religion (Qur'án 2:257). Let him then who will, take the way to his Lord (Qur'án 73:19). (See also 109:6; 27:95; 29:17.)

This verse from the Qur'án clearly encourages an independent search for truth:

> Give then the good tidings to those who hear an utterance and follow the best [they find] therein. These are they whom God guideth and are endowed with wisdom.*
>
> Qur'án 39:19

As the verse implies, a wise person listens (to different points of view) and then chooses the best. Such is the one who receives guidance from God and finds the truth.

> The true beginning of wisdom is the desire to learn (The Wisdom of Solomon 6:17 NEB). A wise man will hear, and will increase learning (Proverbs 1:5).

God's wisdom ordains that people be guided by the power of love and compassion:

> The path to guidance is one of love and compassion, not of force and coercion. This hath been God's method in the past, and shall continue to be in the future!¹³   The Báb

To stay in harmony with the spirit of freedom, Jesus admonished His disciples to teach the truth only to the deserving. He asked them to "look for some worthy person" (Matt. 10:11 NEB), not just *any* person. For if the receiver is not receptive, he may feel pressured or annoyed. Furthermore, truth is noble and divine, it is the honor of the wise and the virtuous, the crown of the righteous. It should not be thrown before those who wish to trample the crown:

> Give not that which is holy unto the dogs, neither cast ye your pearls before swine, lest they trample them under their feet...   Matthew 7:6

In the Old Testament we find again and again that God promises to guide the meek:

---

* Translated by the author. The original word in Arabic is *qawl*, meaning *utterance*. The translations available to the author capitalize the word, thus limiting its meaning only to divine Utterance. This is not the intent of the verse.

The meek will he guide in judgment: and the meek will he teach his way (Ps. 25:9). God arose to judgment, to save all the meek of the earth (Ps. 76:9). (See also Ps. 149:4; Zeph. 2:3.)

When Jesus spoke about His return, He said that He would disclose Himself to those who obeyed His commands (John 14:21). He made no mention of others. Truth unveils itself only to the receptive.

> ...it is He Who leadeth those who...seek the way of righteousness[14] (The Báb). Therefore announce ye the Message unto those who manifest virtue and teach them the ways of the One True God, that haply they may comprehend[15] (The Báb). God guideth all who seek His good pleasure to ways of peace and safety (Qur'án 5:16 Y).

To foster this same spirit of freedom and honor, Bahá'u'lláh repeatedly asks His followers not to offer the water of life unless they find a soul that thirsts for truth and a heart that is pure, worthy, and receptive.

> The wise are they that speak not unless they obtain a hearing...[16]   Bahá'u'lláh

Thus, we see that God never wishes to force anyone, even to the slightest degree, to accept the truth. He simply warns the undeserving of the consequences of their deeds, but does not forcibly remove the barriers that they place between themselves and their Creator. For His Justice, which follows and fulfills His gift of freedom, demands that those who choose darkness stay in darkness:

> He has blinded their eyes and dulled their minds, lest they should see with their eyes, and perceive with their minds, and turn to me to heal them (John 12:40 NEB). Truly we have thrown veils over their hearts lest they should understand this Qur'án, and into their ears a heaviness (Qur'án 18:55). These are they whose hearts and ears and eyes God hath scaled up; these are the careless ones (Qur'án 16:110). (See also Qur'án 14:4.)

In other words, God in His wisdom made humans in such a way as to allow only the deserving (those who do not close their hearts) to see the truth.

When Jesus was with His disciples He often spoke in plain language, but when surrounded by the self-righteous and the prejudiced, He shifted from plain language to parables, for they were not receptive to the plain truth:

> When he was alone, the Twelve and others who were round him questioned him about the parables. He replied, 'To you the secret of the kingdom of God has been given; but to those who are outside everything comes by way of parables, so that (as Scripture says) they may look and look, but see nothing; they may hear and hear, but understand nothing; otherwise they might turn to God and be forgiven.'   Mark 4:10-12 NEB

God's wisdom ordains that those who fail to prepare themselves for the heavenly banquet should not enter therein (Matt. 22:11-14). Bahá'u'lláh too confirms this principle. He states that some people were kept back from the truth "by reason of what their hands have wrought."[17]

This principle is called the law of cause and effect, a law prevailing in every aspect of human life, in fact in every aspect of the universe. If this universal law were nullified, the whole order of the universe would crumble and fall. The law is quite simple, but immutable. Whether it is eyesight or insight, if it is veiled, darkness prevails.

People receive what they choose. They are given many choices:

> Some turned towards Thee...Others recognized Thee and then hesitated, others allowed the world to come between them and Thee...Others disdained Thee...and wished to prevent Thee from achieving Thy purpose. And yet behold how all of them are calling upon Thee...[18]   Bahá'u'lláh

It is always we who hinder ourselves. The Creator would never deprive a true seeker of the Truth.

Consider how at the time of the appearance of every Revelation, those who open their hearts to the Author of that Revelation recognize the Truth, while the hearts of those who fail to apprehend the Truth are straitened by the reason of their shutting themselves out from Him. However, openness of heart is bestowed by God upon both parties alike. God desireth not to straiten the heart of anyone, be it even an ant, how much less the heart of a superior creature, except when he suffereth himself to be wrapt in veils, for God is the Creator of all things.[19]

The Báb

He who shall accept and believe, shall receive his reward; and he who shall turn away, shall receive none other than his own punishment.[20]   Bahá'u'lláh

Freedom is a sublime gift sent from heaven. We must cherish it and invest it for our spiritual growth. Unfortunately, many of us cherish our freedom only as long as it does not concern our religious beliefs. Consequently, when we face a spiritual choice, we often select the stalemate of *in*decision over the agony of decision. We prefer to walk in the ways of our forebears and relinquish our responsibility, acting as if a choice does not exist.

But the truth is otherwise. We are as free to choose our spiritual lives as we are to choose any other aspect of our lives, with one major difference; because we are in essence spiritual beings, we should take our spiritual choices more seriously. For we may ask: what is the difference between 70 or 80 or even 100 years, and eternity? The difference can only be infinite, one that we cannot conceive. What use is it if we serve our perishable bodies, but lose the opportunity to ennoble our spirit, an entity that endures into eternity? Should we not then take our spiritual choices more seriously? Does not the end justify absolute dedication and commitment and our highest endeavor?

For what profit is it to a man if he gains the whole world, and loses his own soul?   Matthew 16:26 NKJ

22

Through Knowledge Shall the Just Be Delivered

Proverbs 11:9

The Gift of Understanding and Knowledge

Besides freedom, God has granted us many other gifts as well, among them the gift of reasoning, understanding, and knowing good and evil (Genesis 3:22). This gift allows us to appreciate knowledge, to uncover the mysteries of the universe.

Knowledge is not gained by acquiring and accumulating an abundance of facts, but rather by ***understanding the***

***unchanging, eternal principles, recognizing the divine
wisdom***. Everyone is born with this potential. The primary
requirement for developing the potential is not high intelligence or scholarship, but a heart that is pure, radiant, and
sincere. The paramount necessity for a pure heart is emphasized in
all the Scriptures:

> ...keep yourselves pure, you who carry the vessels of the
> Lord (Isaiah 52:11 NEB). Blessed are the pure in heart: for
> they shall see God (Christ, Matthew 5:8). Who may ascend
> the hill of the Lord? Who may stand in his holy place?
> He who has clean hands and a pure heart (Psalms 24:3-4 NIV).

> The heart must needs therefore be cleansed from the idle
> sayings of men, and sanctified from every earthly affection,
> so that it may discover the hidden meaning of divine
> inspiration, and become the treasury of the mysteries of
> divine knowledge...This is the prime requisite of whosoever
> treadeth this path. Ponder thereon, that, with eyes unveiled,
> thou mayest perceive the truth of these words.[1]   Bahá'u'lláh

When knowledge strikes a pure heart, it generates the spark
of true understanding. Without a pure heart, knowledge itself
becomes a veil, for it creates vanity and self-satisfaction—
qualities that close the mind. This is what happened to the
religious leaders of Israel at the time of Jesus. As a Christian
scholar observes:

> Jesus offered the Kingdom to Israel, for they were its proper
> heirs...but the religious leaders, followed by most of the
> people, not only refused to enter its blessings but tried to
> prevent others from entering (Matt. 23:13). Nevertheless,
> many tax-collectors and harlots did enter the Kingdom
> (Matt. 21:31).[2]

Bahá'u'lláh shows this source of true knowledge:

> Know verily that Knowledge is of two kinds: Divine and
> Satanic. The one welleth out from the fountain of divine
> inspiration; the other is but a reflection of vain and obscure
> thoughts. The source of the former is God Himself; the

motive-force of the latter the whisperings of selfish desire...
The former bringeth forth the fruit of patience, of longing
desire, of true understanding, and love; whilst the latter
can yield naught but arrogance, vainglory and conceit.[3]

Jesus confirms the same truth:

I thank thee, Father, Lord of heaven and earth, for hiding
these things from the learned and wise, and revealing them
to the simple. Yes, Father, such was thy choice.
Matthew 11:25-26 NEB

Knowledge based on human desire is nothing but fancy,
nothing but a veil. The following passage, which Bahá'u'lláh
quotes from the Islamic Scriptures, points to such a knowledge:

Knowledge is the most grievous veil between man and his
Creator.[4]

This prophecy is about our time:

There will be terrible times in the last days. People will
be lovers of themselves, lovers of money, boastful, proud,
abusive...They are the kind who...are...always learning but
never able to acknowledge the truth.   II Timothy 3:1-7 NIV

To dispel misunderstanding, Bahá'u'lláh often qualifies knowledge with these two attributes: ***understanding*** and ***wisdom***.
Sometimes He says ***true*** knowledge.

To have any value, knowledge must be guided by wisdom
and be tempered with humility: "Knowledge is proud that
he has learned so much; wisdom is humble that he knows
no more." In relation to the events of our time, Daniel was
inspired to say:

...only the wise leaders shall understand.   Daniel 12:10 NEB

Jesus, too, in His parables pertaining to His return, emphasized the attributes of wisdom as an essential prerequisite
for recognizing Him (Matt. 24:45-47; 25:1-13). (These
prophecies are covered in Chapter 1.)

To grant us *spiritual* knowledge and help us uncover the *spiritual* mysteries, God sends Messengers, Teachers, or Redeemers. The reason they are needed is this: *the knowledge of our spiritual nature and destiny stands beyond our reach; we cannot acquire it on our own*. All around us we see people with the most brilliant minds who function on the most primitive spiritual levels, like animals, or even worse. Our world presents us with a perfect example. Our technical advancement is astonishing, but what can we say about our spiritual advancement? The profoundest and most creative minds of our time are baffled and bewildered when they think about the spiritual state of the world. Some of these minds cannot even set their own houses in order.

> Truly man's guidance is with Us [God].   Qur'án 92:12

When the time is ripe, God in His infinite Wisdom bestows divine knowledge, so that He may save us from the agony of not knowing who we are, what we must be doing, and where we are going.

> ...through knowledge shall the just be delivered (Proverbs 11:9). My people perish for want of knowledge (Hosea 4:6 NAB).

The knowledge that God grants to us is expanded progressively by new Messengers. In the Bahá'í Faith this is called *the progressive revelation of truth*.

Knowledge is an essential partner to freedom; one without the other stands incomplete, unfulfilled. It is the purpose of knowledge to mark the boundaries of freedom, to point to its stumbling blocks and to its stepping stones.

Thus we see that God leaves us suspended between the temptations of freedom and the knowledge of the consequences of the proper and improper use of freedom. In the midst of all this He asks us to make choices, to prove ourselves, to try our worthiness.

The idea that God will instantly change the world is a misconception found in many religions. We are the instruments

He has created for carrying out His Plan and Purpose. Our participation is essential:

> Verily never will God change the condition of a people until they change it themselves (with their own souls).
>
> Qur'án 13:11 Y

Our greatest glory lies in serving our Creator, in participating with Him to promote His Purpose. When God reveals new Knowledge through His Messengers and Redeemers, we must arise to promote it.

Christ: Go ye therefore, and teach all nations...

Matthew 28:19

And as you go proclaim the message: "The kingdom of Heaven is upon you."

Matthew 10:7 NEB

Nobody lights a lamp and then covers it with a basin or puts it under the bed. On the contrary, he puts it on a lamp-stand so that those who come in may see the light.

Luke 8:16 NEB

Muhammad: To proclaim a clear message is our only duty.

Qur'án 36:16

Ye shall surely make it known to mankind and not hide it...   Qur'án 3:184

Bahá'u'lláh: ...God hath prescribed unto everyone the duty of proclaiming His Message...[5]

It behoveth you, in this day, to proclaim aloud the Most Great Name among the nations.[6]

The Báb: Proclaim that which hath been sent unto Thee as a token of the grace of the merciful Lord...[7]

Bahá'ís are given the responsibility of spreading the knowledge of the advent of the new Revelation to all the peoples of the world. In sharing the good news of the Kingdom with others, they consider two principles: proclamation, and teaching. They **proclaim** the Bahá'í message to **everyone**, but **teach** only **the receptive**.

The Gift of Responsibility

The partnership between freedom and knowledge gives birth to a third element: responsibility. Responsibility is the inevitable child of freedom and knowledge. If either were wanting, responsibility could never be born:

> If I had not come and spoken to them, they would not be guilty of sin; but now they have no excuse for their sin (John 15:22 NEB). We never punished until we had first sent a Messenger (Qur'án 17:16). Because thou hast rejected knowledge, I will also reject thee (Hosea 4:6).

When knowledge strikes our inborn freedom, the spark of responsibility flashes forth. As soon as we hear the divine Call, our accountability begins to assert itself. In this respect, there is an immeasurable difference between those who hear the divine Call and those who don't. The relationship among the three elements constitutes a spiritual law as definite as the law of gravity: as knowledge and freedom rise or fall, so does responsibility.

> Where a man has been given much, much will be expected of him; and the more a man has had entrusted to him the more he will be required to repay (Luke 12:48 NEB). Say: Shall they who have knowledge and they who have it not, be treated alike? (Qur'án 39:12).

Now how do we demonstrate our sense of responsibility? By the decisions we make. The quality of our decisions determines our destiny both in this world and the next. By our choices we build either a castle that rises heavenward, ultimately crowning us with honor and glory, or a hut that instantly crumbles and crushes us.

The decisions we must make cover a wide spectrum, from the most fundamental to the most trivial, from choosing a profession or a partner to selecting a movie to see or a story to read. One of the decisions we make—or at least we should make—concerns our spiritual destiny. Here many of us wander and waver.

Some people shift the burden of their spiritual responsibilities to others—parents, religious leaders, or the majority. This practice violates the terms of the Covenant:

> "...every man shall bear his own burden" (Gal. 6:5). "No bearer of burdens can bear the burden of another" (Qur'án 39:7 Y). "...every individual must bear his own responsibility, rather than someone else bearing it for him" (the Báb).[8]

Among the responsibilities given to us none is as consequential as that of the search for truth. "Seek ye the kingdom of God" (Luke 12:31). "Seek ye the Lord while he may be found" (Isa. 55:6). "You will find him, if indeed you search with all your heart and soul" (Deut. 4:29 NEB). "Be always on the watch...that you may be able to stand before the Son of Man" (Luke 21:36 NIV). "Blessed are those servants, whom the Lord when he cometh shall find watching" (Luke 12:37). "Behold, I come like a thief! Blessed is he who stays awake" (Rev. 16:15 NIV).[*]

> The essence of all that We have revealed for thee is Justice, is for man to free himself from idle fancy and imitation, discern with the eye of oneness His glorious handiwork, and look into all things with a searching eye.[9]   Bahá'u'lláh

> Let the flame of search burn with such fierceness within your hearts as to enable you to attain your supreme and most exalted goal—the station at which ye can draw nigh unto, and be united with, your Best-Beloved...[10]   Bahá'u'lláh

---

[*] Chapter 1 of this volume is devoted almost entirely to Jesus' emphasis on the necessity of the independent investigation of Truth.

And whoso maketh efforts for Us, in our ways will We
guide them.   Qur'án 29:69

How can we tell if we know and love God?

> Here is the test by which we can make sure that we know
> him: do we keep his commands? The man who says, 'I
> know him,' while he disobeys his commands, is a liar and
> a stranger to the truth; but in the man who is obedient to
> his word, the divine love has indeed come to its perfection.
>   I John 2:3-5 NEB

> If you love me, you will obey what I command. And I
> will ask the Father, and he will give you another Coun-
> selor to be with you for ever—the Spirit of truth...Whoever
> has my commands and obeys them, he is the one who
> loves me. He who loves me will be loved by my Father,
> and I too will love him and show myself to him.
>   John 14:15-17, 21 NIV

Thus the evidence of our knowing and loving the divine
Redeemer is obedience to His commandments. And the
consequence of disobedience is the loss of divine love, in fact,
of the Redeemer Himself. For as the last passage indicates and
as stated earlier, Jesus promises to disclose Himself to those
who honor His commands. He makes no promises to others.
(Chapter 14 of John, which deals primarily with the promise
of the second advent, repeatedly refers to the subject of
obedience, in five verses out of 31.)

How can we be true to our beliefs if we ignore the commandment to search? How can we disregard the awesome
claim made by Bahá'u'lláh that He is indeed the expected
Redeemer of the world, that He fulfills all the prophecies,
and that the proofs of His Mission are so abundant as to be
unparalleled in all human history? Since the consequences are
so fundamental and far-reaching, is it wise to take chances,
to ignore such a claim? Surely we would wish to know, to
prove to ourselves, beyond any doubt, whether the claim is
true or false.

If we find the claim to be false, we have honored our responsibility of obeying the divine commandment; we have also
exercised our right to freedom. We have lost nothing. On the
contrary, we have at least gained something noble, a clear
conscience. However, if we find the claim to be true, then
we have gained something even nobler: a bounty beyond our
fairest dreams, the most glorious reward ever granted by the
Creator to the created, a blessing imperishable and everlasting, a divine gift that defies description. So whatever the
consequences, by seeking we can only win. As for not
seeking, that is something everyone may wish to answer for
himself.

The sacred Scriptures teach us that we all carry the burden
of responsibility for our own deeds, and that we shall all
stand before God's tribunal:

> I will call you to account for your doings... Ezekiel 7:3 NEB

> We shall all stand before God's tribunal.   Romans 14:10 NEB

> ...every one of us shall give account of himself to God.
> Romans 14:12

> By God ye shall be called to account for your devices!
> Qur'án 16:58

> ...they [the dead] take with them the record of their deeds.
> Revelation 14:13 NEB

> ...hereafter shall ye return to your Lord, and he will tell
> you of your works.   Qur'án 39:9

> But I tell you that men will have to give account on
> the day of judgment for every careless word they have
> spoken.   Matthew 12:36 NIV

> Set before thine eyes God's unerring Balance and, as one
> standing in His Presence, weigh in that Balance thine actions
> every day, every moment of thy life.[11]   Bahá'u'lláh

> Ye, and all ye possess, shall pass away. Ye shall, most
> certainly, return to God, and shall be called to account

for your doings in the presence of Him Who shall gather together the entire creation...[12]   Bahá'u'lláh

Know ye that the world and its vanities and its embellishments shall pass away. Nothing will endure except God's Kingdom which pertaineth to none but Him, the Sovereign Lord of all, the Help in Peril, the All-Glorious, the Almighty. The days of your life shall roll away, and all the things with which ye are occupied and of which ye boast yourselves shall perish, and ye shall, most certainly, be summoned by a company of His angels to appear at the spot where the limbs of the entire creation shall be made to tremble, and the flesh of every oppressor to creep. Ye shall be asked of the things your hands have wrought in this, your vain life, and shall be repaid for your doings. This is the day that shall inevitably come upon you, the hour that none can put back. To this the Tongue of Him that speaketh the truth and is the Knower of all things hath testified.[13]   Bahá'u'lláh

O SON OF BEING!
Bring thyself to account each day ere thou art summoned to a reckoning; for death, unheralded, shall come upon thee and thou shalt be called to give account for thy deeds.[14]   Bahá'u'lláh

Like freedom, responsibility is an essential part of being human. By surrendering it, we descend to a lower state of being. Again, any major alteration in the laws of the universe—such as the physical resurrection of the dead—would permanently destroy this gift. God's wisdom conceals many mysteries in order to preserve and honor our freedom:

Should the greatness of this Day be revealed in its fullness, every man would forsake a myriad lives in his longing to partake, though it be for one moment, of its great glory—how much more this world and its corruptible treasures![15]
                                              Bahá'u'lláh

The fourth element of God's covenant with humanity—reward and punishment—is presented in Volume III.

Appendices

Appendix I

Then Shall the Sanctuary Be Cleansed
Daniel 8:14

═══════════════════

Before 1844, tens of thousands believed that "the cleansing of the sanctuary" meant the end of the world and the return of Christ. When Jesus did not descend from the clouds in that critical year, some of those who expected Him desperately reexamined their beliefs. One of them thought of this idea: Daniel's prophecy did not point to the coming of the Master to *the earth*; it pointed to *a heavenly* occurrence. In 1844 an event of great magnitude happened in *the heavenly* sanctuary. (It is far easier to reinterpret *an idea* than a *number*. Numbers are fixed entities; they cannot be reshaped.) This quotation from a Seventh-day Adventists' publication explains this new position:

> Based on his study of the prophecy of Daniel 8:14 [the cleansing of the sanctuary], Miller calculated that Jesus

would return to earth on October 22, 1844. When Jesus did not appear, Miller's followers experienced what came to be called "the great disappointment."

Most of the thousands who had joined the "great second advent awakening" left it, in deep disillusionment. A few, however, went back to their Bibles to find why they had been disappointed. Soon they concluded that the October 22 date had indeed been correct, but that Miller had predicted the wrong event for that day. They became convinced that the Bible prophecy predicted not that Jesus would return to earth in 1844, but that *He would begin at that time a special ministry in heaven for His followers* [emphasis added].[1]

This new idea received a warm welcome from a few disappointed believers whose very faith was on trial, and who could find no other explanation for their unfulfilled hope. It served as the seed from which a new church sprouted. The few disappointed but faithful believers, who welcomed the new interpretation of the prophecy, eventually grew into several million and into a number of churches, who to this day have continued to declare the dawning of a new age in 1844. The Seventh-day Adventists are the largest and best known among them. Since the Great Disappointment of 1844, they have continued to proclaim with zeal and fervor the imminent return of Christ. They have not allowed the light of faith to grow dim or die in the hearts of the faithful. For this they deserve much credit.

The Position Held by Adventists

Based on the teachings of Ellen G. White, the Adventists maintain the following basic principles:

• Jesus' ministry consisted of two phases.

• The marking line between them was the year 1844.

- During the first phase, Jesus' Mission was "*to intercede* for His people."

- During the second phase, His Mission was *to judge* His people.

- Heaven has two "apartments."

- One "apartment" is linked to intercession; the other to judgment.

- In the summer of 1844 Jesus entered the "apartment" linked to judgment.

- At that moment His Mission of judgment began.

- The judgment to which people are subjected is called "investigative judgment."[2] Its purpose is to examine people's character and their readiness for the kingdom of God.

- "The cleansing of the Sanctuary" does not refer to the coming of Christ to the earth, but to a turning point in His Mission.

These quotations further clarify the Adventists' beliefs:

- So when Christ entered the holy of holies to perform the closing work of the atonement [intercession], He ceased His ministration in the first apartment [intercession phase].[3]

- And, as the Second Apartment phase of that ministry, He entered upon the work of judgment in 1844.[4]

- The mistake had not been in the reckoning of the prophetic periods, but in *the event* to take place at the end of 2300 days.[5]

- ...instead of coming to the earth at the termination of the 2300 days in 1844, Christ then entered the most holy place of the heavenly sanctuary to perform the closing work of atonement preparatory to His coming.[6]

What are the issues that this position or interpretation does not address? These are a few:

- The explanation offered does not pertain to the central question. What we need to know is not the various phases of Jesus' ministry, but the meaning of this critical message: *"the sanctuary shall be cleansed."*

- The prophecy declares that at that time (1844) the sanctuary will be cleansed or restored. The words "cleansed" and "restored" are clearly relevant to the terrible conditions of our planet—both physically and spiritually. Are they also relevant to heaven? Does the heavenly sanctuary need restoring or cleansing? Is heaven as defiled or desolated as the earth? Is not where Jesus resides already perfect— pure, radiant, and heavenly?

- It is claimed that in 1844 Jesus entered "the holy of holies," a title synonymous with "the most holy place of the sanctuary," and "the inner sanctuary." But the Gospel declares that Jesus had *already* entered there:

  ...the inner sanctuary behind the curtain, where Jesus, who went before us, has entered on our behalf. He has become a high priest forever, in the order of Melchizedek.   Hebrews 6:19-20 NIV

- As stated, there is no clear relationship between restoring or purifying the sanctuary and entering a new phase of ministry or going from one apartment of heaven to another. Even if we assume there is, what benefit can we gain on earth from knowing that Jesus began a new phase of His ministry in a second apartment in heaven?

- Since heaven is invisible, how can we be sure that something indeed took place there? People can make any claim they wish. What matters most is not the claim but the evidence that supports the claim. The purpose of prophecy is to offer a link between the invisible source (the divine) and the visible (the earthly). Why prophesy about invisible events?

- Prophecies refer to our time specifically as the time of Judgment (Ps. 96:13). But, in general, the time of the advent of every Messenger is a time of judgment, because people are judged by their response to their new Redeemer.

For judgment I have come into this world... John 9:39 NIV

...the Father...has entrusted all judgment to the Son... whoever hears my word and believes him who sent me...will not be condemned... John 5:22-24 NIV

▪ Why would Christ judge His people after 1844 and not before?

The Symbolism of "the Cleansing of the Sanctuary"

This section presents further evidence on the meaning of the chief symbol in Daniel's prophecy of 2300 days. How do we know that "the cleansing of the sanctuary" is synonymous with the coming of the Lord? We are faced with a puzzle: we must seek and assemble all the pieces and then make a judgment. The following are some of the pieces and clues:

1 Perhaps the leading clue is Jesus' own words to His inquisitive disciples who sought to know *the time of His return*. Instead of directly designating the time, He guided His disciples to Daniel's vision of "abomination of desolation," saying that if they referred to it, they would know.

An examination of the Book of Daniel reveals that he has two time visions involving the identifying phrase *the abomination* or *transgression of desolation*. One relates to the prophecy of 2300 days, which specifies the dawning of the New Age (1844 A.D.) inaugurated by the Báb; the other specifies the time of Bahá'u'lláh's public ministry (1863 A.D.).

2 The angel speaking to Daniel states clearly that the vision of 2300 days refers to "the time of the end," a common expression used in the Scriptures to point to the ending of the prophetic cycle, and the dawning of the Day of the Lord.

This fact can be further verified by comparing the evident similarities found between the words of the Gospel *regarding* the vision and some key words found *in the vision itself.* For instance, the disciples asked Jesus about the sign of His coming and "the end of the world," or "the end of the age" (Matt. 24:3). In Daniel's vision we find a similar expression with an identical meaning—"the vision points to the time of the end" (Dan. 8:17 NEB).

3 The sanctuary is the heart of religion, the House of God, the Holy of Holies. "God's sanctuary was His established earthly abode, the place where he chose to dwell among His people."[7]

> And let them make me a sanctuary; that I may dwell among them.   Exodus 25:8

> ...do not withdraw from the sanctuary of His presence...[8]
>   The Báb

Purifying the world is the purpose of every Messenger and Redeemer:

> O peoples of the earth! Verily His Remembrance [the Báb] is come to you...that He may purge and purify you from uncleanliness in anticipation of the Day of the One true God...[9]   The Báb

4 Who, we might ask, has the power and authority to cleanse such a holy and exalted habitation but a God-sent Savior?

The harmony between the prophecy of 2300 days and the fifteen other prophecies, all confirming 1844 as the appointed time, provides us with further evidence.

5 The two time prophecies pertaining to both advents appear together in close succession and share several common clues, such as the desolation or illumination of the sanctuary and the termination of the daily sacrifice.

Even Daniel's inability to comprehend his vision of 2300 days in itself constitutes a clue, indicating its relationship to the last days (see Dan. 12:4; 12:9).

6 Jerusalem is the City of God, and the sanctuary or temple its very heart. Jerusalem sometimes symbolizes the people of Israel and their temporal civilization. The sanctuary or temple symbolizes their spiritual life and heavenly civilization. After the Jews rejected Jesus, He predicted desolation for both the temple and the city until the time of the advent of the Lord, a term frequently used to signify Christ's second coming:

> O Jerusalem, Jerusalem, the city that murders the prophets and stones the messengers sent to her! How often have I longed to gather your children, as a hen gathers her brood under her wings; but you would not let me. Look, look! there is your temple, forsaken by God. And I tell you, you shall never see me until the time comes when you say, "Blessings on him who comes in the name of the Lord!"   Christ (Luke 13:34-35 NEB)

This prophecy clearly links the end of "desolation" of Israel's house of worship or temple to the advent of the Lord. *The New International Version* reads:

> Look, your house is left to you desolate. I tell you, you will not see me again until you say, 'Blessed is he who comes in the name of the Lord.'   Luke 13:35 NIV

By the Báb's advent the sanctuary was spiritually renewed, and Jerusalem began gradually to gather her children. We find the Bahá'í World Center established in the same region and the city itself in a state of continuing growth and prosperity. Once again we see that the end of desolation for the City of God and its Temple is connected to the advent of the Lord. Because Jesus first spoke of the desolation of Jerusalem and its temple, then gave the good news of the advent of the Lord. When Bahá'u'lláh was exiled to the Holy

Land, the vicinity of Jerusalem was literally blessed by the presence of her Lord.

Marvin Rosenthal, a Christian writer, describes the relationship between *the glory of God* and *the temple*. He states that the first temple was built more than nine hundred years before Jesus by David and Solomon. He then continues:

> Although God is omnipresent and "the heaven of heavens cannot contain [Him]" (2 Chron. 6:18), He chose...to dwell among His people within His temple and to manifest His glory there. The children of Israel would be permitted... to see the holiness...and mercy of God—what He was truly like...

> But about four centuries later, the prophet Ezekiel described the departure of the glory of God from the temple. His description is one of the most heartrending stories in all the Word of God. The Sovereign of the universe...who chose Israel as His "peculiar treasure" (Ps. 135:4), was driven out of the temple by His people's grievous sin (Ezek. 8:6).[10]

In the course of several chapters, Ezekiel offers a detailed description of the presence of the glory of God in the temple and His departure from it. Here is a brief summary of those chapters by Rosenthal:

> First, the glory of God departed from over the ark of the covenant...to the threshold of the temple (Ezek. 10:4). It was almost as if the glory of God had paused there at the threshold to say, "Don't drive Me away. I want to be your God. I want you to be My people...Repent of your sin, and I will stay." Then the glory of God moved from the threshold of the temple to the east gate of the Lord's house (Ezek. 10:19). And once again, it was as if the glory of God paused, hesitated, hoping for a repentance that would allow Him to remain...Finally the glory moved from the Eastern Gate...over the Mount of Olives (Ezek. 11:23). The nation had forced the withdrawal of the

presence of God from their midst by their grievous, continuous sin. With that event, over Israel was written the word **Ichabod**, meaning **the glory is departed** (I Sam. 4:21).[11]

Almost six centuries later history repeated itself. The glory of the Father (the glory of God) once again appeared in the temple through His Son. But those who saw themselves as the true custodians of the temple tried to prevent Him from entering and restoring it. They were told that their house would be left desolate until they were ready to say: "Blessed is He who comes in the name of the Lord" (see Matt. 23:37-39 NIV).

People can refuse to enter God's temple, but they cannot prevent Him from building one. By His advent Jesus built a new temple, a new church, which in time would also become desolate.

The Book of Revelation confirms the desolation or disappearance of the old temple and its regeneration by two blessed Beings in the end-time: one called the **Lamb** and the other **the Lord God** or **the glory of God**:

I did not see a temple in the city [of God], because the Lord God Almighty and the Lamb are its temple. The city does not need the sun or the moon to shine on it, for the glory of God gives it light, and the Lamb is its lamp.[*]

Revelation 21:22-23 NIV

Isaiah confirms the same message:

...and he [the Lord Almighty] will be a sanctuary...

Isaiah 8:14 NIV

The Book of Revelation declares that everything will be made new; it refers repeatedly to the temple in the new Jerusalem:

---

[*] Volume II contains a whole chapter devoted to the meaning of the two great Beings with various titles, mentioned repeatedly in the Book of Revelation.

Him who overcomes I will make a pillar in the temple of my God...I will also write on him my new name.

Revelation 3:12 NIV

This verse also points to two great Beings in the temple: *God* and *the Lamb*.

...they [the new believers] are before the throne of *God* and serve him day and night in his temple...*the Lamb* at the center of the throne will be their shepherd; he will lead them to springs of living water.   Revelation 7:15, 17 NIV

(For further references, see *The Relationship Between Heavenly and Earthly "Jerusalem and Sanctuary,"* Chapter 16.)

7   The words *sanctuary, temple, tabernacle, holy of holies,* and *inner court* are often linked to the coming or the presence of the Lord or the Glory of God (Bahá'u'lláh):

O God...I come before thee in the sanctuary to look upon thy power and glory.   Psalms 63:1-2 NEB

And Moses and Aaron went into the tabernacle...and the glory of the Lord appeared unto all the people.

Leviticus 9:23

Behold, I will send my messenger, and he shall prepare the way before me: and the Lord, whom ye seek, shall suddenly come to his temple...   Malachi 3:1
See also Ezek. 8:3-4; 9:3; 10:3-4; 44:4; 43:4-5

The prophetic words of the Old Testament invariably find their counterparts in the New. The mysterious and marvelous Book of Revelation, too, links *tabernacle, temple* or *sanctuary* with the advent of *the Glory of God* in the last days:

And the temple was filled with smoke from the glory of God and from his power...   Revelation 15:8 NIV
See also Isa. 60:13-16

To protect the seeker from misjudging the significance or the meaning of "the opening of the tabernacle," and to prevent him from cherishing the illusion of expecting earthly glory and majesty, soon after revealing the preceding signs, the divine Predictor adds these prophetic words:

That is the day when I come like a thief!

Revelation 16:15 NEB

8 Jesus declared that He would come with power and great glory (Matt. 24:30). The verses quoted from Psalms (63:1-2), Revelation (15:8), as well as many others, refer to the appearance or presence of both power and glory in the sanctuary.

9 The Scriptures indicate that "the cleansing of the temple or sanctuary" was used as a symbol for the inauguration of *the first* advent of Christ. At the beginning of His ministry, Jesus "drove out the unholy business that had defiled the house of God." He cleansed the Temple from those who had transformed the spiritual into the worldly (John 2:13-22). As George Rice, a Christian writer, notes:

The first cleansing of the temple was a carefully planned move by Jesus *to inaugurate His ministry*...[12]

The first public act on the part of Jesus that reflected anything suggesting kingship was the cleansing of the temple at the beginning of His ministry. John 2:13-22... This first cleansing was *the public announcement of His Messiahship and mission*. He acted and spoke with the authority of a king...the first cleansing accomplished its purpose; his mission was announced to the world, and the leaders were made aware of His presence [emphasis added].[13]

10 A prophecy in the New Testament predicts the dawning of the second advent in these terms:

Repent, then, and turn to God...that times of refreshing may come from the Lord, and that he may send the Christ ...He [Christ] must remain in heaven until the time comes for God to restore everything, as he promised long ago through his holy prophets.

Acts 3:19-21 NIV

We are told that Christ will come to refresh and restore every-thing. This is exactly what Daniel's prophecy predicted:

> ...then the sanctuary shall be cleansed *and* restored.
>
> Daniel 8:14 AB

Why is restoration needed? Because of the prevalence of desolation. And that was the original question one saint asked the other:

> ...how long will impiety cause desolation...?
>
> Daniel 8:13 NEB

The words *desolation* and *restoration* are exact opposites. The latter is a logical response to the former. Further, the prophecy from the New Testament states:

> ...the time comes for God to restore everything, as he promised long ago through his holy prophets.
>
> Acts 3:21 NIV

Who were the holy prophets through whom the promise was made? Obviously, one of them must be Daniel, whose book contains many prophecies and promises, including the promise of restoration after 2300 days.

11 This verse from the Book of Revelation clearly links the return of the Redeemer of our age to the tabernacle or sanctuary:

> And I John saw the holy city, new Jerusalem [new Revelation], coming down from God out of heaven...And I heard a great voice...saying, Behold, the tabernacle of God is with men, and he will dwell with them...
>
> Revelation 21:2-3

12 Just before referring to Daniel's vision of "abomination of desolation," Jesus talked about the destruction of the temple (Matt. 24:1-2). That message prompted His disciples to ask Him about the time and signs of His return. Jesus' ominous words concerning the future of the temple—the words that stirred His disciples' curiosity—carried this symbolic message: when I pass away, so will the soul of the temple; when My

body, the temple of My Spirit, is desecrated and destroyed, so will be your temple, which *also* enshrines that Spirit. It will become an empty shell for the worshippers until I come again to restore it with the pearl of My Spirit.

13 The tearing of the veil of the temple at the moment of Jesus' death is one more symbol pointing to the end of opportunity for the people of Israel and the loss of the spiritual powers of their temple. When the veil was rent asunder, a spiritual age ended and a new dispensation dawned; a new church was born to replace the old temple. The daily sacrifice at the altar lost its purpose. The great sacrifice of God who offered His Son as a ransom for the sins of an ungrateful humanity made the ritual vain. According to a Christian source:

> At the moment of Jesus' death, the veil of the Temple was torn from top to bottom (Matt. 27:51; Mark 15:38; Luke 23:45). By His death, Jesus opened a new way into the presence of God. A new order replaced the old. No longer was the Temple in Jerusalem to be the place where men worshiped God. From now on they would worship Him "in spirit and truth" (John 4:21-24).[14]

14 Biblical references as well as Bahá'u'lláh's words indicate clearly that there are two tabernacles or sanctuaries: one in heaven, the other on earth.

> We do have such a high priest [Jesus, the heavenly priest], who sat down at the right hand of the throne of the Majesty in heaven, and who serves in the sanctuary, the true tabernacle set up by the Lord...They [the earthly priests] serve at a sanctuary that is a copy and shadow of what is in heaven. Hebrews 8:1-5 NIV

The following verse links the opening of God's temple in heaven with His covenant. The implication is this: when God opens the gate of a new temple to His people, He also presents them with a new covenant.

> Then God's temple in heaven was opened, and within his temple was seen the ark of his covenant. Revelation 11:19 NIV

In the following prayer, Bahá'u'lláh communicates with God concerning His sufferings, sufferings that touched the heart of heaven:

> He [Bahá'u'lláh]...hath suffered more grievously...than any pen can recount, and been so harassed that He Who is Thy [God's] Spirit [Jesus] lamented, and all the denizens of Thy Kingdom and all the inmates of Thy Tabernacle [heavenly tabernacle] in the realms above cried with a great and bitter lamentation.[15]

As stated in Chapter 10, the vision pertains to the time when the people of Israel will have an opportunity to free themselves from self-imposed humiliation by turning to their Redeemer. Their deeds and destiny are described and predicted by these ominous words:

- Abomination
- Desolation
- Transgression
- Rebellion
- Impiety
- Humiliation

All the words and messages are negative; they are signs of *im*perfection. The vision is a response to this simple question:

> ...how long will impiety cause desolation...?   Daniel 8:13 NEB

To imply that the prophecy pertains to heaven is to associate impiety, rebellion, transgression, and desolation with that divine realm. Heaven has always been the ideal model of purity and perfection. Jesus prayed that God's Kingdom would become as real on earth as it is in heaven. Although impiety, rebellion, transgression, and desolation cannot describe *the heavenly* realm, they *do* describe *the earthly* realm.

The question posed by the saint and the answer given to him both indicate that the vision pertains to an imperfect world. Seeing the response in different translations may further clarify the intent of the vision. Can any of these events relate to heaven?

> ...then the holy place will be properly restored.   Daniel 8:14
> New American Standard

...then the sanctuary shall be restored to its rightful state.
Revised Standard Version

...[the] holy place will certainly be brought into the right condition.
New World Translation

...then the sanctuary shall have its rights restored.
The Jerusalem Bible

...then shall the sanctuary be cleansed. King James Version

15 Common codes point to a common message concealed in the two parts of the vision. These six key codes are found in both parts of Daniel's vision; the part that points to the first advent, and the part that points to the second:

The First Advent	*The Second Advent*
1. daily sacrifice (9:27)	1. daily sacrifice (8:13)
2. transgression (9:24)	2. transgression (8:13)
3. desolation (9:18; 9:17; 9:27)	3. desolation (8:13)
4. sanctuary (9:17)	4. sanctuary (8:13; 8:14)
5. restore (9:25)	5. restore and cleanse (8:14 AB); cleanse (8:14 KJV)
6. the city that bears thy name, Jerusalem, the holy city (9:18; 9:25)	6. the fairest of all lands (Jerusalem) (8:13 NEB)

Some translations such as *The New English Bible* read "desolation of both the Holy Place (the sanctuary) and the fairest of all lands" (Jerusalem). Others, such as *New International Version*, read "the desolation, and the surrender of sanctuary and of the host" (the Jews). If we substitute "the host" for "the fairest of all lands" (Jerusalem), then we can find another common clue in place of Jerusalem. The clue is "thy people" (9:24), and "the host" (8:13), both of which refer to the people of Israel.

For further evidence linking "the cleansing of sanctuary" with the return of Christ see Chapter 10.

Tabernacle and Sanctuary in Bahá'í Scriptures

The words tabernacle and sanctuary appear repeatedly in Bahá'u'lláh's Writings, and are in perfect harmony with biblical usage. By them He conveys these meanings:

- The spiritual domain of the world
- The unifying power of God, His "collective center for humanity"
- The religion of God
- The spiritual abode of the divine Messengers
- The seat of God's love in humans
- The domain of divine protection
- The instrument of God's presence among humans, His Manifestation

These few examples demonstrate Bahá'u'lláh's usage of the word tabernacle:

> O thou who art waiting, tarry no longer, for He is come. Behold His Tabernacle and His Glory dwelling therein. It is the Ancient Glory, with a new Manifestation.[16]

> The tabernacle of unity hath been raised; regard ye not one another as strangers. Ye are the fruits of one tree...[17]

> How vast is the tabernacle of the Cause of God! It hath overshadowed all the peoples and kindreds of the earth, and will, erelong, gather together the whole of mankind beneath its shelter.[18]

> They who dwell within the tabernacle of God, and are established upon the seats of everlasting glory, will refuse, though they be dying of hunger, to...seize unlawfully the property of their neighbor...[19]

...behold Them [the divine Messengers] all abiding in the same Tabernacle...[20]

Know thou that he is truly learned who hath acknowledged My Revelation, and drunk from the Ocean of My knowledge, and soared in the atmosphere of My love, and cast away all else besides Me...Verily, such a man is blessed by the Concourse on high, and by them who dwell within the Tabernacle of Grandeur...[21]

Biblical prophecies pointing to sanctuary and tabernacle and the presence of the glory of God in them were fulfilled by Bahá'u'lláh not only symbolically but literally as well. For Bahá'u'lláh had a tent called *the Tabernacle of Glory*. He pitched that glorious tent on Mt. Carmel. That was one of His specific earthly abodes.

We should note that Israel's earliest sanctuary, like Bahá'u'lláh's, was a movable tent:

Israel's earliest sanctuary was the movable tent known as the tabernacle where the ark containing the tablets of the covenant was housed (Ex. 25:8 etc.).[22]

Carmel, in the Book of God, hath been designated as the Hill of God, and His Vineyard. It is here that, by the grace of the Lord of Revelation, the Tabernacle of Glory hath been raised. Happy are they that attain thereunto; happy they that set their faces towards it.[23]   Bahá'u'lláh

And again:

This is the Day whereon He Who is the Revealer of the names of God [Bahá'u'lláh] hath stepped out of the Tabernacle of Glory...[24]   Bahá'u'lláh

Blessed the wayfarer who directeth his steps towards the Tabernacle of My glory and majesty...and [blessed] the needy one who entereth beneath the shadow of the Tabernacle of My wealth.[25]   Bahá'u'lláh

Appendix II

William Miller's Dream

I dreamed that God, by an unseen hand, sent me a curiously wrought casket about ten inches long by six square, made of ebony and pearls curiously inlaid. To the casket there was a key attached. I immediately took the key and opened the casket, when, to my wonder and surprise, I found it filled with all sorts and sizes of jewels, diamonds, precious stones, and gold and silver coin of every dimension and value, beautifully arranged in their several places in the casket; and thus arranged they reflected a light and glory equaled only to the sun.

I thought it was not my duty to enjoy this wonderful sight alone, although my heart was overjoyed at the brilliancy, beauty, and value of its contents. I therefore placed it on

454 I Shall Come Again

a center table in my room and gave out word that all who had a desire might come and see the most glorious and brilliant sight ever seen by man in this life.

The people began to come in, at first few in number, but increasing to a crowd. When they first looked into the casket, they would wonder and shout for joy. But when the spectators increased, everyone would begin to trouble the jewels, taking them out of the casket and scattering them on the table.

I began to think that the owner would require the casket and the jewels again at my hand; and if I suffered them to be scattered, I could never place them in their places in the casket again as before, and felt I should never be able to meet the accountability, for it would be immense. I then began to plead with the people not to handle them, nor to take them out of the casket; but the more I pleaded, the more they scattered; and now they seemed to scatter them all over the room, on the floor and on every piece of furniture in the room.

I then saw that among the genuine jewels and coin they had scattered an innumerable quantity of spurious [fake] jewels and counterfeit coin. I was highly incensed at their base conduct and ingratitude, and reproved and reproached them for it; but the more I reproved, the more they scattered the spurious jewels and false coin among the genuine.

I then became vexed in my physical soul and began to use physical force to push them out of the room; but while I was pushing out one, three more would enter and bring in dirt and shavings and sand and all manner of rubbish, until they covered every one of the true jewels, diamonds, and coins, which were all excluded from sight. They also tore in pieces my casket and scattered it among the rubbish. I thought no man regarded my sorrow or my anger. I became wholly discouraged and disheartened, and sat down and wept.

While I was thus weeping and mourning for my great loss and accountability, I remembered God, and earnestly prayed that He would send me help.

Immediately the door opened, and a man entered the room, when the people all left it; and he, having a dirt brush in his hand, opened the windows, and began to brush the dirt and rubbish from the room.

I cried to him to forbear, for there were some precious jewels scattered among the rubbish.

He told me to "fear not," for he would "take care of them."

Then, while he brushed the dirt and rubbish, false jewels and counterfeit coin, all rose and went out of the window like a cloud, and the wind carried them away. In the bustle I closed my eyes for a moment; when I opened them, the rubbish was all gone. The precious jewels, the diamonds, the gold and silver coins, lay scattered in profusion all over the room.[1]

Interpretation

The jewels, gold, and silver symbolize the truths revealed to us by God's great Messengers:

> Thus We...bestow upon thee the **gems** of divine wisdom, that haply thou mayest soar on the wings of renunciation to those heights that are veiled from the eyes of men.[2]
>
> Bahá'u'lláh

> He [Bahá'u'lláh] it is Who hath laid bare before you the hidden and treasured **Gem**, were ye to seek it.[3]   Bahá'u'lláh

At the beginning, the gems are pure and radiant, but as time goes on people begin to tamper with them. They "trouble the jewels," take them out of their context, conceal them under their illusions, scatter them, and abuse them for their selfish ends. They devise their own counterfeit doctrines, denominations, and sects, and then package them, and present them as genuine. This desire to abuse the divine truths entrusted to the human hand is so powerful and pervasive that no one can stop it. William Miller felt frustrated at his inability to protect the jewels. We can see a clear example of this in his life. He was the first to discover and proclaim the date of Christ's return. After the Great Disappointment, although perplexed and disillusioned, he remained loyal to the Word of God. He continued to believe in the accuracy of his findings, supported by so much evidence that no one could refute them. But those around him distorted his findings by saying that the great event associated with 1844 happened in heaven. The purity of the truth he had discovered was lost under the dust of selfish ends, theological assumptions, arguments, and illusions. Despite his strenuous efforts, Miller failed to keep people on course. In the end, he experienced rejection and ridicule. He was abandoned by the very people who had followed him. He became an outcast.

A true seeker who carries enough "oil" of wisdom (Matthew 25:1-13) can always find his Beloved. He can always recognize the gems of true knowledge. He can always see the difference between the genuine and the fictitious:

> Each and every thing, however small, would be to him a revelation, leading him to his Beloved, the Object of his quest. So great shall be the discernment of this seeker that he will discriminate between truth and falsehood, even as he doth distinguish the sun from shadow. If in the uttermost corners of the East the sweet savors of God be wafted, he will assuredly recognize and inhale their fragrance, even though he be dwelling in the uttermost ends of the West. He will, likewise, clearly distinguish all the signs of God— His wondrous utterances, His great works, and mighty deeds—from the doings, the words and ways of men, ***even as the jeweler who knoweth the gem from the stone***...[4]
>
> Bahá'u'lláh

God is patient. He always gives people a chance. But at the precise moment, He steps in, scatters the forces of darkness, removes the rubbish, gathers His gold, jewels, and pearls together, and allows them once again to glitter in the utmost glory and splendor. The parable of the vineyard (Matthew 21:33-41) proclaims this same divine drama. Isaiah summarizes the same message:

> On that day sing to the pleasant vineyard, I the Lord am its keeper, moment by moment I water it for fear its green leaves fail. Night and day I tend it...   Isaiah 27:2-3 NEB

Jesus predicted that He would come on the clouds. In his dream, William Miller saw all the counterfeit jewels and coins rise like a cloud and disappear. As Bahá'u'lláh teaches, the clouds on which Christ was promised to ride are superstitions, false dogmas, beliefs, illusions, and assumptions that prevent the peoples of the earth from beholding the Glory of God. What an astonishing dream! At the end, Miller was blessed with seeing a glimpse of the glorious Kingdom that God has promised to humankind:

> He then placed on the table a casket, much larger and more beautiful than the former, and gathered up the jewels, the diamonds, the coins, by the handful, and cast them into the casket, till not one was left, although some of the diamonds were not bigger than the point of a pin.
>
> He then called upon me to "come and see."
>
> I looked into the casket, but my eyes were dazzled with the sight. *They shone with ten times their former glory.* I thought they had been scoured in the sand by the feet of those wicked persons who had scattered and trod them in the dust. They were arranged in beautiful order in the casket, every one in its place, without any visible pains of the man who cast them in. I shouted with very joy...

* * *

For these are the words of the Lord of Hosts...I will shake heaven and earth, sea and land, I will shake all nations; *the treasure* of all nations shall come hither, and I will fill this house with glory; so says the Lord of Hosts, and *the glory of this latter house shall surpass the glory of the former*, says the Lord of Hosts. In this place will I grant prosperity and peace. This is the very word of the Lord of Hosts.   Haggai 2:6-9 NEB

Should the greatness of this Day be revealed in its fullness, every man would forsake a myriad lives in his longing to partake, though it be for one moment, of *its great glory*— how much more this world and its corruptible treasures![5]
                                                            Bahá'u'lláh

It [the City of God] shone with *the glory of God*, and its brilliance was like that of a very precious jewel, like a jasper, clear as crystal.   Revelation 21:11 NIV

The moon will shine like the sun, and the sunlight will be seven times brighter, like the light of seven full days...
                                                            Isaiah 30:26 NIV

The moon shall grow pale and the sun hide its face in shame; for the Lord of Hosts has become king.
                                                            Isaiah 24:23 NEB

Great, immeasurably great is this Cause! Mighty, inconceivably mighty is this Day! Blessed indeed is the man that hath forsaken all things, and fastened his eyes upon Him Whose face *hath shed illumination upon all who are in the heavens and all who are on the earth*.[6]
                                                            Bahá'u'lláh

Appendix III

I Shall Come Upon You Like a Thief

Revelation 3:3 NEB

Part II

Among the most critical instructions Jesus gave about His return were these:

- I shall come upon you like a thief!
- Watch!

In Chapter 1 we examined several of Jesus' parables to show that "Watch!" means "Search!" or "Investigate!" Similarly in Chapter 2 we studied several biblical references to indicate that coming "like a thief" means coming *secretly*.

How do Christian writers and scholars interpret the first instruction, which compares Jesus' coming to that of a thief? Many of them say that the intent of the prophecy is not to say that Christ comes *secretly*, but rather to say that He comes *suddenly*. They say this because other prophecies point to His sudden return. How do they interpret the second instruction "Watch!"? They simply say it means to *be ready.*

What those Christian interpreters accomplish is this: they eliminate the commandment "Watch!" as *a special* instruction. They make it subordinate to the general command "Be ready!" They do the same with "I shall come upon you like a thief." They eliminate it as a *special* sign and make it subordinate to the word "suddenly." They act as if "Watch!" and "like a thief in the night" do not add anything new to other signs and commandments. They simply ignore the unique purpose for which they were given.

Other Christian writers and scholars admit that "Watch!" means "Investigate!" For instance, a widely distributed Christian magazine explains that the command to "Watch!" means to keep up with the news, with what is happening around the world. Then it adds that one way this can be done is to read that magazine. Unfortunately, the magazine has failed to inform its readers of the news of the coming of the Báb and Bahá'u'lláh.

Similarly in recent times some Christian writers and scholars have accepted the idea that Christ will initially return in secret. This may eventually open the door to many seekers of truth to investigate the Bahá'í message. The first obstacle for many Christians in testing Bahá'u'lláh's Revelation is their expectation that there will be a display of great power and glory at *the very outset* of the advent. It should be noted that those who accept the initial secret coming of Christ still insist that Christ will make a visible and dramatic descent from heaven at a later date. Will their position on this issue also eventually change?

The following statement from Dr. Ray Stedman offers a rationale behind his belief in the initial secret coming of Christ:

> A key to understanding the teaching of the New Testament on this subject is the Greek word *parousia*. This word is commonly translated "coming," which in the mind of the reader projects the vision of the single dramatic appearance described above. But *parousia* should properly be translated "presence." This is the meaning given first by both Thayer and Arndt and Gingrich lexicons and includes the idea of an entrance, a consequent duration, and either an exit or a continued presence. It is not, therefore, a single event (\ /), but a continuation (|_____ |) of unspecified duration.
>
> This meaning is the only way to make sense of Jesus' revelation in Matthew 24 of His return to earth in the last days. There He describes a coming in power and glory immediately following the terrible time of trouble that He calls "the great tribulation" and the darkening of the sun and moon and the falling of the stars from heaven (Matt. 24:28-30). *But it would be impossible for such a coming to take anyone by surprise who knew of our Lord's description. For in the same chapter Jesus speaks of His coming as unexpected and sudden as the flood came upon the people of Noah's day; and He likens it to a thief creeping into a household at night, without warning, and surreptitiously removing its treasure (vv. 36-44). Yet how could His coming be both unexpected and preceded by such cosmic events of dramatic character?* [Emphasis added.]
>
> The only answer is that one passage describes His initial, totally unheralded and unexpected appearing while the other describes the disclosure of His presence by a dramatic display of power and glory...
>
> ...Thus His initial, thieflike coming, His continued presence behind the scenes on earth, and His final revelation in power would all be covered by the term *parousia.*[1]

Many of those who believe in the initial secret coming of Christ, also believe that during His secret presence He will start to take the faithful believers secretly to Himself, one or a few at a time. They call this "the rapture," which literally means "to snatch away." This idea is popular and has many supporters.

This is how a Christian source describes the rapture:

> According to this belief, Jesus will return to this earth in two phases. First, He will return secretly to whisk away all true Christians to heaven to protect them from the time of "great tribulation" Jesus foretold. Therefore, it is believed that the Church will be protected not on this earth, but up in heaven. The second phase is believed to be His "public" coming, at which time all will be able to see and hear Him.[2]

Some Christian writers have portrayed the rapture in graphic and dramatic terms. Here is a passage from Dr. Ivor Powell, a believer in bodily rapture:

> I shall always remember the woman who came to me at the end of a meeting in California. She said, "I hope the Lord will not return when my husband is coming across the Atlantic with his passengers. He is a pilot with United Airlines. He is a Christian, and furthermore, his co-pilot is also a Christian. What would happen to that plane load of people if the pilot and his co-pilot were suddenly removed?" I could only reply, "Friend, that plane would crash!" Probably hundreds of planes will crash, hundreds of thousands of automobiles will crash, railway trains will crash, and from all parts of the world will come news of unprecedented disaster. Every radio and television program, every newspaper, will tell stories of strange events which will have taken place all over the earth.[3]

Strict literalism has led Dr. Powell and many other Christians to expect such strange and dramatic events. They fail to recognize that spectacular dramas do not serve a thief's purpose. The heavenly thief is interested in His servants' inner essence: their spirits. If He can quietly lift their immortal spirits, why should He concern Himself with their perishable bodies?

The rapture is spiritual. It relates to the hearts and souls of humankind. As soon as the awakened ones acknowledge their Lord, they rise to a new realm invisible to others. We know too well that a married couple may live in the same house for fifty years yet fail to discern each other's private invisible world.

Moreover, we know the heavenly thief is extremely kind and gentle. He respects people's right of freedom. He would never disturb a sleeper's sweet dreams—one who prefers rest over rapture. His goal is to be seen by "every eye," by every householder who stands at the door praying and watching for his heavenly thief:

> Two men will be in the field; one will be taken and the other left. Two women will be grinding with a hand mill; one will be taken and the other left. Therefore keep watch...   Matthew 24:40-42 NIV

If "watch" means "look carefully," what benefit can come from seeing people raptured (lifted to heaven)? Only a *spiritual* rapture requires watching or investigating.

The thief's peerless skill lies in this: to rapture the ripe spirits before the gazing eyes of others without being detected. He does His work so efficiently that even those who live and work together in the same field fail to discern each other's disappearance, fail to detect the thief's marvelous workings.

Aside from taking the wakeful servants to Himself, the thief accomplishes still another goal. He tries to awaken His sleeping servants by gently calling them. If they refuse to rise and accompany Him, *He takes their spiritual possessions away from them*. The parable of the talents makes this quite clear.

These two verses are quite instructive:

> On that ***day*** no one who is on the roof of his house, with his goods inside, should go down to get them...I tell you, on that ***night*** two people will be in one bed; one will be taken and the other left [emphasis added].

Luke 17:31, 34 NIV

What does Jesus mean by "that day," and what does He mean by "that night"? He uses "the day" in relation to the urgency of the news of His return and the need for immediate action. He applies "the night" to the secret "rapture" of the believers' hearts and souls in the dark of confusion, fear, and the stress and distress of living.

Let us explore the sign "like a thief" and the commandment "Watch!" a little further. Among the most critical signs Jesus gave concerning His return were that He would return ***suddenly*** and ***secretly***. And in relation to each of those signs He gave special instructions or commandments. In relation to the first sign (coming suddenly) He said "Be prepared!" According to the dictionary, the word "suddenly" means "quickly and without warning." Preparation is especially required when an event happens without prior notice. When people are asked to expect a sudden event, they cannot excuse themselves at any given time by saying "I don't need to be ready now. I will either know in advance to prepare before the event, or I will do so after the event." If a team is told that they may be called at any time to play a game, they cannot say, "We will prepare on the day of the game."

In relation to the second sign (coming like a thief in the night), Jesus gave the commandment: "Watch!" Watching is required when an event can escape one's attention. This is how *The American Heritage Dictionary* defines "watch:" "to look or observe attentively or carefully, be closely observant, be on the look out or alert; be constantly observant or vigilant, look at steadily, observe carefully; observe the course of; keep up on or informed about..." For instance, to a child we say, "When you cross the street watch for cars, look both ways." We say this because his attention span and perception are limited. We remind him that *careful* and *close* observation is essential. It would seem strange indeed if on a sunny day and at noon we asked someone to watch for the sun! Similarly, we say, "Watch for the news of..." Can a person remain watchful but uninformed? The following verses clarify the meaning of "Watch:"

> ...unto them that look for him shall he appear the second time... Hebrews 9:28

> ...be ye yourselves like unto men looking for their Lord... Luke 12:36 ARV

> ...Christ...will appear a second time...to those who are watching for him. Hebrews 9:28 NEB

Once people are asked to "Watch!" they cannot abandon their responsibility to investigate the truth. They cannot say, "When Jesus comes I will know." Because *a clearly visible event does not require watching.*

Let us explore the analogy of the thief further. The most critical question we must ask is this: what is *the goal* of a thief? *To carry away precious goods without being detected.* To attain that goal the thief devises and follows a special strategy. He knows he must come:

• Suddenly (without warning)
• Quietly
• At a time when people do not expect him
• In the darkness of the night

The thief may also wish to wear dark clothes and a mask, and even carry some electronic devices. These are all part of *the strategy.* But a thief does not come just for the sake of executing *a strategy.* He comes to execute *a goal*, to accomplish *an objective*. The means he uses are to help him attain that objective. Aside from that, the means have no significance. *The coming of a thief must always be in harmony with his goal.*

A thief's sole purpose is to *steal* precious property, and his only concern is to observe secrecy. Secrecy is so critical to him that he even kills and destroys to conceal the evidence.

The thief comes only to steal and kill and destroy...

John 10:10 NIV

Let us review this brief quotation from Dr. Stedman:

He [Jesus] likens it [His coming] to a thief creeping into a household at night, without warning [unexpectedly], and surreptitiously [secretly], removing its treasures (Matt. 24:36-44).

What would a thief gain if he came suddenly or in any other way but failed to carry away precious goods? Therefore, the interpretation that "coming like a thief" simply means "suddenly" carries these weaknesses:

• It disregards *the objective* of the thief, it puts *the strategy* in place of *the goal.*

• It replaces a thief's *all-inclusive* strategy with *a partial* strategy.

It is obvious that if a thief announces his coming he cannot observe secrecy. But to remain secret he must do more than that. All the necessary things he must do are covered by the word *secrecy* but not *suddenness.*

Furthermore, the words "night" and "awake" in these two prophecies point clearly to *secrecy:*

The day of the Lord will come like a thief in *the night.*.

I Thessalonians 5:2 NIV

Behold, I come like a thief! Blessed is he who stays *awake*...   Revelation 16:15 NIV

A thief can choose to come **suddenly**, but not secretly, before the wakeful and astonished eyes of the householder, and take everything by force. But this is not what Jesus and Paul imply. Paul uses "night" to suggest "concealment and secrecy," and Jesus uses "awake" to imply a state of consciousness required to counteract the strategy of secrecy. Both words show that the "householder" can indeed **miss** the thief and never be aware of His parousia (presence).

Paul addressed these words to the enlightened believers:

> ...you know perfectly well that the Day of the Lord comes like a thief in the night...But you, my friends, are not in the dark, that the day should overtake you like a thief. You are all children of light, children of day. We do not belong to night or darkness, and we must not sleep like the rest, but keep awake and sober. Sleepers sleep at night, and drunkards are drunk at night, but we, who belong to daylight, must keep sober...
>
> I Thessalonians 5:2-8 NEB

Paul's words clearly show that recognition of the promised Redeemer requires **enlightenment**. If a person is deprived of that, he cannot recognize the Lord. Paul's words contradict the literal coming of Jesus from the sky. Who are the "children of light"? They are the enlightened people. Only **they** see the thief. Who are the "sleepers"? The unenlightened people. Why do the "sleepers" remain unaware? Why do they miss the thief? Clearly, their handicap is spiritual, not physical, because both the enlightened and the unenlightened have physical eyes.

If the Master came suddenly from the sky, what would be the purpose of wakefulness? All people—whether they are physically or spiritually asleep—would know. In fact, the open and sudden descent of Christ from the sky would require less wakefulness than the perception of any other event in history.

Jesus points out that the obstacles that prevent people from recognizing Him are spiritual:

> Be careful, or your hearts will be weighed down with dissipation, drunkenness and the anxieties of life, and that day will close on you unexpectedly like a trap...Be always on the watch, and pray that you may be able to escape all that is about to happen, and that you may be able to stand before the Son of Man.   Luke 21:34-36 NIV

What does Jesus mean by saying "your hearts will be weighed down with drunkenness"? Being "drunk" resembles being "asleep." Both states imply spiritual unawareness. How can one "escape all these things"? How can one stay out of the snare of unawareness, complacency, and unconcern, or the terrible trap of the denial of the Lord and its everlasting consequences? The remedy, as Jesus instructs, is this:

- Keep your hearts sober

- Never allow the worries and the anxieties of life to entrap you

- Never allow the worldly pleasures (dissipation) to entrap you

- Always watch or investigate

- And pray

This emphasis on wakefulness would suggest a secrecy that requires investigation. The following verses further encourage alertness and action:

> *Wake up*! Strengthen what remains and is about to die... But if you do not wake up, I will come like a thief [emphasis added]...   Revelation 3:2-3 NIV

> *Arise*...your light has come, and the glory of the Lord rises upon you. See, darkness covers the earth and thick darkness is over the peoples [emphasis added]...
>   Isaiah 60:1-2 NIV

> ***Wake up***, you drunkards, and lament your fate [emphasis added]...   Joel 1:5 NEB

The following prophecy, which pertains to our time, clearly expresses the meaning of staying asleep:

> The Lord has brought over you ***a deep sleep***...For you this whole vision is nothing but words sealed in a scroll [emphasis added].   Isaiah 29:10-11 NIV

All these instructions indicate that the coming of the Lord and the day of the Lord are like the coming of a thief in the night. The whole Gospel confirms this interpretation. When Jesus compared His second coming ***and*** His presence (parousia) among the people of our time to the coming and presence of Noah and Lot among the ancient people, what did He intend to convey? If Christ came from the sky, both His coming and presence among us would be in stark contrast to the coming and presence of Noah and Lot among ancient people. Indeed the station of both Noah and Lot were veiled to most of the people of their time. Only ***the enlightened*** people "saw" them. Only those who had "eyes" discerned their glory.

> ...without holiness no one will see the Lord.
>   Hebrews 12:14 NIV

> I counsel you to buy from me...salve to put on your eyes, so you can see.   Revelation 3:18 NIV

The following verses indicate that recognizing Christ in the second advent, as in the first, is private and personal. It does not come from a public display of glory. The Master "knocks," if the host opens his heart, then He comes in:

> Here I am! I stand at the door and knock. If anyone hears my voice and opens the door, I will come in and eat with him, and he with me.   Revelation 3:20 NIV

The Master shows Himself only to those who love Him and obey Him:

> I will not leave you as orphans; I will come to you...
> Whoever has my commands and obeys them...I...will...
> show myself to him.   John 14:18, 21 NIV

Showing must be spiritual, because all people—both the
faithful and the unfaithful—have physical eyes, but only those
who truly love their Master and obey Him have spiritual
eyes. Only they see Him. Only those who have spiritual hearing will hear the knocking. Only they will open their hearts.

> The people walking in darkness have seen a great light...
> For to us a child is born...he will be called...Prince of
> Peace...   Isaiah 9:2, 6 NIV

Who will see the light? Those who walk and seek in the dark
of unbelief. What light do they see? Spiritual. With what
eyes? Spiritual.

As we noted in Chapters 1 and 2, Jesus recounted many
parables to clarify the meaning of "Watch!" and "thief in
the night." Who were the five maidens who entered the
banquet of the Kingdom? They were *the enlightened* ones.
The Bridegroom appeared and left while other people remained
unaware. The parable clearly points to secrecy.

Jesus also used the parable of the talents. Who received the
most severe punishment from the Master? The fearful servant
who failed to invest his talents, who said "I was afraid" (Matt.
25:25 NIV). The parables and prophecies of Jesus clearly point
to His knowledge of the prevailing fear among His followers
at the time of His return. We see the full realization of that
knowledge in the response of many Christians to the Message
of Bahá'u'lláh.

In summary, Jesus issued several simple instructions to His
faithful followers. One of them was that "I will come suddenly." We can read all these messages in that instruction:
Always be ready in spirit and in deed, be just and humble,
have an open heart and mind. Spiritual receptivity cannot be
gained on short notice; it is a lifelong endeavor. Someday

you may stand before Me. When that day dawns, I will appear *suddenly* on the horizon of your soul. Do not allow yourself to be entangled in the mesh of tradition, fantasy, and the pressures of daily living.

Another clue Jesus gave was that "I will come *secretly*." This clue implies that "To find Me you must search, inquire, and investigate. God does not wish to impose the gift of Himself on unwilling, complacent, ungrateful, and apathetic people."

Independent investigation of truth (Watch!) is the master key that opens all the treasuries of heaven. It is the seed from which everything good and noble grows and multiplies; it is the essence of wisdom, the wellspring of knowledge.

The essence of all that We have revealed for thee is Justice, is for man to free himself from idle fancy and imitation, discern with the eye of oneness His glorious handiwork, and look into all things with a searching eye.[4]   Bahá'u'lláh

References

Foreword

1. *The Hidden Words of Bahá'u'lláh*, Arabic, No. 8.
2. *Tablets of Bahá'u'lláh*, p. 66.
3. Taherzadeh, Adib. *The Revelation of Bahá'u'lláh*, Oxford: George Ronald, 1988, vol. 4, p. 236.
4. *Selections from the Writings of 'Abdu'l-Bahá*, p. 12.
5. *Epistle to the Son of the Wolf*, p. 46.
6. *The Proclamation of Bahá'u'lláh*, p. 94.
7. *Gleanings from the Writings of Bahá'u'lláh*, p. 16.
8. *The Proclamation of Bahá'u'lláh*, p. 63.

He Who Overcomes

1. *Living By the Book*, CBN Center, Virginia Beach, Virginia, p. 2.
2. *The Plain Truth*, August 1991, pp. 9-10
3. Pratney, Winkie and Barry Chant. *The Return*, Chichester: Sovereign World, 1988, pp. 242-243.

4. Ibid., p. 243.
5. *The Book of Certitude*, p. 3.
6. *The Hidden Words of Bahá'u'lláh*, persian, No. 82.
7. Adler, Ronald and Neil Towne. *Looking Out Looking In*, New York: Holt, Rinehart and Winston, 1987, p. 96.
8. *The Book of Certitude*, pp. 3-4.
9. Dyer, Wayne. *You'll See It When You Believe It*, New York: Avon Books, 1983, pp. 167-168.
10. Ibid., pp. 164-165.
11. *Epistle to the Son of the Wolf*, p. 139.
12. *The Book of Certitude*, p. 3.
13. *Selections from the Writings of the Báb*, p. 134.
14. *The Book of Certitude*, p. 89.

Chapter 1

1. Stedman, Ray. *What's This World Coming To?* Ventura: Regal Books, 1986, pp. 120-167.
2. Unger, Merrill F. *Unger's Bible Dictionary*, Chicago: Moody Press, 1985, p. 632.
3. *Gleanings from the Writings of Bahá'u'lláh*, p. 143.
4. Haynes, Carlyle B. *Our Lord's Return*, Nashville: Southern Publishing Association, 1964, p. 6.
5. Achtemeier, Paul J. (ed.). *Harper's Bible Dictionary*, San Francisco: Harper and Row, 1985, p. 751.
6. *Tablets of Bahá'u'lláh*, p. 16.
7. MacPherson, Dave. *The Great Rapture Hoax*, Flecher, N.C.: New Puritan Library, 1983, pp. 125-127.
8. Ibid., p. 57.

Chapter 2

1. *Gleanings from the Writings of Bahá'u'lláh*, p. 216.
2. Stedman, Ray C. *Waiting for the Second Coming*, Grand Rapids: Discovery House, 1990, pp. 84-85.
3. Ibid., pp. 91-92.
4. *Selections from the Writings of the Báb*, p. 27.
5. *Tablets of Bahá'u'lláh*, p. 186.
6. *Selections from the Writings of the Báb*, p. 15.

7. The analogy is adopted from the Words of Bahá'u'lláh.
8. *Selections from the Writings of the Báb*, p. 86.
9. *Tablets of Bahá'u'lláh*, p. 238.
10. Ibid., pp. 240-241.
11. *Selections from the Writings of the Báb*, p. 112.
12. *The Book of Certitude*, p. 177.
13. *Selections from the Writings of the Báb*, p. 112.
14. *The Book of Certitude*, p. 142.
15. *Gleanings from the Writings of Bahá'u'lláh*, p. 75.
16. *Selections from the Writings of the Báb*, p. 22.
17. *The Hidden Words of Bahá'u'lláh*, Persian, No. 41.
18. *Gleanings from the Writings of Bahá'u'lláh*, p. 197.
19. *Selections from the Writings of the Báb*, p. 68.
20. *The Book of Certitude*, p. 53.
21. The analogy is adopted from the Writings of Bahá'u'lláh.
22. *The Book of Certitude*, p. 8.
23. Ibid., pp. 195-196.
24. *The Seven Valleys and the Four Valleys*, p. 7.
25. Stedman, Ray. *What's This World Coming To?* Ventura: Regal Books, 1986, pp. 54-56.
26. *The Kitáb-i-Aqdas*, p. 49.
27. *Tablets of Bahá'u'lláh*, p. 47.
28. *The Kitáb-i-Aqdas*, p. 57.
29. *Tablets of Bahá'u'lláh*, p. 155.
30. *The Hidden Words of Bahá'u'lláh*, Arabic, No. 6.
31. *Tablets of Bahá'u'lláh*, p. 156.
32. *Epistle to the Son of the Wolf*, p. 25.
33. *The Seven Valleys and the Four Valleys*, p. 9.
34. *Tablets of Bahá'u'lláh*, p. 156.

Chapter 3

1. Lindsell, Harold. *God's Incomparable Word*, Minneapolis: World Wide Publications, 1977, p. 5.
2. *Gleanings from the Writings of Bahá'u'lláh*, p. 218.
3. *Gleanings from the Writings of Bahá'u'lláh*, p. 106.
4. *Selections from the Writings of the Báb*, p. 109.

5. Ibid., p. 134.
6. Kennedy, James. *Why I Believe*, Waco: Word Books, 1980, p. 14.
7. Ibid., p. 14.
8. Chant, Barry, and Winkie Pratney. *The Return*, Chichester: Sovereign World, 1978, p. 101.
9. *Paris Talks*, p. 101.
10. *Living By the Book*, CBN Center, Virginia Beach, Virginia, 23463.
11. *Tablets of Bahá'u'lláh*, p. 75.
12. *Bahá'í Prayers*, Wilmette, Illinois: Bahá'í Publishing Trust, 1982, p. 19.
13. Ibid., p. 22.
14. Ibid., p. 55.

Chapter 4

1. White, John Wesley. *Re-entry*, Minneapolis: World Wide Publications, 1971, p. 14.
2. Ibid., p. 8.
3. *The Proclamation of Bahá'u'lláh*, p. 27.
4. *Tablets of Bahá'u'lláh*, p. 12.
5. Shoghi Effendi. *The World Order of Bahá'u'lláh*, Wilmette: Bahá'í Publishing Trust, 1980, p. 104.
6. *Gleanings from the Writings of Bahá'u'lláh*, p. 45.
7. Smith, Peter. *In Iran*, Los Angeles: Kalimát Press, 1986, p. 163.
8. *Gleanings from the Writings of Bahá'u'lláh*, pp. 12-13.
9. *The Proclamation of Bahá'u'lláh to the Kings and Leaders of the World*, Haifa: Universal House of Justice, 1967.
10. *Tablets of Bahá'u'lláh*, p. 11.
11. Ibid., p. 11.
12. *Gleanings from the Writings of Bahá'u'lláh*, p. 16.
13. Ibid., p. 136.
14. Ibid., pp. 10-11.
15. Ibid., p. 11.
16. *Tablets of Bahá'u'lláh*, pp. 9-10.
17. Lockyer, Herbert Jr. (ed.). *Nelson's Illustrated Bible Dictionary*, New York: Thomas Nelson Publishers, 1986, p. 66.
18. Tenney, Merrill C. (ed.). *The Zondervan Pictorial Bible Dictionary*, Grand Rapids: Zondervan Publishing House, 1977, p. 466.

19. *Tablets of Bahá'u'lláh*, pp. 235-236.
20. *The Book of Certitude*, p. 211.
21. Ibid., p. 3.
22. *Gleanings from the Writings of Bahá'u'lláh*, p. 143.
23. Ibid., p. 143.
24. *The Proclamation of Bahá'u'lláh*, p. 91.
25. *Gleanings from the Writings of Bahá'u'lláh*, pp. 85-86.
26. Ibid., p. 57.
27. *Selections from the Writings of the Báb*, pp. 63-64.
28. *The Promulgation of Universal Peace*, p. 86.
29. *The Proclamation of Bahá'u'lláh*, p. 96.
30. *Some Answered Questions*, p. 121.
31. *Tablets of Bahá'u'lláh*, p. 138.
32. *Gleanings from the Writings of Bahá'u'lláh*, p. 7.
33. You will find some of these quotations and many others in *The Bahá'í World*, Volumes viii and ix.

Chapter 5

1. Adler, Ronald, and Neil Towne, *Looking Out Looking In*, New York: Holt, Rinehart and Winston, 1987, p. 152.
2. Ibid., p. 152.
3. Pratney, Winkie and Barry Chant. *The Return*, Chichester: Sovereign World, 1988, p. 135.
4. *The Hidden Words of Bahá'u'lláh*, Arabic, No. 56.
5. *The Proclamation of Bahá'u'lláh*, p. 89.
6. *The Kitáb-i-Aqdas*, p. 49.
7. *The Dawn-Breakers*, New York: Bahá'í Publishing Committee, 1953, p. 608.
8. *The Kitáb-i-Aqdas*, p. 64.
9. *Gleanings from the Writings of Bahá'u'lláh*, p. 169.
10. *Tablets of Bahá'u'lláh*, p. 182.
11. Ibid., p. 11.
12. *Gleanings from the Writings of Bahá'u'lláh*, p. 36.
13. *Tablets of Bahá'u'lláh*, p. 107.
14. Shoghi Effendi. *The World Order of Bahá'u'lláh*, Wilmette: Bahá'í Publishing Trust, 1980, p. 105.
15. *The Proclamation of Bahá'u'lláh*, p. 27.

16. *Gleanings from the Writings of Bahá'u'lláh*, p. 100.
17. *Prayers and Meditations by Bahá'u'lláh*, p. 278.
18. *The Book of Certitude*, p. 192.
19. Ibid., pp. 14-15.
20. *Gleanings from the Writings of Bahá'u'lláh*, p. 16.
21. Ibid., p. 169.
22. *Tablets of Bahá'u'lláh*, p. 16.
23. Ibid., pp. 16-17.
24. *Gleanings from the Writings of Bahá'u'lláh*, p. 213.
25. Biederwolf, William E. *The Second Coming, Bible Commentary*, Grand Rapids, Michigan: Baker Book House, 1985, p. 321.
26. Ibid., p. 321.
27. *Tablets of Bahá'u'lláh*, p. 17.
28. *Gleanings from the Writings of Bahá'u'lláh*, p. 248.
29. Ibid., p. 313.
30. *The Book of Certitude*, p. 60.
31. Graham, Billy. *World Aflame*, Minneapolis: The Billy Graham Evangelical Association, 1965, p. 211.
32. *Appreciations of the Bahá'í Faith*, Wilmette: Bahá'í Publishing Committee, 1947, pp. 9-10.
33. Esslemont, J.E. *Bahá'u'lláh and the New Era*, Wilmette: Bahá'í Publishing Trust, 1980, p. 39.
34. *The Book of Certitude*, p. 131.
35. Kennedy, D. James. *Why I Believe in Christianity*, Fort Lauderdale: Coral Ridge Ministries, 1977, p. 2.
36. Moayyad, Heshmat (editor). *The Bahá'í Faith and Islam*, Canada: Association for Bahá'í Studies, 1990, p. vii.
37. *Gleanings from the Writings of Bahá'u'lláh*, p. 203.
38. *Tablets of Bahá'u'lláh*, p. 12.
39. *Gleanings from the Writings of Bahá'u'lláh*, p. 85.
40. *Prayers and Meditations by Bahá'u'lláh*, p. 154.
41. Pratney, Winkie, and Barry Chant. op. cit., pp. 241-242.
42. Sper David (ed.). *Knowing God Through the New Testament*, Grand Rapids: Thomas Nelson, Inc., 1982, p. 23.
43. Robertson, Norman K. *Understanding End Time Prophecy*, Chichester, England: Sovereign World Ltd., 1983, p. 95.
44. *Epistle to the Son of the Wolf*, p. 25.

45. Pratney, Winkie, and Barry Chant. op. cit., p. 135.
46. Ibid., p. 131.

Chapter 6

1. *Tablets of Bahá'u'lláh*, p. 244.
2. *The Hidden Words of Bahá'u'lláh*, Arabic, No. 56.
3. *Gleanings from the Writings of Bahá'u'lláh*, p. 44.
4. Ibid., p. 41.
5. Ibid., p. 255.
6. *Prayers and Meditations by Bahá'u'lláh*, p. 189.
7. Dyer, Wayne W. *You'll See It When You Believe It*, New York: Avon Books, 1989, p. 64.
8. Vandeman, George. *Winds on a Leash*, Thousand Oak: it is written, pp. 12-13.
9. *The Plain Truth*, April 1991, p. 7.
10. Pratney, Winkie, and Barry Chant. *The Return*, Chichester: Sovereign World, 1988, p. 116.
11. Church J. R. *Hidden Prophecies in the Psalms*, Oklahoma City: Prophecy Publications, 1986, p. 206.
12. Berns, Roberta M. *Child, Family, Community*, New York: Holt, Rinehart and Winston, 1985, p. 85.
13. *Tablets of Bahá'u'lláh*, p. 90.
14. *Gleanings from the Writings of Bahá'u'lláh*, p. 43.
15. *Tablets of Bahá'u'lláh*, p. 10.
16. Ibid., p. 11.
17. Ibid., p. 14.
18. *The Book of Certitude*, p. 31.
19. White, John Wesley. *Re-entry*, Minneapolis: World Wide Publications, 1971, p. 110.
20. Ibid., p. 113.
21. Ibid., p. 117.
22. Ibid., p. 117.
23. *The Plain Truth*, April 1991, p. 6.
24. Armstrong, H.W. *What Is the True Gospel?* Worldwide Church of God, 1972, p. 1.
25. Pratney, Winkie, and Barry Chant. op. cit., p. 127.
26. Graham, Billy. *Till Armageddon*, Minneapolis: World Wide, 1981, p. 7.

27. Griffin, Mary, and Carol Felsenthal. *A Cry for Help*, Garden City: Doubleday and Company, Inc., 1983, p. 11.
28. *Gleanings from the Writings of Bahá'u'lláh*, pp. 39-40.
29. Dadd, Debra Lynn. *Let's Live*, "How the Global Environment Affects Our Health," April 1991, pp. 18-20.
30. Fox, Matthew. *The Cosmic Coming of Christ*, New York: Harper & Roe, p. 15.
31. Carson, Robert, James Butcher, and James Coleman. *Abnormal Psychology and Modern Life*, Glenview: Scott, Foresman and Company, 1988, p. 4.
32. De Haan, Martin. "Things are not as they seem," *Radio Bible Class News*, October 1989.
33. *Gleanings from the Writings of Bahá'u'lláh*, p. 213.
34. *The Book of Certitude*, pp. 30-31.
35. Carson, Robert, James Butcher, and James Coleman. op. cit., p. 4.

Chapter 7

1. Vandeman, George E. *Showdown at Armageddon*, Boise: Pacific Press Publishing Association, 1987, p. 93.
2. Ibid., p. 75.
3. *The Plain Truth*, March 1991, p. 1.
4. *The Hidden Words of Bahá'u'lláh*, Arabic, No. 56.
5. *The Book of Certitude*, pp. 3-4.
6. *Gleanings from the Writings of Bahá'u'lláh*, p. 198.
7. *Bahá'í World Faith*, p. 254.
8. Peale, Norman Vincent. *Plus*, April 1988, vol. 39, no. 3 (Part I), pp. 6-7.
9. Vandeman, George, op. cit., p. 66.
10. Haynes, Carlyle B. *Our Lord's Return*, Nashville: Southern Publishing Association, 1964, pp. 100-101.
11. Stedman, Ray C. *Waiting for the Second Coming*, Grand Rapids: Discovery House, 1990, p. 117.
12. Kennedy, James. *Why I Believe*, Waco: Word Books, 1980, p. 152.
13. McKeever, Jim. *The Coming Climax of History*, Medford: Omega Publications, 1982, p. 274.
14. Stedman, Ray C. op. cit., p. 88.
15. *The Book of Certitude*, p. 34.
16. *The Seven Valleys and the Four Valleys*, p. 10.

17. *The Book of Certitude*, p. 20.

18. *Selections from the Writings of the Báb*, p. 163.

19. *Tablets of Bahá'u'lláh*, pp. 78-79.

20. Lindsey, Hal. *The Promise*, New York: Bantam Books, 1984, p. 19.

21. Ibid., p. 19.

22. Ibid., pp. 19-20.

23. Ibid., p. 23.

24. Ibid., p. 26.

25. Himes, Joshua V. *Views of the Prophecies and Prophetic Chronology Selected from Manuscripts of William Miller*, Boston: Published by Joshua Himes, 1842, p. 288.

26. Ibid., p. 284.

27. Ibid., p. 284.

28. Ibid., p. 284.

29. McDowell, Josh. *More than a Carpenter*, Minneapolis: World Wide Publications, 1977, p. 43.

30. Ibid., p. 43.

31. Himes, Joshua, op. cit., p. 284.

Chapter 8

1. Gale, Robert. *The Urgent Voice*, Washington D.C.: Review and Herald, 1975, p. 119.

2. Ibid., p. 49.

3. Ibid., p. 49.

4. I wish to acknowledge my debt to Dr. A. Misbáh for finding and introducing this source to me.

5. Froom, Leroy. *The Prophetic Faith of Our Fathers*, Washington, D.C.: Review and Herald, 1950, vol. 3, p. 12.

6. Ibid., p. 750.

7. Meister, Charles W. *Year of the Lord, A.D. Eighteen Forty Four*, North Carolina: McFarland and Company, Inc., 1983, p. 17.

8. Clarke, Jerome. *1844*, Tennessee: Southern Publishing Association, 1968.

9. Froom, Leroy. op. cit., vol. 3, p. 495.

10. Meister, Charles W. op. cit., p. 18.

11. Ibid., p. 17.

12. *Selections from the Writings of the Báb*, p. 12.

13. Ibid., p. 74.
14. Ibid., p. 73.
15. Froom, Leroy. op. cit., vol. 4, p. 474.
16. Meister, Charles W. op. cit., p. 20.
17. Ibid., p. 21.
18. Ibid., p. 22.
19. Gale, Robert. op. cit., p. 101.
20. Ibid., p. 121.
21. Ibid., p. 121.
22. Ibid., p. 50.
23. Ibid., p. 82.
24. Ibid., p. 88.
25. Ibid., pp. 114-115.
26. Ibid., p. 87.
27. Ibid., p. 122.
28. Froom, Leroy. op. cit., vol. 4, p. 855.
29. Gale, Robert. op. cit., p. 123.
30. Meister, Charles W. op. cit., p. 33.
31. Gale, Robert. op. cit., p. 123.
32. White, E. G. *The Triumph of God's Love*, Washington, D.C.: Review and Herald, 1957, p. 133.
33. Gale, Robert. op. cit., p. 133.
34. Vandeman, George. *Winds on a Leash*, Thousand Oaks: it is written, p. 12.
35. White, E. G. *The Great Controversy*, California: Pacific Publishing Association, 1971, p. 359.
36. Ibid., p. 359.
37. Meister, Charles W. op. cit., p. 35.
38. Froom, Leroy. op. cit., vol. 4, p. 858.
39. Lindsey, Hal. *The Promise*, New York: Bantam Books, 1984, pp. 79-80.
40. Stedman, Ray C. *Waiting for the Second Coming*, Grand Rapids: Discovery House, 1990, p. 88.
41. Ibid., p. 88.
42. Vandeman, George. op. cit., p. 12.
43. Ibid., pp. 12-13.

Chapter 9

1. Guinness, Henry Gratten (Dr. and Mrs.). *Light for the Last Days*, London: Marshall, Morgan & Scott LTD, 1934, p. 65.
2. Archer, Gleason L. Jr. *Encyclopedia of Bible Difficulties*, Grand Rapids: Zondervan Publishing House, 1982, p. 289.
3. Ibid., p. 291.
4. Himes, Joshua V. *Views of the Prophecies and Prophetic Chronology Selected from Manuscripts of William Miller,* Boston: published by Joshua Himes, 1842, p. 72.
5. Clarke, Adam. *Clarke's Commentary*, New York: Abingdon Press, 1825, vol. 4, p. 602.
6. Archer, Gleason L. Jr. op. cit., p. 289.
7. Biederwolf, William E. *The Second Coming, Bible Commentary*, Grand Rapids: Baker Book House, 1985, p. 217.
8. Froom, Leroy. *The Prophetic Faith of Our Fathers*, Washington, D.C.: Review & Herald, 1946, vol. 3, p. 11.
9. Ibid., p. 11.
10. Smith, Uriah. *Thoughts, Critical and Practical on the Book of Daniel*, Battle Creek: Seventh Day Adventist Publishing, 1881, p. 247.

    The dates of the four decrees according to *Evidence that Demands a Verdict* are: 539 B.C., 519 B.C., 457 B.C., and 444 B.C. (Josh MacDowell, Volume I, 1986, p. 172).
11. Ibid., p. 105.
12. Smith, Uriah, op. cit., pp. 144-145.
13. Ibid., p. 273.
14. Vandeman, George E. *Showdown at Armageddon*, Boise: Pacific Press Publishing Association, 1987, p. 22.
15. Baker, Kenneth and John Kohlenberger (editors). *Zondervan NIV Bible Commentary, Volume 1: The Old Testament*, Grand Rapids, MI: Zondervan Publishing House, 1994, p. 1389.
16. *Selections from the Writings of the Báb*, p. 87.
17. *Gleanings from the Writings of Bahá'u'lláh*, p. 328.
18. *Some Answered Questions*, p. 41.

Chapter 10

1. *Some Answered Questions*, p. 42.

2. White, E. G. *The Triumph of God's Love*, Washington, D.C.: Review and Herald, 1957, p. 240.
3. Robertson, Norman K. *Understanding End Time Prophecy*, Chichester: Sovereign World, 1989, pp. 205-206.
4. Lindsey, Hal. *The Promise*, New York: Bantam Books, 1984, pp. 144-145.
5. Smith, Uriah. *Thoughts, Critical and Practical, on the Book of Daniel*, Battle Creek: Seventh-Day Adventist Publishing Association, 1881, p. 242.
6. Froom, Leroy. *The Prophetic Faith of Our Fathers*, Washington, D.C.: Review and Herald, 1950, vol. 3, p. 273.
7. Ibid., p. 749.
8. Himes, Joshua V. *Views of the Prophecies and Prophetic Chronology Selected from Manuscripts of William Miller*, Boston: Published by Joshua Himes, 1842, p. 62.
9. Ibid., p. 297.

Chapter 11

1. Biederwolf, William E. *The Second Coming, Bible Commentary*, Grand Rapids: Baker Book House, 1985, p. 275.
2. Kennedy, James. *Why I Believe in Christ*, Fort Lauderdale: Coral Ridge Ministries, 1977, p. 1.
3. *The Hidden Words of Bahá'u'lláh*, Arabic, No. 1.
4. *The Seven Valleys and the Four Valleys*, p. 36.
5. *Selections from the Writings of the Báb*, p. 53.
6. Esslemont, J. E. *Bahá'u'lláh and the New Era*, Wilmette: Bahá'í Publishing Trust, 1980, p. 23.

Chapter 12

1. "Herzel, Theodore." Britannica CD. Version 97. Encyclopaedia Britannica, Inc., 1997.
2. "Israel." Britannica CD. Version 97. Encyclopaedia Britannica, Inc., 1997.
3. Noah, M. M. *Discourse on the Restoration of the Jews*, New York: Harper & Brothers, 1845, pp. iii-v.
4. Ibid., p. vii.
5. Ibid., p. viii.
6. Ibid., pp. 9-10.

7. Ibid., p. 11.
8. Ibid., pp. 37-38.
9. "Herzel, Theodore." Britannica CD. Version 97. Encyclopaedia Britannica, Inc., 1997.
10. "Oliphant, Laurence." Britannica CD. Version 97. Encyclopaedia Britannica, Inc., 1997.
11. "Herzl, Theodor." Britannica CD. Version 97. Encyclopaedia Britannica, Inc., 1997.
12. Robbins, Anthony. *Giant Steps*, New York: Simon & Schuster, 1994, p. 39.
13. "Turkey and Ancient Anatolia." Britannica CD. Version 97. Encyclopaedia Britannica, Inc., 1997.
14. Sours, Michael. "The 1844 Ottoman Edict of Toleration in Bahá'í Secondary Literature," *The Journal of Bahá'í Studies*, vol. 8, no. 3, March-June 1998, p. 70.
15. Ibid., p. 72.
    I am indebted to George Townshend for recognizing the relevance of this Edict to the Bahá'í Faith, to William Sears who did further research on this topic, and to Michael Sours for introducing and evaluating the Edict in *The Journal of Bahá'í Studies*.
16. Guinness, H. Gratten (Dr. & Mrs.). *Light for the Last Days*, London: Marshall, Morgan & Scott Ltd., 1934, pp. 114-115.
17. Froom, Leroy. *The Prophetic Faith of Our Fathers*, Washington, D.C.: Review and Herald, 1950, vol. 4, pp. 1194-1195.
18. Guinness, H. Gratten. op. cit. pp. 230-232.
19. Noah, M. M. *Discourse on the Restoration of the Jews*, New York: Harper & Brothers, 1845, p. 33.
20. Ibid., pp. 51-52.
21. Reagan, David. *The Master Plan*, Eugene, OR: Harvest House Publishers, 1993, p. 46.
22. *Some Answered Questions*, p. 65.
23. *Gleanings from the Writings of Bahá'u'lláh*, p. 60.

Chapter 13

1. Cobb, Stanwood. *Islamic Contributions to Civilization*, Washington, D.C.: Avalon Press, 1965, p. 5.
2. Townshend, George. *Christ and Bahá'u'lláh*, London: George Ronald, 1957, p. 40.

3. Ibid., p. 41.
4. *Selections from the Writings of the Báb*, p. 69.
5. Parrinder, Geoffrey. *Jesus in the Qur'án*, New York: Barnes & Noble Inc., 1965, p. 15.
6. Nuqabá'í, H. *Bishárát-i-Kutub-i--Ásmání* (Persian), Tihrán, Bahá'í Era 124, p. 226.
7. Smith, Peter. *In Irán*, Los Angeles: Kalimát Press, 1986, p. 163.
8. *Gleanings from the Writings of Bahá'u'lláh*, p. 101.
9. Taherzadeh, Adib. *The Revelation of Bahá'u'lláh*, Oxford: George Ronald, 1988, vol. 4, p. 97.
10. *Tablets of Bahá'u'lláh*, p. 9.
11. Parrinder, Geoffrey. op. cit., p. 15.
12. Lockyer, Herbert Sr. (ed.). *Nelson's Illustrated Bible Dictionary*, Nashville: Thomas Nelson Publishers, 1986, p. 683.
13. Unger, Merril F. *Unger's Bible Dictionary*, Chicago: Moody Press, 1985, p. 702.
14. Achtemeier, Paul J. (ed.). *Harper's Bible Dictionary*, San Francisco: Harper & Row, 1985, p. 611.
15. *Gleanings from the Writings of Bahá'u'lláh*, p. 197.
16. *Selections from the Writings of the Báb*, p. 56.
17. Tenney, Merrill C. (ed.). *The Zondervan Pictorial Bible Dictionary*, Grand Rapids: Zondervan Publishing House, 1977, p. 387.
18. Unger, Merrill F. op. cit., p. 450.
19. Morse, Joseph Laffan. *Funk and Wagnalls Standard Reference Encyclopedia*, New York: Standard Reference Works Publishing Company, Inc., 1960, vol. 14, p. 5043.
20. Achtemeier, Paul J. op. cit., p. 432.

Chapter 14

1. *Some Answered Questions*, p. 49.
2. Suleimání, A. *Masábíh-i-Hedáyat* (Persian), vol. 7, p. 272.
3. *Gleanings from the Writings of Bahá'u'lláh*, p. 60.
4. *Selections from the Writings of the Báb*, p. 74.
5. Pratney, Winkie and Barry Chant. *The Return*, Chichester: Sovereign World, 1988, p. 121.
6. Neff, Leroy. *Where Are We Now In Prophecy?* "Is There Any Place of Safety?" Passadena: Worldwide church of God, p. 20.

7. Schonfield, H.J. *Readers' A to Z Bible Companion*, New York: New American Library, 1967, pp. 94-95.

8. McClaim, A. J. *Daniel's Prophecy of Seventy Weeks*, Grand Rapids: Zondervan Publishing Co., 1940, p. 62.

9. *Some Answered Questions*, p. 51.

   The center of the Umayyad's dominion was Syria and Jerusalem, "and it was here that the religion of God and the divine teachings first disappeared."

10. Pratney, Winkie. op. cit., p. 121.

11. Taherzadeh, A. *The Revelation of Bahá'u'lláh*, Oxford: George Ronald, 1988, vol. 4, p. 210.

12. *Some Answered Questions*, p. 70.

13. Ibid., p. 70.

14. Lockyer, Herbert Sr. (ed.) *Nelson's Illustrated Bible Dictionary*, New York: Thomas Nelson Publishers, 1986, p. 477.

15. *Some Answered Questions*, p. 71.

16. Biederwolf, William E. *The Second Coming, Bible Commentary*, Grand Rapids: Baker Book House, 1985, p. 6.

17. Ibid., p. 635.

18. Ibid., p. 635.

19. Froom, Leroy. *The Prophetic Faith of Our Fathers*, Washington, D.C.: Review & Herald, 1950, vol. 3, p. 638.

20. *The Proclamation of Bahá'u'lláh*, p. 87.

21. *Gleanings from the Writings of Bahá'u'lláh*, p. 60.

22. *Selections from the Writings of the Báb*, pp. 51-52.

23. Riggs, Robert. *The Apocalypse Unsealed*, New York: Philosophical Library, 1981.

   See also *New Keys to the Book of Revelation*, by Ruth Moffet, 1971, Bahá'í Publishing Trust, India.

Chapter 15

1. Stedman, Ray C. *Waiting for the Second Coming*, Grand Rapids: Discovery House, 1990, p. 78.

2. Toffler, Alvin. *Future Shock*, New York: Random House, 1970, p. 26.

3. Ibid., pp. 26-27.

4. Bernard, H.W. *Child Development and Learning*, Boston: Allyn and Bacon, Inc. 1973, p. 4.

5. Meister, Charles W. *Year of the Lord*, North Carolina: McFarland and Company, Inc., 1983, p. 12.
6. Kane, Joseph Nathan. *Famous First Facts*, New York: The H.W. Wilson Company, 1981, p. 635.
7. Clarke, Jerome. *1844: Religious Movements*, Tennessee: Southern Publishing Association, 1968, pp. 388-389.
8. Ibid., p. ii.
9. Ibid., p. i.
10. Smith, Uriah. *Thoughts, Critical and Practical, On the Book of Daniel*, Battle Creek: Seventh-Day Adventist Publishing Association, 1881, pp. 388-389.
11. *Gleanings from the Writings of Bahá'u'lláh*, p. 36.

Chapter 16

1. Himes, Joshua V. *Views of the Prophecies and Prophetic Chronology Selected from Manuscripts of William Miller*, Boston: published by Joshua Himes, 1842, p. 16.
2. Ibid., p. 23.
3. Lindsey, Hal. *The Promise*, New York: Bantam Books, 1984, p. 179.
4. Himes, Joshua V. op. cit., p. 262.
5. *Encyclopedia Judaica*, 1971, vol. 11, p. 854.
6. Ibid., p. 854.
7. Smith, William. *Smith's Bible Dictionary*, Old Tappan: Fleming H. Revell Company, 1979, p. 371.
8. Himes, Joshua V. op. cit., p. 80.
9. Ibid., p. 45.
10. Achtemeier, Paul J. (ed.). *Harper's Bible Dictionary*, San Francisco: Harper and Row, 1985, p. 599.
11. *Encyclopedia Judaica*, op. cit., pp. 852-854.
12. Froom, Leroy. *The Prophetic Faith of Our Fathers*, Washington, D.C.: Review & Herald, 1946, vol. 4, p. 473.
13. Himes, Joshua, op. cit., p. 45
14. Ibid., p. 80.
15. Froom, Leroy. op. cit., vol. 3, p. 634.
16. Ibid., p. 633.
17. Nuqabá'í, H. *Bishárát-i-Kutub-i-Ásmání* (Persian), Tihrán, Bahá'í Era 124, p. 281.

18. Guinness, Henry Gratten (Dr. & Mrs.). *Light for the Last Days*, London: Marshall, Morgan & Scott LTD, 1934.

19. Ibid., p. 44.

20. Tenney, Merrill C. (ed.). *The Zondervan Pictorial Bible Dictionary*, Grand Rapids: Zondervan Publishing House, 1977, p. 425.

21. Shoghi Effendi. *The World Order of Bahá'u'lláh*, Wilmette: Bahá'í Publishing Trust, 1955, p. 105.

Chapter 17

1. *Epistle to the Son of the Wolf*, p. 47.

2. *Gleanings from the Writings of Bahá'u'lláh*, p. 36.

3. *Selections from the Writings of the Báb*, p. 105. See also pp. 89, 107, and 118.

4. *Epistle to the Son of the Wolf*, p. 141

5. Ibid., p.141.

6. Ibid., p. 152.

7. Ibid., p. 142.

8. Shoghi Effendi. *God Passes By*, Wilmette, IL: Bahá'í Publishing Trust. 1957, p. 29.

9. Ibid., p. 29.

10. Church, J. R. *Hidden Prophecies in the Psalms*, Oklahoma City: Prophecy Publications, 1986, p. 247.

11. Biederwolf, William E. *The Second Coming Bible Commentary*, Grand Rapids: Baker Book House, 1985, p. 346.

12. Ibid., p. 346.

13. Ibid., p. 346.

14. Ibid., p. 346.

15. *Selections from the Writings of the Báb*, p. 56.

16. Biederwolf, William E. *The Second Coming Bible Commentary*, Grand Rapids: Baker Book House, 1985, pp. 365-366.

17. Shoghi Effendi. *God Passes By*, Wilmette, IL: Bahá'í Publishing Trust. 1957, pp. 5-6.

18. Ibid., pp. 6.

19. Nabíl. *The Dawn-Breakers*, New York: Bahá'í Publishing Committee, 1953, p. 65.

20. *Epistle to the Son of the Wolf*, p. 21.

490 I Shall Come Again

21. Nabíl. *The Dawn-Breakers*, New York: Bahá'í Publishing Committee, 1953, pp. 315-316.
22. *Epistle to the Son of the Wolf*, p. 29.
23. Ibid., pp. 42-43.
24. Ibid., p. 119.
25. Ibid., p. 46.
26. Vandeman, George. *Winds on a Leash*, pp. 12-13.
27. Stedman, Ray, C. *Waiting for the Second Coming*, Grand Rapids: Discovery House, 1990, p. 117.
28. Pratney, Winkie, and Barry Chant. *The Return*, Chichester: Sovereign World, 1988, p. 27.
29. White, John Wesley. *Re-entry*, Minneapolis: World Wide Publications, 1971, p. 110.
30. *Gleanings from the Writings of Bahá'u'lláh*, p. 103.

Chapter 18

1. Suhráb, E. *Mabádí-i-Estedlál* (Persian), Tihrán, Bahá'í Era 130, p. 251.
2. Nuqabá'í, H. *Bishárát-i-Kutub-i-Ásmání* (Persian), Tihrán, Bahá'í Era 124, p. 94.
3. Ferraby, John. *All Things Made New*, London: Ruskin House, 1957, p. 171.
4. Nuqabá'í, H. op. cit., p. 61.
5. Kahn, A., O. Karsh, and B. Mundy. *Four Remarkable Indian Prophecies*, Healdsburg: Naturegraph Co., p. 8.
6. Ibid., p. 10.
7. Cameron, Glenn and Wendi Momen. *A Bahá'í Chronology*, Oxford: Geroge Ronald, 1996, p. 57
8. *The Hidden Words of Bahá'u'lláh*, pp. 51-52.
9. *Prayers and Meditations by Bahá'u'lláh*, p. 284.
10. *Selections from the Writings of the Báb*, p. 68.
11. *Epistle to the Son of the Wolf*, p. 97.
12. *Selections from the Writings of the Báb*, p. 42.
13. *Gleanings from the Writings of Bahá'u'lláh*, pp. 103-104.
14. Shoghi Effendi. *Guidance for Today and Tomorrow*, London: Bahá'í Publishing Trust, 1953, pp. 149-150.

Chapter 19

1. Froom, Leroy. *The Prophetic Faith of Our Fathers*, Washington, D.C.: Review and Herald, 1950, vol. 3, p. 11.
2. Meister, Charles W. *Year of the Lord*, North Carolina: McFarland and Company, Inc., 1983, p. 30.
3. Clarke, Jerome. *1844, Religious Movements*, Tennessee: Southern Publishing Association, 1968, vol. 1, Preface.
4. Froom, Leroy. op. cit., vol. 3, p. 671.
5. Ibid., p. 675.
6. Ibid., p. 677.
7. Ibid., p. 677.
8. Ibid., p. 674.
9. Ibid., p. 674.
10. Kennedy, James D. *Messiah: Prophecies Fulfilled*, Ft. Lauderdale: Coral Ridge Ministries, p. 71.
11. Froom, Leroy. op. cit., pp. 479-480.
12. Ibid., p. 463.
13. Ibid., p. 480.
14. Ibid., p. 463.
15. Ibid., p. 472.
16. Ibid., p. 481.
17. Ibid., p. 481.
18. *The Hidden Words of Bahá'u'lláh*, Persian, No. 39.
19. *Selections from the Writings of the Báb*, p. 110.

Chapter 20

1. *Tablets of Bahá'u'lláh*, p. 129.
2. *Epistle to the Son of the Wolf*, p. 15.
3. Townshend, George. *Christ and Bahá'u'lláh*, London: George Ronald, 1957, p. 116.
4. *The Proclamation of Bahá'u'lláh*, p. 79.
5. *The Book of Certitude*, p. 17.
6. *Gleanings from the Writings of Bahá'u'lláh*, pp. 56-57.
7. *The Book of Certitude*, pp. 3-4.
8. *Selections from the Writings of the Báb*, pp. 90-91.

Chapter 21

1. Lockyer, Herbert Sr. (ed.). *Nelson's Illustrated Bible Dictionary*, Nashville: Thomas Nelson Publishers, 1986, p. 259.
2. Ibid., p. 259.
3. *Selections from the Writings of the Báb*, p. 87.
4. *Prayers and Meditations by Bahá'u'lláh*, p. 284.
5. *Selections from the Writings of the Báb*, p. 65.
6. *The Book of Certitude*, p. 13.
7. *Selections from the Writings of the Báb*, p. 68.
8. *Gleanings from the Writings of Bahá'u'lláh*, p. 157.
9. *Selections from the Writings of the Báb*, p. 15.
10. *The Hidden Words of Bahá'u'lláh*, Persian, No. 41.
11. *Epistle to the Son of the Wolf*, p. 97.
12. *Gleanings from the Writings of Bahá'u'lláh*, p. 130.
13. *Selections from the Writings of the Báb*, p. 77.
14. Ibid., p. 160.
15. Ibid., p. 162.
16. *The Hidden Words of Bahá'u'lláh*, Persian, No. 36.
17. *Prayers and Meditations by Bahá'u'lláh*, p. 76.
18. Ibid., p. 97.
19. *Selections from the Writings of the Báb*, p. 133.
20. *Gleanings from the Writings of Bahá'u'lláh*, p. 339.

Chapter 22

1. *The Book of Certitude*, p. 70.
2. Tenney, Merrill (ed.). *The Zondervan Pictorial Bible Dictionary*, Grand Rapids: Zondervan Publishing House, 1977, p. 466.
3. *The Book of Certitude*, p. 69.
4. Ibid., p. 69.
5. *Gleanings from the Writings of Bahá'u'lláh*, p. 278.
6. *Tablets of Bahá'u'lláh*, p. 13.
7. *Selections from the Writings of the Báb*, p. 62.
8. Ibid., p. 91.
9. *Tablets of Bahá'u'lláh*, p. 157.
10. *Gleanings from the Writings of Bahá'u'lláh*, pp. 323-324.

11. Ibid., p. 236.
12. Ibid., p. 247.
13. Ibid., p. 125.
14. *The Hidden Words of Bahá'u'lláh*, Arabic, No. 31.
15. *Gleanings from the Writings of Bahá'u'lláh*, p. 197.

Appendix I

1. McFarland, Ken. *Let's Get Acquainted*, Boise: Pacific Press Publishing Association, 1987, pp. 6-7.
2. White, E. G. *The Triumph of God's Love*, Washington, D.C.: Review and Herald Publishing Association, 1957, p. 252.
3. Ibid., p. 253.
4. Johnson, William C. *Why I Am a Seventh-day Adventist*, Washington, D.C.: Review and Herald Publishing Association, 1986, pp. 28-29.
5. White, E.G. op. cit., p. 250.
6. Ibid., p. 249.
7. Tenney, Merrill C. (ed.). The Zondervan Pictorial Bible Dictionary, Grand Rapids: Zondervan Publishing House, 1977, p. 751.
8. *Selections from the Writings of the Báb*, p. 53.
9. *Selections from the Writings of the Báb*, p. 62.
10. Rosenthal, Marvin. *Pre-Wrath Rapture of the Church*, Nashville: Thomas Nelson Publishers, 1990, pp. 92-93.
11. Ibid., p. 93.
12. Rice, George E. *Christ in Collision*, Mountain View: Pacific Press Publishing Association, 1982, pp. 49-50.
13. Ibid., p. 105.
14. Lockyer, Herbert Sr. (ed.). *Nelson's Illustrated Bible Dictionary*, Nashville: Thomas Nelson Publishers, 1986, p. 1038.
15. *Prayers and Meditations by Bahá'u'lláh*, p. 285.
16. Esslemont, J. E. *Bahá'u'lláh and the New Era*, Wilmette: Bahá'í Publishing Trust, 1980, p. 23.
17. *Tablets of Bahá'u'lláh*, p. 164.
18. *Gleanings from the Writings of Bahá'u'lláh*, p. 92.
19. Ibid., p. 298-299.
20. Ibid., p. 52.
21. *Epistle to the Son of the Wolf*, p. 83.

22. Douglas, J. D. (ed.). *New Bible Dictionary*, Wheaton: Tyndale House Publishers, Inc., 1986, p. 1070.
23. *Epistle to the Son of the Wolf*, p. 145.
24. *Gleanings from the Writings of Bahá'u'lláh*, p. 32.
25. *Tablets of Bahá'u'lláh*, p. 16.

Appendix II

1. White, Ellen G. *Early Writings*, Washington D.C.: Review & Herald, 1945, pp. 81-83.
2. *The Book of Certitude*, p. 97.
3. *Gleanings from the Writings of Bahá'u'lláh*, p. 30.
4. Ibid., p. 268.
5. Ibid., p. 197.
6. Ibid., p. 245.

Appendix III

1. Stedman, Ray C. *Waiting for the Second Coming*, Grand Rapids: Discovery House, 1990, pp. 156-157.
2. Tkach, Joseph W. (ed.). *The Ambassador College Bible Correspondence Course*, "The Dramatic Return of Jesus Christ!" Lesson 3, p. 4.
3. Ibid., pp. 61-62.
4. *Tablets of Bahá'u'lláh*, p. 157.

Permissions

Grateful acknowledgment is made for permission to use material from the following:

Index

of God   64-65
of truth   30
Fearful   28
Fig tree, the   360
Fire, meaning of   56-57, 163,
    166, 168-170
Flee   137
Freedom   107, 393, 396, 414,
    416-417, 419, 422
    gift of   414, 420
    of choice   162, 208, 230,
        396-397, 414
    of conscience   399
    religious   418
Future, the glorious   126

G

Galileo Galilei   52
Gate of the Gate, the   321, 363-
    364
Gate, the   96, 321, 364, 370
Gentiles   263, 265, 301-303, 348
    times of the   263-266, 277,
        279, 280, 301, 303, 336,
        343-344, 346, 355, 373
Glory   58, 106, 108, 111, 114-
    116
    God, of   12, 87, 96, 320
    the meaning of   110, 116
God - most manifest and most
    hidden   52
God's guidance, need for   414,
    419
    law of visibility and
        invisibility   51-53

Gospel   28
    confirmed   16
    proclaimed   385, 388-389,
        391
Gratten, Dr Henry Guinness
    212, 273, 299, 345-346
Great tribulation, the   462

H

Heart, the pure in   70, 72, 77, 92,
    112, 255, 258-261, 416,
    424
Heaven, descending from   87,
    108-109, 208, 320
    symbolism of   310, 320,
        405, 415
Herod   45, 312
History, learning from   74, 90,
    96, 161, 172
"Hour," the time of the   318
Householder, the   44-46, 48,
    463, 467
Human standards of judgment
    161, 164, 172, 176
Humility   54, 57, 61, 78-80, 90,
    106, 132
Hushidar   370

I

Instruments of God   44-45, 415,
    426, 450
Interpret, the right to   97, 119-
    121, 124, 194
Investigation of truth   26, 73, 407,
    429, 460, 465, 468, 471

Index of Bible Verses Used in this Book

Contents of Volumes
II and III

Volume II
Lord of Lords

Volume III

King of Kings

Sources for Information and Literature

1. To receive information or a recorded message on the Bahá'í Faith, call: 1-800-228-6483.

2. Visit these Bahá'í Web Sites:
   - www.bahai.org
   - www.onecountry.org
   - www.bahai-library.org

3. Check the white and yellow pages for the Bahá'í Faith or a community listing.

4. To receive free literature on the Bahá'í Faith, call us at: 1-800-949-1863.

5. To receive a free catalog of Bahá'í books or to order Bahá'í books in the United States, call Bahá'í Distribution Service: 1-800-999-9019, or write to:

   Bahá'í Distribution Service
   4703 Fulton Industrial Boulevard
   Atlanta, GA 30336-2017
   USA

A Few Bahá'í Centers

Alaska
13501 Brayton Drive
Anchorage, Alaska 99516
USA

Australia
Bahá'í Publications
173 Mona Vale Road
Ingleside, NSW 2101
Australia

Canada
7200 Leslie Street
Thornhill, Ontario
L3T 6L8 Canada

England
27 Rutland Gate
London SW7 1PD
United Kingdom

Hawaii
3264 Allan Place
Honolulu, Hawaii 96817
USA

India
Bahá'í House
5 Canning Road
Post Box 19
New Delhi 110 001
India

New Zealand
P.O. Box 21-551
Henderson 1231
Auckland
New Zealand

United States
536 Sheridan Road
Wilmette, IL 60091
USA

About the Author

Dr. Motlagh is Professor Emeritus at Central Michigan University. His background is in psychology with a specialty in educational psychology.

It has taken the author over 30 years to write the current six-volume series. And the work is not yet finished. At one point when he had completed the first volume, he sent it to a publisher who would not even respond. When he called, he was told that the book had been rejected. But the bad news soon turned into good news. The next morning shortly after he woke up, he had a magnificent vision the like of which he had never seen. The vision gave him hope and the promise of assistance; it strengthened his determination to continue. He persisted for some 25 more years to complete the next five volumes.

To Dr. Motlagh it seems ironic that his Jewish ancestors met many Christians who would say: "The Messiah has come! His name is Jesus." Now he is saying to the descendants of those same Christians: "The Messiah has come again! His name is Bahá'u'lláh (The Glory of God)." Many of his close relatives live in Israel. They are still praying for the coming of their Messiah.

He hopes his readers will not wait that long! He prays that they will study this book in the same spirit in which it was written: an unshakable determination to persist.